Food in Global History

GLOBAL HISTORY SERIES

Bruce Mazlish, Carol Gluck, and Raymond Grew, Series Editors

Food in Global History

Edited by
Raymond Grew

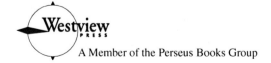

Westview PRESS

A Member of the Perseus Books Group

Global History

Copyright © 1999 by Westview Press, A Member of the Perseus Books Group

Published in 1999 in the United States of America by Westview Press, 5500 Central Avenue, Boulder, Colorado 80301-2877, and in the United Kingdom by Westview Press, 12 Hid's Copse Road, Cumnor Hill, Oxford OX2 9JJ

Find us on the World Wide Web at www.westviewpress.com

Library of Congress Cataloging-in-Publication Data
Food in global history / edited by Raymond Grew.
    p.   cm. — (Global history)
    Includes bibliographical references.
    ISBN 0-8133-3884-0
    1. Food—History.   I. Grew, Raymond.   II. Series.
TX353.F64   1999
641.3'09—dc21   99-38889
                                                                                         CIP

The paper used in this publication meets the requirements of the American National Standard for Permanence of Paper for Printed Library Materials Z39.48-1984.

10   9   8   7   6   5

Contents

Tables and Figures

Acknowledgments

The essays in this book were first prepared as papers for a conference held at the University of Michigan, and they have benefited in revision from the discussions that took place there. Many valuable points that now nestle in these chapters, as well as the sense of discovery often reflected in them, owe much to the participation of scholars who do not appear here as authors: **Rajen S. Anand**, Director, Program Development, Center for Nutrition Policy and Promotion, United States Department of Agriculture; **Professor Robin Barlow**, Professor of Economics and Population Planning, University of Michigan; **Professor Alison Cornish**, Department of Romance Languages, University of Michigan; **Professor John D'Arms**, President, American Council of Learned Societies; **Professor Stanley Garn**, Emeritus, School of Public Health, University of Michigan; **Professor Kenneth Kiple**, of History, Bowling Green University; **Dr. Rachel Laudan**, Mexico; **Professor Harvey Levenstein**, Department of History, McMaster University; **Professor Bruce Mazlish**, Department of History, Massachusetts Institute of Technology; **Professor Marion Nestle**, Department of Nutrition and Food Studies, New York University; **Professor Paul Rozin**, Department of Psychology, University of Pennsylvania; **Professor Wolf Schäfer**, Department of History, SUNY-Stony Brook; **Professor Thomas N. Tentler**, Department of History, University of Michigan; **Professor Rafia Zafar**, Department of English and Afro-American Studies, Washington University. We want especially to acknowledge the spirited participation of **Dr. Gerald Gaull**, Director, Center for Food and Nutrition Policy, Georgetown University, whose sudden death prevented his completing his essay and who is very much missed.

The conference was prepared by a committee consisting of Alison Cornish, Adam Drewnowski, and Raymond Grew, with special help from John D'Arms, Homer Rose, James Schaefer, and Steven Soper; and it was part of a theme semester at the University of Michigan, which featured a score of courses on food in global history taught in nearly as many departments, in addition to a lecture series, a film series, and special exhibits in the Clements Library (featuring the Jan Longone collection of American cookbooks published in each of the last two hundred years), the Kelsey Museum of Archaeology, the Harlan Hatcher Graduate Library, and the University of Michigan Museum of Art. These activities were an invaluable stimulus to the entire project and brought a well-informed audience to the conference itself.

The skill, tact, and perserverance of James Schaefer have been essential to this project from its inception to the preparation of the manuscript.

A project on this scale required untold contributions of time from a great many people and significant contributions of funds from The Horace H. Rackham School of Graduate Studies at the University of Michigan, the College of Literature, Science, and the Arts of the University of Michigan, the Gerber Foundation, the Toynbee Prize Foundation, and *Comparative Studies in Society and History*. We thank them all.

Chapter One

Food and Global History

Raymond Grew

The history of food is a fashionable topic, and so is global history. Although they come together naturally, their combination is explosive. They intersect so easily because each sends forth tentacles of relevance that reach across conventional limitations of time, region, and scholarly specialization. Both employ vocabularies applicable everywhere. As subjects of study, however, food and global history begin from opposing points of departure and move along contrasting intellectual trajectories—with different purposes, methods, and prejudices. Remarkably, these complex, erudite, demanding topics appeal to a broad public. Articles and programs on the history of food appear in all the media, and allusions to it decorate patriotic speeches and advertising. A reference to globalization (and therefore some conception of global history) has become a talisman of wise engagement with the modern world and regularly inserted in economic forecasts, political statements, and sociological analyses. Although this double popularity has been a stimulus to this book and understanding the challenge in combining two such universal interests was essential to the project it represents.

I
The Appeal of Food as a Subject of Study

Readers who would not normally wade through the abstractions of social analysis and for whom the details of history are a burden will nevertheless eagerly read about the foods and eating habits of other eras and cultures. There are many reasons for this appeal. Descriptions of other societies seem more immediate and concrete when they treat the common experiences of hunger and eating, inevitably invoking personal memories, sentimental associations with familiar foods, and a shock of delight or revulsion at descriptions of strange foods. Travel accounts, novels, and motion pictures all use food to measure social distance and to give immediacy to penury or plentitude. At home or abroad, colorful food markets are taken to represent something essential and real about culture and society that becomes masked or artificial in supermarkets.[1]

This universality of food gives it enormous potential as an indicator of cultural differences and historical change.[2] All societies must produce and distribute food.[3] Their ways of doing so define the societies themselves. All societies construct elaborate rules about the preparation and consumption of food, rules that reveal internal structure and tensions; and apparently no region has been so poor as not to have special foods for festivals or holidays or family occasions. Necessity, taste, social distinction, opportunity, and values all intersect at the table, dictating who sits where, what is on the plate and whether there is one, who prepares the food and who serves it. On great public occasions, the order of service expresses this formally; but food operates as a social indicator even more powerfully with daily repetition. Everyone in Western societies recognizes the social implications of whether a household normally eats caviar or hot dogs, truffles or frozen dinners and whether they do so standing or sitting and in a kitchenette or under a chandelier. In other societies other signs are no less clear.[4]

The production of food is so fundamentally integrated with labor systems and property arrangements and so clearly tied to available technology that diet is often taken to be a measure of economic development (with effects ranging from the elimination of famine to clogged arteries and obesity). Advancing science has not merely affected what people eat but has made diet a concern of public policy, and fortifying foods with vitamins may be one of the most successful, and beneficial, efforts at social control. Of course, the connections between food and the environment and between food and social organization change with the systems of agriculture, food preservation, and transport and are altered by new knowledge about the principles of nutrition, plant genetics, and biological needs. Diet depends on more than wealth and knowledge, however; and experts have sometimes mistaken cultural preference for scientific or economic indicators of the level of development—mistaking the discouragement of breast feeding, a preference for big breakfasts, or the high consumption of milk and meat for universal signs of progress.

Historians find in food's ties to economics, technology, commerce, and religion particularly satisfying evidence of how ordinary, daily activities are related to larger historical trends. Until the high middle ages, Europeans reclined while eating, at least on formal occasions. The change to a seated position, two leading historians of food point out, freed the left hand, facilitating the use of a knife, which opened the way to the fork, adopted in the fourteenth century following the Black Death. The change in food manners was connected to changes in social relations, furniture, wealth, and technology. Current historical scholarship on food and diet, they add, seeks,"to touch upon all aspects of human action and thought."[5]

That scholarship can proceed in many different ways. There are excellent studies of foods in single cultures.[6] Specific foods and the customary ways of eating them have been tellingly analyzed as an aesthetic, cultural, semiotic code; and changes in eating can be related to important social and psychological changes, something Sidney Mintz suggests when he asserts that a new conception, the idea that a person could become different by consuming differently, first emerged with tobacco, tea, and sugar—stimulants and products of empire.[7] Interestingly, the urge to make food historically significant is not just the penchant of scholars; in every society, folk histories accompany particular dishes and, like folk etymologies, associate the local and familiar with famous figures, great events, and historical turning points.[8]

The attention to food in literature and art reinforces the impression that whole cultures divulge themselves through their way with food;[9] and the sense of food's significance comes so readily, perhaps from deep within the psyche, that claims for cuisine as evidence must be accepted with some grains of salt. Modern nations, for example, tend to stress the antiquity and distinctiveness of their regional cuisines, especially at times when, for other reasons, regional differences seem important. In reality, however, the promotion of certain dishes to a place in regional identity is often quite modern, following rather than preceding the creation of a nation and the establishment of a national cuisine.[10]

Harvest rituals, communal celebrations, religious and family feasts all use food to infuse social ties with a sense of plentitude and well-being. Foods thereby define and reinforce group membership, and they provide an instrument for exposing the processes of assimilation. Migration, often in part a search for food, carried special foods with it; and there is much to be learned from the capacity of cuisines to spread, to change, and to absorb elements of other cuisines, while preserving their distinctiveness and remaining powerful symbols of identity.[11] Food remains at home in melting pots.

Strongly associated with women's domestic roles, the preparation and serving of food within the family conveys bonds of affection and tends to assert male authority and female power—thus the modern concern that these meanings may be eroded by the spread of packaged foods and the practice of eating in restaurants[12] (where professional chefs, like the corporate executives who produce and distribute packaged food, are likely to be men).

In all these respects, the study of food demonstrates how deeply processes of political and social change can reach into society. No wonder then that commentary on contemporary cuisine is often also a comment on politics, commercialization, the ecology, and cultural decline.[13] Books on the history of food can be fascinating and delightful as they set unusual and interesting details about the daily life of an era within grand (and satisfyingly familiar) historical narratives. Unfamiliar information on a commonplace subject often has an impact greater than its import, and historical lore about food can readily acquire an aura of significance and erudition it may not merit.

Only rarely does the study of food reveal historical processes previously slighted. Can thinking in terms of global history make a significant difference? The chapters that follow address questions of historical importance.

These essays constitute something of an experiment, neither because they engage a neglected subject nor because their authors are scholars from many different fields. The study of food has tended to stimulate interdisciplinary research. The fresh achievement here lies with the engagement of scholars from many disciplines using the latest work in their own fields to think about the history of food within a framework of global history. In doing that they discuss topics of great general interest, subjects discussed in the mass media, matters of official policies normally considered in congressional committees and international agencies, and issues of medical science more at home in seminars and antiseptic corridors. The authors have in common their command of great bodies of knowledge that partially overlap, their willingness to take part in this experiment, and their desire to reach a broader audience.

The Interest in Globalization

Increasing attention to things global may reflect increasing curiosity about the rest of the world; but globalization refers to a fundamental historical process. Admittedly, the weight of the term is lessened by the frequency and intellectual lightness with which labels are used to declare modern times a new epoch—the Computer Age, the Atomic Age, the Age of Totalitarianism, the Age of the Automobile, the Age of Anxiety—but this obsessive labeling may in itself be an important sign of our times. Almost everyone agrees, a little uncritically, that the pace of historical change has become faster; and the need for such labels indicates how fundamentally modern thought is shaped by conceptions of historical change as well as by contemporary concern about where that process of change is taking us. Globalization has much of the appeal of science fiction.

Usually assumed to be propelled by new technologies and by mechanisms internal to capitalism, globalization is sometimes described in the language of progress, with echoes of Enlightenment confidence in the power of reason and of nineteenth-century hope for science and technology. Globalization so conceived brings societies closer together, with benefits that include the elimination of famine and the enjoyment of foods from around the world. Diets that once featured chestnuts, taro, or turnips were imposed by nature; now those limitations have been overcome. From a common biology and through a shared human experience, this progress allows more diverse diets and makes them more widely available as they also become internationally more similar, achieving through food what Esperanto attempted through language.

More often, however, references to globalization are accompanied by allusions to the sorcerer's apprentice and by warnings of dehumanized commerce and environmental disaster. An ungainly term, globalization often suggests a troubling determinism, a juggernaut that destroys rain forests while multinational agribusinesses plow under family farms and capitalism forces peasants to move into cities and work for wages, thereby eroding social relations, undermining local customs, and subverting taste in culture and food. This globalization involves an assault on nature. With respect to food, technology violates the natural rhythm of the seasons and modernity undermines the convivial rituals and religious meanings associated with eating. Ever more available, food loses the savor preserved only in memories of produce fresh from the garden and prepared in mother's kitchen from recipes so traditional they were never written down. Ultimately, this litany compares the barbarism of gulping hamburgers with the refinements of family feasts and contrasts fruit freshly picked with processed foods deficient in flavor and nutrients. Admittedly, the spread of McDonald's restaurants around the world would seem to imply some universal attraction or need; yet that expansion is more famous as a symptom than as a success. Part of the interest of this book's topic lies in the fact that, at the end of the twentieth century, discussions of globalization and food encapsulate such conflicting assessments of the present and the future.

II
Constructing Global Histories (of Food)

Concerns with globalization today have obviously stimulated interest in global history. As a field of study that uses historical methods to analyze global connections and processes of historical change, global history has other intellectual roots as well, among them eighteenth-century Scottish and French philosophers, much of nineteenth-century social science (including August Comte, Karl Marx, and the birth of anthropology), and twentieth-century studies of modernization and world systems. As a distinctive field, however, global history can be said to be new; and there is an ongoing debate among interested historians as to whether or not global history is a way of studying all of history or should be limited to study of the modern period.[14]

For some, the global connectedness of our age is its distinguishing characteristic, a new reality and a change in consciousness of which interest in global history is but one manifestation.[15] This global era and its origins, including perhaps the last 50 or 100 years, should therefore be the subject matter of global history. For others, historians, thinking globally as a result of contemporary experience invites a new look at all periods of the past, probing for global connections and recognizing global historical processes of change that may have been underestimated. Such new research would in turn deepen understanding of the modern period itself and should lead to new categories of analysis and new theories of change.

The study of food in global history is unlikely to resolve this issue of periodization. Some themes—such as agribusiness, global marketing, fast foods, environmental concerns, and genetic engineering—are very much part of global history understood as the history of modernity. Others—such as trade in food stuffs over great distance, even in prehistory; the response of subsistence economies to global changes in climate and disease, and the spread across societies and continents of techniques for producing and preserving food (beginning in ancient times)—extend through history. That human beings around the world are tending to grow taller and live longer is related to the global history of food in the modern era, that food is a crucial element in the relations of economies and empires and religions has been a part of global history much longer.

Some patterns of change are clear. Undeniably there has been an historic increase in the amount of food available (with enormous implications for population and longevity and all of social life), and there has been an increase in the range of foods in prosperous countries and in the distribution of food among social classes. Conceived on a grand scale, global history tends to privilege long-term and highly visible factors like conquest, technology, and economic necessity. The importance of food in human history is not limited, however, to material factors. Eating together, sharing certain foods, and eschewing others have helped groups define themselves and religions maintain community. Shamans and doctors have relied on foods, specially prepared as medicines, to sustain their social roles. Patterns of consumption have been principle indicators of social position from soup kitchen to bourgeois banquet. Family life, peasant festivities, and rulers' displays of power have always featured food; and the symbolic power of food is expressed in everyday preferences, religious proscriptions, works of art, and modern advertising.

Perhaps food can be used as a kind of trace element, tracking the direction of change, revealing the complex intersections of old and new that demark the global and the local but belong to both. The history of food can be thought of as beginning with biology and the hard realities of climate, soil, property, and labor; but it continues through social structure, economic exchange, and technology to embrace culture and include a history of collective and individual preferences. This global history of food need not reject contingency nor deny the efficacy of human choices.

Thinking in terms of global history nevertheless generates significant tensions. When global historians look for connections, they are looking at established subjects of research and are especially dependent on the work of others for the knowledge they have assembled, the theories they have generated, and the very topics being studied. Each of these topics has its own lore, sets of questions, bodies of knowledge, and particular methods that come to be thought of as part of the topic itself and serve to give it boundaries. The study, for example, of a single manufacturing company is always understood to be a subtopic of larger topics: a kind of product, a form of production, the economy of a nation.[16] Such topics are normally explored within an established conceptual framework and a well-developed scholarly literature. To consider them on a global scale is not only to be unusually dependent on the work of others but to use that research in ways for which it was not intended.

In practice this search for connections often challenges established categories of thought and conventional boundaries between topics. Thus, while relying on the work of others, the global historian is also often subverting it. That may result simply from reversing the emphasis, stressing the connections more than the things connected, an analysis that often reveals unexposed relationships that cut across established categories. It may result more fundamentally from a new perspective, a new angle of vision that significantly modifies the topics connected, that reveals assumptions which need rethinking, and that identifies historical processes largely overlooked. Or, most ambitious of all, it may result from the application of theories about global relations that explain historical processes in new ways. (The essays in this book function at the more moderate of these levels, although the attentive reader will note some striking possibilities for larger theories). Even when happily convinced of having something new and important to say, the global historian cannot forget the great risks in transgressing distinctions that have resulted from specialized knowledge and disciplined methods.

Global connections are not necessarily hard to find, and scholars often know in advance where to look for them. Most obvious are the connections across space, from country to country, across continents, and around the globe. These attract our attention for two reasons. The first is modern experience. The ease of movement and communication, the increase in both the pressures of international markets and concern for the environment have made us aware that all the world is connected. Globalization is on everyone's lips, shibboleth and excuse, often loosely used; and serious thought cannot afford to avoid the obvious. Connections across space attract our attention for a subtler reason as well. The study of society has been shaped by the fact that travel and communication were for so long difficult and slow, that customs and languages tend to amplify the sense of distance and difficulty, and that cultures are so often noticed and described in terms of difference. The prominence of state and nation, with historiography its product and chronicler, has obscured many continuing connections. When the response to information about global connections is one of surprise, that surprise comes as much from the realization that important ties had been overlooked as from the discovery of their existence.

The analysis of global connections must be attentive to time as well as space. Connections formed in one era tend to shift in form and meanings with the passage of time. The visible exchange of goods may have its most important effects through the ideas and customs that accompany it but only slowly take effect. Ties that were once imperial may outlast the political connections that formed them. Explanations of how specific global connections began are often easier to establish than why they persist, are transformed, or peter out—promising areas for research in global history. The reminder to be alert for connections across space and over time can be a useful prod to further investigate but is both too easy and too grand to shape research.

Because global history, conceived of as a kind of historical research, does not aspire to create a narrative of world history that leaves no island out, it can tolerate lots of gaps. But global historians face other difficulties. In their search for connections, global historians need an explicit rationale for delimiting their inquiry. Once accepted categories have been denied their truncating power and habits of thought no longer define the boundaries of research, connections can become infinite. The two most common devices for avoiding an endless loop of connections are either to focus on a closely defined subject treated as an example of other nodes of multiple connections or to study a specific system of connections, for which it is then necessary to provide some theoretical support. [17] Both are used in the chapters that follow.

The global historical framework one chooses will go far to determine what evidence is relevant; the theories and methods employed will shape its interpretation. There are, it seems to me, essentially four broad approaches to building a global, historical framework. One begins from universal experiences. Human beings everywhere construct shelter, ward off or survive disease, and, of course, eat. Environmental and economic factors have, for example, led many societies at different times to depend heavily on a single dietary staple. Whether that staple was wheat, rice, potatoes or something else, the production, distribution, and consumption of that staple was integral to social organization and cultural values. Changes in any of these elements affected the others in a process that can be studied. Similarly, urban living, set working hours, and restaurants are now nearly universal experiences that have implications for food and its cultural meanings. Constructing a global history on the basis of a selected set of universal experiences has important advantages. It encourages comparison of how societies meet similar needs and how different social systems respond to change, and it tends to favor research that is empirical and open-ended. Nutritional studies, with their foundation in biology and medicine and their concerns for public health, frequently work this way; and a number of chapters in this book illustrate its effectiveness. Defining historical problems on the basis of common experiences can be done in a way to avoid imposing Western models on non-Western societies.[18] The selection of which universal experiences to study and which comparisons to make is not automatic, however, but requires some carefully elaborated conception of historical change to avoid the dull simplifications that assumptions about universal experience can encourage.

A second way to way to build a framework of global history is to trace the diffusion of materials, techniques, ideas, and customs from one place to another. William McNeill's study of the global diffusion of plagues is an outstanding example[19]; and several of the essays in this volume establish their problematic from instances of diffusion. The spread of previously unknown foods from the New World to Europe and Asia provides one of the great historical examples of diffusion,[20] the contemporary spread of fast foods, one of the most talked about. An important element in historical change, diffusion is a natural preoccupation of global history. Tracking the movement of something specific from place to place over time allows a measured concreteness and chronological clarity that facilitates the comparison of diverse responses to similar opportunities and challenges. Tracing such contacts has a further importance, because every item carries some culture with it and patterns of contact thus have wider historical significance.

Within a framework of diffusion a global history of food might investigate the spread of plants and animals, agricultural techniques (from irrigation, the plow, and animal husbandry to tractors, fertilizers, and genetically engineered plants); the food preferences and taboos carried by religion; or the specific dishes, ways of cooking, and table manners disseminated by travelers, migrants, and merchants. Studies of diffusion tend to favor the concrete and readily identifiable, churches more than religious beliefs, inventions more than social organization, certain foods more than social relations. That can be a serious limitation, as can the fact that the thing disseminated may itself be changed in the process. In global histories of diffusion, significant issues and findings arise less reliably from study of the idea or object diffused than from exploration of the responses to it, which often reveals a great deal about the process of change. In that way research into the diffusion of people, businesses and markets, labor systems, knowledge and techniques, religious or political movements, or public policies can contribute significantly to global history.

A third approach to building a framework for global history uses the formal ties of politics, economics, or culture to explore the creation of global webs of connections. These are most often thought of in terms of trade or empire, relations that lie at the core of many of the best known and most influential global histories published in the last thirty years. Such close attention to economic ties opens the study of global history to an extensive literature on economic theory. Variants of Marxism in particular have contributed to theories of dependency and the world-capitalist system that have been effectively applied to examples from around the world. Similarly, political ties are central to global histories of the shifting balance of power and of competing hegemonies, and modern studies of imperialism have enriched our understanding of the lasting impact of webs of connection. Among the various approaches to global history, the search for webs of connections is the one most inherently attentive to power, another respect in which it fits well with contemporary social science, and is useful for the kind of ecological analysis in some of the following chapters.

Webs of connection built on trade in food (and in tobacco, tea, and opium) have been crucial in many periods of history. Trade in wine and olive oil in the ancient world, the flow of grain in the Roman empire, the demand for spices in the middle ages, and the transatlantic exportation of meat and grain have often structured accounts of European history. Food was also an important commodity on the comparably important trade routes of Asia and the Middle East. Investigating global connections through food underscores the importance of cultural and social factors such as language, religion, and migration in sustaining webs of connections. From Japan to the European Union and North America, battles over the quality and effects of foreign foods show the continuing importance of symbolic associations as well as economic interests. Intimately related to personal style and social practice, food consumption (like a preference for wine, beer, espresso, or Coca-Cola) flourishes at the intersection of the local and the global. These examples also point to significant changes in the contemporary world; for the global history of food brings to the fore the role of international marketing in today's economy, when the capacity to create demand and to domesticate imported products is one of the marks of corporate capital. There is a dangerous tendency, however, to confuse connection with hegemony and to assume that vectors of influence flow in only one direction. Global historians (unlike nativists who fear the effects of importing foreign foods) cannot assume that imported practices arrive unfiltered or that such encounters transform culture, for there is exciting research to be done on when elective affinities do and do not obtain and when they form webs of connection.

A fourth way of building toward a framework of global history looks at cultural encounters, not simply as conflicts but as a process of change in which cultural identities are formed and altered. Many elements of this can be found in what is thought of as the history of civilizations, global history differing primarily in a lesser commitment to seamless narrative and a greater focus on the processes of historical change. Global history constructed around cultural encounters, which uses established work on religion, language, and society, has strong resonance with late-twentieth-century concerns about nationalism, fundamentalism, and ethnic identity.[21] Applied to the place of food in global history, it probes the ways in which foods function as cultural symbols and markers of difference. The array of examples (rice, the beef of old England, couscous, rye bread, curry, borscht, tortillas) is extraordinary, and so is the range of purposes to which they have been put. Foods can demark cultural difference and define community. Specific foods have long been associated with particular groups, and it has been common to associate the foods of a region with its climate and terrain as the basis for a description (and implied explanation) of the character of the inhabitants. In the nineteenth century, as the choice of food increased, nationalism flourished, and the limited diets of the poor became all the more noticeable, proletarian foods quickly became a (usually disparaging) nickname for other nations: potato-eaters, limeys, frogs, and krauts.

The examples are so interesting that they are often cited on the way to conclusions already familiar, but the study of cultural encounters has much more to offer to global history. The process of codification whereby the diets of ordinary people came to be a mark of identity associated with particular festivals and ethnic groups is historically important. Increased awareness of others and greater freedom of choice provoked issues of identity; consciousness of change stimulated inventive uses of the term, traditional. Global cultural encounters expand and alter that consciousness and those choices. Distinctive foods, recodified in ethnic restaurants around the world, became part of shifting balances between the exotic and the familiar,[22] as several chapters here demonstrate. Food provides a sensitive indicator of the melding of global and local; and study of how cuisines adapt to new circumstances (or are adapted by elites, restauranteurs, migrants, advertisers, and international social agencies) can provide a useful counterweight to the tendency to think of global history in terms of impersonal, predictable, and irresistible forces. The intersection of larger trends and individual choices, of great forces and local groups, of structures and cultures that has given vitality to all forms of history remains essential for global history, too.

Constructing Histories of Food (in a Global Context)

Global historical frameworks developed from histories of universal experiences, diffusion, webs of connections, or cultural encounters are all applicable to global histories of food. There is much to build on. The historical literature on food is considerable; and although most of it was written independent of any special concern for global history, its extension to global frameworks follows logically. This potential can be found in the histories of single foods; of food, famine and demography; of human nutrition; of food as a cultural marker, distinguishing one culture from another; of the trade in food and of the systems of landholding and labor on which it rests; and of agribusiness and the international capital and marketing it involves.

There are marvelous histories of particular foods that, by reaching across vast expanses of time and geography, reveal continuities and relationships that are the ligaments of global history. One of the most impressive is Redcliffe Salaman's history of the potato, and there are a number of others. [23] The intellectual pleasures of contemplating the multiple and often surprising ways a single food connects to social history can be savored in Toussaint-Samat's encyclopedic account of foods, which considers the berries and animals of the wild, cultivated grains and fruits, locally varied yet ubiquitous alcoholic drinks, and more exotic products, some of which like spices and coffee, became featured items of world trade.[24] Sydney Mintz's remarkable study of sugar begins with the universal human appeal of sweetness; follows the diffusion of techniques used to cultivate and consume sugar; examines the trade in sugar and the imperial connections, plantation systems, and slavery that developed around that trade; and explores the cultural changes associated with sugar consumed as medicine, condiment, and luxury but differently by different social classes. "Uses," he notes, "determine meanings," a point crucial in thinking about food in global history precisely because the cultural habit is to think of that relationship in reverse. [25]

Scarcity and famine are also topics that invite a global outlook. At the beginning of the modern, industrial era, the Reverend Malthus argued that only war, disease, and famine prevented overpopulation, which otherwise would foster all three scourges on an unprecedented scale. Ever since, as populations continued to increase, the question of whether scientific knowledge, technology, and social organization could provide the food to sustain such growth has remained central. This concern—important to contemporary discussions of economic development, population planning, international aid, and environmental policies—has also greatly added to historical research and understanding. Much as tree rings register the quality of each growing season, a society's system of food supply can be read as the skeletal remains of its social structure and the vicissitudes that it had to meet. Archaeologists and historians study the ratios of population to land, the efforts to establish an adequate water supply (crucial elements in the development of the fertile crescent between the Tigris and Euphrates and in the stability of Asian, Roman, and pre-Columbian civilizations), the impact of technology from animal harnesses and moldboard plows to gasoline engines, new fertilizers, and pesticides. Scholars have learned to give close attention to the importance of food stuffs for the development of trade routes and empires from the date palms of the ancient world and the spice trade of the middle ages to developmental change in the last fifty years.[26] Issues of food supply run through history from the most ancient periods to the present.[27]

Famine is often thought of as a natural disaster about which little could be done. Historians, however, find that for the last several centuries at least governments could make all the difference, and thus famine should not be dismissed from historical analysis as an external pressure on society but should rather stimulate questions about the human policies that made it possible.[28] The effects of famine are far-reaching, and responses to its tragedy have served political, imperial, and political interests. The demographic effects of famine tend to be statistically minor compared to its psychological and social effects; but population growth, one of the great themes of global history, is due in part to the increasing provision of sufficient food to strengthen resistance to disease. Like demography, the science of nutrition examines universal aspects of human biology in very specific contexts. Nutritionists know the physiological effects of specific foods and the nutritional elements they contain; for recent times, at least, these researchers know a great deal about the effects of dietary change. And they have considerable experience of public policy; of the impact on it of cultural, economic, and political factors; and of its often unexpected outcomes. This can be a tool for uncovering large-scale historical trends. Food, the object of considerable record keeping, makes an invaluable historical indicator.

Which plants and animals are considered to be food varies with culture; and what is eaten, how it is prepared, and who eats it, often needs to be studied in quite local terms yet raises important questions about how societies function. Anthropologists have long made use of this,[29] and food practices can be the basis for stimulating comparisons between societies, including some very distant in time,[30] and for analyzing patterns of change.

Food has been an important item of trade since ancient times; and increasing global trade has spread plant and animal varieties, added greatly to the variety of foods available in wealthier societies, and created powerful networks of distribution and processing.[31] These developments have not all pointed in one direction, however. It can be argued that economic ties have also reduced the variety of foods available in developing countries, pushing them to produce single crops for international markets.[32] International agribusiness can also drive peasants into city slums, favor high-yield grains that provide reduced nutrition, and harm the environment as well as health by making regions once self-sufficient (admittedly at low levels) dependent on imported foodstuffs and the exportation of goods produced at low wages.[33] These are primarily modern phenomena, and there is disagreement about their extent and long-term effects, a disagreement that is in effect an argument about their place in global history. Many current practices are clearly extensions of patterns developed following the great European expansion of the sixteenth century. Staple foods and foods that are major exports have always been closely tied to a society's labor system, and dramatic examples include the latifundia of ancient Rome, the labor-intensive production of rice in China and Japan, and the reliance on slavery in the sugar islands. From the nineteenth century to the present, the modern food industry has often relied on cheap labor in poor countries to produce foods sold in rich markets.

As a subject, then, food lends itself especially well to the study of global historical patterns, connecting elements of history that are more often studied in isolation. Because foodways intersect so concretely with economics, politics, social structure, and culture, the history of food is remarkably suggestive. Yet histories of food must accomplish more than that if they are to add to the understanding of global history.

III

This conjunction between histories of food and global history facilitates our project but says little about how specific studies should be formulated. Although this is not the place for a disquisition on methodology and global history, it is useful while reading the chapters that follow to bear in mind the concerns that shaped them. Like all good history, global histories should address important historical problems. Identifying those to be considered is a critical step. The four, broad global historical frameworks discussed above, used with whatever degree of deliberation and whether separately or in combination, can be helpful but are not enough. Theories, or at least certain conceptions, of global historical processes direct the scholar's attention to the kind of events and practices likely to be important. Investigating those more closely provokes a series of questions, leading to further explorations. And all of this, from beginning to end, evolves from the author's initial interests, which are necessarily delimited in time and place and topic. Influenced by available data and current discussions, these interests also reflect the traditions and methods of particular academic disciplines. Along the way, this posing of questions and persistent probing leads to the recognition of significant problems in global history that can be given the definition and delimitation necessary for systematic investigation.

Finding coherent patterns in history is a resounding challenge, tracing them through time and space an enormous satisfaction, and attaching them to specific cases a critical contribution to historical understanding. For that to work, global history, as a field of study, must be able to proceed from the specific to the general as well as the reverse. The essays that follow do that. They emphasize different global connections. Their authors do not always agree about the global historical processes that matter most. Yet all attend to ecology, economics, technology, and politics and are alert to issues of culture, social class, and gender as they track the interaction of global and local factors. Writing on diverse societies and starting from different fields of research with their own vocabularies, data, and methods, these authors nevertheless address related, and important, issues about food in global history.

The Processes of Global History

The four essays in this section all analyze processes of change in foodways but do so on very different scales, moving from a truly global conception of change through human history, to a comparative study of Chinese and Indian responses over several centuries to new foods from the Americas, to an assessment of restaurants and travel as agents of change, to the cultural constructions of an ethnic minority that moved from North Africa to metropolitan France. Each essay uses all of the approaches to building a global framework discussed above; yet each begins from an emphasis on one of them.

In Chapter Two, "Going in Circles: The Political Ecology of Food and Agriculture," Harriet Friedmann starts from the universal, the complex balance of nature that evolves in place and purpose. This framework leads to an evolutionary perspective on how human beings, seeking the sustenance life requires, have benefited from, worked with, and battled against various ecological niches. That provides a way to identify major historical transformations; and Friedmann emphasizes in the last three centuries the Columbian exchange (the subject of Chapter Three), the global expansion of European power, and the decline of the household economy with industrialization, a radical break that made food a commodity. The themes she identifies are taken up again and again in this volume. Through her focus on ecology, she outlines a chain of being from bacteria to human relations that connects environment, economy, social system, urban-rural relations, techniques of production, family structure, and social values. Her political ecology becomes an impassioned warning against miscalculations of efficiency and profit (consider mad cow disease, discussed in Chapter Fourteen) and against the dangers of losing genetic diversity. Attention to place, primarily Great Britain and the United States, provides evidence for a social vision and a cultural program (echoed in the last chapter of this book).

The global framework that Sucheta Mazumdar uses in Chapter Three starts from the most visible example of diffusion in the history of food, the spread of plants from the New World following European exploration. She then identifies a significant historical problem, for "The Impact of New World Food Crops on the Diet and Economy of China and India, 1600–1900" explores two strikingly different responses to these new crops, especially sweet potatoes, maize, and peanuts. The contrast between China and India was not the matter of a moment but lasted for centuries. It began with China's agricultural revolution, much earlier than Europe's, and it had implications for demographic growth and political revolts as well as national cuisines. Attentive to plant histories, ecology, and local economies, Mazumdar's analytic comparison emphasizes the importance of land-holding patterns, peasant proprietors, and the role of the state (providing valuable background for the discussion in Chapter Thirteen of Japan's response to imported foods). Institutions, policies, and ordinary people created the difference, using crops differently and in ways that affected the history of great civilizations.

Global frameworks can thus point to, and clarify, critical, long-term processes. They can also illuminate transformations that occur on a shorter time scale. Rebecca Spang also writes about diffusion in Chapter Four, but her emphasis is on the restaurant as a site of cultural encounter, between people from the provinces and urban sophisticates, consumers from different social classes, and travelers from different cultures. "All the World's a Restaurant: Gastronomics of Tourism and Travel" contains a number of surprises. Placed in a global context, the restaurant is seen to be far from universal and hardly some artless, natural development; its rise needs to be explained. Associated from birth with travel, it was then inventively made a kind of substitute for it. This is a modern story, in which modern concerns for health and the technologies of modern travel intersect with commerce and the wealth and taste of the middle class to create an institution—the restaurant—that codifies cuisines and makes the exotic accessible and safe. In the process of becoming global, this orchestrated form of cultural encounter preserved something of older, local ways the representation of social and ethnic identities and an essential marker of the modern way of life around the world.

Cultural encounter is also central to Joëlle Bahloul's close study of North African Jews. But Chapter Five, "On Cabbages and Kings: The Politics of Jewish Identity in Post-Colonial French Society and Cuisine," builds its global framework from the webs of connections within which the Jews of North Africa have for centuries been situated. Their eating patterns recapitulated their position between Muslim neighbors and French governors. Subsequently carried into France, that way of eating underwent further compromises between ancient Jewish law and the attractive opportunities of French republican society. Bahloul's research on food practices that developed, informally and in the home, weighs the impact of migration, economic development, and political climate as well as issues of ethnic, religious, and class identity in a case study of responses to modern social change. It reveals a subtle and complex process that intermingles rituals with shifting symbolic meanings and constructs changing boundaries within the fields of tension created by the promises and threats of integration.[34] In four frameworks of different chronological and geographic scale, these studies of food reveal much about global historical processes.

Public Policy and Global Science

The chapters in this section constitute a rather different experiment. International agencies and programs for world health and economic development are in themselves forces for global change. Global thinking is, in a sense, built into the disciplines represented here, while the policies they advocate must deal with immediate, often pressing, local issues. Written by experts who study universal nutritional needs and design public policies to meet those needs, these chapters concentrate on modern conditions, especially in countries undergoing rapid change. These authors assess their own fields of research and the policies they have fostered with remarkable critical balance. Placing those practices within global patterns, uncovers trends that influence research itself as well as policies on nutrition and food supply. Public policies formulated in the name of science and public welfare, are often shaped by fashions, ideologies, commercial interests, and political considerations that reach around the world. Two generations ago, protein deficiency was a principal target, one now overshadowed by concern for nutritional balance and the risks from excessive consumption of sugar and fat. That change results from new knowledge, of course, but also from the experience of the developed world with the worrisome indulgences of prosperous people. While acknowledging the dangers of imposing on one society standards derived from another, policy makers face shifting targets; for the societies they seek to help, whether rich or poor, are rapidly changing through their participation in global historical trends.

The production of food has always been one of society's most important purposes, and Elisabet Helsing begins with that historical perspective in Chapter Six on "Food and Nutrition Trends, East and West." Governments have always had to be concerned about supplies of food; and in those terms, as she points out, food policy is nothing new. The idea that governments should establish national policies based on the latest findings in nutrition science is, however, quite new and itself a product of global historical trends. The results are mixed. Policies, even those favored by United Nations agencies, may be influenced by commercial interests and political considerations for which public health benefits are at best secondary. Nutrition science itself reflects the cultures from which it comes as well as the theories currently in vogue. Helsing develops these points with courageous independence, starting with a look at Europe as a whole, contrasting the greater autonomy of nutrition scientists in the United States from commercial pressures, then more closely studying differences among the Nordic countries. They offer a rare instance in which per capita food production has been declining and where governments, starting with Norway, the first nation to have a nutrition policy, have pioneered in applying nutritional standards. She then turns to the telling and troubled case of the Soviet Union. Its subsequent breakup reveals in contemporary crisis how nutrition policies were frozen in the knowledge and ambitions of the 1930s, to be maintained for food as for industrial organization or the arts within the amber rigidity of Soviet bureaucracy. In all these instances, the results in terms of what people eat and the state of their health demonstrate the importance of public policies but also the degree to which these policies in turn reflect global influences on politics, economics, and science itself.

In Chapter Seven Della McMillan and Thomas Reardon address classic issues of development and international economic aid as it affects "Food Policy Research in a Global Context: the West African Sahel." The impact of global trends stand out starkly in a region where even the harsh constraints of poverty and aridity do not lessen the variety of factors—economic, social, and cultural—involved in changing the production of food. Keenly aware of this complexity, McMillan and Reardon ponder the efficacy of research itself in bringing about desirable change. Policies stimulated by international agencies and external ideologies are inevitably transformed as they function within specific societies. Cultures and social structures remain tightly tied to a distinctive environment, and local leaders have their own sets of ideologies and ambitions. The path from international research and experts' recommendations to the creation of local jobs and higher living standards is not direct. For all that, McMillan and Reardon sustain a sense of calling that leaves them optimistic about the value of research. Research, they conclude, can, by acknowledging its practical limitations, contribute to the more efficient production and better distribution of food in difficult and undeveloped regions, even as global patterns of aid, trade, and urbanization sweep over them.

Issues of nutrition, development, and global processes come together differently and with particular clarity in Chapter Eight, by Noel Solomon, on "Childhood Nutrition in Developing Countries and Its Policy Consequences." Focusing sharply on the special, and morally compelling, issues of child nutrition, especially in the Caribbean, he expands on the impact of imperialism and such international agencies as the World Bank and the World Health Organization that was mentioned in the preceding two chapters. He measures development in terms of the peoples newly affected by it and warns against Eurocentrism and the adoption of North American standards for the normal height and weight of children. He views the shifting equilibria established within local ecologies in response to global pressures as a cultural achievement; and, while recognizing the opportunities (including better health) that arise from global change, he never forgets that the knowledge of Western science is limited and its dogmas usually impermanent. The very training given experts in nutrition is, he notes, a reflection of global pressures. Applying the latest findings of nutrition science, nevertheless, Solomon lays out the multiple elements essential to childhood diet and offers alternative assessments of what balanced diets mean and how they can be achieved. That opens a prospect that, he shows, is relevant to many regions of South America, Africa, and Asia—and an open-ended perspective on global history, past and future.

Global Systems and Human Diet

The essays so far, on the global processes affecting the production and availability of food and on public policies reflecting preferences for some foods over others, have all mentioned some changes in what people actually eat. That is brought to the fore in the next three chapters, all of which address the question of why there are global patterns of dietary change and their relationship to health.

Here, too, the conceptual challenge lies in the complexity of multiple interconnections that give food a place in global history. Jeffrey Sobal directly addresses that complexity in Chapter Nine. "Food System Globalization, Eating Transformations, and Nutrition Transitions," provides an ambitious overarching schema for comprehending global patterns in dietary change. The familiar evolution from hunting and gathering to settled agriculture to industrial society and to global exchange is analyzed as a series of intersecting systems. Food and nutrition in a given society also constitute a system, composed of subsystems of producers, consumers, and nutritional results. The foods any group consumes come primarily from surrounding regions, called foodsheds, but these have expanded as cheaper, faster transport and new techniques of preservation draw food stuffs from ever larger areas and eventually the entire world. This process, Sobal declares, has created major historical changes, which he labels eating transformations, nutrition transitions, and health outcomes. Concentrating on the period since industrialization, he notes the role of taste (closely analyzed in the next chapter) and restaurants (the subject of Chapter Four) and assesses the impact on health (continuing the discussion in Chapters Six and Eight). This schema, which reviews economic, political, and cultural approaches to globalization, pulls together much that has gone before (in a view more optimistic than Friedmann's in Chapter One) and points to much that follows in the subsequent chapters.

Adam Drewnowski is concerned with a specific but fundamental, historical change in "Fat and Sugar in the Global Diet: Dietary Diversity in the Nutrition Transition." Chapter Nine considers one of the most talked-about issues of diet and health, the (dangerously excessive) consumption of sugar and fat. As he makes clear, the subject, mentioned in several other chapters as well, is not merely controversial but ideologically sensitive, the product of differing definitions of good health and of differing attitudes toward modern change. Using the concept of transition, adapted from demography, he treats dietary change as a general transition from one pattern of consumption to another. That transition, he argues, is a cross-cultural one, the result of an inherent and healthy human preference for variety. Moving from the familiar North American experience, he uses empirical evidence to expose a similar pattern in Asia, with evidence from China and Japan (the subject of Chapter Fourteen). Drewnowski thereby makes the case that the taste for sugar and fat is universal in human beings, that consumption of them both has indeed tended to increase over time, that this pattern of increase is remarkably transcultural (however much its fame in the United States may be related to cultural traditions of meat and potatoes), and that this universal, historical tendency to consume more sugar and fat can be correlated with increased wealth—a stunningly clear and global, historical pattern.[35] The disagreement, then, is about values, about whether this transition is good or harmful, as many international agencies (and as the many Americans discussed in Chapter Fourteen) assume.

The relationship between global systems and the choice of food made recent headlines around the world with reports of a mysterious and catastrophic disease; and in Chapter Eleven on "The 'Mad Cow' Crisis: A Global Perspective," Claude Fischler lucidly exposes its relationship to industrial production (the availabilty and use of bone meal in feed), to the scientific analysis of the causes of Bovine Spongiform Encephalopathy and its transmissibility, and to the role of governments in the regulation of food production and public health measures. As news reports circled the globe, the disease created a world-wide scare, with dramatic effects on international markets and the sale of meat. Within this impressively global context, each society responded somewhat differently and in ways that reflected its own traditions of eating, public health, and general suspiciousness; and Fischler notes in particular the contrast between attitudes in northern and Mediterranean Europe. Prejudices (toward other nationalities, modern science, or urban life) and ideologies (about the dangers of free markets, the industrial production of food, and the eating of meat—a subject of taboos from prehistory to the present)— came into play. These reactions, not always closely tied to real risks, exemplify another aspect of global connections, one that echoes through the history of public health regulations. Similar outbreaks of concern can be expected in the future, too, as new techniques such as the genetic alteration of plants, themselves products of international efforts, can be expected to spread rapidly and to provoke greater contentiousness, mobilizing scientists, interest groups, and health experts to do battle in ideological conflicts often inflamed by exaggerated claims, misplaced certitude, and ancient fears.

Eating Together Globally

Of all food's connections to human society, none is more interesting than its ties to culture. As symbol, center of ritual, and marker of cultural boundaries, it is universally understood to be an expression of identity and the representation of a social group. The food that matters is shared commensally, within the family or at a public feast;[36] and the foods employed in these daily and seasonal rituals evoke family ties, Denmark community, and seem to embody culture in some immemorial way. Yet the foods served, the ceremonies that go with them, and the meanings constructed around them do change nevertheless and for all the reasons discussed in previous chapters. What people eat, under what circumstances, and what they believe about these actions is important to this volume because global and local meet at the table.

The family is the great instrument for the construction of these complex meanings, even when it does not invent them. Alex McIntosh considers food and the changing roles of the family in Chapter Twelve, "The Family Meal and Its Significance in Global Times." The change is important and needs emphasis because of the constantly restated myths about the strength of the family in the past. As McIntosh points out, self-conscious emphasis on the family is in itself a relatively modern phenomenon. He thus wants to concentrate on recent history, and he accepts that ours is already a global era. He finds, however, that scholarship on family eating is surprisingly limited and that he must construct a framework for placing the family meal in global history. Reviewing the vast literature on the family, McIntosh notes the variety of functions the family meal serves or is thought to serve, and he considers some of the ways these functions are expressed through gender roles or parental discipline or seating arrangements. The question that follows— what have been the effects, on the family and on society, of the changes in eating patterns that we associate with recent global history?—deserves the attention from scholars that it receives in popular discourse. Assertions about the impact on family life of packaged food and fast foods, nearly always alleged to be deleterious, are commonplaces of late-twentieth-century commentary. On subjects as sensitive as food and family, the fears of global changes are clearer than the changes themselves.

In fact, of course, the global and the local construct each other, creating something new, as Emiko Ohnuki-Tierney emphasizes in "We Eat Each Other's Food to Nourish our Body: The Global and the Local as Mutually Constituent Forces," Chapter Thirteen. After comparing anthropological and historical approaches to global history, she traces Japan's response over the centuries to three different sets of food practices. All of them—eating rice, meat, and American fast foods—were imported; yet as symbols and metaphors, these food practices express intensely felt conceptions of identity, modernity, and the Other. External influences have been absorbed, changing society by becoming critical constituents of it. Art, poetry, rituals, proclamations, and popular culture have reinforced the association of rice with the land and an ancient past, of meat with modernity, and fast food with a new generation in a global culture. Even so, something of older beliefs and taboos has mingled with new practices. Ohnuki-Tierney's examples have the richness of anthropological fieldwork; by placing them in the context of a broader literature, she makes her study of Japan a statement about global processes more generally.

The final chapter, "Food and the Counterculture: A Story of Bread and Politics," treats the current history of one country, the United States; yet Warren Belasco's lively study is also an essay on, and example of, truly global thinking. It explains the intellectual and cultural origins of a movement that constructed a countercultural conception of globalization. Using the twentieth-century's increased knowledge of other cultures, the world economy, nutritional needs, the agricultural and biological sciences, and issues of identity—the very kinds of knowledge that led to assertions that mass-produced food, globally distributed were an inevitable necessity—this movement created an alternative vision. While maintaining much of the apocalyptic tone of those it opposes, that movement has, as Belasco shows, deeply American roots. In turn, it has found notable resonance in much of the rest of the developed world, as so much of American culture has. The call for radical change comes not simply as a reaction to global forces but from the sense of liberation that can come from awareness of them. An account of ecological and global connections that stimulate a countercultural movement centered on food and then facilitates new marketing strategies by international corporations, Belasco's chapter about the choices of some young, middle-class Americans is also about global history on many levels. Written with the wit and insight of a sympathetic participant, it relates to all the other chapters in this book.

IV
The Results

This project on food in global history did not require, it is worth noting, that everyone agree or that all issues be resolved. Global history does not imply a particular methodology or ideology. Globalization remains an imprecise term, its sources, direction, antiquity, and inevitability all subject to dispute. Nevertheless, these authors, experts looking anew at topics they know well, found it useful to relate their analyses to global historical processes. Nor does global history require massive coverage of all human experience but only the establishment of global frameworks within which to set the historical problem to be analyzed. Such frameworks then help determine the theories and data relevant to the problem's solution. The study of food encourages construction of such frameworks both because there is so much information on which to build and because histories of food touch on so many aspects of social life.

Connecting food to social life while placing that relationship in a global context encourages the use of evidence and methods often kept apart by the habits of academic disciplines. As many of these chapters indicate, the fact that with regard to food some similar issues arise in all societies facilitates unusual comparisons between distant societies and stimulates more systematic comparisons of societies known to be connected. Recognizing foodways as part of large-scale patterns of historical change makes it possible to relate the food practices of one place at one moment to theories about global change.

There are hints in these essays that food itself be made the basis for a periodization of human history, and some of these chapters show to good effect how that might be done. Assessing contemporary change in light of historical turning points can be salutary, and historical understanding is deepened with recognition of food's importance in the history of civilization. Food was a central factor in the transition of hunters and gatherers to settled agriculture, irrigation, and the domestication of animals; in evolution of new systems of land holding and increased division of labor; in the development and diffusion of agricultural technology; and in the rise of commerce around the world. In such an outline, European settlement of the New World stands out for the wealth of new foods carried to Europe and Asia as well as for the building of empires. A periodization based on foodways would stress the massive migrations that came later and then, especially in the last one hundred years, the improved means of transporting and preserving foods. Such periodizations, which can be worked out in greater detail for single societies or particular foods, are helpful in relating foodways to political and cultural change. Like all efforts to place food in a global, historical context, they usually are more valuable when they lead to fresh thinking about the nature of historical processes than when they attach data on food to conventional conceptions of change or, in laying claim to historical significance, treat food as an independent cause of long-term change. (Whole civilizations can also be categorized in terms of the foods that are their dietary staples, emphasizing the ties to social structure and culture built around wheat, rice, or potatoes. Such efforts, however, tend to be more interesting than explanatory and in fact to rely on conventional historical frameworks).

In many of these chapters, a global historical framework leads to the identification of problems needing fresh analysis, exposing, for example, parochial assumptions that had flourished unchallenged and sometimes unnoticed. This is most evident in accounts of public policy but applies elsewhere as well. By moving beyond the nation, which provides the framework of most historical writing, national and regional practices that seemed simply natural or necessary are often shown to need fuller explanation. In the same way, extending analysis through time exposes hidden assumptions common to contemporary thinking (including many within the social sciences and global history itself). Global history can similarly help overcome the habits of Eurocentricism, although that benefit is by no means automatic.

The history of food invites some generalizations about global history more generally. The rules of material necessity do apply to the production of food and the need for nutrition. There are limits to the possible. Material conditions, which both inhibit and stimulate change, circumscribe history but do not determine it. As these chapters illustrate, rarely do such constraints explain more than the most basic elements of a society's eating patterns. Foods and cuisines—like technologies, ideas, and fashions—spread beyond the circumstances of their creation to other environments, altering the receiving societies in the process even as they themselves are transformed. Cuisine is never fixed. The meanings of food derive from the way eating intersects with community, and expressions of those meanings matter; for cultures are real, but cultural boundaries are shifting, social creations. Food is a useful marker of difference and cultural purity would be an impoverishment. When the study of food reveals more clearly the interdependence of ecology, property, social structure, international trade, scientific knowledge, public policy, taste, custom, belief, and life style and when that study shows how those interconnections reach around the world, then the history of food has revealed ligatures of global history.

Not surprisingly, historical interest in food turns out to have extraordinary relevance to our own times, illuminating issues of development, international cooperation, multinational corporations, public policy, human health, and social identity, while revealing the tensions between tradition and change within specific cultures. These intense contemporary concerns should open up new avenues of historical research that will in turn affect our understanding of the present. Notably, these issues fall within five areas in which global historical scholarship, empirical and theoretical, is particularly strong: the global restructuring of cultures as the result of mass communications, increased leisure, and salient issues of identity; the global networks of production that depend on and locally demand particular structures of land holding, labor relations, and systems of production; the global role of state policies in shaping international connections through empire, international agencies, trade policies, tariffs, and regulations that favor certain interests in the name of public welfare or national need; the global systems of distribution that foster global fashions and patterns of consumption; and the global environmental constraints that become more pressing as technology mines resources around the globe. The chapters in this volume touch on all these areas, indicating both the fruitfulness of current scholarship on global history and the contribution to that history that can come from the study of food.

Some conclusions do emerge. Historically, food has tended to become more available, its distribution increasingly a matter of market rationality, and its consumption increasingly self-conscious and codified. Its availability has increased in a double sense. Despite ever-growing populations, a greater quantity of food is accessible to a larger proportion of human beings; and in nearly every market, there is an ever-greater choice of foods. But these chapters point to other trends as well. The variety of local species may be diminished, with important ecological, evolutionary, and social losses. Capitalist distribution makes access to specific foods primarily a matter of means, thinning some of its cultural symbolism. Food becomes a product, produced and even redesigned for markets that advertising has helped create. At the same time, the ethnic and regional identity of food has become increasingly codified, less a matter of local custom or of the foods available at a given moment than of a representation collectively agreed upon: a cuisine defined in a certain way, served in restaurants with a certain decor, usually at set hours to fit urban needs at predictable prices and to the expected customers.

Several chapters deal with the remarkable spread of cuisines that were once identified with a single country. The result of migration, touring, marketing, and wealth, this dissemination of cuisines does not strike our authors as the homogenization so many fear. It may be that the foods consumed with minimal ritual in their homelands (or at least, like tea, easily stripped for export of the rituals that sustained them at home)—hamburger, french fries, pizza, hot dogs—are the ones that travel best. In any case much of the fear about the globalization of eating habits and taste seems misplaced. Food cultures have always intermixed and overflowed political or cultural boundaries, and their symbolic importance makes it easy to exaggerate their cultural effect. Sushi bars on every continent do not replace other cuisines; and if McDonald's hamburgers have found a niche on the Champs Elysées and in Tokyo and Istanbul, their impact on national eating habits has been rather less revolutionary than many feared.[37]

These chapters also help to correct the presumptions of determinism, driven by technology and markets, that many discussions of global history invite. The contributors here do not find the global and the local to be in mortal combat but see their intersection as part of a continuing process of creativity. They identify the distinctiveness of our era in the range and pace of change but consider any dichotomy between homogeneity and heterogeneity more false than helpful. Cultures, it is clear, give very unreliable testimony as to which behaviors are new or old; and societies are deceptive about the distinctions between the foreign and the indigenous. Several authors show that much considered to be timeless (styles of regional cooking, for example) often has quite recent origins and that much heralded as new (such as the transcontinental spread of foods, pushed by economic interests and pulled by fashion) often has many precedents.

These studies of food in global history demonstrate anew the humbling relevance of the past, connect society to ecology and time, reveal the persistent power of human choice, employ knowledge of nutrition and evidence from history to challenge received opinions in both areas, provide critical assessments of public policies affecting food and health, and explore the continuing concern for cultural identity while revealing some of the contrivances from which identities are constructed. The history of food invites a tolerant relativism by underscoring how much of culture consists of taste and mores combining necessity with convention. Although omnivorous and adaptable, human beings choose to erect taboos and prejudices against certain foods; and the tension between preference for the familiar foods of home and attraction to the luxury of imported variety adds its energy to the process of change. Because something so simple as food is so thoroughly woven into the fabric of social life, foodways provide a remarkable instrument for tracking critical patterns in global history.

Notes

1. Emile Zola's novel, *Le Ventre de Paris*, about the markets of Les Halles is a classic elaboration of these themes.

2. *The Cambridge History and Culture of Food and Nutrition*, Kenneth F. Kiple and Kriemhild Coneè Onelas, eds. (New York: Cambridge University Press, forthcoming) will be a major reference. Among the important and reflective works on the meanings of food: P. Caplan, *Feasts, Fasts, Famine: Food for Thought* (Providence: Berg, 1994); *Food: Multidisciplinary Perspectives*, Barbara Harris-White and Raymond Hoffenberg, eds. (Oxford: Blackwell Publishers, 1994); Peter Frab and George Armelagos, *Consuming Passions: The Anthropology of Eating* (Boston: Houghton Mifflin, 1980); Jack Goody, *Cooking, Cuisine, and Class: A Study in Comparative Sociology* (New York: Cambridge University Press, 1982); *The Sociology of Food and Eating*, Stephen Mennell, Anne Murcott, and Anneke H. Van Otterloo, eds. (Beverly Hills: Sage Publications, 1993).

3. That fact alone can provide a broad framework for global history: Charles B. Heiser, Jr., *Seed to Civilization: The Story of Food* (Cambridge: Harvard University Press, 1990); Otto T. Solbrig and Dorothy J. Solbrig, *So Shall You Reap: Farming and*

Crops in Human Affairs (Washington, D.C.: Inland Press, 1997); *Agriculture, Resource Exploitation, and Environmental Change*, Helen Wheatley, ed. (Brookfield, Vt: Ashgate, 1997).

4. These points are developed in William Alex McIntosh, *Sociologies of Food and Nutrition* (New York: Plenum, 1996).

5. *Histoire de l'Alimentation*, Jean-Louis Flandrin and Massimo Montanari, eds. (Paris: Fayard, 1996), 13. Studies of food have particular resonance in the historiography of ancient and medieval Europe: *L'Alimentazione nel mondo antico*, Gabriele Barbieri, ed., 4 vols. (Rome: Istituto poligrafico, 1987); Rudolph M. Bell, *Holy Anorexia* (Chicago: Chicago University Press, 1985); Caroline Walker Bynum, "Fast, Feast, and Flesh: The Religious Significance of Food to Medieval Women," *Representations* (Summer 1985) and *Holy Feast and Holy Fast* (Berkeley: University of California Press, 1987); M.P. Cosman, *Fabulous Feasts: Medieval Cookery and Ceremony* (New York: Braziller, 1976); Gillian Feeley-Harnik, *The Lord's Table: The Meaning of Food in Early Judaism and Christianity* (Washington, D.C.: Smithsonian Institution Press, 1994); Peter Garnsey, *Famine and Food Supply in the Graeco-Roman World* (New York: Cambridge University Press, 1988); Bernard Rudofsky, *Now I Lay Me Down to Eat* (Garden City: Doubleday, 1980); F.J. Simoons, *Eat Not this Flesh: Food Avoidances in the Old World* (Westport, Ct: Greenwood Press, 1981) and *Eat Not This Flesh: Food Avoidances from Prehistory to the Present* (Madison: University of Wisconsin Press, 1994).

6. The list is endless, but in addition to works already mentioned, the following are particularly notable: C. Anne Wilson, *Food and Drink in Britain from the Stone Age to the Present* (London: Constable, 1973); K.C. Chang, *Food in Chinese Culture* (New Haven: Yale University Press, 1977); Arjun Appadurai, "How to Make a National Cuisine: Cookbooks in Contemporary India," *Comparative Studies in Society and History*, 30:1 (January, 1988); *European Food History: A Research Review*, Hans J. Teuteberg, ed. (Leicester: Leicester University Press, 1992); *Storia d'Italia: Alimentazione* (Turin: Einaudi, 1997); Paolo Sorcinelli, *Gli italiani e il cibo* (Bologna: CLUEB, 1995); E. Ohnuki-Tierney, *Rice as Self: Japanese Identities Through Time* (Princeton: Princeton University Press, 1993); *Dining in America*, Kathryn Grover, ed. (University of Massachusetts Press, 1987); Harvey Levenstein, *Paradox of Plenty: A Social History of Eating in Modern America* (New York: Oxford University Press, 1993) and *Revolution at the Table: The Transformation of the American Diet* (Oxford University Press, 1988).

7. The work of Mary Douglas has been particularly influential, see her "Deciphering a Meal," in *Myth, Symbol, and Culture*, Clifford Geertz, ed. (New York: Norton, 1971). Sidney Mintz, *Sweetness and Power: The Place of Sugar in Modern History* (New York: Viking, 1982), 185.

8. Flandrin and Montanari, *Histoire de l'Alimentation*, 8–10.

9. As an example: Sabry Hafez, "Food as a Semiotic Code in Arabic Literature," Zubaida and Tapper, eds., *Culinary Cultures of the Middle East*, 257–80; the use of food by individual artists can be revealing, too, as in Maggie Lane, *Jane Austen and Food* (London: Hambledon Press, 1995).

10. In France, for example, the most noted regional dishes are often based on foods that only arrived from the New World in the sixteenth and seventeenth centuries. Jean-Louis Flandrin and Philip Hyman, "Regional Tastes and Cuisines: Problems, Docu-

ments, and Discourses on Food in Southern France in the 16th and 17th Centuries," *Food and Foodways: Explorations in the History and Culture of Human Nourishment* (June, 1986), 1–31. Similarly, the case for an Italian cuisine was made during the Risorgimento in Artusi's famous cookbook, which borrowed from French models.

11. The multiple connections of food and migration are apparent in another volume in this series: *Global History and Migrations*, Wang Gungwu, ed. (Boulder: Westview Press, 1997).

12. For an unexpected example, see Ianthe MacIagan, "Food and Gender in a Yemeni Community," in *Culinary Cultures of the Middle East*, Sami Zubaida and Richard Tapper, eds. (London: T.B. Tauris Publishers, 1994), 159–72. The topic has a remarkable range and important theoretical implications: C. Adams, *The Sexual Politics of Meat: A Feminist-Vegetarian Critical Theory* (Cambridge: Polity, 1990); M. Buitelaar, *Fasting and Feasting in Morocco: Women's Participation in Ramadan* (Oxford: Berg, 1993); J. Dubisch, "Culture Enters Through the Kitchen: Women, Food, and Social Boundaries in Rural Greece," in *Gender and Power in Rural Greece*, G. Dubisch, ed. (Princeton: Princeton, 1986); J. Kaplan, *A Woman's Conflict: The Special Relationship Between Women and Food* (Englewood Cliffs: Prentice Hall, 1980); Anna S. Meigs, *Food, Sex and Pollution: A New Guinea Religion* (New Brunswick: Rutgers University Press, 1984).

13. Sidney W. Mintz, *Tasting Food, Tasting Freedom* (Boston: Beacon Press, 1996) is a notable example.

14. Bruce Mazlish, Wolf Schäfer, and I have sustained an ongoing debate on this subject for some time. Initial positions can be found in our chapters in *Conceptualizing Global History*, Bruce Mazlish and Ralph Buultjens, eds. (Boulder, Colo.: Westview Press, 1933). Schäfer's sense of global history is more fully developed in his book, *Ungleichzeitigkeit als Ideologie* (Frankfurt: Fischer Taschenbuch Verlag, 1994). Some of the available theories and ideological differences are discussed in the 1995 special issue of *History and Theory*.

15. Arjun Appadurai, *Modernity at Large: Cultural Dimensions of Globalization* (Minneapolis: University of Minnesota Press, 1996); *Reading the Shape of the Modern World*, Henry Schwartz and Richard Dienst, eds. (Boulder: Westview Press, 1996); Robert K. Schaeffer, *Understanding Globalization: The Social Consequences of Political and Economic Change* (Lanham, Md.: Rowman and Littlefield, 1997); Peter Taylor, *The Way the Modern World Works: World Hegemony to World Impasse* (New York: John Wiley and Sons, 1996).

16. Reay Tannahill, *Food in History* (New York: Stein and Day, 1973) treats individual companies.

17. The most influential example is Immanuel Wallerstein's conception of a world system, *The Modern World-System*, vols. I-III (New York: Academic Press, Inc., 1974–89). There are many others on systems of economic connection or world power, often emphasizing the ascendency of Europe.

18. Victor Liberman achieves this in "Transcending East-West Dichotomies: State and Culture Formation in Six Ostensibly Disparate Areas," *Modern Asian Studies*, 31 (1997), 463–546. He compares the internal development in the early modern period of selected Asian and European countries, and the parallels he finds are all the more suggestive because they do not start from the search for a connection between the cases (a preoccupation of global history).

19. William H. McNeill, *Plagues and Peoples* (Garden City, N.J.: 1977).

20. Alfred W. Crosby, *The Columbian Exchange: Biological and Cultural Consequences of 1492* (Westport: Greenwood Press, 1972); Jack Weatherford, *Indian Givers: How the Indians of the Americas Transformed the World* (New York: Fawcett Columbine, 1988).

21. A good introduction is *Global Culture: Nationalism, Globalization, and Modernity*, M. Featherstone, ed. (London: Sage, 1990).

22. The subtleties of Jewish adaptations are particularly interesting: Judith Friedlander, "Jewish Cooking in the American Melting Pot," *Revue française d'études américaines*, 11 (February, 1986), 87–98; Joëlle Bahloul, *Le culte de la table dressée: Rites et traditions de la table algérienne* (Paris: A.-M. Métaillé, 1983); Claudia Roden, "Jewish Food in the Middle East," Zubaida and Tapper, eds., *Culinary Cultures of the Middle East*, 153–58.

23. Redcliffe Salaman, *The History and Social Influence of the Potato* (New York: Cambridge University Press, 1949, 1985). See also S.A.M. Adshead, *Salt and Civilization* (New York: St. Martin's Press, 1992); Kaj Birket-Smith, *Origin of Maize* (Copenhagen: E. Munksgaard, 1943); *Spices in the Indian Ocean World*, M.N. Pearson, ed. (Brookfield, Vt.: Ashgate, 1997); H. Garrison Wilkes, "Maize and Its Wild Relatives," *Science*, 177 (September 1972), 22.

24. Maguelonne Touissant-Samat, *History of Food* (Cambridge: Blackwell Publishers, 1992).

25. Mintz, *Sweetness and Power*, 6.

26. For a valuable recapitulation of this research, see Ester Boserup, "The Impact of Scarcity and Plenty on Development," *Hunger and History: The Impact of Changing Food Production and Consumption Patterns on Society,* Robert I. Rotberg and Theodore K. Rabb, eds. (New York: Cambridge University Press, 1993), 185–93. Also see Gigi M. Berardi, *World Food, Population, and Development* (Totowa, N.J.: Roman and Allanheld, 1985); Jared Diamond, *Guns, Germs, and Steel: The Fates of Human Societies* (New York: W.W. Norton, 1997); Philip D. Curtin, "Nutrition in African History," ibid., 172–84, shows how African history can be understood in light of these issues.

27. On the contemporary issues: *A 20/20 Vision for Food, Agriculture, and the Environment* (Washington, D.C.: International Food Policy Research Institute, 1995); Phillips Foster, *The World Food Problem: Tackling the Causes of Undernutrition in the Third World* (Boulder: Lynee Rienner Publishers, 1992); David Grigg, *The World Food Problem* (Oxford: Blackwell Publishers, 1993); Susan George, *Ill Fares the Land: Essays on Food, Hunger, and Power* (Washington: Institute for Policy Studies, 1984); *Population and Food in the Early Twenty-first Century: Meeting Future Food Demand of an Increasing Population*, Nurul Islam, ed. (Washington, D.C.: World Bank, 1995); *World Hunger and Morality*, William Aiken and Hugh LaFollette, eds. (New York: Prentice Hall, 1996).

28. David Arnold, *Famine: Social Crises and Historical Change* (Oxford: Blackwell Publishers, 1988); David W. Fogel, "The Conquest of High Mortality and Hunger in Europe and America: Timing and Mechanisms," in *Favorites of Fortune: Technology, Growth, and Economic Development*, Patrice Higonnet, David S. Landes, and Henry Rosovsky, eds. (Cambridge: Harvard University Press, 1991), 38–39; Susan George, *How the Other Half Dies: The Real Reasons for World Hunger* (Har-

mondsworth, Engl: Penguin Books, 1976), and see Amartya Sen,"Nobody Need Starve," *Granta,* 52 (Winter, 1995), 213–20, for a provocative assessment of international economic and political practices today.

29. The classic of the rich anthropological literature is, of course, Claude Lévi-Strauss, *The Raw and the Cooked* (New York: Harper and Row, 1975), but the following can suggest some of the range of the work done since: M. Arnott, *Gastronomy: The Anthropology of Food and Food Habits* (The Hague: Mouton, 1975); Peter Farb and George Armelagos, *Consuming Passions: The Anthropology of Eating* (New York: Washington Square Press, 1980); Marvin Harris, *The Sacred Cow and the Abominable Pig: Riddles of Food and Culture* (New York: Simon and Schuster, 1986); C. Hugh-Jones, "Food for Thought: Patterns of Production and Consumption in Pira-Parana Society," in J.S. La Fontaine, ed., *Sex and Age as Principles of Social Differentiation* (Academic Press, 1978), 41–66.

30. Two interesting examples appeared in *Comparative Civilizations Review,* 5 (Fall, 1980): Lowell Edmunds, "Ancient Roman and Modern American Food: A Comparative Sketch of Two Semiological Systems," 52–69, and William E. Naff, "Some Reflections on the Food Habits of China, Japan, and Rural America," 70–95. But see also R.S. Khare, *The Eternal Food: Gastronomic Ideas and Experiences of Hindus and Buddhists* (Albany: University of New York Press, 1992); *South Asian Food Systems: Food, Society, and Culture,* R.S. Khare and M.S.A. Rao, eds. (New Haven: Yale University Press, 1977) and Stephen Mennell, *All Manners of Food: Eating and Taste in England and France from the Middle Ages to the Present* (Oxford: Blackwell Publishers, 1985).

31. Marcel Mazoyer and Laurence Roudart, *Histoire des Agricultures du Monde: du Néolithique à la crise contemporaine* (Paris: Seuil, 1998).

32. See Getel H. Pelto and Pertiti J. Pelto, "Diet and Delocalization: Dietary Changes since 1750," in Rotberg and Rabb, *Hunger and History,* 309–30.

33. Discussed in *The Age of Transition: Trajectory of the World System, 1945–2025,* Terence K. Hopkins and Immanuel Wallerstein, eds. (London: Zed Books, 1996) by Sheila Pelizzon and John Casparis, "World Human Welfare," 126–32, 143–45; and Immanuel Wallerstein, "The Global Picture," 209–225.

34. For a comparable response to global changes affecting a local society, see Marie-Claud Mathias, "Milk and Its Transformations in Indian Society," *Food and Foodways,* 2 (1988), 265–88.

35. There is, of course, a whole literature on the development of taste, see *Taste, Experience, and Feeding,* Elizabeth D. Capaldi and Terry L. Powley, eds. (Washington, D.C.: American Psychological Association, 1990); Hans Deutsch-Renner, *The Origin of Food Habits* (London: Faber and Faber, 1944).

36. Elias Canetti, *Crowds and Power* (New York: The Viking Press, 1962) speaks of feasts, crowds and the special importance of abundance, 62–63.

37. Holly Chase, "The Meyhane or McDonald's? Changes in Eating Habits and Evolution of Fast Food in Istanbul," Zubaida and Tapper, eds., *Culinary Cultures of the Middle East,* 73–85.

Part One

*The History of Food
in Global Perspectives*

Chapter Two

Circles of Growing and Eating: The Political Ecology of Food and Agriculture

Harriet Friedmann

After three million years of culling food from the natural life cycles of other species, the human species undertook a vast series of uncontrolled experiments in reshaping the earth. Five to ten thousand years ago, bands of human foragers began to control the reproduction of plants and animals, marking the most profound shift in human relations to the earth, more significant than electricity or nuclear fission (Mintz 1994:106). Tied to their cultivated fields, human beings soon divided into stable groups which I shall call households: hierarchical groups of human beings and dependent species attached to, and deriving sustenance from, specific places in the earth. Our ancestors selected a small number of the 5,000 plant species that have ever fed the human species (and these are only a fraction of 1 percent of the world's flora); over the millennia since domestication, we have reduced the number of plants that feed us or our dependent animals to about 150 (Wilkes 1988: 68). Human beings, the "most adaptable and therefore most widely distributed . . . large land animals" (Crosby 1986: 13), began to push back the frontiers of self-organizing life, of evolution.

Domestic plants and animals are our dependents, even our "wards" (Wilkes 1988:67). Human beings have always altered forests, grasslands, and waterways; changed the flows of water and air; yet depended on these cycles to absorb the wastes of monocultural plantations of species, including human beings. The human species must interact with ecological processes, but the question is whether we do so wisely or dangerously. What, then, can the history of agriculture and food tell us about the choices open to the human species in taking responsibility for our power to shape the earth?

The essay is in four parts: first, an ecological interpretation of agriculture and food; second, an interpretation of the enlarging circles of food and agriculture from the Neolithic Revolution to industrialization, with a focus on the effects of colonization and commodification in reconstellating households in relation to land; third, an account of the fundamental social and ecological shift in human relations to the earth entailed by industrial agriculture; and, fourth, a suggestion of practices which prefigure ways of life and work which might replace food and agriculture at the center of human economy, what Colin Duncan (1996) argues is the next step in the long journey of humankind from local to planetary ecosystem.

Ecology of Agriculture

Having converted much of the face of the earth into monocultural grasses to feed ourselves and our dependent animals, the human species has emerged from the local ecosystems whose features provide our inherited, distinct cultural experiences. Past human disturbances have destroyed the wild containers of natural ecosystems. We now face the challenge of managing our planet's intertwined cycles of water, soil, air and a vastly reduced number of species. "Seed eaters have responsibilities," writes Duncan (1996:183) as he concludes his brilliant analysis of agriculture as the key to regulating human relations with the rest of nature.

Agriculture is the human activity that simplifies the mix of species in a defined area of soil (a field) "with a view to. . . . organized harvesting" (Duncan 1996: 13).[1] In other words, a farmer destroys the interdependent mix of species naturally growing in a meadow and tries to make it grow only wheat or rice (or, with slightly different effect, intercropped maize, beans, and squash). To grasp the implications of this definition, let us begin with an ecosystem relatively undisturbed such as that which existed when human beings foraged and hunted like other large mammals. Before agriculture, hunter-gatherers lived by taking food from living beings without actively trying to control their cycles of life; though vulnerable to climate and predators, they usually did not work very hard (Sahlins 1972).[2]

In a natural ecosystem, there occurs a biological succession of species, each creating a niche for another organism, with plants dominating. Each of these sets of organisms changes the soil and other conditions by using up substances and by eliminating wastes, thus creating additional niches for other sets of organisms. These stages of succession continue until a more or less stable community of species called the "climax" establishes itself. This climax community is a breathtakingly complex web of life, in which minerals, soil, water, air, and light pass through and are changed by the organisms living with and through each other. In this view, human beings are not at the top of a linear food chain but a point in the web: Although we have killed our large predators, both alive and dead, we are food for micro-organisms.

The earth's major ecosystems are named for distinct climax communities: tropical forest, savanna, arid land, temperate forest (deciduous and coniferous), temperate grassland, seashores, plus high altitude and marine ecosystems (Collinson 1977). A climax community is generally an extremely diverse ecosystem that is not a very efficient source of human food, as anyone walking through a temperate forest without a packed lunch will realize. Most of the "biomass" (weight of living organisms) is woody matter inedible to human beings, which is why hunter-gatherers can sustain themselves only by finding such extremely large areas to cull enough food from climax ecosystems.

Agriculture reverses the ecological process of succession. It removes the diverse organisms from forest or grassland and creates a simple ecosystem that consists of one or a few plants. Human beings cultivate plants, particularly the seeds of grasses (grains) and the roots of tuberous plants (such as potatoes) whose cycles create a dense biomass that human beings can eat. In ecological terms, grains are annual grasses that have evolved to bear many seeds, thus ensuring that at least some survive the dangers from one generation to the next. Annuals characterize an early stage of succession, full of niches ready for invasion by other organisms. Annuals naturally tend to give way to perennials. So, agriculture not only creates its own constant source of "pests" (weeds, molds, fungi, and insect and larger competitors for cultivated plants). It also creates plant competitors (weeds) which are hardier perennials compared to the more fragile cultivated annuals. Farmers may inadvertently expel complementary species, for instance pollinating insects, and then must recruit replacements (Duncan 1996:14–18). Whether caused by angels or population pressure or human curiosity, the expulsion from Eden is grounded in ecological science: Human beings cultivating fields must get food by the sweat of their brows (Heiser 1990:1).[3]

Herding is slightly less disruptive of grassland ecosystems. Grazing animals eat plant matter which human beings cannot digest. To avoid overgrazing, herding requires cyclical migration over large territories. Still, the temptation to overgraze remains: The dry, rocky terrain of the Mediterranean was created over thousands of years by several civilizations, which caused soil erosion by overcutting forests, then allowed their herds to overgraze the plants that occupied the disrupted terrain. Even without this overgrazing, herds of animals, domestic or wild, destroy plants with hooves and teeth, making room for colonizing plants (weeds) and the organisms whose cycles mesh with theirs. This aspect of grazing animal herds will be an important part of the story below of European "ecological imperialism", both intended and unintended (Crosby 1986).

Weed species and disease organisms are at the crux between the intended and the unintended effects of agriculture. Botanists define a weed as "any plant that spreads rapidly and outcompetes others on disturbed soil" (Crosby 1986:149). Some cultivated crops, such as rye and oats (which still

grow "wild" in wheat fields) were originally weeds; some Neolithic cultivars, including crabgrass, have been abandoned to become weeds. Weeds stabilize disturbed ecosystems and prevent soil erosion. Observed in the waste
areas surrounding early human habitations, weeds are one suggested source
of plant domestication (Heiser 1990:15). Human beings disrupt ecosystems
first of all by tilling the soil, which can be done with varying degrees of disruption, depending on the type and number of species and the techniques of
working the soil. Servant animals, particularly grazers, disrupt soil and
plants by trampling and nibbling. When plants and animals introduced to an
alien ecosystem disturbed by colonization become naturalized—go wild—
they change the habitat for all the native species, including the human beings, who then create the enemies they fight (Crosby 1986:145–70). What is
true for weeds is also true for disease organisms: the greater the simplification, the greater the struggle.

Over the millennia of householding agriculture, human beings have
gained experience in each habitat, which has led to more or less stable farming systems. They moved slowly with their *portmanteau biota* (Crosby
1986:287–88) over land and sea, readapting basic neolithic patterns of cultivation and cuisine wherever they settled. The basic pattern across cultures
was centered on grain, both to grow and to eat. The soil had to be renewed
with the nutrients used up by the grain, either by allowing it to lie fallow to
renew itself or by mixing or rotating complementary plants or animals
whose life processes restored fertility to the grainfields. The cycles of the extended family of human beings, animals and plants had to be mutually sup-
portive, often with the help of wild organisms, such as pollinating insects,
for life to continue.

Human beings have also adapted their farming to the nutritional requirements of the human body, having discovered them by experience long before
science gave them names. A protein to supplement the incomplete versions
in each grain was cultivated (or reared) and prepared in some form everywhere. Beans, corn and (for vitamins) squash were grown and prepared together in Mexico (along with early cultivars such as chili pepper). Fermentation allowed for the maximum digestion of sorghum protein in African beer
and in Asian soybean curd. Yeast in these foods and in breads added plant
protein in Europe (Wilkes 1988:68). And of course, in Europe, the centrality
of animals in the diet and in the farming system was to be decisive in the unequal meeting and reconstellating of ecosystems led by European colonialism. But even then, the diet remained Neolithic in form: a "core" of starchy
staple, a "fringe" to give flavor, and a complementary meat or vegetable protein (Mintz 1994:106). Agriculture and cuisine formed a (sometimes reconstituted) circle.

The monumental shift to cultivation helps us to re-imagine the human
species as the dominant large animals in all ecosystems. We have achieved
this distinction because of culture, which in biological terms may be under-

stood as a vastly increased ability to change quickly by "storing and altering patterns of behavior not in the molecules of the genetic code but in the cells of the brain" (Crosby 1986:14). Each culture stores patterns of behavior from experience in guiding a local ecosystem, usually based on cereal cultivation. Can we find, or imagine, a common organizational form that emerged with this shift in all the various parts of the world?

Households: Key to the Past

The Greek word *oikos*, meaning household, is the root of both "economy" and "ecology": the management and knowledge of the household (Waring 1988). Although there may be variations in marriage, residence, descent, status, and power, it is reasonable to see the emergence of lineages, usually tracking descent in the male line, and the relocation of one marriage partner, usually the wife, as connected with settlement and cultivation (Chevillard and Leconte 1986). Domestication refers both to control over reproduction and to the habitations of human groups with their dependent species. Thus, oikos in Western thought refers to the group living with the lineage head; in classical Athens, the citizen was a male owner of property, with his wives, children and slaves arranged in various relations of dependence (Coontz and Henderson 1986; Saliou 1986). Departing from my earlier emphasis on distinctions among households (Friedmann 1980, 1986), I shall use the word household to name the common experience initiated with the Neolithic revolution.

The Neolithic Revolution divided human societies as it allocated areas of the earth. Before the domestication of other species, human beings, like other primates, related to their habitats as whole societies. All individuals were woven into a single fabric of mating and descent. Domestication— human control over reproduction of other species—not only created hierarchies among species but also among human beings. Households consist of "extended families" of human beings and our servant species (Crosby 1986: 25), who are attached to specific sites. Households, including not only kin but also servants (and slaves) of both human and other species, have been the enduring institution for the managing and inheriting of, and living from, the land. From this perspective, plantations, manors and other direct hierarchical relations all stem from the Neolithic household.

Settled cultivation inaugurated hierarchies of inherited patriarchal wealth and rule.[4] Just as preindustrial masters (or latterly, heads of households) depend on wives, children, tenants, servants and slaves, human beings depend on servant species, such as cattle and wheat, and their companions, such as insects, birds, and bacteria, of which we may be less aware. Just as the presence of some kinfolk is unappreciated, domestication also creates unwanted dependent species—weeds, predators, and disease organisms. The household—until the development of the modern, capitalist, industrial society—

was the army in the war against natural succession. Recent centuries and decades have both shifted the nature of human relations (industry) and undermined the enduring unit of social life (the household).

Deeply embedded in inherited thought, the household still presents itself as a natural unit, even after the individualization brought by wage relations and the extension of political rights.[5] Despite his profound understanding of the ecological divide between agriculture and industry, Duncan stops short of a full appreciation of this social transformation. He defines modernity (1996: 26) as "a society . . . modern to the extent that its *households* consume little of what they themselves produce and produce little of what they themselves consume" (added emphasis). The separation of households that produce and consume already implies their disintegration as fundamental social units. Duncan's phrasing obscures the obvious shift of production to nonhousehold units, such as factories, shops, warehouses, and offices, which are far more fluid in composition and function. Even more, it masks the fluidity in units of consumption, as households shrink in membership, even to consist of single persons, and have the function of making the arrangements to share dwellings.

I find useful Duncan's distinctions among modernity (enabling freedom), capitalism (compelling infinite expansion), and industry ("a qualitatively distinct mode of interacting with nature") (Duncan 1996: 29). Yet his insightful proposals for new social forms appropriate to harmonious, conscious management of natural cycles, are limited by his failure to understand the historical importance of the crisis of Neolithic households. Duncan's proposal (1996: 29) to "drop capitalism, control industrialism, but retain modernity" is improved by an appreciation of the importance and decline of households. It is to understand our present situation in an ecohistorical context that we interpret the experience of the long period of householding, from the Neolithic to the industrial era.

Enlarging the Circles of Growing and Eating: Colonization

Until the European conquest of new worlds, human beings moved slowly over land and water, sometimes leaving members behind, sometimes adopting new dependent species, usually bringing along their stowaway weeds and varmints (rats, roaches, houseflies, and the like) as well as their personal vermin (lice, fleas, internal parasites). If they were lucky, as were the first migrants to America and Australia, they left behind their large and microscopic enemies and adapted to foraging or created complex households in new ecosystems. Taking the long ecological view, Crosby (1986) emphasizes the independent evolution of Old and New Worlds for several million years before the parallel Neolithic Revolutions. Until 500 years ago, then, and for most purposes, even 50 years ago, extended agrarian households became re-established in new habitats and found ways to sustain their cultivation and diets.

For millenia, the circles of growing and eating were contained by the lands on which human beings managed the dependent species which fed them; as ingredients of cuisines, dependent plants and animals linked human bodies and human cultures to the earth. Food, therefore, was for most of human history inseparable from close relations with servant (and parasitic) species and with the lands they cohabited. Each Neolithic cuisine centered on a starchy staple made from one of the small number of grasses or tubers domesticated by parallel Neolithic cultures—wheat, rice, maize, barley, oats, millet, quinoa, rye, cassava, yams, sweet potatoes, or potatoes—plus complementary ingredients both cultivated and wild (Mintz 1994:105). Descendants of these cuisines, like peasant cultivators, are still the familiar ones we call traditional.

The first stage in breaking the apparent reciprocal dependence between the human species and local ecosystems, along with the widening of the circles of growing and eating, began with colonial conquest and settlement 500 years ago. Europeans failed in their first colonizing efforts, succumbing to diseases in Africa (notably in the Crusades) and Asia, whose biota evolved in a contiguous land mass and resisted displacement. But human beings and other species in the New Worlds were helpless to resist the intensive colonization by aggressive Old World biota, both large and small, especially microscopic, disease organisms. European settlers, cattle, wheat, weeds, and vermin went wild in what became the Neo-Europes of the Americas and Australia and New Zealand. Crosby (1986: 271) calls this "a revolution more extreme than any seen on this planet since the extinctions at the end of the Pleistocene."

What Crosby calls Neo-Europes were created through the transplantation of colonies of European human beings and their portmanteau biota, in other words, all the species they intentionally and unintentionally carried with them (Crosby 1986: 279). European households had evolved with an unusually large number of animals, and especially the cow, which offered European human beings, with their comparatively rare capacity to digest milk, a steady source of protein, animal power to pull plows through heavy soils, and abundant manure to replenish intensively cultivated soils. The complementary adaptations of human beings, animals and plants gave the European complex an advantage in conquering most New World ecosystems. The animals disturbed the soil and stripped away local grasses, allowing European weeds (opportunistic plants which colonize disturbed soils) to take root, since they were adapted to disturbed soils over centuries of plowing. Some cattle interbred with native breeds, such as those in Argentina; some went feral; and some replaced hardy native species like the bison only by the systematic slaughter at the hands of their human masters. Thus, the New World environments were Europeanized, by which Crosby (1986: 291–92) means:

a condition of continual disruption: of plowed fields, razed forests, overgrazed pastures, and burned prairies, of deserted villages and expanding cities, of human beings, animals, plants, and microlife that have evolved separately, suddenly coming into intimate contact . . . an ephemeralized world in which weed species of all phyla prosper and the other life forms are to be found in large numbers only in accidental enclaves or special parks . . . weeds, in the broadest sense of the word, are more characteristic of the biotas of lands anciently affected by the Old World Neolithic than any others.

With the wheat came Hessian flies; with settlers and their livestock came weeds such as dandelion and burdock, honeybees to pollinate, rats to compete for stored wheat flour, and myriad Old World species wanted and unwanted.

With colonization there also began the "Columbian Exchange" of Old and New World species, which became woven into the natural and social fabric of most ecosystems (Crosby 1972). European traders created new complexes of transplanted human beings and other species in the New World, speeding up the rate of movement and widening the circles of origin of the new extended households. In the Americas, European masters commanded the labour of African slaves and Indian indentured labourers or reorganized the remnants of defeated indigenous societies in monocultural plantations tied to European markets. Columbus brought sugar cane cuttings to Hispaniola in 1494 (Brockway 1988: 53). Carried back to Europe from the Middle East by Crusaders 200 years earlier, sugar cane was transplanted successfully in the Mediterranean islands, Iberia, and Atlantic islands; and honey replaced Renaissance sugar as a sweetener (Crosby 1986:67–68). Coffee, which had come to Holland from its Ethiopian origins via Arab plantations in India, reached Brazil via Dutch colonies in the Americas. Bananas, from Asia, were transplanted in America. Cacao, a New World crop, was organized into the plantations in America and peasant farms in Africa and combined with sugar to become chocolate, a popular food in Europe.

Human beings also brought their own foods to America from their origins in Europe, Africa and Asia. Europeans brought citrus fruits, grape vines, olives, melons, onions, and radishes, many of which failed in the climate (Brockway 1988). Africans and Indians brought fruits, such as mangoes, herbs, and spices from home. Thus began the Creole cuisines of America. As the wild places and indigenous cultivators were pushed back, as the number of plants in the world was reduced and as the ecosystems homogenized, the transplanted peoples and dependent species multiplied the types of cultural food practices.

European colonial empires also hastened and deepened the reconstellation of local agriculture and diets in the Old World. In Europe and the European colonies, cultivation—and the mixture of human beings and dependent species—in many ecosystems reconstellated around New World crops such as potatoes, maize, and other staples. Old World cuisines now called traditional contained transplanted New World fringes such as tomatoes, capsicum (chili peppers), and peanuts.

Colonial conquests—the first new stage in human homogenization of the life processes on earth (Crosby 1986: 172)—created a common, though highly contentious, conflictual, and varied story for humankind. Many threads of the story can be traced, as households—recombined with complex new elements of race, gender and generational hierarchies, and changed notions of agriculture—were reconstituted with imported and domestic species coexisting in varying states of harmony and conflict. These resulted in transformations of interdependence among species and among earthly cycles of soil, water, and air, now organized across the globe.[6] The thread I follow here is the deepening of commodity relations and attendant stresses on households in England, the most intensive site of industry and capitalist reorganization, and in North America, the most intensive site of simplification and relocation of agricultural households.

Enlarging Circles of Growing and Eating: Commodification

The blending and simplification of ecosystems results from the global integration of human activities and needs through anonymous markets. Households and farming, the unified and local bases of human life since the beginning of civilization, became differentiated and marginalized. Increasingly, though with reversals, specialized markets connected farms, like factories, to anonymous markets. Wage relations connected individuals directly to anonymous markets, bypassing or penetrating households. Individuals cast out of rural households moved into cities, what Crosby (1986:30) calls "single stands of human beings," along with their pests and micropredators. When they could, migrant human beings found work, along with the money to buy what they could no longer acquire directly, in industries that worked into commodities inert substances taken from fields and mines in distant regions of the earth. The breakdown of household organization and direct, observable effects of human activity on earthly cycles were thus intertwined. The climax came with industrial agriculture in the middle of the twentieth century.

During the transition to industrial agriculture, changes in agriculture were paradoxical: ecologically sound but socially devastating high farming in England, early capitalist agricultural ventures there, and socially progressive but ecologically disastrous family farms in North America. Duncan emphasizes the importance of laws regulating land use, since these are crucial to the formation of an understanding of how human techniques affect the rest of nature. This leads him to laud the virtues of high farming, since it encouraged a long view of receiving returns from the land. Similarly, Duncan berates the ecological devastation of monocultural settler agriculture in North America. This is useful, in that social and economic histories generally ignore the role of "soil mining," a cause of such ecological catastrophes as the Dust Bowl in the North American grasslands only about two generations after settlement (Friedmann 1978; Bonnifield 1979). In search of a balanced and unified account, I look briefly to the stresses on households as an aspect of the ecological histories.

High Farming.   Duncan (1996: 64–80) reinterprets the history of English high farming in ecological terms: The four-crop rotation (wheat, turnip, barley, and clover crops) was scientifically integrated with sheep rearing (and horses for pulling plows) in such a way that the condition of the land was maintained indefinitely. Previously infertile land was improved and brought into sustainable production, all the while increasing the yield per acre of wheat. This seems indisputable. The key to this achievement was "biological or ecological, as opposed to industrial (chemical), methods" (1996:65). The orientation of the farmer, despite the fully capitalist nature of the enterprise, was to achieve the proper balance between wheat output and animal manure, which in turn required including winter forage crops for the animals in the rotation. Turnips and clover added nutrients to the soil, allowing wheat yields to rise. Most importantly, sheep were "mobile fertilizer factories" (1996:64). "Folds", or movable fences, enclosed sheep in desired locations; after grazing on hillsides by day, the "folded" sheep dropped their manure in the required fields by night, transferring nutrients from uncultivated to the cultivated soils. Experience showed how to adjust rotations to achieve what is now called biological pest control.

The consolidation or "engrossing" of farms, together with the enclosure of the common lands, was necessary to this rational reorganization of farming. Land size was dictated by the area which could be supervised on horseback and by the ideal balance of crops and animals. Labour was abundant and cheap, since villagers deprived of traditional lands had few alternatives except to emigrate. As a result, the variation in the size of English farms was related to the ecological characteristics present in each district. All of this came to be part of the local knowledge of both farmers and laborers in each locality.

Duncan attributes this achievement, first, to reliable markets for wheat, the main source of income for the farm, and for wool, which in this account was a byproduct of the system of production rather than its motive.[7] Second, and most important, after a period of relatively free land markets, the practice of "strict settlement" revived the medieval practice of entail. This restricted the heir of an estate from selling the core of the landholding or from using it in ways that reduced its natural wealth, for instance, by overcutting timber or by converting arable land to pasture. By requiring each heir to pass the land on to the next generation in stable or improved condition, the institution instilled a long view. It prevented farmers from focusing only on getting the maximum revenues in volatile wheat, wool, and other specialized markets. Third, technologies based on fossil fuels did not yet exist. The science and technologies used on the farm continued to follow natural cycles, but human caretaking was improved by careful observation and experimentation; human power was replaced by animal power, with inputs that were part of the rotation and the outputs from which entered into renewal of the soil.

T.P. Bayliss-Smith (1982: 37–55), by contrast, locates the extraordinarily benign and productive ecology of English high farming in the context of displacement of agrarian households by the classes of capitalist farmers and impoverished farm laborers. His analysis, which centers on the ratios of energy inputs and outputs, is consistent with Duncan's declaration that English high farming is the most efficient and ecologically benign agricultural system ever devised. By his measure, a Wiltshire (southern England) farm of 1826 was three times more efficient in the ratio of human energy input to human food energy than that of the shifting cultivation in New Guinea, which is probably comparable to the Neolithic. The improvement in human productivity was mainly due to the use of horses as "energy slaves." The output per unit of land was four times higher because the use of animal manure and rotations allowed the English system to dispense with fallow periods.

Yet Bayliss-Smith refuses to accept as useful the "abstract" measure of gross energy productivity (total food energy, including fodder, divided by total population)—eight times higher than New Guinea labor—because of the unequal distribution of the product compared to egalitarian shifting cultivators. He offers in addition the calculation that the labor contributed by an English farmworker yielded five times the food energy that he and his family consumed. The ratio between his work energy input and food energy consumption was slightly worse than the New Guinea cultivator. His lot was considerably harder in insecurity and subservience; and unlike the surplus of the New Guinea cultivators, which enabled them to maintain large pig herds and hold redistributive feasts, the Wiltshire farm laborer was fortunate if he could afford to keep even one pig for his family's use.

Bayliss-Smith's conclusion (1982: 55,52) is, therefore, that English high farming overcame the ecological limits to agriculture before and since but faced fatal limits set by social instability. In 1830 workers rioted against labor displacing technology. In the famous Luddite, or Captain Swing, movement, unemployed and underemployed men marched through the countryside smashing threshing machines and demanding higher wages. The threshing machine is key, since it was ecologically benign in its use of horses for power (as were early harvesters and other machines). When it was used, feed and manure could be included in the rotation, although it was socially impoverishing to the majority of the rural population, as was the whole system of improved agriculture. Social resistance led for several decades to the postponement of the introduction of the machines. Duncan (1996: 68) insists that the threshing machine was a technical innovation not intrinsic to capitalist farming because it processed the wheat after it was harvested, though he "acknowledges that it was "gratuitously disruptive." For Duncan, the social limits to English high farming came from the world market.

In my view, both Bayliss-Smith and Duncan are correct. Bayliss-Smith's argument does lead to the profound understanding that English ecological success broke out of the container of the household, which had organized human interaction with nature since the Neolithic revolution. English farmers and landlords had broken the old bonds of obligations to their workers, and villagers evicted from ancestral holdings lost their former bonds to masters and the land. Without a new container, class conflict and cheap imports led to the demise of high farming.

Settler Farming.   Emigrants fleeing the poverty of late-nineteenth-century Europe rode the new railways across the plains of North America to farm the unplowed earth recently cleared by force of their human and buffalo inhabitants. Duncan (1996: 102–3) makes the significant point that settler agriculture, which supplied the New World market from 1880 onwards, revived "unsophisticated farming." Settlers were granted blocks of land that were huge by European standards. Starting with little but their own labor and that of their wives and children, the "masters" of the shrunken households deposited in the treeless prairies built sod huts, cleared the fields of stones, and broke the soil which had been grazed and manured by wild herds for millenia. American low farming could rely little on experience, since it would not have been transferable from distinct and distant ecosystems. What they depended on was the fertility stored naturally over eons in lands never farmed but over which roamed human hunters and large grazing mammals as they continuously returned nutrients to the soil. Prairie grain was cheap because of "methods more akin to mining than to proper farming" (1996:102).

States and railways intent on organizing vast expanses of land into national territories and international markets encouraged extensive land use. Prairie farms, the abundant produce from which drove European farmers into cities or into specialized products for several decades, always had low yields per acre. Their high yields per person were due to a combination of scarce labor and depletion of natural fertility. The shortage of labor was managed at harvest by the use of improved horse-drawn mechanical reapers and binders, often owned by specialized custom operators who followed the season from southern to northern plains, selling their harvesting services to farmers (Giedeon 1969: 146–62; Friedmann 1978a).[8] Because it took from the soil without returning, prairie agriculture inevitably reached ecological limits. Because grasslands are inherently more fragile than the cleared forests

of Europe, the Dustbowl crisis came within five decades, barely two generations later.

Settler farmers were not the first to wreak local ecological havoc. The
uniqueness of settler agriculture was its place in emerging world commodity
markets. Settler farms depended entirely, for the first time in agricultural history, on selling their products to distant markets and buying what supplies
they needed from these same markets. In contrast to the commodification of
labor in English high farming, American settler farming was fully commodi-
fied in its relation to all inputs and outputs. Given the impoverished origins of
most settlers, who were fleeing the slums and villages of industrializing Europe, money was scarce. The governments and railways pushing settlement
placed ever-growing numbers of competing farmers on the prairies, not only
in the United States and Canada but also in Argentina, Australia, Siberia, and
the Punjab. The ability to buy inputs or even animals to renew soils was limited by the short-term pressure to survive. At the same time, settlers were not
part of integrated village communities. Although they invented cooperative
practices and institutions with their new neighbors and even built important
political movements in the larger society, settler farms were shrunken households caught in a monoculture (see Friedmann 1978a,1978b, 1980). The
household was preserved, although in an extremely simplified version, both in
its composition of species and its tie to the land.

The world wheat market which emerged in the late nineteenth century
linked unsustainable prairie farming with English high farming. The latter
began to specialize in animal production for markets rather than renewing the
wheat-centered rotation. As the English population began to depend on imported wheat, English farmers began to intensify their efforts to raise livestock
through the use of industrially produced, often imported, feeds. This undermined the self-contained renewal of species and soil which had characterized
high farming (Duncan 1996: 95–99). English wheat production adapted, receiving massive state support during the World Wars and the Depression between, to take on the shrunken form of "family farms" (Friedmann 1978a).
During and after World War II, both American and English wheat farms took
on the industrial characteristics of a mechanical-chemical intensive monoculture because the ever-larger concentration on intensive animal production was
concentrated in ever-larger operations requiring the purchase of larger quantities of feed. Farms specialized in grains or livestock. The latter yielded not manure but waste. The former needed chemical fertilizer(Berlan 1991; Giedeon
1969; Bayliss-Smith 1982: 98–109). By the 1960s, monocultural grain production dependent on (imported) industrial inputs was introduced to many parts
of the world through the Green Revolution (Shiva 1993: 9–59).

The households engaged in monocultural farming depended on families
increasingly similar to, and integrated with, urban households. As a result,
family farms now carry the paradoxical legacy of being the keepers of the
link to the earth, even as they are the agents of the break with the rest of

nature. As commercial enterprises, a few operations have retained a family connection, often through contracts with large industrial input and purchasing firms. Those engaged in commercially successful monoculture have sacrificed local knowledge to the instructions accompanying packages of seeds and associated chemicals. The upgrading of skills on the farm has more to do with accounting and the use of computers than with agronomy. Farm families often live in cities most of the year and experience the same gender and generational conflicts as non-farm families (Friedmann 1987). Everything wrong with the family is also wrong with the family farm.

At the same time, the majority of farms are part-time, often mixed enterprises; and their owners are linked into the activities of urban life (Whatmore 1991). The new movement in the so-called advanced societies is breaking down the ancient cultural divide between urban and rural dwellers. Although much will have to be done to reclaim the simplified, often poisoned fields of monoculture—both grain and livestock—the social bases for reconfiguring urban and rural communities may emerge from the changes in work, family, and values that unite them. Both equality and freedom, included in Duncan's term modernity, undermine households and create opportunities for new forms of intentional community. English high farming and American settler agriculture each broke with one of the remaining institutions of Neolithic agriculture: English agriculture with the complex household of human beings, American agriculture with the integration of species and soil. Settlement and trade had begun the process of homogenizing agricultural systems and melding cuisines. Industrialization deepened the separation of agriculture and diets from ecosystems. The circles began to expand to the breaking point.

Industrial Agriculture: Break with the Past and with the Earth

The reconstellation of agricultural ecosystems (and cuisines) in the colonial period thus gave way to the interdependent specialization of production. Farms using standard seeds and packages of inputs produce raw materials for industrially produced standard edible commodities sold on world markets. Food industries seek generic ingredients—sweeteners, fats, thickeners, stabilizers, and artificial flavors—from around the world as substitutable inputs (Goodman, Sorj, and Wilkinson 1987). The global diet created in this way sacrifices (or standardizes) distinct cuisines under the dictates of price and physiologically maladaptive human desires for sugar and fat and, of course, salt. Mintz (1994: 113) calls this the second revolution, the first being domestication. Farms and consumers are linked to industry throughout the globe at the level of inputs as well as markets but divorced from specific cycles of species, soil, water, and air in their ecosystems.

When agriculture adopts techniques borrowed from industry, it incorporates the contradiction between self-organizing processes and inert substances. Duncan (1996:116) follows the distinction of the Physiocrats which claims that "agriculture necessarily rides on living ecological cycles, whereas industry transforms dead matter, changing only its form." The defining feature of industry is a linear processing of "inputs" into "outputs."[9] A factory buys inputs of energy, raw materials, and labor and organizes them to create products. The decisive factors in choosing, for instance, cotton or nylon are the relative costs of purchasing, processing, and selling the final product. The radical substitutability of inputs—and as diets become flexible through separation from traditional meanings of interlinked cultures and ecosystems (Duncan 1996:116)—of outputs, may define industrial agriculture. The radical substitutability itself makes possible the abstract language of inputs and outputs.

Industrial agriculture chooses inputs in relation to relative prices, replacing animals with tractors, for instance, according to the relative costs of each. According to Duncan, it was the desperation of surviving Depression farmers to reduce costs that led them to adopt mechanical and chemical inputs promoted by machinery and chemical industries. Agricultural historian Erik Kerridge (1969, cited in Duncan 1996:90) writes:

> There has been [since 1914] a revolution in the introduction of machinery integrated with the internal combustion engine and of chemical fertilizers, pesticides, and weed killers, but this has originated in the chemical and engineering industries, not in farming, and farmers have been less than passive in these developments, mostly having to be bribed into participation by vast and wholly unjustified outpourings of public money.

Two key elements in artificial fertilizer, potassium and phosphorous, must be mined, so they are finite resources. Tractors, unlike animals or human beings, require non-renewable energy to run. Pesticides kill organisms beyond the control or intention of the manufacturers or farmers and create niches for more pests to appear. Socially, the substitution of purchased inputs for renewable cycles locks farmers into markets; and relative costs become embedded in farming practices at the expense of agronomic knowledge.

The contradiction between living cycles and the linear transformation of inputs into outputs makes it difficult to reverse the process of simplification. Once chemical fertilizers replace organic matter and machinery compacts soil, the billions of living organisms involved in the self-renewing processes diminish in number and vitality and mutual interdependence. To revert towards diversification and self-organization requires massive effort, knowledge, and attention to the specifics of the field, something unlikely to arise in the conditions that led to industrial techniques. The farmer eventually becomes as dependent on the knowledge of the chemical manufacturer as does the effect of a fertilizer or pesticide on the crop itself. She or he moves farther from active involvement in the self-organizing cycles of organisms, air and water toward the search for the advice of experts in the use of particular seeds, chemicals, and machines, often in complex combinations.

Substitutability thus occasions another feature of industry in agriculture: radical indifference to place.[10] Put another way, this makes it possible for industry to ignore or adapt a place to its activities; a key innovation of industry was the movement of coal, oil, or electricity to an industrial site instead of accepting the restrictions implicit in such fixed locations as those of mills driven by water or wind. This locational flexibility allows greater distance from the consequences of handling wastes. Industrial agriculture creates wastes which are easier to ignore (chemical fertilizers and pesticides become "externalities" when they flow into watersheds) than in the preindustrial farming system. Of course, industrial agriculture did not invent pollution, which happens for instance when soil becomes salinated as the result of irrigated preindustrial agriculture. However, it systematically externalizes the effects.

Of course, technology restructured farming, indeed the whole of life, long before industry. For instance, the medieval plow invented in the seventh century cut the earth so deeply that cross-plowing fields became unnecessary, but the number of animals required to pull it prevented easy turning at the end of rows. As a result, the entire field system was reorganized into long strips to accommodate the tool, and village and social structures were transformed (White 1962: 1995).

Industrial agriculture goes further, however, to standardize conditions of soil to accommodate packages of seeds and chemicals, as well as large machines. It attempts to render the life cycle of the plant into as technical a process as possible and to make the soil an inert receptacle for the synthesized elements of growth. All the soil on earth must be renewed or restored, and human beings need the help of the specific species that make it. It is sobering to recall that soil is made by the casting of earthworms and consists of billions of microorganisms—the more, the healthier. Yet soil compaction by giant machines, chemical replacement of specific elements for plant growth, and of course, the poisons intended for the specific pests invited by ecologically simplified fields, destroy the habitat of this creature that sustains us. If industry began the process of breaking up the extended family of human beings and dependent species and industrial diets contribute to the breaking up of the diminished human family, the industrialization of agriculture breaks up the web of connections among the species which was (and remains) the basis of domestication, as it is of life.

The manifest advantage of industrial agriculture is the increase in the productivity of labor. We marvel that a tiny fraction of the U.S. labor force can produce grain for so much of the world. Yet hidden by this spectacle are several sobering facts. First, our fascination with reduced labor distracts from paying attention to the effects on the land.[11] The concentration of commercial grain farming in North America, South America, and Australia, is based on extensive land use, in contrast to most peasant and, as we have seen, early capitalist, agriculture. Second, labor has not so much shifted out of food production as it has moved into supporting industries. The replacement of human and animal labor by machines and chemicals depends on an army of petrochemical, industrial, and transport workers. As farm products have become ingredients in manufactured food rather than final consumer goods, another army has been employed in food processing. The combined labor in the whole food system, therefore, is closer to a quarter of the U.S. labor force.

Finally, as energy has shifted from living to mechanical and therefore from renewable to nonrenewable sources, the efficiency of energy conversion has plummeted. In comparing a modern English farm with the Wiltshire farm documented by William Cobbett in 1826 (compared above to New Guinea), Bayliss-Smith (1982: 107–9) calculated that the ratio of food and energy output to the combined energy inputs (by human beings, animals, and machines) fell from 40:1 to 21:1 in less than a century and a half. The difference is accounted for by the energy used in manufacturing the fuels used by machines, the manufacture and transport of fertilizers, herbicides, and pesticides. The food systems of industrial countries now account for nearly 20 percent of their energy use (Payne 1994:98–99). The advances depend on a very partial accounting.

The most compelling danger of industrial agriculture is the loss of genetic diversity. Wilkes (1988:76) argues that "the technological bind of improved varieties is that they eliminate the resource upon which they are based." Pathogens multiply far more quickly than the crops (or the human beings) they attack. In preindustrial farming, many varieties of wheat, rice, or maize exist in the microecosystems of fields. The plants cross-pollinate themselves with the help of insects or human beings and human-directed adaptations by selection and breeding. Most major grains, which also feed most animals in industrial feedlots, are grown not in their native habitats but in habitats where they are transplants. Wild and traditionally cultivated varieties, called Landraces, continue to evolve only in their rather small areas of origin, known as Vavilov centers, and only in relatively undisturbed habitats. Gene banks have been created to store all known landraces, but if they cease to adapt in co-evolution with human beings, there is a danger that the pathogens will outpace them far beyond the capacity of genetic engineers. The Irish potato famine was the first major disaster of a transplanted monocropped food staple: In the absence of its native predators, the potato flourished in its new home; but since its genetic base was narrow, having not been renewed by wild or varied domestic varieties, the entire population of potatoes succumbed when a pest appeared. Similar disasters have been narrowly averted and not widely publicized in recent years, due to the genetic uniformity of wheat and maize (Wilkes 1988:75). It follows, then, that survival of at least some farmers working with Landraces in their native habitats is the only assurance of continuing adaptation and evolution of our small number of grains. As farmers live in real cultures, biodiversity requires respect and support for the lifeways of pre-industrial civilizations.

Industrial agriculture has accelerated the damage to ecosystems over millennia (as in deforestation of the Mediterranean) to mere decades. Although it occupies merely one half of 1 percent of the duration of agriculture, the industrial period has greatly accelerated human impact on earthly cycles. The speed has changed its nature, finally threatening to break the cycles of knowledge and practice, of habitat and species (notably human). Human beings can—and must, if we are to survive—become fully aware of our place in the web of species and of the effects of our food practices on our earthly habitat.

Industrial agriculture is not the only alternative to premodern agrarian societies with their vulnerabilities and oppressions. The particular constellation of technologically driven (applied) sciences and monoculture that characterizes industrial agriculture is recent and not at all inevitable. It is worth remembering that Darwin began his *Origin of Species* with a discussion of "variation under domestication." What he projected onto nature from observations of scientific farming of the middle of the nineteenth century has come full circle. With ecology, a science which grew out of evolutionary theory, we can now reinterpret domestication in the context of self-organizing life on earth.

Opportunities: Intentional Bioregional Communities

Global integration, as Philip McMichael (1996) puts it, reconstellates localities. If they are not sustainable, industrial diets and industrial agriculture must mark a transition from Neolithic extended family households and starchy staple diets to something new but not yet formed or fully constellated. The dissolution of Neolithic patterns over the past 500 years, intensively in the past 50 years, opens up the possibility of developing an awareness of the effects of human farming and diets upon the earth. It therefore opens for the first time the possibility—and the necessity—of exercising choice, of taking responsibility. If the Neolithic Revolution occurred because hunter-gatherers had occupied all the available areas and grown beyond the ability of their habitats to support them (Cohen 1977), then the common experience of all human beings in our shared planetary habitat suggests the necessity for a shift comparable to that in the Neolithic Age.

Making Agriculture Central

As local effects have merged, the human species now confronts the challenge of managing the resources of this planet. Guided by the science emerging from industrial practice, the effort to manage these resources needs to explore the route of further homogenizing ecosystems: Biotechnology, often designed to resist pesticides, contributes to the genetic modification of organisms that can then kill everything else in the field and to the development of information and communications technology so microvariations in soil composition can be identified by satellites, which can then also direct machines to apply specific mixes of chemicals accordingly.

Ecological science points instead to a return to the specifics of place. Communities committed to specific places are in a better position to take responsibility, monitoring the absorption of wastes, the integrity of flows, and the balances between the simplicity of guided food-bearing species and the complexity of habitats. Duncan (1996:38) recommends that "henceforth, industry must be subordinate to agriculture, which must be everywhere locally attuned to the environment . . . .[This] is the only way to ensure that we do not unknowingly wreak some local havoc that turns out to be global." Theory cannot be tested, of course, only in its propositions. But we make the world we believe in by selective attention and organized practices. That chemically restored soil is lifeless affirms the theories that guide its destruction. Increasing the diversity, number, and liveliness of organisms in the soil affirms theories exploring the self-organizing webs of living organisms (Prigogene 1997).

Duncan concludes that we must begin with awareness of our role in disrupting natural cycles through industrial economies which "externalize" the depletion of natural inputs and the pollution of unnatural wastes. Accordingly, awareness requires acknowledging the centrality of agriculture in human management of the life cycles of human beings, other species, water, and air. By agriculture, Duncan would like us to mean processes that are "life produced" rather than "field produced" (1996: 177). This requires relinking production and consumption, thus closing the circles, so that their effects on the earth can be observed. It means recasting our understanding of soil and water not as an "inert substrate for our activities" (1996:143), but as a living web of which we are the most powerful, most conscious part. It means re-embedding the activities we call "economic" within social relations with each other and the rest of nature. Only then can we use agriculture to monitor locally—always marking where they begin and where they appear—the effects of *all* our productive and consuming activities on soil, water and air. By coordinating local knowledge and activities, communities of human beings can take common responsibility for sustaining the life-support system of the planet.

This does not mean returning in North America to hard labour in the fields and wrinkled apples in winter. Although it receives little funding or attention in scientific circles, new techniques that give farmers new skills and unite science and cultivation are being developed by pioneers. The most radical, admired by Duncan, is Fukuoka's system of substituting attention and precisely timed interventions for labor. In his One Straw Revolution, this extraordinary man accounts for his chance discovery in the late 1940s of the natural growth of rice within the mix of wild species, based on observation of an abandoned field he passed each day on his way to an office job. Fukuoka observed patterns of water flows and their effects on weeds. Devoting himself to an experiment lasting several decades, he found a way to imitate the fortuitous benefits of nature in that field and to devise a method applicable to other fields. Fukuoka departs from traditional farming, which battles succession with massive effort. His method "recognizes biotic complexity and deliberately exploits it." He uses tree and crop polyculture for careful intervention, relying on timing rather than effort, with mulching and watering to kill weeds and to help the desired mix of crops prosper. Duncan (1996: 156) argues that the principles are applicable to any bioregion: "What is required is a polyculture of plants whose lifecycles are sufficiently different but that can be interlocked to our advantage."

Habitats can never again be separate places buffered by wilderness. But future links need not be homogenizing. Connections can be respectful of the autonomy of each culture, taking responsibility for its part of the global ecosystem. This bottom-up universalism is quite different from what Vandana Shiva (1993:10) names the "globalizing local," which hides the local bias of homogenizing and simplifying theories in false claims to universality. As responsible human beings redistribute settlements in relation to watersheds and other natural formations, human social organization will, with attention and intention, evolve; already international initiatives to regulate air and water quality recognize the artificiality of present borders. Sustainable communities will be responsible for the wastes of organisms and industrial production. This requires new relations among human societies, as well as new relations between those societies and the elements they confront in their environment.

The Gift Economy.   By revaluing places and the lively earth, by adapting to bioregions, intentional communities are better able to revalue time and to orient practices towards the vitality of life across generations. The practices of communities centered on agriculture use different measures of efficiency in acquiring monetary gain. When he addressed the use of energy rather than money as a measure, Bayliss-Smith (1982: 108) concluded that "only in fully industrialized societies does the use of energy become so profligate that very little more energy is gained from agriculture than is expended in its production."

To refocus food system energy in agriculture, human energy supplemented by solar energy will begin to replace nonrenewable fossil fuel energy. It cannot be predicted how the shift of labor to ecological agriculture will compare to its decline in the industrial agro-food system. But the consideration of the leisure available to earlier agrarian societies is suggestive. Moreover, retraining agricultural laborers among ecological farmers to refocus communities on agriculture implies highly intelligent, attentive, scientific labor. Based on the ecological sciences, site-specific knowledge can requalify workers in the earth, reacquainting the laboratory and the field; and work in cooperation with natural cycles implies cooperation among human beings. The "original leisure" of foragers, it seems, can be recaptured by renewing the notion of a society based on living cycles but redefined by applying a scientific and democratic ethos.

The shrinking and breakup of human households in the industrial world can be seen as the final stage of the breakup of extended families of animal species mastered by some human beings. The dangers are no greater than the opportunities. The freedom from traditional inequalities between genders and generations of patriarchal households, what Duncan calls modernity, opens possibilities for taking responsibility for our species' continued existence. If the household is the broken key to the past, then new forms of community among free, responsible individuals must be the key to the future.

A sustainable, indeed a good, life can be based on enduring (though flexible and freely negotiated) social relations. Such relations allow for planned rather than violent reduction in the numbers of human beings and our dependent animals, to the point that our wastes can be absorbed in natural cycles. Such reductions suggest the manufacture of durable objects, whose origins are known and appreciated and whose disposition matters. All possessions can become treasured. As treasures, they can be passed on to those we love or honor and received from those who love and honor us. Arguably, consumerist society, far from being too materialistic, is not materialistic enough.

An awareness of where everything comes from includes a deep appreciation for the aeons of evolution and the precious human effort and talents contained in each object. An ecologically responsible society makes objects that endure, so that we nurture the yields of natural cycles and the labour that guides them, creating as little waste as possible. Enduring objects, unlike fashion, are artful: They embody deep, slowly changing perceptions of beauty and of function. A truly materialistic consciousness, unlike the acquisition and discarding of endless unsatisfying commodities, values matter. Our dwellings, our garments, our decorations, our tools—like our ideas, songs, and dances—are more likely to endure if they are beautiful as well as useful. If we love them and imbue them with our experience in using them, we care what happens to them when we separate from them. When their life is finally ended, we can return them to the earth for renewal; while they are alive in use, we attend to the relations they carry with other human beings.

A world that values matter also values human creative effort. Goods can become like services, where the gift of the maker is realized in passing it on; the scientist whose ideas engage with the community of thinkers, the teacher whose gift inspires the student, the healer whose gift cures the sick, the artist whose handiwork combines function with beauty (Hyde 1979; Giedeon 1969). It is a way of life in which new forms of money equalize and balance gender roles, unifying what present money now separates: Caring work—which is unpaid or low-paid, unappreciated, and usually done by women—is differentiated from impersonal work, which is paid and confers power and status (Raddon 1998). A gift economy keeps objects moving, as ideas and artistic expression still do today. It is based on fundamental attitudes of faith and gratitude that are quite different from those of arrogance (based on fear) that has led to the mania to control.

Conclusion

Of the 80,000,000,000 *Homo sapiens* estimated ever to have lived on earth, only about 6 percent have lived in agricultural societies and only 3 percent in industrial ones (Bayliss-Smith 1982: 25). Each human has always been connected to all human beings, all species, all flows of air, water, minerals—and even, over geologic time, mountains. Once the connection, local and unconscious, was built into practices of gathering, herding, domesticating, preserving, so that they were transformed into culturally meaningful and nourishing cuisines and returned matter and energy from human bodies to the earth. Through transplantation, the connection became more conscious, and yet allowed for greater—or different—illusions about the mutual dependence between human beings and the rest of nature. Now the deepening unity of world production through specialization and trade, through the integration of agriculture in more and more ecosystems via industrial inputs and distant markets, makes possible and necessary a conscious, shared awareness of earthly interconnectedness.

The insights of ecology, still a young science, carry some of the emerging consciousness of humanity and suggest ways for human beings to take responsibility for the powers we have acquired. I take hope from the impulses of more and more human beings to recover healthy, nourishing, culturally enriching food, along with their parallel impulses to recover direct experience of our interconnectedness with the flows of life on the planet and even with the cosmos (Swimme 1996). The reader who drinks a cup of tea is taking into her or his body water that has passed through the bodies of innumerable ancestors and myriad species and will pass from him or her into the cycles of life anew. As she or he breathes in and out, the reader engages with the plants of the earth, all dancing in the wind flows that can carry our awareness as well as our lives.

Notes

1. The description of ecology and agriculture below summarizes Colin Duncan (1996:14–24), with occasional additions from other sources as noted.

2. Fire was used to change large areas, but this cannot be compared to the work of farming or herding (Duncan 1996:14). For a detailed account of shifting cultivation which may have been continuous over 9,000 years, see Bayliss-Smith (1984: 25–36).

3. The difficulty of agrarian life in subarid regions, argues Paul Shepard (1982), created in the culture of Judaism, Christianity, and Islam a sense of nature as ungenerous, even dead. Cited in Duncan (1996:18).

4. Matriarchal remnants in, say, South India (Agarwal 1994) suggest an alternative historical path in some places or perhaps for all humanity. The New Guinea cultivators analyzed by Bayliss-Smith (1982: 17–24) are egalitarian and quite similar to their Neolithic ancestors of about 9,000 years ago. It is civilization, built on the transition from shifting to stable cultivation, that probably inaugurated hierarchical households.

5. Feminist and other thinkers have of course denaturalized the family and household, probing the gender and generational issues opened by the profound individualization of society.

6. Pioneers include Salaman, Mintz, Wolf, and Friedland. For some other places to begin, see the references in my earlier articles (Friedmann 1978a, 1978b).

7. This suggests revising the many accounts of the enclosures and the industrial revolution that emphasize sheep are key to evicting labour from the countryside and wool as the commodity that inspired profit-seeking landlords and farmers.

8. The same system exists today but with giant, self-propelled combine harvester-threshers.

9. This is true of both "batch" and "continuous processing" industries. Some industries, of course, recycle their by-products, such as heat, into the manufacturing system. In this they mimic the self-organization of nature. Perpetual motion machines and solar, wind, and water sources of energy are the closest to ecological agriculture in integrating with natural cycles.

10. Much of my understanding of industrial agriculture comes from Colin Duncan's brilliant analysis, *The Centrality of Agriculture: Between Humankind and the Rest of Nature* (1996).

11. In response to the extensive, wasteful practices which resulted in the Dust Bowl of the 1930s, conservation practices introduced by the government in conjunction with price supports allowed resumption of agriculture. However, farmers, increasingly dependent on industrial inputs and industrial markets, have forgotten the past, particularly in the high-price years of the 1970s. Erosion as well as pollution of soil is once again a major concern.

References

Agarwal, Bina. 1994. *A Field of One's Own: Gender and Land Rights in South Asia*. Cambridge: The University Press.

Bayliss-Smith, T.P. 1982. *The Ecology of Agricultural Systems*. Cambridge: The University Press.

Berlan, Jean-Pierre. 1992. "The Historical Roots of the Present Agricultural Crisis," in William H. Friedland, L. Busch, F.H. Buttel and A.P. Rudy, eds., *Towards a New Political Economy of Agriculture*, 115–36. Boulder CO: Westview.

Berry, Thomas. *1990. The Dream of the Earth*. San Francisco: Sierra Club Books.

Bonnifield, Paul. 1979. *The Dust Bowl: Men, Dirt, and Depression.* Albuquerque NM: University of New Mexico Press.

Brockway, Lucille. 1988. "Plant Science and Colonial Expansion," in Jack R. Kloppenburg, Jr., ed., *Seeds and Sovereignty: The Use and Control of Plant Genetic Resources*, 49–66. Durham: Duke University Press.

Chevillard, Nicole; and Sebastian Leconte. 1986. "The Dawn of Lineage Societies: The Origins of Women's Oppression," in Stephanie Coontz and Peta Henderson, eds., *Women's Work, Men's Property: The Origins of Gender and Class*, 76–107. London: Verso.

Cohen, M.N. 1977. *The Food Crisis in Prehistory: Overpopulation and the Origins of Agriculture.* New Haven: Yale University Press.

Collinson, A.S. 1977. *Introduction to World Vegetation.* London: George Allen and Unwin.

Coontz, Stephanie; and Peta Henderson. 1986. "Property Forms, Political Power and Female Labour in the Origins of Class and State Societies," in Stephanie Coontz and Peta Henderson, eds., *Women's Work, Men's Property: The Origins of Gender and Class*, 108–55. London: Verso.

Crosby, Alfred W. 1972. *The Columbian Exchange: Biological and Cultural Consequences of 1492.* Westport CT: Greenwood Press.

_____. 1986. *Ecological Imperialism:The Biological Expansion of Europe, 900–1900.* Cambridge: Cambridge University Press.

Dahlberg, Kenneth A. 1993. "Regenerative Food Systems: Broadening the Scope of Sustainability," in Patricia Allen, ed., *Food for the Future.* New York: John Wiley and Sons.

Friedmann, Harriet. 1978a. "World Market, State, and Family Farm: Social Bases of Household Production in the Era of Wage Labor." *Comparative Studies in Society and History*, 20:4, 545–86.

_____. 1978b. "Simple Commodity Production and Wage Labour in the American Plains." *Journal of Peasant Studies*, 6:71–100.

_____. 1980. "Household Production and the National Economy: Concepts for the Analysis of Agrarian Formations." *Journal of Peasant Studies*, 7:158–84.

_____. 1983. "State Policy and World Commerce: The Case of Wheat, 1815 to the Present," in Pat McGowan and Charles Kegley, eds., *Foreign Policy and the Modern World-System*, 125–55. San Francisco: Sage.

_____. 1986. "Patriarchal Commodity Production." *Social Analysis, Special Issue: Rethinking Petty Commodity Production*, Alison MacEwen Scott, ed., 20:47–55.

_____. 1991. "Changes in the International Division of Labor: Agri-food Complexes and Export Agriculture," in Friedland, *Towards a New Political Economy of Agriculture*, 65–93.

_____. 1992. "Distance and Durability: Shaky Foundations of the World Food Economy." *Third World Quarterly*, 13:2, 371–83.

_____. 1994. "International Relations of Food," in Barbara Harriss-White and Sir Raymond Hoffenberg, eds., *Food: Multidisciplinary Perspectives*, 174–204. Oxford: Blackwell.

Giedeon, Siegfried. 1969. *Mechanization Takes Command.* New York: Norton.

Goodman, David; B. Sorj; and J. Wilkinson. 1987. *From Farming to Biotechnology.* Oxford: Basil Blackwell.

Hyde, Lewis. 1983. *The Gift: Imagination and the Erotic Life of Property*. New York: Vintage, Random House.

Kerridge, Erik. 1969. "The Agricultural Revolution Reconsidered." *Agricultural History*, 43:4, 463–75.

Leiss, William H. 1972. *Domination Over Nature*. New York: George Braziller.

McMichael, Philip. 1996. *Development and Social Change: A Global Analysis*. Thousand Oaks CA: Pine Forge.

Merchant, Carolyn. 1989 [1980]. *The Death of Nature: Women, Ecology and the Scientific Revolution*. San Francisco: Harper-San Francisco.

Mintz, Sidney. 1994. "Eating and Being: What Food Means," in Barbara Harriss-White and Sir Raymond Hoffenberg, *Food: Multidisciplinary Perspectives*, 102–15. Oxford: Blackwell.

Payne, Philip. 1994. "Not Enough Food: Malnutrition and Famine," in Barbara Harriss-White and Sir Raymond Hoffenberg, *Food: Multidisciplinary Perspectives*, 77–101. Oxford: Blackwell.

Prigogene, Ilya. 1997. *The End of Certainty: Time, Chaos and the New Laws of Nature*. New York: Free Press.

Raddon, Mary-Beth. 1998. "Love is Like a Magic Penny: Reconciling Money Value and the Value of Women's Caring Work." Paper prepared for the Canadian Learned Societies, Ottawa. June.

Sahlins, Marshall. 1972. "The Original Leisure Society," in *Stone Age Economics*. Chicago: University of Chicago Press.

Saliou, Monique. 1986. "The Processes of Women's Subordination in Primitive and Archaic Greece," in Stephanie Coontz and Peta Henderson, eds., *Women's Work, Men's Property: The Origins of Gender and Class*, 169–206. London: Verso.

Shiva, Vandana. 1993. *Monocultures of the Mind: Perspectives on Biodiversity and Biotechnology*. London: Zed.

Swimme, Brian. 1996. *The Hidden Heart of the Cosmos: Humanity and the New Story*. Maryknoll NY: Orbis.

White, Lynn. 1995. "Historical Roots of our Ecological Crisis," in Mary Heather MacKinnon and Moni McIntyre, eds., *Readings in Ecology and Feminist Theology*. Kansas City: Sheed and Ward.

_____.1962. *Medieval Technology and Social Change*. Oxford: Oxford University Press.

Waring, Marilyn. 1988. *If Women Counted: A New Feminist Economics*. San Francisco: Harper-San Francisco.

Whatmore, Sarah. 1991. *Farming Women: Gender, Work, and Family Enterprise*. London: Macmillan.

Wilkes, H. Garrison. 1988. "Plant Genetic Resources over Ten Thousand Years," in Jack R. Kloppenburg, Jr., ed., *Seeds and Sovereignty: the Use and Control of Plant Genetic Resources*, 67–89. Durham: Duke University Press.

Chapter Three

The Impact of New World Food Crops on the Diet and Economy of China and India, 1600–1900

Sucheta Mazumdar

The celebration of the New Year on the lunar calendar is more important to the Chinese than the celebration of Christmas to the Western people. Many kinds of special foods are prepared in advance for it. From the beginning of the twelfth month all the women in the village are busy grinding wheat and other cereals to make the holiday cakes, wheat flour rolls, vegetable balls, and bean curd. A certain kind of cake is so large that it takes two adults to lift one. The cakes are made from two kinds of glutinous millet, boiled sweet potatoes, and yeast. When these ingredients have been mixed and fermented, the dough is put into a big round container and steamed in a deep boiler. When the cake is done it is about six inches thick and two and a half feet in diameter.[1]

Martin Mou-ch'un Yang goes on to describe the ritual of steaming sweet-potato cakes in his Shandong village in the 1930s: Doors were locked to prevent inauspicious interruptions; the children were hushed and walked on tiptoes while adults lowered their voices; sticks of burning incense marked the exact time that the cake needed to be steamed, and all invoked the kitchen god to ensure the success of the steaming. A Chinese New Year's ceremonial cake made with sweet potatoes from the Americas seemingly from time immemorial. How and when did this come to be?

This essay begins with the history of the introduction of American food crops to parts of Asia, then explores the ways in which these crops transformed the diets of China and India. The perils of attempting to write a comparative history of the world's two largest agrarian economies are many, but the divergent trajectories of the history of consumption, adoptions, and uses in these two countries allow us to ask more fundamental questions: To what extent does the local context determine the significance of the global stimulus? Why was the peasant economy of China more open to the rapid adoption of American crops than its Indian counterpart?

Crops from the Americas

Christopher Columbus carried several plants, including sugar cane, on his second voyage to the Americas in 1493 and returned with animals and fruits along with ten Caribs and gold.[2] We do not know if Vasco da Gama, in his "four ships that went in search of spices" carried any plants or animals in 1498. When da Gama arrived in Calicut, India, the gifts he brought included, besides some cloaks, a bale of sugar, honey, and two barrels of butter.[3] In the following century, however, the Portuguese, and to a lesser extent, the Spanish and the Dutch were to become agents for introducing a number of American plants. The Spanish and the Portuguese were the more important sources for bringing the plants into southeastern coastal mainland China via the Philippines, while the Portuguese and Dutch made most of the introductions to India.

There were two major periods of introduction of American plants into Asia. The first wave, in the sixteenth and seventeenth centuries, included sweet potatoes, maize, potatoes, jicamas, capsicums (chile peppers), squashes, and peanuts, cashews, custard apples, guavas, avocadoes, tomatoes, papayas, passion-fruit, pineapples, and sapodillas, all part of the global history of the accelerated pace of crop diffusions in this period. Within Asia, the history of diffusion was uneven. For example, plants like the cassava (*Manihot utilissima*) were probably first introduced in the seventeenth century into the Philippines but arrived in India only in the nineteenth century via Africa.[4] Other plants, such as the papaya and sapodilla, were introduced to the Philippines by the Spanish and from there spread to Malaysia, where the Portuguese picked them up and brought them to India.[5] In the second wave, American plants, such as cocoa and the sunflower (as a commercial crop for edible oil), were brought to India even more recently in the twentieth century, appearing after other new varieties developed elsewhere, such as the sunflower varieties cultivated since the 1970s that were introduced via Russia.[6]

The Portuguese, who arrived in Asia somewhat earlier than the Spanish, had control of several Asian ports such as Diu, Goa, Colombo, Melaka and Macao by the middle of the sixteenth century. Although they did not have direct control of other ports, such as Hughli and Chittagong (Bengal), the Portuguese were given permission to settle and trade there at this time. The first phase of American plant introductions therefore started out in the maritime areas where the Portuguese had the most contact: in India, the areas around Goa, Surat, and Cochin on the west coast, and Bengal on the east; in China, the southeastern coastal provinces of Guangdong and Fujian. Some of the American crops, as examined below, also crossed over into the Chinese provinces of Yunnan and Sichuan via the trekking routes from Bengal and Assam, which attest to a far more active overland trade nexus between easternmost India and southwestern China than has been commonly suggested.

In India, the Portuguese introductions can be traced through their etymology, such as *ata* (custard apple, *Annona suqamosa,* known sometimes as *ate* in Mexico), *peyara* (guava), and *pepe* (papaya), all listed as Portuguese words in standard Bengali dictionaries.[7] Carib and Aztec words that entered the local vernacular by the same route include *caju* (cashew, from the Tepic *acaju*), *tomater* (tomato, from the *Nahuatl tomatl*), and the fruit of the tree producing chicle gum used by the Aztec for chewing, now known as *sapota* in southern Indian vernaculars and *cheeku* in northern India vernaculars from its Meso-American name *chicosapote*. And, of course, the use of the generic term, *batata,* for both kinds of potatoes, is common practice in the western Indian vernaculars as well as those of Portuguese. [8]

The chronicles of the Mughal emperor, Akbar, indicate that pineapples were already a regular item in the imperial kitchen by 1590 in North India. Called *kathal i safari* (durian of travellers) perhaps because the young plants were grown in pots to mature en route, pineapples came to be more commonly known in India by the Portuguese name, *ananas* (modified as *anarus* in the north Indian vernaculars). Fruits listed in the imperial larder also note *amrud,* the present-day term for guavas in the north Indian vernacular as a fruit from "Hindustan" (as opposed to fruits from Afghanistan and Iran). Unfortunately, a description of the fruit is not provided, so we cannot be sure whether this was indeed the newly introduced guava or the older Indian pear, for which the term amrud was also sometimes used.[9] The English physician, John Fryer, who visited India in the 1670s, clearly found the fruit, *guiavas,* in Madras,[10] although they could have been introduced from the Americas by the Dutch, given their greater presence than the Portuguese on the Coromandal coast. The swift adoption of various fruits in India may have been due to the personal interest of the Mughal emperors in horticulture. As the court historian noted, "His Majesty looks upon fruits as one of the greatest gifts of the Creator, and pays much attention to them."[11]

The emperor was fond of a variety of flavors, but food preparations at the court still used black pepper (Portuguese, *nigrum*) although the Portuguese introduced the chile pepper (*capsicum annum*) into Goa also by the first half of the sixteenth century. Known as "Pernambuco pepper," which acknowledged its Brazilian connection, the use of the chile pepper spread throughout the subcontinent and was indigenized primarily by adding adjectives such as "red" or "green" or "goa" to the local terms for black pepper (Sanskrit *maricha*). The Carib term for chile peppers, (*axi* or *achi*) also became part of the subcontinental vocabulary in the form of *achar* (pickles)[12]; John Fryer noted that seamen at Surat laid in stocks of a soft cheese and achar.[13]

Like the chili peppers added as condiments, potatoes were also added as supplements to the main course and continued to be used as a vegetable rather than a staple in the Indian subcontinent. The sweet potato (*Ipomoea batatas*) and probably also the common or white potato (*Solanum tuberosum*) were both introduced there in the sixteenth century. The first-recorded mention of either kind of potato in India is in 1615, when it was apparently served to Sir Thomas Roe, the British ambassador to the Mughal court, at a banquet in Ajmer, Rajasthan.[14] John Fryer also noted that "potatoes are their usual banquet" when he was travelling through south-central India in the 1670s.[15] In both of these cases, this was probably the sweet potato, since the white potato was far from a widespread crop in England at this time and the only potato the Englishmen would have been sufficiently familiar with to recognize straightaway would have been the sweet potato introduced almost a century before.[16] The cultivation of the white potato, by far a more common crop than the sweet potato in India today, seems to have spread very slowly. Even as late as 1780 a basket of white potatoes was presented as a special gift to Warren Hastings, the governor-general of India.[17] In fact, as explored below, maize may have been the only American crop to have had a significant impact on the pattern of subsistence-crop cultivation in the subcontinent.

The cultivation of tobacco, in contrast to the food crops, spread very rapidly. It was smoked, chewed, used as snuff, and quickly added to the other recreational drugs *afim* (opium) and *bhang* (*cannabis sativa*) to produce *madak*. Introduced as early as 1508 to the Deccan, by the early seventeenth century it was grown in many regions throughout India extending from Surat in the west to the Coromandel coast in the southeast. By the 1620s, Indian tobacco had become an export item in the inter-regional trade to Pegu (Burma).[18] So many fields had been turned over to the cultivation of tobacco that the Mughal emperor, Jehangir, even issued a prohibition against its use in 1617.[19] The proclamation seems to have had little effect. As the intrepid traveller and merchant, Jean Baptiste Tavernier, noted in 1652, "You meet many women on these roads, some of whom always keep a fire to light the tobacco of passers, and even to those who have no tobacco they give a pipe."[20]

The Spanish, who arrived via the Pacific and established themselves in Manila by the 1570s, introduced many American plants into Asia. One of Miguel Legaspi's first official acts, after he established the Spanish settlement at Cebu in the Philippines, was to plant "Castilian seeds" that probably included a good many seeds from the Americas.[21] The Philippines consequently became a major source of diffusion within Asia. In addition to words already mentioned, such as papaya and the others mentioned above that entered the Indian languages, a number of other Aztec and Carib words entered the various other Asian languages to identify the origin of the plants being introduced: The sweet potato is known in all the languages of the Philippines by its Aztec name, *camotl*.[22] In China most of these introductions were marked by adding the prefix *fan* (foreign) to a familiar fruit or vegetable, for example, using "foreign yam" for sweet potatoes and so on.[23]

Below, I discuss the introduction of the primary crops into China. There is, however, a striking difference when we compare the history of cultivating American food crops in India with that of China. Although some of the new plants such as the potato were clearly known quite early in some regional pockets of India, for the most part the cultivation of the American plants, other than tobacco and some maize, remained limited until the nineteenth century. In contrast, not only did the cultivation of maize and sweet potato start expanding in China almost immediately after their introduction in the sixteenth century, these crops became, along with the peanut, part of what I propose was the second agricultural revolution in China. By the oft-used term revolution, I mean not just the introduction of technical inputs such as new plants but the underlying social transformation that enabled the adoption and promotion of these new technologies. I begin with an outline of the fundamental features of the first agricultural revolution in China and the generally acknowledged "revolution in farming" that occurred between the tenth and twelfth centuries.[24] This will help us clarify the socioeconomic dimensions of what I call China's second agricultural revolution of the seventeenth and early eighteenth centuries. Then, in the final pages of this chapter, I will turn to an examination of the very different history of cultivation of American food plants in India, where the processes of social transformation occurred primarily in the late nineteenth and twentieth centuries under colonial aegis.

American Foods in China

The first agricultural revolution in China came with the fundamental social changes that took place during the Song dynasty (960–1279). A new class of elites emerged from the southern landed gentry whose access to political privilege and bureaucratic office increasingly depended on the reorganized imperial examination system. During this transition, the old aristocracy and local magnates—the "famous families of the Northwest," with their endogamous marriage connections and military-based networks—lost many of their exclusive privileges including preemptive access to political office. Several members of the new Song gentry owned vast estates administered by managers and worked by serfs or bonded tenants. These members were often actively interested in developing their properties, improving agriculture, and increasing their surplus during periods of rapid urbanization.[25]

The Song government also sought to promote agriculture through state-aided endeavors designed to help sustain the tax base of smallholders. Apart from those concerns arising from Confucian ideological proclivities that may have made the Chinese state more interested in agriculture than other contemporary states, pragmatic issues dictated the need to sustain the peasants' tax base. Military expenses in the north and the costs of paying tribute to the semi-nomadic Liao-Khitan from Central Asia, who had gained control of parts of north China, had escalated dramatically by the early eleventh century. The state's efforts resulted in several initiatives, including the provision of tax breaks to open up derelict and new fields, tax exemptions to develop agricultural products and encourage the use of new implements, and of irrigation systems to boost agricultural output.[26]

Simultaneously, as more of the north came under the control of Central Asian nomadic groups and more people moved south, for the first time in China's history the population base of the country heavily shifted to the temperate and sub-tropical zones along the Yangzi river and to its southern regions. Coincidentally, a higher percentage of the population also began to live in cities and towns. Of the estimated population of around 100 million in 1102, approximately 21 percent of the population south of the Yangzi may have been urban.[27] The longer growing season of the South altered food availability and food habits, and urbanization produced new consumers. Improved techniques of water transportation and an extension of the main transportation routes meant that scores of fruits and vegetables once only grown for local consumption could now be sold in the hundreds of markets in the cities and towns. Tea and sugar, for example, came into general use in the Song; and northerners relocating to the urban centers of central China began to consume new vegetables and fruits such as litchis, apricots, and bananas brought in from the south. Above all, the widespread adoption of a new variety of rice marked the agricultural revolution underway.

Champa rice, from a kingdom that is now part of modern Vietnam and Cambodia, had long been known in southern China as an early ripening variety of rice that grew to maturity within 80 to 120 days of transplantation. The Song state's interest in expanding its agrarian base and state income initially led to official promotion of this new variety of rice in 1012. Then, in the 1020s, in response to a famine, the state undertook a massive distribution of the new Champa rice seeds. Song agricultural officials went from village to village, distributing free seeds and explaining the appropriate cultivation methods. For a brief period, low-interest loans were even provided to help smaller producers. Publication projects were undertaken to popularize new techniques. Between state-sponsored projects and those of the gentry, no fewer than 105 new illustrated agricultural treatises were published in the Song period. Often written in accessible vocabulary by those members of the gentry involved in agriculture, these texts provided information on a broad variety of subjects ranging from fertilizers, crop rotations, sugar manufacturing, litchis, and equipment to process foods. The *Gengzhi tu* (Illustrated Guide to Agriculture and Sericulture), with twenty drawings on the various stages of rice cultivation, and presented to the emperor in 1145, was a particular favorite and went through a series of editions.

Champa rice was a forerunner of the subsequent "green revolution" varieties. Its shorter growing period made double-cropping possible in many of the areas established in cultivating rice, especially since it could be cultivated on poor soils and was even drought resistant. As a result, the area of total land under rice cultivation expanded dramatically in the Song. Although it encouraged the cultivation of Champa rice for daily consumption of the masses, the state continued to collect tax in *geng mi* (*japonica* rice), a slower-maturing and harder variety of rice with a moderate gluten content that grew only on richer soils but kept longer in storage. A vibrant trade in rice for supplying the cities also emerged. Involved in the rice trade via brokers and merchants, estate owners began to collect such large amounts of rice from tenants immediately after the harvest as debt payment and to build such enormous storehouses for holding hundreds of thousands and even millions of piculs of rice that some officials expressed concern that the poor had no stocks of rice left.[28]

Dramatic as it was, the Song agricultural revolution was nevertheless a revolution from above. The state and the elites took a major role in generating all of its facets. In the sphere of agriculture, the new rice seeds, new designs of seed drills, water pumps and treadle pumps were all popularized due to the efforts of the state and the gentry-literati. Needless to say, the gentry, with their official connections and access to resources, were often best able to take advantage of these measures. The efforts of the state notwithstanding, tax-free elite estates comprised as much as 70 percent of all arable land by the middle of the twelfth century.

The second agricultural revolution in China, commencing at the end of the sixteenth century, had very different roots. Small producers dominated the social forces underpinning this revolution. The technological transformations that occurred in its wake, from crop selections to techniques of irrigation, were therefore predicated on very different impulses than those of the Song revolution.

The consolidation of land and resources at the elite level during the later Song, although restructured during the fourteenth century by peasant rebellions and then through the initiatives of the state in the early Ming (1368–1644), reached unprecedented levels of concentration in many of the more economically developed parts of the country by the middle of the sixteenth century. In the Yangzi river delta region, contemporaries noted that "among the people of Wu, one in ten owns land while nine out of ten work as tenants for the others."[29] The majority of these tenants were bonded to the landlords. By the last decades of the sixteenth century, various types of servile relations further increased in the countryside. Smallholders, unable to meet the tax demands of the state, commended themselves, their lands, and their children to wealthy estate owners whose official status exempted them from land-and-corvée taxes. The depletion of the ranks of independent smallholders only increased the tax burden for the surviving few, aggravated the fiscal crisis of the state, and set in motion the enserfment of yet other smallholders. Then, at the end of the sixteenth century and the early decades of the seventeenth, the country exploded. Hundreds of peasant rebellions broke out. Squatter movements developed in several parts of the country; elsewhere, serfs and bondservants burned down the houses of their masters along with the deeds of their enserfment. As an eyewitness account of a riot in Jiangsu in 1645 commented, "Among the bondservants, some are cunning and they are stirring up a movement for the annulment of their bonds of servitude, saying that the dynasty is changing so how can the regulations for bondservants be as they used to be."[30]

The Manchu who had been engaged in expanding their territorial control over parts of northeastern China through the early decades of the seventeenth century were invited to enter Beijing in 1644 by a Chinese general of the Ming to help put down the most troublesome of the peasant leaders who had just crowned himself emperor. As the new rulers of imperial China, the Manchu emperors actively sought to pacify the country, demilitarize peasant communities, and reestablish the fiscal viability of the state. This included a range of state policies to ensure that smallholders did not disappear from the tax rolls. From the perspective of state ideology vis-à-vis the smallholders, the Qing shared both Confucian ideals and the pragmatic logic of the Song. But a significant difference now underlined the relationship of the ruling dynasty and the regional elite. Large and wealthy gentry estates had been particularly common in the prosperous regions of the Yangzi Delta and the southern province of Guangdong. Many of the gentry in the same areas harbored sentiments loyal to the Ming and opposed to the Manchu; several of them had even supported armed resistance. As I have argued in detail elsewhere, stripping the southern gentry of their serfs, hauling them in for tax evasion, and curtailing their privileges of wide-ranging tax exemptions served to discipline the gentry and bolster the smallholder in ways that had not been attempted in the Song.

While the Qing state continued to uphold the rights of the landlord to collect rent, it took from individual landlords the legal right to punish recalcitrant tenants. The state also prohibited enserfment and bonding as payment on loans and also made efforts to limit landlord usury.[31] Most important, the state sought to provide land to as many smallholders as possible by sponsoring controlled migrations and military colonization schemes throughout the country and awarding tax waivers to all those who undertook land reclamation. Unlike previous dynasties, which limited such efforts to the initial period of peace following transitional upheavals, Qing resettlement policies continued to supervise migrations of civilians for almost all of the mid-seventeenth century through to the end of the nineteenth century.[32]

There were, in addition, three items of legislation passed by the Kangxi emperor (reigned 1662–1722) with far-reaching consequences for the small-holders. First, tax payments were switched from grain, corvée, and cloth to consolidated payments in silver. Second, the poll tax was abolished; and, third, in a supreme gesture of imperial benevolence, the tax rates were set at the levels of 1711 for eternity. The switch to tax payments in silver drew peasant producers into a more intimate market nexus with implications for non-food crop production while freeing them from the necessities of rice cultivation for tax payment. The abolition of the poll tax removed restrictions on both labor mobility and fertility. Peasant producers and the heads of households could now use all the labor of the family. More sons could translate into more available labor, although down the line this led to greater fragmentation and the division of agricultural land into parcels in a system that did not have primogeniture but recognized the hereditary rights of all sons, including those whose mothers who may have never even been recognized formally as concubines.

Individual smallholders were able to retain access to their means of subsistence through a range of stratagems that included permanent or temporary migration to other provinces and, most relevantly, making their small plots yield more by increasing the number of crop choices. Simultaneously, local social formations such as lineage developed greater coherence. These and other patterns of community organization strengthened the peasants' rights to land and even allowed tenancy rights to become inheritable. The tie to the land was so successfully maintained that, on the eve of the twentieth century, China was less urbanized than it had been some 800 years before; less than 8 percent of the population was urban in the 1890s.[33] It was also this class of smallholders and their needs, I suggest, that ushered in the second agricultural revolution by making use of the new crops from the Americas.

The sweet potato was introduced into mainland China during the last decades of the sixteenth century through three channels. Two of the channels—from Vietnam into Dianbai county near the Leizhou peninsula and into Dongguan county in the Pearl River Delta—were both in Guangdong province; the third was from Manila into Changle county of Fujian province.[34] A wealthy merchant with trade connections in the Philippines, Jin Chenlung, apparently imported the plants into Fujian; and his son presented them to the governor of Fujian province during the famine of 1594. Soon cultivation of the plant spread to other provinces up north along the coast to Zhejiang and Shandong as well as inland to Henan.[35] The sweet potato was also introduced directly from Manila by the Spanish in the early seventeenth century to the colony they had in northern Taiwan. By the middle of the century, the plant had spread so extensively throughout Guang-dong, Taiwan, and Fujian that several commentators noted, "It is treated like grain in Fujian and Guangdong." In the areas where commercial crop cultivation had already expanded, such as south China, by the end of the seventeenth century it was cultivated along with a host of other food and non-food crops such as rice, sugarcane, cotton, hemp, ramie, abaca, mulberry, indigo, yellow ginger [*curcuma* or turmeric, used for food flavor, coloring, and cloth-dyes], barley, cabbage [*brassica*] and rape, bananas, litchis, oranges, pomelo, and so on, besides sericulture and aquaculture.[36] Many of the areas that took to the sweet potato continued to cultivate varieties of Chinese yam as well as varieties of taro, but the sweet potato emerged as the primary staple in addition to rice.[37]

As cultivation and consumption spread, Chinese dietary preferences adapted the sweet potato to many different food preparations. Taiwan's Chu-lo county gazetteer of 1717 notes that the sweet potato was eaten directly baked or boiled; made into a fresh gruel; cut and dried into pieces, and then cooked; dried and made into a flour for noodles and steamed cakes; and also brewed into a kind of wine.[38] Other types of tubers continued to be cultivated, but only the sweet potato became a staple. As the 1819 edition of the district gazetteer of Xin'an county in Guangdong's Pearl River Delta pointed out: "There are several types of yam grown in the county: there is the sweet yam, the mountain yam, the sweet potato, the linen yam, the hairy yam, the red yam, the white yam, and the greater yam. Of these the sweet potato is used by the local people as a substitute for rice. It is an extremely nutritious food characteristic of the area."[39] Even the imperial authorities recognized the transformed diet. By the early eighteenth century, the Yongzheng emperor (1723–35) estimated the regional food sufficiency of Guangdong province and its need to import food in terms of both rice and sweet potatoes.

The earliest available rural surveys of south China are from the 1920s, and their data all point to the fact that sweet potatoes regularly provided a supply of at least three to four months' worth of food for practically everybody living in the countryside. The poor ate sweet potatoes everyday throughout the year in both the south [40] and parts of the north. In Shandong province, besides providing the primary ingredient in the New Year's cake, sweet potatoes were eaten at "every meal, every day, throughout the year," with valiant efforts made to provide some variety in this monotonous diet.[41] For a few months after the late fall harvest and until the early spring, they were eaten fresh, baked, boiled, or mashed with pickles. During late spring and summer, dried slices of sweet potatoes would be eaten boiled; ground into flour and made into noodles, bread, or a gruel with barley flour and peanut powder; or stirred into a hash with chopped turnips and soybean juice. In Shandong, unlike Guangdong, women did not have to do extensive work in the fields, but they did have to know how to slice sweet potatoes with a special slicer and to dry them properly, a task that was even a required qualification for a daughter-in-law.[42]

Numerous factors influenced this rapid adoption of the sweet potato in China, including its ability to grow in marginal soil, resist drought conditions, be relatively immune to pests like locusts, and require low levels of labor input and soil fertility.[43] In South China, the warmer climate allows farmers to grow at least two, even three, crops of sweet potato. Better yet, the sweet potato does not need to be transplanted like rice; and preparations for new crops are cheap because one bulb can provide a dozen or so shoots for new plants.[44] Twentieth-century studies from Taiwan show that growing sweet potatoes took only a little over one-tenth of the effort needed for that of rice: One crop of rice requires 85.92 male labor days, 18.75 female labor days, and 15.79 animal labor days per hectare (2.47 acres); but a sweet-potato crop requires only 9.47 male labor days, 2.47 female labor days, and 2.05 animal labor days.[45] The cultivation of sweet potatoes also requires a minimum of care, and the specific details such as trimming the tendrils of the plant to prevent excess leaves and smaller roots in the south can be almost completely done by women.[46]

Yields of sweet potato in China in the twentieth century averaged 278 *jin* per *mu* (almost 370 pounds per one sixth of an acre) of land or twice that of *gaoliang* (Chinese sorghum), millet, barley, or wheat.[47] In terms of calories provided per mu, sweet potatoes are twice as productive as other dry-land crops and have more calories than rice and the ordinary potato. The sweet potato has more dry, starchy and sugary matter than the ordinary white potato; and chemical analysis shows it to have a sugar content of 10 to 20 percent and a starch content of over 16 percent.[48] While the caloric content of sweet potatoes differs slightly with the gluten content of rice, an eight-ounce cup of cooked white rice provides only 185 calories, while a cup of mashed potatoes contains 291 calories. The availability of a highly caloric, nutritious, but inexpensive and readily cultivable food crop arguably freed up land and labor which would otherwise have been needed for growing food at a time of expanding cash-crop cultivation in the seventeenth century. Hence, the sweet potato became ubiquitous, the basic staple of the smallholder in many provinces across China.[49]

Two other crops from the Americas, maize and the peanut, similarly had a significant impact on the Chinese countryside. Maize, *fan mai* (Western or foreign wheat), was introduced into China before the mid-sixteenth century, both overland from India and Burma via Yunnan province and also through the coastal provinces of Fujian and Zhejiang.[50] Given the preference for glutinous cereals in many regions of Asia, a glutinous variety has developed through natural selection.[51] If the sweet potato was most closely identified with the smallholder food culture of the coastal parts of the country, maize was the staple of the people living in the inland highlands.

Already widespread in Sichuan and Hubei provinces before 1700, it was brought to Shanxi by the several million immigrants from these regions who moved to the north in the eighteenth century in state-sponsored migration initiatives. Like newcomers elsewhere, these immigrants did not have access to the best lands in the long-settled valleys. Instead, they found land in the dry, less fertile uplands, so maize became the basic subsistence food of the smallholder economy of this region. A hardy, easy-to-cultivate crop capable of producing high yields with minimal investment, maize had greater tolerance for cold temperatures than the buckwheat grown earlier in these areas. Although the sweet potato was also introduced into this area under government sponsorship, it did not displace maize, since the latter requires a growing period of only four months, compared to the six-month period of the sweet potato in this area. Instead, both were added to the diet. Like the sweet potato, maize requires an amount of time that is only the half that of other staple food crops in these areas, such as barley, wheat, or millet.[52] Although not a preferred staple, maize was cultivated in areas as widely dispersed as upland Shanxi in the northwest down to Yunnan in the southwest. By the nineteenth century it was also a primary crop in the inland provinces of Hunan and Jiangxi. As a local gazetteer from Jiangxi province noted, "The leading crop of the hills and mountains . . . is maize . . . which provides half a year's food for the mountain dwellers. . . . In general, maize is grown on the sunny side of hills, sweet potatoes on the shady side."[53]

While eaten as a snack food of roasted half-ripe cobs throughout China,[54] maize proved to be no less versatile than the sweet potato in the regional cuisines of those areas where it became the staple. Given the range of other familiar staples such as barley, millet, and sorghum, the consumption of maize remained far more differentiated by class. Like the sweet potato, it was adapted to culinary preferences. Ground into flour, maize was made into a gruel eaten with pickled turnips and cabbage. It was also made into steamed buns, rolled into flat cakes, and made into boiled noodles. Today, maize-and-wheat noodles are often eaten with fiery chili pepper sauces by the poor in Hunan and Hubei, a culinary footnote commemorating the common overland routes by which both plants entered China.[55]

The peanut (*lo huasheng*), listed as a local product as early as 1538 in Changshu county near Suzhou, is usually considered a Portuguese introduction to China. The availability of many other types of edible vegetable oils from varieties of brassicas species such as rape and turnip initially slowed the expansion of peanut cultivation in China. But by the seventeenth century, smallholder peasants were using all the available properties of the peanut in their cultivation, for in many ways the second agricultural revolution was predicated on the maximum utilization of all crops and the development of complementary patterns of crop selection. In southern provinces like Guangdong, for example, peanuts were often cultivated in the same localities as sugarcane, setting up a long-term pattern that combined the use of the two products. As Eugene Anderson has noted, "Ground or broken peanuts abound in pastries, candies and sweets, and when a new sweet is borrowed from the West, a large dose of peanuts is often a step in making the borrowing into a true Chinese product."[56]

Sugarcane is a voracious consumer of nitrogen, requiring between 50 and 200 pounds of nitrogen per acre. The nitrogen-fixing properties of the

Leguminosae family that includes peanuts, makes this a most suitable crop for growing in conjunction with cane.[57] Peanut meal (remnants after oil extraction) is a highly desirable fertilizer for sugarcane.[58] Peanut cake was also useful as a high-protein feed for hogs. As complementary products on the market that shared similar types of processing methods and were grown in rotation, peanuts and sugarcane were cultivated in ways that prevented soil depletion. Elsewhere, as in Shandong, the peanut became the cash crop of choice for smallholders cultivating sweet potatoes for their subsistence. Planted in alternate rows, peanuts enriched the soil for sweet potatoes while providing the benefit of fodder for farm animals. Peanut cultivation expanded rapidly in the Guangdong delta and Taiwan in the eighteenth century, then increased markedly throughout the country in the nineteenth and twentieth centuries, due to an increase in world market demand.[59]

Of the American food crops, I would suggest that the sweet potato had the greatest impact on the social and economic structure of China. Just as in the more thoroughly studied examples of the impact of the potato crop in Western Europe, the sweet potato also invites closer examination, since it could sustain larger populations while increasing fertility by providing more calories.[60] Indeed, it could feed a larger number of people per unit of arable land.[61] The massive demographic increase of China was a fairly rapid process. Beginning with the last years of the seventeenth century, there was marked population growth that escalated through the course of the eighteenth century, increasing from a population base of approximately 180 million in 1750 to that of a base to well over 425 million by 1850.[62] The intensification of non-food crop agriculture in the Qing and the expanded production of silk, tea, and sugar for the world market that began accelerating with the seventeenth century in China was thus based on a subsistence food which required much less labor than rice and other cereals. Extensive cash crop cultivation for both domestic use and the export market, the hallmark of this second agricultural revolution, was accommodated without a fundamental transformation of property relations and without devastating or continuous subsistence crises until the late nineteenth century.[63] The small peasant producer transformed the Chinese countryside into small parcels of land and minute terraced fields and adapted the sweet potato to provide for all subsistence needs of the producer household while cultivating rice and other crops for the market.

American Foods in India

Patterns of landownership in India differed considerably from those of China in the late seventeenth and eighteenth centuries, for there was no formal separation of civil and military authority, either at the level of the national government or at the level of the village.[64] Broadly, without elaborating on regional differences and the many variations that existed, two rural classes are typically identified: One group was small but had hereditary transferable rights to collect revenue from land (*zamindari ra'iyats, maliks, muqaddam*). The members of this group received their rights of revenue and rent collection from the second group, comprised of the ruler or his deputies and the vast majority of direct producers who cultivated the land on the basis of customary rights.[65] As previously pointed out here, "the property of one [group] and the rights of the other are in a measure held at discretion."[66] In contrast to China, however, all of India remained a militarized society that made both sets of rights far more malleable and contested. When the central authority of the Mughals decayed and military activity increased throughout the region in the eighteenth century, these trends were amplified.

Other distinctive features of the subcontinent included the vast abundance of fertile arable land even in the nineteenth century and a relatively slow population growth between 1600 and 1850.[67] That entire villages set off on vast migrations without any state supervision to escape war or an oppressive zamindar was therefore possible and quite common. Long-settled areas could be abandoned for decades, with fertile areas never reclaimed.[68] This happened even in the heartland of the empire: After the famine of 1783–84, some 600 villages in Delhi Territory were depopulated; in 1820, at least 200 of them still stood empty.[69] Pre-colonial Indian society was therefore unusually mobile for a peasant economy, a feature, I suggest, that combined with the availability of arable land and low demographic pressure to shape the seventeenth- and eighteenth-century responses to American food crops. The subsistence sector did not require an intensification of agriculture, but cash crops were typically grown by the bigger peasants or small zamindars.[70] In the colonial period, in contrast, peasant migrations were sharply curtailed. The state sought to promote stability by reconfiguring land rights, establishing permanent settled communities, indeed trying to "fix" people in their place by every measure possible. Colonialism set in motion a new agrarian and demographic regime that included a rapid commercialization of the agricultural economy and an increase in the number of smallholders.

It was also in the nineteenth and twentieth centuries that the food crops of the Americas started making major inroads into the food cultures of India. As we have seen, the potato and the sweet potato were well-known; but neither became a miracle food that provided daily subsistence or even insurance against famines as in China. Then, in the nineteenth century, the colonial government took an active role in the propagation of the potato. In some areas such as Assam, along with the development of tea plantations, the sweet potato was introduced very widely in the 1830s; but these efforts met with limited success until an acclimatized variety was developed. Although today one can scarcely imagine an urban Indian middle-class meal cooked entirely without using either tomatoes or potatoes, these foods entered the general repertoire only in the last century as the rate of urbanization increased. As George Watt, reporter on economic products to the Government of India noted at the end of the nineteenth century, "As an article of food, potatoes are now valued by all classes, especially the Hindus on days when forbidden the use of grain. At first potatoes were eaten by the Mohammadans and Europeans only, but for some years past they have got into universal usage, and it is now not uncommon circumstance to find cooked potatoes offered for sale at refreshment stalls, in various cold preparations, to be eaten along with so-called sweetmeats that form the midday meal of the city communities."[71]

The closest parallel to the Chinese history of the state-sponsored promotion in terms of an American food crop in India is a relatively recent example from the southern state of present-day Kerala. The local ruler in the 1880s promoted the use of cassava and personally conducted demonstrations to show how the bitter compounds could be leached out before consumption.[72] With the economy recovered and rice cultivation expanded in India's southern states, the use of cassava as a staple, however, remained limited to this one region of India. Today it is widely grown and casually eaten as a flavored pilaf in some parts of the country, while the flour is more often used in conjunction with arrowroot (*C. angustifolia*) as a recuperative food for children.

Of all the American food crops, only maize had a wide distribution in India prior to the nineteenth century. Called *makkai* or *makkhi* (Mecca corn) in the north Indian languages, the vernacular term for maize suggests a connection with the Mughal court. The Portuguese were the probable avenue of its introduction.[73] Soon cultivated in western India in the hinterlands of Bombay, maize is listed among the crops assessed for revenue in 1664 in eastern Rajasthan.[74] Despite its supposed connection with the court, maize was not a food of the aristocracy. Instead, as in China, maize became a food for people living in the poorer highlands of the Himalayas reaching into Nepal and for the aboriginal tribes living in the hilly tracts throughout the country well before British colonial agricultural surveys were started in the middle of the nineteenth century.

Maize was also a standby food in other states. In the plains of Uttar Pradesh and Bihar, those too poor to have fuel everyday with which to cook their main meal ate *sattu*, (roasted and ground maize mixed with roasted barley flour) with a side of chillies, onions, and salt. In the Punjab province, an area where wheat, millet, and sorghums provided the primary staples, the expansion of wheat exports to Europe in the late nineteenth-century initially led to an increase in maize cultivation.[75] But, here too, even though used more often as a staple than in other parts of the country, maize remained a marginal subsistence crop and varieties of millet and barley were far more commonly cultivated. Eating *makkai ki roti* (corn flat breads) with *sarson ka sag* (mustard greens) in the spring is more of a symbolic statement of Punjabi regional identity today that nostalgically celebrates the rural roots of its sons of the soil rather than an accurate reflection of the levels of maize consumption in Punjabi history.

In most areas of India, maize is commonly eaten as a snack food of roasted unripe cobs. This type of maize consumption became so common throughout urban India that special varieties evolved that were only suited to being eaten in unripe form. This variety only took three months to grow. As one late-nineteenth-century source noted, "Nearly every peasant grows a few plants near his homestead."[76] Roasted cobs were popular in every town, village railway station, and market; and selling them could apparently be lucrative as a line of business. Maize was, thus, transformed from a primary staple into a casual fast food in much of India; its impact by the same token remained limited.

Peanuts, too, entered the diet of the vast majority throughout the country as a casual food, often to be added to a spicy concoction of puffed rice, roasted gram, and chillies, or eaten as sweet peanut brittle. Peanuts arrived in India by several different routes in the eighteenth century: via Africa to Western India; via China to Bengal, where it is still called Chinese nuts (*chinebadam*); and via Manila to South India, where it is known as *manila kottai* (manila nuts).[77] Peanuts were widely cultivated in parts of southern India by the nineteenth century, but unlike maize, the major expansion of peanut cultivation came under direct British colonial aegis and its interest in expanding the market for Indian food products in Europe. As a 1879 report on the Indian peanut queried, "The question now is whether India should be content to leave France to draw all her supplies of this valuable food-stuff from Africa or whether she should not enter actively into commercial competition for at any rate a substantial portion of the trade."[78]

The two areas of India where the British established the *ryotwari* system (peasant proprietor system versus *zamindari* or landlord proprietor system) in the nineteenth century, the Bombay Presidency and Madras Presidency eventually became the major centers of peanut production in India.[79] By the twentieth century, in addition to the export market, the growing urban populations of mill cities like Bombay and Ahmedabad served as markets for peanut oil, so indigenous capitalists began developing both oil mills and rice mills. By 1950, over half the oil consumed in India was made from peanut oil.[80]

In a pattern that was now somewhat similar to that of China, smallholders producing cash crops for the world market on marginal lands in the late nineteenth and early twentieth centuries found that the peanut was a viable and valuable crop. In the Bombay presidency in particular, the best land was given over to cotton cultivation in order to meet escalating market demands for that crop; and the traditional pattern of crop rotation involving lentils, millet, and sorghum was replaced with the rotation of cotton and peanuts.[81] A late-nineteenth-century survey found that among the slightly well-to-do peasants in this area, peanuts were regularly rotated with sugarcane and chillies, and occasionally with white potatoes and eggplants.[82] As this last list shows, American food crops had indeed transformed the diet of the Indian subcontinent, since three out of the five crops listed were from the Americas. Yet the agrarian regime and the period of local history in which this expansion in cultivating new world crops took place is equally relevant to the saga of change.

By the end of the nineteenth century, India was integrated into the world market and entered a period of rapid capitalist transformation. The peanut became an important cash crop that propelled the transformation of certain local economies in tandem with certain other changes already underway, including the rise of an industrial sector. In China, on the other hand, the availability of crops like the sweet potato may have enabled peasant resistance to these same changes. In many areas the success of the smallholder in maintaining a hold on the subsistence sector slowed proletarianization.[83] As I have tried to show, the different rates of adoption of the American crops in China and India and the very different trajectories that followed also highlight the problems of ignoring the impact of the specificities of local histories on the study of global history. Ultimately, it would seem, it is the local social formation that determines the outcome of the global impetus.

Notes

1. Martin Yang, *A Chinese Village* (New York: Columbia University Press, 1945), 35.

2. Noel Deerr, *The History of Sugar* (London: Chapman and Hall, 1949), 1:116; Redcliffe Salaman, *The History and Social Influence of the Potato* (reprint; Cambridge: Cambridge University Press, 1987), 131.

3. Sanjay Subrahmanyam, *The Career and Legend of Vasco da Gama* (Cambridge: Cambridge University Press, 1997), 83, 136.

4. K. T. Achaya, *Indian Food: A Historical Companion* (New Delhi: Oxford University Press, 1994), 226.

5. Ibid., 224.

6. Except for the dates of introduction of the major food plants and tobacco, for which there are well-established eye-witness sources from China and India, the dates of introduction for the minor plants are rather vague because adequate research has not yet been done in the primary sources, particularly in the history of the Philippines. I have arrived at the general chronology proposed here by comparing such Chinese and Indian references as given in Eugene Anderson, *The Food of China*, 97–98 (New Haven: Yale University Press, 1988); Ho Ping-ti, *Studies on the Population of China*, 183–95 (Cambridge: Council on East Asian Studies, Harvard University, 1959); Ho Ping-ti, "The Introduction of American Food Plants into China," *American Anthropologist*, 57:2 (1955), 191–201; Francesca Bray, *Agriculture*, vol. 6, pt. 2, 456, 518, 530 of Joseph Needham, ed., *Science and Civilization in China* (Cambridge: Cambridge University Press, 1984); Hsu Wen-hsiung, "Aboriginal Island to Chinese Frontier: The Development of Taiwan before 1683," in Ronald Knapp, ed., *China's Island Frontier*, 18 (Honolulu: University of Hawaii Press, 1980); Zhou Xianwen, *Qingdai Taiwan jingji shi*, 27 (Taipei: Taiwan yinhang, 1957); Achaya, *Indian*

Food, 218–38; George Watt, *The Commercial Products of India*, 265 (reprint; New Delhi: Today and Tomorrow Printers, 1966). J. E. Spencer, "The Rise of Maize as a Major Crop Plant in the Phillippines," 13–28, and Jean Andrews, "Diffusion of Meso-American Food Complex to Southeastern Europe," 1–11, of Helen Wheatley, ed., *Agriculture, Resource Exploitation, and Environmental Change* (Brookfield: Ashgate Publishers, 1997).

7. Rajshekhar Bose, ed., *Chalantika, Adhunik Bangabhashar Abhidan* (Calcutta: 1976).

8. Salaman, *The History*, 132.

9. Ain i Akbari, *Abul Fazl Allami*, H. Blochmann, trans., 1:64, 66, 68 (Calcutta: Baptist Mission Press, 1873). The word translated as *guava* is given in the Persian text as the Hindi word *amrud*, a common term for guava today. But it has been suggested that the word could have referred to the older Indian pear in Akbar's time: Achaya, *Indian Food*, 224.

10. John Fryer, *A New Account of East India and Persia*, 40 (1698; Delhi, 1985).

11. *Ain i Akbari*, 64.

12. Watt, *The Commercial Products*, 265.

13. Fryer, *A New Account*, 119.

14. Watt, *The Commercial Products*, 1028.

15. Fryer, *A New Account*, 179.

16. Salaman, *The History*, 424, 445–50.

17. Achaya, *Indian Food*, 226.

18. William H. Moreland, *From Akbar to Aurangzeb*, 80–81 (reprint, New Delhi, 1972).

19. Watt, *The Commercial Products*, 796.

20. Jean Baptiste Tavernier, *Travels in India*, 2:282 (1676, V. Ball, trans.; reprint, Lahore: Al-Biruni, 1976).

21. James A. Robertson, "Spaniards Brought Animals, Fruits, Vegetables and All Manner of Plants," in Lewis Hanke, ed., *History of Latin American Civilization*, 36, 40 (Boston: Little, Brown and Company, 1973); Spencer, "The Rise of Maize," 17–19.

22. Anderson, *The Food of China*, 97; Achaya, *Indian Food*, 222–5.

23. The word *fan*, besides meaning "foreign," can also be translated as "barbarian"; and some authors discussing New World plant introductions have translated it as such (such as Anderson, *The Food of China*, 97–98). I have, however, preferred to translate the word as "foreign," since to use the prefix "barbarian" for yams and wheat and eggplants and so on unnecessarily exoticizes the language.

24. Mark Elvin, *Pattern of the Chinese Past*, 113 (Stanford, 1973).

25. Japanese scholarship on the Song is particularly rich and the most comprehensive discussion in English of these trends, drawing on the Japanese scholarship, can be found in Elvin, *Pattern of the Chinese Past*, and Shiba Yoshinobu, *Sôdai shôgyôshi kenkyû* (Tokyo: Kazama Shobô, 1968).

26. Bray, *Agriculture*, 597–9.

27. Kang Chao, *Man and Land in Chinese History*, 60 (Stanford: Stanford University Press, 1986); G. William Skinner, ed., *The City in Late Imperial China*, 225 (Stanford: Stanford University Press, 1977); Elvin, *Pattern*, 178.

28. Shiba Yoshinobu, *Commerce and Society in Sung China*, Mark Elvin, trans., 51, 69, 70 (Ann Arbor: University of Michigan, Center for Chinese Studies, 1970).

29. Gu Yanwu cited in Oyama Masaaki, "Large Landownership in the Jiangnan Delta Region During the Late Ming-Early Qing Period," in Linda Grove and

Christian Daniels, eds., *State and Society in China*, 103 (Tokyo: University of Tokyo Press, 1984).

30. *Yantang jianwen zalu*, Wang Jiazhen (ca. 1664), cited in Chu Mi, "Lord and Peasant: The Sixteenth to the Eighteenth Centuries," *Modern China*, 6:1 (1980), 27–28. Similar sentiments were expressed by *nupu* (serfs) and *dianpu* (bonded tenants) all the way from Anhui province to Guangdong province: Ye Xian'en, *Ming Qing Huizhou nongcun shehui yu dianpu zhi*, 284–8 (Anhui: Anhui renmin chubanshe, 1983). The following section is based on Sucheta Mazumdar, *Sugar and Society in China: Peasants, Technology and the World Market*, ch. 4 (Cambridge: Harvard University, Asia Center, 1998).

31. K*ang Yong Qian shiqi chengxiang renmin fankang douzheng ziliao*, Zhongguo Renmin Daxue Qingshi yanjiusuo, comp., (Beijing: Xinhua shuju, 1979), 74; Baling Xianzhi, excerpted in Li Wenzhi, ed., Zhongguo jindai nongyeshi zhiliao, 1:78 (Beijing: Sanlian shudian, 1957).

32. Ho, *Studies of Population*, 136–168.

33. Kang Chao, *Man and Land*, 60; Skinner, *The City*, 225; Elvin, *Pattern*, 178. Dwight Perkins, *Agricultural Development*, 290–5, suggests only 4 percent of the population lived in cities by 1900.

34. Liang Jiamian and Qi Jingwen, "Fanshu yin zhong kao," *Huanan nongxue yuan xuebao*, 1.3(1980), 74–78; Liang Fangzhong, "Fanshu shuru zhongguo kao," in *Liang Fangzhong jingji shi lunwenji pubian*, 227–9 (Henan: Zhongzhou guji qubanshe, 1984). The introduction to Fujian is better recorded and has therefore received more attention than the introductions into Guangdong. Ho Ping-ti has suggested that there was an overland route for the sweet potato from India into Yunnan in the 1560s and 1570s. But this is difficult to establish, particularly because in Bengal the closest point of contact with the New World is via the Portuguese, so the sweet potato is known as *chine alu* (Chinese potato) or *chini alu*, "chini" being the word for both China and "Chinese sugar." The introduction into Yunnan may have been the *Dioscorea fasciculata*, a reddish kidney-shaped yam from Burma called the "Karen Potato."

35. Shinoda Osamu, *Chugoku shokomotsu shi*, 236 (Tokyo: Shibata Shoten, 1974).

36. *Guangdong xinyu*, Qu Dajun (preface, dated 1700; reprint, Hong Kong: Zhonghua shuju, 1974), juan 14, pp. 370–1.

37. British Parliamentary Papers, *General Correspondence*, Area Studies Series, China, 39:10–11 (Shannon: Irish University Press, 1972)

38. *Chulo xianzhi*, section on *wuchan zhi*, 193

39. *Xin'an xianzhi*, juan 3, p. 122. See also Ho Ping-ti, *Studies on the Population*, 187.

40. Guoli Zhongshan daxue nongke xueyuan, *Guangdong nongye gaikuang diaocha baogaoshu*,1:7,25; 2:59, 119, 297; 3:5,9 (Guangzhou: n.p., 1925–1933). Rubie Watson, *Inequality*, 78, found many who recalled the past as "the time when we ate sweet potatoes." A 78-year-old woman remembered that when she married into a poor household in Ha Tsuen in 1918, the family ate nothing but sweet potatoes at every meal.

41. Martin Yang, *A Chinese Village*, 32 (New York: Columbia University Press, 1945).

42. Ibid., 32–36.

43. Xu Guangqi was a great supporter of the yam (*Dioscorea esculenta*) and sweet potato and wrote extensively about their virtues in his *Ganshu su* (1608 comp., now lost) and the *Nongzheng quanshu,* juan 27, zhong ce, 688–95 and juan 51, xia ce, 1517. Though he correctly identified the *Ipomoea batatas* as a new introduction by the Portuguese, he uses the term *ye shan yao* rather than the term *fanshu.*

44. J. W. Purseglove, *Tropical Crops: Monocotyledons,* 1:98 (New York: Halstead Press Division, 1972); British Parliamentary Papers, *General Correspondence,* 10.

45. Lu Nien-tsing ed., *Statistics of Crop Cultivation Survey in Taiwan* (Taipei, Taiwan tudi yinhang, 1962) Appendix 1, p. 487. Discussion of crop rotation in Taiwan based on Chen Chung-min, *Upper Camp: A Study of a Chinese Mixed Cropping Village in Taiwan* (Nangang: Institute of Ethnology, Academia Sinica, 1977).

46. Rubie Watson, *Inequality among Brothers,* 77 (Cambridge: Cambridge University Press, 1985); Franklin H. King, *Farmers of Forty Centuries,* 229 (reprint, New York: St. Martins Press, 1988).

47. Dwight Perkins, *Agricultural Development in China, 1368–1968,* 48 (Chicago: University of Chicago Press, 1969), is inaccurate when he suggests that sweet potatoes were only a hedge against disaster. The survey data that he used did not record the output of marginal lands, which is where the potatoes were grown.

48. Watt, *The Commercial Products,* 688. The common misconception that the sweet potato was nutritionally deficient comes from the fact that entirely starch-based diets all lead to vitamin deficiencies and that the dietary deficiencies noted among the Chinese poor came from eating very little other than sweet potatoes. But acre for acre, the sweet potato provides more calories than rice.

49. King shows how widespread the cultivation of the sweet potato was on the mainland in the first decade of the twentieth century. See also British Parliamentary Papers, *General Correspondence,* 10.

50. Amano Motonosuke, *Chûgoku nôgyôshi kenkyû,* 929 (Tokyo: Nôgyô sogo kenkyûjo, 1962), points out that Anhui, Henan, Zhejiang, and Fujian were all provinces that cultivated maize by the early sixteenth century. Ho Ping-ti, *Studies on the Population,* 187, based on the evidence of the 1574 edition of the provincial gazetteer, points to its cultivation in Yunnan. Bray, *Agriculture,* 456–9, 530, has looked at maize and its cultivation in detail. See also Watt, *The Commercial Products,* 686–7, 1132 (s.v.).

51. Bray, *Agriculture,* 457–8.

52. Laura May Kaplan Murray, "New World Food Crops in China: Farms, Food and Families in the Wei River Valley, 1650–1910," 317 (Ph. D. dissertation, University of Pennsylvania, 1985).

53. Ho, *Studies on the Population,* 146.

54. Bray, *Agriculture,* 458–9. Bray suggests that maize was never really popular and was used mostly for fodder and chicken feed in the rice-growing regions of the southeastern coast. Anderson, *The Food of China,* however gives a somewhat different impression, and I agree with him.

55. Anderson, *The Food of China,* 203.

56. Ibid.,153.

57. Purseglove, *Tropical Crops,* 1:199, 236. Many species of legumes have nodules on their roots containing bacteria with the property of fixing atmospheric nitrogen, which is then available to the host plant. Further nitrogen is added to the soil as these nodules slough off and disintegrate.

58. Negishi Benji, *Minami shina nôgyô keizairon*, 122 (Tokyo: Nihon Hyôronsha-pan, 1940).

59. *Zhujiang sanjiaozhou*, 5:66.

60. K. H. Connell, "The Potato in Ireland," *Past and Present*, 23 (1962), 62–63.

61. Jan de Vries, *The Economy of Europe in an Age of Crisis, 1600–1750*, 74 (Cambridge: Cambridge University Press, 1976).

62. Ho, *Population*, 281–2.

63. Contrast, for example, the devastating subsistence crisis of mid-eighteenth century Zhili and the various other famines that occurred in North China: see Pierre-Etienne Will, *Bureaucracy and Famine in Eighteenth Century China*, Elborg Foster, trans. (Stanford: Stanford University Press, 1990).

64. I am indebted to Vasant Kaiwar for his help in explicating the Indian land tenure system.

65. Tapan Raychaudhuri, "The Mid-Eighteenth Century Background" in Dharma Kumar and Meghnad Desai, eds., *The Cambridge Economic History of India*, 2:11 (reprint, Hyderabad: Orient Longman, 1982).

66. Raychaudhuri, "The Mid-Eighteenth Century Background," 13.

67. Tapan Raychaudhuri and Irfan Habib, eds., *The Cambridge Economic History of India*, 1:225 (Hyderabad, Orient Longman, 1984); Leela Visaria and Pravin Visaria, "Population," in Kumar and Desai eds., *Cambridge Economic History*, 523.

68. Mountstuart Elphinstone, *Territories Conquered from the Paishwa, A Report*, 3–4 (1821; reprint, Delhi, Oriental Publishers, 1973).

69. Eric Stokes, "Agrarian Relations, Northern and Central India" in Kumar and Desai eds., *Cambridge Economic History*, 45.

70. Habib, *The Cambridge Economic History of India*, 222.

71. Watt, *Commercial Products*, 1030.

72. Achaya, *Indian Food*, 226.

73. Watt, *Commercial Products*, 1133

74. Habib, *The Cambridge Economic History of India*, 217.

75. Imran Ali, *The Punjab Under Imperialism, 1885–1947*, 228 (Princeton: Princeton University Press, 1988).

76. Watt, *Commercial Products*, 1134.

77. Ibid., 74.

78. Ibid.

79. George Blyn, *Agricultural Trends in India, 1891–1947*, 116, 298–9 (Philadelphia: University of Pennsylvania Press, 1966).

80. K. T. Achaya, *The Food Industries of British India*, 132 (Delhi: Oxford University Press, 1994).

81. Vasant Kaiwar, "Social Property Relations and the Economic Dynamic: the Case of Peasant Agriculture in Western India, ca. mid-Nineteenth to mid-Twentieth Century," 139–40 (Ph. D. disser., UCLA, 1989).

82. Watt, *Commercial Products*,75.

83. See Chapter 7 of my book, *Sugar and Society in China* (1998). Also, see Robert Eng, *Economic Imperialism in China*, ch. 1 (Berkeley: Institute of East Asian Studies, University of California, 1986).

Chapter Four

All the World's a Restaurant: On the Global Gastronomics of Tourism and Travel

Rebecca L. Spang

"The visitor to Mexico can choose his climate and scenery as one selects a meal à la carte." So wrote Duncan Hines in the 1945 edition of his guidebook for motorists, *Adventures in Good Eating*.[1] Begun, according to Hines, as "a new game that would intrigue my wife," the task of inventorying North America's restaurants, inns, and motels quickly grew into a thriving business that involved Hines in publishing ventures, product endorsement, and cartography. Throughout the 1930s and 1940s, Hines reviewed roadside eateries even more quickly than Howard Johnson could franchise them. ("Well liked by many," was, however, all he had to say about the restaurants with the cupolas, blue-green shutters, and orange roofs, the "similar architectural pattern" of which he deemed more remarkable than the ice cream.[2]) Traversing the United States, Mexico, and Canada with remarkable thoroughness, Hines' itinerary treated the continent as à-la-carte menu, banquet menu, and smorgasbord all in one.

If it was Duncan Hines who brought a sense of the map as menu (and, by extension, of the menu as map) to the American dining and driving publics, his was hardly a novel comparison—as the multiple meanings of the French word *carte* (both "menu" and "map") make evident. Already in 1809, Pierre Jouhard (a successful lawyer in Napoleon's Paris) had asserted that a restaurateur's *carte* transported every customer to "the land that saw his birth, and seated him at the table of his forefathers." In the famous restaurants of the

Parisian Palais Royal, Jouhard claimed, an Englishman could have his roast beef and a Frenchman could have his salmon, while if "you were born in those burning lands watered by the Indus . . . you are offered a *carrick à l'indienne.*"[3] Long before Duncan Hines sent traveling salesmen to collect the autographs of obliging restaurateurs or Rian James wrote of the varied pleasures of dining in New York City—in 1930, these observations ranged from watching a "long-haired Parsee waiter pour roseleaf wine into a low squat glass" to eating "genuine English Sole from the skillet of a one time Royal Chef"—numerous writers had treated the restaurant table as a mode of transportation only slightly less marvelous than a flying carpet, only vaguely more costly than an omnibus.[4]

An intimate connection seems to link restaurants and travel, voyaging and eating, whether one thinks of "Diners Club" or recalls that Michelin makes tires in addition to awarding stars. On one level, there is of course the simple fact that people away from their places of residence still need to eat and that if "eating out" is something done only from necessity, it will primarily be travelers who do so (though it will also be the case that the homeless always "eat out"). In addition, however, there is a sense in which eating—especially, though not necessarily—in a restaurant has come to be a stand-in for travel, or an enticement to it. Avowedly "ethnic" restaurants are often decorated with posters that might just as well grace a travel agency's walls. The rebranding of British identity may be effected, in part, by offering tasty samples of "new British cuisine" to arriving international passengers at airports and ferry landings. During the mass tourism boom of the 1960s and early 1970s, several airlines participated actively in the publication of cookbooks and restaurant reviews.[5]

In all of these examples, restaurants are privileged locations for the experience of global variety and are sites where it is possible to overcome physical distance and cultural difference in order to experience a "taste of the Orient" or "olde Englishe fayre." If, as many studies have asserted, food and diet are among the more striking markers of cultural identity, then a visit to a restaurant is one of the easiest ways to encounter the Other. In a restaurant, as in the themed environments of the "Viking" Jorvik Centre or Disneyland's "Bear Country," difference is "locationally and perceptually convenient."[6] So understood, restaurants offer the framework for a comparative study of cooking and cuisines. The comparison may take the form of Patricia Wells naming the ten finest restaurants in the world; or it may allow someone else to decide that he does, or does not, like Thai (or Cajun or Portuguese) food.[7] In both cases, the public fare of restaurants is taken as the standard unit of comparison.

This, however, is not the way in which this chapter conceives of the relationship between restaurants, food, and global history; for while restaurants, and urban agglomerations of them, may both be worldly, restaurants are hardly a world-wide institution. In responding to a 1987 survey by the International Labour Organisation, the government of Chad counted but 6 restaurants within its borders (for a population of 3.3 million); while that of Tanzania (17.5 million) noted 18. In the same year, Finland had considerably more restaurants than Australia, which had three times as many people; Yugoslavia (22.5 million) had twice as many as the United Kingdom (55 million); and in 1987, the Philippines had the same number as the state of Nevada in 1933.[8] Eating and eating out are certainly phenomena of global proportions, but restaurants, just as clearly, are not. The point here is neither to use restaurants in order to compare cuisines nor to consider restaurants as vehicles for the globalization of once local diets. Rather, this essay is concerned to identify how restaurant service differs from other, arguably worldwide, forms of eating out and to consider the ways in which other forms and vectors of globalization—such as the transport revolutions of the nineteenth and twentieth centuries and the concomitant growth of tourism—have served to make restaurants into an increasingly widespread, but by no means universal, phenomenon.[9]

Local Restaurants

Restaurants are neither spread uniformly across the planet nor encountered regularly throughout history. The common, perhaps intuitive, sense of restaurants as a global phenomenon, found wherever people are hungry, masks a much more telling historical specificity. If Hangchow in the Sung period had establishments that functioned much like modern restaurants, Victorian London did not.[10] The mid-nineteenth-century *London at Table, or How, When, and Where To Dine and Order Dinner*, published for the Great Exhibition of 1851, mentioned not a single "restaurant" and instead directed visitors to the capital's hotels, private clubs, and chophouses. John Richardson's *The Exhibition London Guide and Visitor's Pocket Companion* of the same year also noted no restaurants and guided its readers to two-shilling tavern dinners where meat was carved from a common joint and served with the utterly predictable side dishes of two vegetables and potatoes.[11] London in the mid-nineteenth century—like Avignon or Moscow—was as bereft of restaurants as Havana in the 1970s or Rhodesia in the 1950s. Indeed, the author of *London at Table* found that the British Empire's capital had so few public establishments to hold his interest that he gave his fullest attention to describing not public eateries but dinner parties in private households (rather an unlikely venue in which to "order dinner," whatever the book's subtitle might have suggested).

If a city has no restaurants, that does not necessarily indicate that all food eaten there is consumed within the home. Street vendors around the world sell a wide range of edibles, and drinking establishments often make simple sustenance available to sop up brandy, beer, or coffee. In medieval and early modern Europe, religious houses and local elites all extended some measure of hospitality to travelers in need of bed and provender.[12] Nineteenth-century

London was home to innumerable public houses, chophouses, and gin palaces. Even in France, where a 1982 study revealed that half of those interviewed had eaten at least one midday meal outside their homes during the past week, it was further specified that while 11 percent had had at least one meal in a restaurant or cafeteria, 25 percent had eaten a meal in someone else's home.[13] All of these experiences and locations may fall within the broad rubric of "eating out," but few speakers of English would term a cart from which roast chestnuts were sold (or a medieval monastery, for that matter) a "restaurant."

The *American Heritage Dictionary* defines a restaurant in a very general fashion as "a place where meals are served to the public," but most native speakers—like those cited in industry-wide surveys and government-compiled statistics—easily distinguish restaurants from fast-food vendors, cafeterias, or even diners. Though such categories are not rigidly fixed, and words may circulate and gain new connotations over time (often contradicting earlier denotations, such that we now have bistros where the service is not particularly quick), the differentiation of a restaurant from a cafeteria is as intuitive for most speakers as it is schematic for most surveys.

The generalization of the term restaurant to refer to all public eateries depends on the same sort of linguistic slippage that gives us *brasseries* where no beer has ever been brewed, for the first *restaurants* were not actually places to dine but to purchase special foods to eat—or, more properly speaking, soups to sip. Opened in the 1760s in central Paris, the first restaurants were, in a sense, also the first health-food restaurants, taking their names from the "restorative bouillons" in which they specialized. Stressing their menus' specific curative and medicinal properties (as well as more general restorative ones), these early restaurants capitalized on the medical sensibility that was so central to the Enlightenment's commercial and popular success. Like patent-medicine sellers, or Mesmer with his wands and tubs, the first restaurateurs brought science into the urban marketplace.[14]

The first "restaurateurs' rooms" (as they were then called) made much of their healthful menus, but their real and enduring innovation was in their style of service. In these restaurants of the 1760s and 1770s, the frail, the ailing, and others in need of restoration were first given the option of ordering food "at any time, by the dish, and at a fixed price."[15] So standard have these features now become, common to every restaurant around the world, (be it a *restaurant* in France, a *ristorante* in Italy, a *restoran* in Russia, a *restoracja* in Poland, or a *restoraan* in Iran) that we may find it difficult to imagine them having once been remarkable. Yet they marked a radical break from the established format of the innkeeper's or cook-caterer's table d'hôte. At a table d'hôte (or "ordinary," as such service was more commonly called in Britain at the time), all the dishes were placed on a single large table at one set time, and customers paid a flat sum per head, no matter how much food they ate. As the table d'hôte was laid with a finite amount of food, this system benefited the first to arrive and those sharp in the use of an elbow but might leave vexed and hungry a less-prompt or less-aggressive patron: The English agronomist, Arthur Young, grumbled about a Rouen innkeeper who served "a soup, three pounds of boiled meat, one fowl, one duck, a two-pound roast of veal, and two other small plates with salad" at a table set for sixteen.[16]

In contrast to the shared experience and potential mayhem of a table d'hôte, a restaurant's separate tables, printed menus, and flexible hours all emphasized and depended on the patrons' individual needs, desires, and preferences. Though initially advertised as especially suited to the convalescent, restaurants could appeal to anyone who thought his or her needs somehow special or unique. Denis Diderot welcomed the possibility of being left alone with his thoughts, while an English visitor, Stephen Weston, was glad to have the "printed bill of fare," which allowed him to "order what he liked." Another visitor from Britain, who bemoaned the common French custom of bartering, was happy that the menu listed prices as well as dishes; the German playwright, Augustus von Kotzebue, noted that a menu made it possible to order dinner without speaking French.[17] Yet despite all these advantages, restaurants long remained a Parisian oddity. In 1815, a commercial directory with listings for all of France noted few outside the capital; in 1851, nearly two-thirds of French departments included no restaurants; a dictionary from the 1870s remarked that they were exclusively found in the largest cities.[18] When clever entrepreneurs in the 1840s opened a restaurant adjacent to the new Rouen railway station, they hastened to advertise that the cuisine, the prices, and the style of service were all identical to those found in Paris.[19]

Throughout the nineteenth century, travelers to Paris spread word of the French capital's strange eateries, seeing them as proof of the frivolity, fickleness, and love of display common to the French "national character."[20] Restaurants addressed travelers' emotional, as well as physical, needs; visitors needed to eat but also needed to affirm that they were someplace new and different. Writing in 1844, John Durbin, the reasonably well-traveled President of Dickinson College (Carlisle, Pennsylvania), remarked that "the system of these establishments is in many ways peculiar to Paris."[21] Durbin, who had lived most of his life in Philadelphia and New York, had toured Great Britain extensively before arriving on the Continent; but he was still surprised to find public-eating establishments where one never sat with strangers, always ordered specific dishes from an extensive printed listing, and often saw "ladies as well as gentlemen." It is important to note that it was the fact of eating in a restaurant, and not the food served, that struck Durbin as so strange and forcibly French: His *Observations in Europe* said nothing whatsoever about the food served in Paris restaurants. For the first-time patron, eating in a restaurant was anything but a simple matter of cuisine. Instead, it was the meal's structure, and the surrounding environment, that proved most remarkable and made it into such a novel experience.

Today, of course, "table service" is what one expects from any restaurant, anywhere, and discerning culinary variation between restaurants is a topic for expatiation by guidebook authors and travelogue writers. Seated at their "own" tables within a public forum, restaurant customers—who, unlike patrons at a table d'hôte, do not have to brawl for drumsticks or make chitchat with strangers—can concentrate on their table companions and the foods before them, politely oblivious to the meals and interactions of those at other tables. But it was when restaurants no longer proved so astonishing a way of organizing social space that authors routinely devoted pages to the foods they sampled there. Gradually accustomed to being in a room with people who did not (noticeably) stare at them nor share their meals with any one, restaurant patrons came to speak and write increasingly about cuisine.

Restaurant-style service has only very slowly become a more proto-global phenomenon: Bostonian Samuel Topliff thought it a novelty when he encountered it in Italy. In 1911, his *The Gourmet's Guide to Europe* said this phenomenon was barely to be found in Switzerland at the beginning of this century.[22] When, in the mid- and late-nineteenth century, western European and American travelers (and armies) used recently completed railroads to reach a wide range of new destinations, they certainly found people eating, but not at local, indigenous restaurants. Rather, those railroads, as well as other transport revolutions of the nineteenth and twentieth centuries, contributed much to spreading the model of restaurant service more widely around the globe.

Instances of this relationship are evident in many different contexts. Consider, for example, the resort hotels and lavish restaurants built single-handedly by the Canadian-Pacific Railroad (CPR). Having first laid track across a vast stretch of minimally populated countryside, the CPR then built attractions—the most famous being the Banff Springs Resort in Alberta and the "largest hotel in the British Empire" (the Royal York in Toronto). Even in places where people were not expected to make extended stays, the CPR built restaurants, for dining cars were too heavy to drag economically or quickly over the Canadian Rockies.[23] (A somewhat different story might be told about the southwestern United States, where "Harvey House" restaurants proliferated, once Fred Harvey signed a contract with the Atchison, Topeka, and Santa Fe Railroad.[24])

North American railroad companies were scarcely the only ones to recognize that benefits might be reaped by providing a variety of amenities (though it may usually have been European and North-American tastes that were catered for): In the first decade of this century, the Chinese Eastern Railroad (a branch of the trans-Siberian) guaranteed that every major train station in Manchuria had a restaurant serving "European" foods and that "its excellent bread and butter" were "the pride" of the newly constructed town of Harbin.[25] By 1914, every express train or long-distance through-train in Japan had a dining car with à-la-carte service of European foods and sparkling water.[26]

Even in the most luxurious surroundings, restaurant service could be an added attraction: Promotional literature for the 1906 launch of the Hamburg-American Line's new transatlantic steamer, the *Kaiserin Auguste Victoria*, made much of the shipboard restaurant that supplemented the traditional dining room. According to the publicity brochures, the latter had always obliged passengers "to sit next perfect strangers, and either make themselves agreeable or be conscious that they are regarded as bores." In contrast, the *Kaiserin*'s new restaurant, "one of the most novel and striking features of the ship," permitted passengers the "comfort of ordering their own meals from a French kitchen, and of having them at separate tables, at their own times, with their own friends."[27] Fully 140 years after the first restaurateur hung out his shingle and set his small tables, eating what one wanted, when one wanted it, in the company of people one knew, was still a radical innovation in shipboard catering.

Global Travel

Trains and steamships, airplanes and automobiles—all are obvious technological inventions that have changed the world profoundly since the eighteenth century.[28] On a level that is much less frequently noted, but equally significant, menu language and restaurant service are technologies as well: More often than not, they are the means by which geographical difference comes to be articulated as a matter of cuisine. Cuisines—ways of cooking that are defined by rules, routines, social stratification, and, most importantly, codification in print—are no more a world-wide phenomenon than are restaurants.[29] Nor are they timeless or spontaneous: They are imagined communities that may (but do not necessarily) overlap with the imagined communities known as nations.[30] Most attention to this point by culinary historians has focused on cookbook production and recipe writing, but restaurants and, most clearly, their menus, have served an equally significant role. According to K.C. Chang, while there are many different ways of dividing Chinese foods into regional specialties, all of the divisions are based on restaurant cooking.[31]

Numerous scholars have commented on the ways in which diet contributes to a sense of shared community and individual identity, but they have rarely noted that actual encounters with and knowledge about the cuisine of others is often mediated through (often begins with) a restaurant meal. Many a nineteenth-century Anglophone traveler to France remarked with surprise that frog legs were not to be found on restaurant menus there and concluded that popular prejudice had erred in imagining that the French ate such things, never considering the possibility that "the French" ate frogs' legs at home but did not serve them in restaurants. From the perspective of restaurant menus, it may seem that late-twentieth-century Americans eat neither "Cap'n Crunch" breakfast cereal, peanut-butter-and-jelly sandwiches, nor popcorn. These are American foods, but they may be only tangentially part of American cuisine.

Restaurants made (and make) variety available by making it intelligible and dependable, subject not to the haphazard growing seasons of certain foodstuffs but to the desires of the menu-wielding eater. The specific format of a restaurant meal facilitates the perception of particular and specific cooking styles and culinary traditions in a way that reflects neither the innkeeper's table of the eighteenth century nor the supermarket shelves of the twentieth. The lengthy menu found in many restaurants does initially suggest nearly endless variety: If cookbooks belong, as Arjun Appadurai has argued, "to the literature of exile, of nostalgia, and of loss," gastronomy's other prime generic invention, the restaurant menu, counterbalances them, promising a fullness, a presence, and a plenitude that threatens to overwhelm the inexperienced and baffle the uninitiated.[32] But the "soups, thirteen sorts" and the "poultry and game, under thirty-two various forms" that so amazed early nineteenth-century restaurant patrons in Paris should also be seen as part of the work of standardization that distinguishes a "cuisine" from mere "cooking."[33] The four-column menu, in folio, of the Restaurant Véry in the Palais Royal, like a Chinese-restaurant menu enumerating 136 dishes today, may have increased the number of dishes available but only by minimalizing the variation among different preparations given the same name. Restaurant recipes and restaurant language must be standardized.[34] At the intersection of print capitalism and travel capitalism, a menu standardizes difference.[35]

The presentation of difference in any given restaurant may take many different forms: A single restaurant or a group of restaurants in a given city or region may provide some elements of unique distinction based on variety or cultivated taste. In Pierre Jouhard's Paris (cited above), restaurants as we know them were still comparatively novel, so a single restaurant could cater to all conceivable tastes. According to Jouhard, the Englishman had his roast and the Frenchman his salmon filet—European peace, in short, was possible. From one unseen kitchen, magic sprites of all flavors and nationalities might issue forth. Jouhard's description did not, however, name any particular restaurant; instead, his was a composite picture of the city's finest, meant to demonstrate the Empire's successes and triumphs. Nor did Jouhard imagine a Frenchman eating steak or a Briton craving fish; instead, the restaurateur's menu transported customers to their homelands and left them there. (Were the alimentary structures of nationality as fixed as he presumed, it would be impossible to imagine "fish and chips" as a British dish or "beefsteak and fries," a French one.[36]) A similar logic informed the Hamburg-American shipping line's promotion of the restaurant aboard the

Kaiserin Auguste Victoria, in which the Englishman was guaranteed his grilled meats; the German, his delicatessen; and the American, "his special dishes, shellfish, and fruit." (The French patron should be satisfied to know that the kitchen staff had been trained by Escoffier and that the restaurant was the only room to have been decorated by a French firm.)

In Jouhard's Palais Royal and aboard the Hamburg-American Line's *Kaiserin,* a single restaurant provided many different customers with a "home away from home." Like the bread and butter in Harbin, a restaurant could make travelling safe, pleasant, and familiar. (Arguably, a comparable function is performed today by the Pizza Huts and Burger Kings scattered around the globe.) Such accounts are, of course, cozily dependent on particular, even stereotypical, understandings of national difference and on a marked sense of just whose needs must be met. Regional variety and medically imposed or religious dietary restrictions were not taken into account on the *Kaiserin;* despite the firm's claim of "ALL TASTES CONSULTED [sic]," no special provision was envisioned for Irish, Norwegian, or Japanese passengers.

In Los Angeles of the 1930s, it was decor that offered the most important clue to ethnic identity; and it was performance in the dining room that was privileged over skill in the kitchen. *Eating 'Round the World in Los Angeles* (1939) told its readers and prospective diners practically nothing about the dishes served in various restaurants but promised atmosphere and adventure, nonetheless. La Conga, "a little bit of gay Havana," was touted for its rumba band on a revolving stage; the Hofbrau Garden featured "musicians attired in fascinating Swiss costumes [who] play romantic waltzes and rollicking drinking songs"; the Csarda had strolling "gypsies." A cosmopolitan restaurant was one where the jet set was seen: At the Cocoanut Grove, "distinguished visitors from all corners of the globe" could be seen chatting with Bette Davis or Hedy Lamar (and though the restaurant guide said nothing about the food there, it did specify "dresses by Molyneux, Schiaparelli, Adrian").[37]

The premise of *Eating 'Round the World* was the opposite of that on which the Hamburg-American Line's restaurant was based: The latter made it possible to feel at home while traversing the Atlantic, and the former intimated that no such arduous voyage would be necessary. Ethnic or exotic restaurants in one's hometown may promise the pleasures of the faraway in a local, familiar, and convenient format; but a restaurant frequented by tourists must provide the comforts of the familiar and the regular within the framework of the foreign. Fodor's *China* (1984) says that there are "no suitable restaurants" in Shijiazhuang (capital of Hebei Province and an important railroad junction) but then grants that "Chinese-speaking visitors of an adventurous spirit might care to try a meal at one of the 'masses' restaurants."[38] In order to be a "suitable restaurant," an eatery must at least be recognizable as a restaurant in which one is safe from the hazards and confusions posed by sharing a meal with strangers or eating whatever is proffered. Other essays in this volume note that as processes of globalization produce more complex, increasingly mediated, versions of local life, consumers often attempt to reject the unknown and invisible (be this in the form of the gastro-counterculture of organic bioregionalism studied by Warren Belasco or the anxiety surrounding the "mad cow" disease analyzed by Claude Fischler). Much restaurant culture, however, marks a departure from this pattern. Faced with only all-too-visible flies hovering around the visibly unrefrigerated fare of street vendors in many cities, travelers retreat to the comfortingly familiar and *invisible* food preparation characteristic of a "proper" restaurant.[39]

Seemingly identical in format, restaurants today can be treated as comparable on the basis of their food and wine lists alone, such that Patricia Wells can authoritatively list "The Ten Best Restaurants in the World." As a restaurant-like structure has been imposed on eateries around the world, social differences have been transformed into culinary ones; and competing ways of organizing social space, replaced by the "civilized" clash of gastronomic sensibilities. The experience of a restaurant meal has come to be understood almost exclusively as a question of cookery, hence anyone who can follow a recipe can reproduce it "at home" and restaurant chefs moonlight as the authors of cookbooks.

The spread of restaurants of the sort with which we are familiar and which make it possible to conceive of cuisine as one of a culture's key identifying features has been among the processes that make it possible to think in terms of a global gastrosphere encompassing both the oft-decried "McDonaldization" of our planet *and* the more genuinely spontaneous, chaotic and charismatic locales that the Golden Arches have presumably replaced.[40] The bounty promised by restaurant culture has two simultaneous effects: It involves both expanded variety (often at the higher end of the price range) and increased uniformity (generally at the lower end). Like the World Wide Web's ability to provide an electronic menu of menus, the effect is neither a simple increase in inequality nor an utopian democratization.

Notes

1. Duncan Hines, *Adventures in Good Eating,* 27th printing (Bowling Green, Kentucky: Adventures in Good Eating, Inc., 1945), 133.

2. Ibid., 132.

3. Pierre Jouhard, *Paris dans le XIXm siècle, ou Réflexions d'un observateur* (Paris: J.G. Dentu, 1809), 137.

4. Rian James, *Dining in New York* (New York: John Day, 1930), 4–5.

5. The Demos Report (often considered the blueprint for Tony Blair's "Cool Britannia") envisioned feeding "morsels" to the jet-lagged, see, *The Independent* (Lon-

don), Sept. 8, 1997, p. 1; Jerome Klein, *Views to Dine By* (Long Island City, N.Y.: View Books, 1961) with the co-operation of Alitalia Airlines; Sandy Lesberg, *Great Classic Recipes of the World* (New York: Dial Press, 1972) with the co-operation of BOAC and a foreword by the airline's General Manager of Cabin Services; Charlotte Adams, *The SAS Worldwide Restaurant Cookbook* (1960); on the rise of "mass tourism" since the 1950s, see Gareth Shaw and Allan M. Williams, *Critical Issues in Tourism* (Oxford: Basil Blackwell, 1994), 174–200; Maxine Feifer, *Tourism in History* (New York: Stein and Day, 1986); and United Nations Conference on International Travel and Tourism (Rome, Aug. 21-Sept. 5, 1963), *Recommendations on International Travel and Tourism*.

6. I have borrowed the notion of "perceptually convenient" from Shaw and Williams, *Critical Issues*, 171.

7. Patricia Wells, "Rating the World's Best Restaurants," *International Herald Tribune*, Jan. 17, 1994, p. 7 (first of a series).

8. Restaurant statistics from International Labour Organisation, Sectoral Activities Programme, *General Report, Hotel, Catering, and Tourism Committee* (Geneva: International Labour Office, 1989), 63; population figures from (U.N.) Department of International Economic and Social Affairs, Statistical Office, *Demographic Yearbook* (United Nations: New York, 1987); U.S. Bureau of the Census, *Census of American Business Retail Distribution*, Food Retailing (Washington: Bureau of the Census, 1933), 12.

9. This essay focuses on the experience of eating in a restaurant, not working in one; for studies of the latter, see the classic, William Foote Whyte, *Human Relations in the Restaurant Industry* (New York: McGraw-Hill, 1948); Gary Fine, *Kitchens: the Culture of Restaurant Work* (Berkeley: University of California Press, 1996); Philip Crang, *Spaces of Service* (London: Routledge, forthcoming).

10. For an evocation of eateries in thirteenth-century China, see Jacques Gernet, *Daily Life in China on the Eve of the Mongol Invasion, 1250–1276,* H.M. Wright, trans. (London: George Allen and Unwin, 1962), 48–51, 133–39; Michael Freeman, "Sung," in Kwang-Chih Chang, ed., *Food in Chinese Culture* (New Haven: Yale University Press, 1977), 158–63.

11. *London at Table, or How, When, and Where To Dine and Order Dinner* (London: Chapman and Hall, 1851); John Richardson, *The Exhibition London Guide and Visitor's Pocket Companion* (London: Simpkin, Marshall, and Co., 1851), 144.

12. Felicity Heal, *Hospitality in Early Modern England* (Oxford: Clarendon, 1990).

13. Marie-Annick Mercier, "Repas à l'extérieur et au domicile en 1982," France, *Les Collections de l'insée,* 130 (France: Institut National de la Statistique et des Etudes Economiques).

14. For more on the first restaurants, see my "Rousseau in the Restaurant," *Common Knowledge* 5:1 (1996), 92–108, and my forthcoming book, tentatively titled *The Invention of the Restaurant: Paris and Modern Gastronomic Culture* (Cambridge, Mass.: Harvard University Press).

15. [Mathurin Roze de Chantoiseau], *Tablettes de renommée ou Almanach général d'Indication* (Paris, 1773?), n.p.

16. Arthur Young, *Travels in France* (New York: Doubleday, 1969), 82.

17. Denis Diderot, *Oeuvres complètes* (letter of Sept. 28, 1767), J. Assézat and M. Tourneux, eds. (Paris: Garnier, 1876), vol. 19: 254; Stephen Weston, *Letters from Paris during the Summer of 1791* (London: Debrett, 1792), 169; J.G. Lemaistre, *A Rough Sketch of Modern Paris* (London: J. Johnson, 1803), 278–80; Augustus von Kotzebue, *Travels from Berlin, through Switzerland to Paris* (London: Richard Phillips, 1804), vol. 2: 94.

18. *Almanach du commerce* (Paris: De la Tynna, 1815); Archives Nationales (Paris), F⁷ 3025 (census des débitants, 1851–1852); W. Duckett, ed., *Dictionnaire de la conversation* (Paris: Firmin Didot, 1875), vol. 15: 378.

19. *Charivari*, May 5, 1843, p. 4.

20. Spang, *Invention of the Restaurant;* Paul Gerbod, *Voyage au pays des mangeurs de grenouilles* (Paris: Albin Michel, 1991).

21. John Durbin, *Observations in Europe* (New York: Harper Brothers, 1844), vol. 1, 38–39.

22. Samuel Topliff, *Letters from Abroad in the Years 1828–1829* (Boston: Athenaeum, 1906), 191; Richard Newnham-Davis, *The Gourmet's Guide to Europe* (New York: Brentano's, 1911), 310.

23. E. J. Hart, "See this World Before the Next: Tourism and the CPR," in Hugh A. Dempsey, ed., *The CPR West* (Vancouver and Toronto: Douglas and McIntyre, 1984), 151–69; Harold Kalman, *The Railway Hotels and the Development of the Château Style in Canada* (Victoria, British Columbia: University of Victoria Maltwood Museum, 1968).

24. Richard Pilsbury, *From Boarding House to Bistro: the American Restaurant Then and Now* (Boston: Unwin Hyman, 1990), 44.

25. *An Official Guide to Eastern Asia* (Tokyo: Imperial Japanese Government Railways, 1913), vol. 1: 13, 31–32.

26. Ibid., vol. 2: xxxiv, xxxviii.

27. Hamburg-American Line, "Ritz's Carlton Restaurant on Board the S.S. *Kaiserin Auguste Victoria*" (University of Michigan Libraries), n.p.

28. For an especially interesting analysis, see Wolfgang Schivelbusch, *The Railway Journey: The Industrialisation of Time and Space in the Nineteenth Century* (Leamington Spa: Berg, 1977).

29. Jack Goody, *Cooking, Cuisine, and Class* (Cambridge: Cambridge University Press, 1982).

30. Benedict Anderson, *Imagined Communities* (London: Verso, 1983).

31. Chang, "Introduction," in Chang, ed., *Food in Chinese Culture*, 14.

32. Arjun Appadurai, "How to Make a National Cuisine: Cookbooks in Contemporary India," *Comparative Studies in Society and History* (1988), 3–24, at 18.

33. *Paris as it Was and as it Is* (London: C. and R. Baldwin, 1803), vol. 1: 443; Jack Goody, *Cooking, Cuisine, and Class* (Cambridge: Cambridge University Press, 1982).

34. For other discussions of how our contemporary food regime "diminishes contrasts and increases variety," see the concluding sections of Stephen Mennell, *All Manners of Food* (Oxford: Basil Blackwell, 1985); Sidney Mintz, *Tasting Food, Tasting Freedom* (Boston: Beacon Press, 1996).

35. On the contribution of "print capitalism" to nationalist understandings of difference, Anderson, *Imagined Communities;* see too, József Böröcz, "Travel-Capital-

ism: The Structure of Europe and the Advent of the Tourist," *Comparative Studies in Society and History* (1992), 708–41.

36. John K. Walton, *Fish and Chips and the British Working Class, 1870–1940* (Leicester: Leicester University Press, 1992); on the semiotics of French steak, Roland Barthes, *Mythologies* (Paris: Seuil, 1957).

37. Tad Cronquist, *Eating 'Round the World in Los Angeles, Hollywood, and Vicinity* (Los Angeles: Tad Cronquist, 1939), 6–8, 12.

38. John Summerfield, *Fodor's People's Republic of China* (New York: Fodor's Travel Guides, 1984), 458.

39. Consider, by way of contrast, situations in which the preparation of a potentially risky food is explicitly exposed: the revealed kitchen area that was central to the design of McDonald's (where the very low prices might leave patrons skeptical), John Love, *McDonald's, Behind the Arches* (Bantam: Toronto and New York, 1986), 16; and the virtuoso performances of sushi chefs, Roland Barthes, *In the Empire of the Senses.*

40. I thank Wölf Schaeffer for suggesting the term "gastrosphere"; George Ritzer and Allan Liska, "'McDisneyization' and 'Post-Tourism': Complementary Perspectives on Contemporary Tourism," in Chris Rojek and John Urry, eds., *Touring Cultures* (London: Routledge, 1997), 96–109; George Ritzer, *The McDonaldization Thesis: Explorations and Extensions* (London and Thousand Oaks, Calif.: SAGE Publications, 1998).

Chapter Five

On *"Cabbages and Kings"*: *The Politics of Jewish Identity in Post-Colonial French Society and Cuisine*

Joëlle Bahloul

The symbolic articulation of cultural, ethnic, religious, or socio-economic identity in food practices has been investigated widely in the social sciences for the last few decades.[1] The social and cultural processes that it generates take a global dimension when elaborated in the historical context of migration and decolonization. The late twentieth century's extensive globalization of food markets has, paradoxically, allowed migrants to transport their diet in their travels and to install it in the local socio-cultural context that hosts them, paradoxically in an era of dietary patterns made universal through the economic power of the multinational food industry. The ultimate result of this multi-directional mobility of food symbolism and ingredients has evolved in a double process: The globalization of dietary patterns has produced both the universalization of some particular practices and the particularization of universal practices.

In my view, the place of food in global history, especially as it relates to migration and ethnic identity, has to be explored through this inductive approach, that is, as constituting a wide-scale structural system of "groups of transformation"[2] or recurrent schemes of behavior found in different social contexts and in different "forms." The historical context of decolonization and the large-scale migrations it has triggered constitute an insightful example of this double-sided process. Identity is articulated here as a dual relation:

One identifies oneself *vis-à-vis* someone else or another identified entity.[3] Thus, food in global history, as it relates to identity processes, necessarily involves a dialectic relation of opposition, often antagonism, conflict, or exchange in various forms. This chapter proposes a case study of the global processes in which food is elaborated as a "field" of identity formulation.

The historical context is the French colonial experience in North Africa and its aftermath in French society and culture. This includes over a century of political, economic, and cultural domination and resistance, and the massive migrations towards France that decolonization triggered between the mid–1950s and the early 1960s. Among the migrants were a large variety of populations that had cohabitated in the colonial period and within a social system characterized by marked social, economic, geographical, linguistic and cultural frontiers. Politically, these migrating populations were located within colonial society on each side of the power game. Both colonizers and colonized were represented in the migrations that also included populations "in between", neither colonizers nor colonized: *petits blancs*, native Maghrebian Jews and descendants of Mediterranean peoples who had immigrated in North Africa during the flourishing years of declining colonialism in the late nineteenth and early twentieth centuries. The cultural and historical diversity of the migrants was proportionate to the range of their political allegiances. The largest part was, however, of Mediterranean origin, West and East, and established in North Africa by various historical processes. Among them, those who migrated to France included descendants of French military personnel and early rural colonizers, of Spaniards, Italians, Maltese and Portuguese lower-middle-class and working-class populations, of Jewish craftsmen, petty traders and emancipated professions, as well as some Arab-Moslem peoples who had acquired French citizenship during the colonial period or who were attracted by the potential working opportunities in decolonizing French society. These diverse groups found themselves in French metropolitan melting pots with new socio-economic barriers and their families scattered across France and sometimes beyond the French borders across the Mediterranean. The post-colonial situation has generated a complex politics of identity. The process involves both maintaining and reproducing ethnic, religious, or historical identity and affirming the group's irreversible membership in French culture and society. I argue that the post-colonial integration of migrants from former colonies into the French metropolis has the following effects:

First, it has generated among immigrants and French peoples, the sense of a "melting-pot" climate, and a process of permanent negotiation of cultural boundaries;

Second, it has reformulated former colonial power relations, and the social status of all actors involved;

Third, as in other socio-historical contexts profoundly changed by colonialism and decolonization, the question of identity in French post-colonial society is dialectically articulated.

Not only the immigrants' identity was challenged in the migration and integration processes, but French (and European) identity[4] as a cultural entity was reformulated or affirmed in the media, in political partisan discourse and agendas, in social scientific scholarship,[5] and in the practices of daily life.

These three dimensions of the French post-colonial experience are articulated in a number of social and cultural practices. French and immigrant cuisines have been especially marked by these processes and have actually contributed to their development. On the one side, there exists in France a dramatic sense of the existence of a national cuisine expressed in opposition to other European cuisines and to the various diets of immigrants from former French colonies.[6] This cuisine carries French identity abroad, as it is exported internationally, especially on the Western side of the Atlantic.[7] On the other hand, immigrant cuisines have long engaged in seeking cultural legitimization by developing and operating a nationwide network of restaurants and grocery stores that specialize in the distribution of ethnic ingredients and foods. Nowadays, couscous and Vietnamese dishes have become full-fledged parts of the French urban culinary landscape. The politics of taste is one of power and its manipulation and is used as a terrain for constant negotiations between the dominant and the immigrant cultures. Similarly, in French multicultural urban society, the culinary melting-pot is actually not melting so much as discriminating between subtly combined ingredients and flavors circumscribed within fine classificatory gustatory boundaries. In addition, as an example of cultural fusion, the process is by nature not limited to the French context. By being exposed to each other in the post-colonial situation, each of these culinary cultures (the French and the immigrants') constitutes a response with a global dimension. One illustration is the emergence in Paris of a few restaurants claiming to serve Chinese Kosher cuisine. Here several cultural geographies are symbolically articulated to form a new taste among both Jewish kosher and Chinese eaters. Food practices among immigrants in France will be analyzed in three major functions[8]:

1. food practice as resistance to colonial domination, especially in its cultural dimension;
2. food used as a practical terrain for identity formulation;
3. food used as a strategy of integration into a dominant society.

I shall discuss the specific ethnographic example of North African Jewish immigrants, among whom I have conducted field work in the last twenty years. My methodology involves the analysis of the response to the global procedure of culinary change in terms of its idiosyncratic articulation in the North African Jewish diet. The ethnographic history of these Jewish migrants is exemplary of the diverse characteristics of the colonial system and of post-colonial history. Although the Jewish presence in North Africa is ancient and dates back to the sixth century BCE, there have been successive immigrations of Jews from all the Mediterranean and up to the early part of the twentieth century. Before the Arab invasion, Jews had developed a specific indigenous tradition in North Africa through their contacts with Berber populations. Similarly to its effects among other North African populations, medieval Arabization and Islamization of the western Mediterranean profoundly affected regional Jewish cultures, with the Jews' progressive integration and active participation in Arabic language and culture. French colonization of Northern Africa has brought irreversible changes in the long-established experience of the Jews and their gradual political emancipation and Frenchification. By the middle of the twentieth century, the Jews of the Maghreb had been profoundly influenced by the French in language, cultural practices, and in education. But they had also retained major assets of Arab-Maghrebian culture in a selective form of everyday practice, including their food habits and ritual celebrations. Their cultural integration into French society has generated a system of ethnic and religious identity with a dualist structure designed to trace symbolic and practical boundaries between the self and the world of Otherness. With their immigration to France in the 1950s and early 1960s, North African Jews have completed over a half-century-long process of socio-cultural advancement and Europeanization; but their contact with French culture in situ changed their status in the colonial system. In North Africa, they were exposed to the aspects of French culture and culinary practices imported as the result of the process of colonial domination. There, French culture was exposed to a number of cultural, religious, and nutritional influences. In North Africa, French culture was part of a European generic category which in fact constituted a pan-Mediterranean fusion of diverse food cultures. Now in France, North African Jewish food cultures are detached from their original local food markets and must compete in French national ideology with the culinary traditions of the French *terroir*, which they encounter in the metropolitan cultural and commercial landscape. In addition, North African Jewish food cultures are now exposed to a number of other ethnic cuisines that have migrated in the decolonizing process: Arab-Muslim, South-East Asian, Eastern Mediterranean, African, and others. Now they have been included in the category of ethnic cuisines as opposed to French cuisines of the terroir.[9] This form of ethnicizing the immigrants' culture in terms of their food practices is a direct heritage of French colonial history and of the French politics of colonialism and decolonization. I will take this colonial historical approach in my attempt to develop a case study of the dialectic relation between identity and cuisine in a global experience.

Colonial Domination Inscribed in the Menu: Religious Identity and Socio-Cultural Barriers

The first part of this chapter discusses the processes shaping Jewish identity in North African colonial society as they are elaborated in the organization of their cuisines. I shall emphasize the religious dimension of the identity process, along with an analysis of the observance of dietary laws among Jewish communities in the process of socio-political emancipation. With their progressive Frenchification after the European takeover of these regions in the nineteenth century, Jews in North Africa experienced the following changes in their social status and their daily lives:

First, colonization abolished the status of dhimmi established early on by Moslem rulers, which had involved both the partial exclusion of Jews from Moslem-dominated society and allowed them to practice their religion within self-enclosed quarters;

Second, throughout the second half of the nineteenth and the early twentieth centuries, Jews were progressively emancipated politically when granted French citizenship under various legal procedures;

Third, on the socio-economic level, Jews were progressively able to enter occupations that had long been closed to them and the liberal professions and government jobs on particular;

Fourth, on the cultural level, the major change in the Jews' daily experience was their massive enrollment in the secular French educational system which, in contrast with their traditional religious educational system, allowed young women to acquire higher levels of education.

This process also resulted in a progressive shift in daily linguistic practice from traditional Judeo-Arabic languages to French. Within the same process, traditional dress codes were given up; and the naming system was Frenchified.[10] Ultimately, religious practice did not disappear but was profoundly eroded in an effort to adjust to the new dominant culture that the Jews yearned to be integrated into.

This process slowly evolved throughout the twentieth century. Its forms varied according to the families' social status and to the reluctance of rabbis in certain geographical areas, who were striving to keep the Jewish tradition intact. Also, until the period after World War II, Jews were only partially integrated into the European community, since popular and political anti-Semitism erected barriers that could not be breached, especially during the interwar period.[11] Only after the Second World War can one notice a profound degree of Frenchification among Jews of North Africa. By that time, most of them were primarily Francophone (though also bilingual or multilingual), had elevated their level of education in a noticeable manner, and improved their material condition similarly. In addition, kinship and matrimonial practices had been discernibly modified with the emancipation of women and changing gender roles within the family and, more important, with the increasing practice of intermarriage with Christians, especially among the middle and upper-middle classes.

Within these regional historical processes, dramatic changes in the North African Jewish diet occurred concurrently with other socio-cultural developments. Typically, food practices were affected by the widespread process of Frenchification and the introduction of new ingredients brought with colonization and socio-economic advancement. That was particularly significant in the consumption of meat: In general, a wider variety—including veal, introduced in the 1950s—was consumed and in greater quantities, even by those at the lowest levels of the social ladder. But most important, the consumption of religiously prohibited meats began to characterize the Frenchification of the diet of emancipated Jews. They not only ate the flesh of animals not slaughtered according to Jewish religious laws but also that of animals the Jews considered "abominable," [12] such as pork, rabbit, shellfish, and shrimp. As if intended to connect to changes in kinship and sexual practices, [13] these changes in cuisine have historically been associated with the emergence of intermarriage between Jews and French Christians. One has to notice here that these prohibited meats quite significantly represent some of the regional symbols of French urban cuisine. Another important observation to make is that, with the exception of pork, rabbit and shellfish are present in the traditional Arab cuisine in North Africa, yet they had not been included in the Jewish diet during the centuries of Judeo-Moslem cohabitation and that Jewish-Moslem intermarriage had been extremely rare. Although they did not adopt these prohibited meats as items from the Moslem cuisine, Jews did accept them as representations of French archetypal culture.

The dietary modifications described above did not occur unconditionally. Analogous to the barriers that Jews were facing in colonial society, prohibited meats—because they represented the dominant European culture—appeared only on non-religious occasions, that is, on the ordinary days of the week and at non-ritual gatherings outside the family. Religious practices, though suffering from Frenchification, was preserved within the limits imposed by the Jews in order to fulfill their goal of being integrated into French culture. So the Frenchification of the Jewish diet was organized along symbolic principles that aimed to trace boundaries between that which was designated as the core of Jewish identity in colonial society and that which was symbolic of the European Christian world. Thus, the required consumption of "kosher" meats in ritual menus remained in opposition to the selective integration of certain religiously prohibited foods.

Even in times of emancipation and much-desired Europeanization, a pork stew would have been an aberration on a Sabbath table, even one that did not comply strictly to the rules of ritual observance. Within a similar symbolic procedure, dishes served at ritual gatherings that included kosher ingredients were cooked at home by the family for family members and relatives. In addition, each family was extremely proud to maintain its own regional and local *'ada*, or custom, which meant using the ingredients and recipes pertaining to the gastronomic range of the forbears' regional origins. Indeed, the table was organized as a structured narrative system in which the strategy and politics of identity were dramatized and formulated in a practical manner.

Politics on the table aimed to distinguish the Jews not only from the dominant European culture but also from the Moslem community identified as the ultimate native, the person excluded from the Europeanization process in which the Jews yearned to be included. So mutton, for example, though a highly ritualized meat in the Moslem diet, would never have appeared in a Jewish ritual menu.

One interesting aspect of this dramatic ritualization of certain meats is illustrated by the increasing religious value assigned to beef. As I have mentioned earlier, the period after World War II witnessed a significant increase in the consumption of meats, such as beef and veal, valued by the European middle class in North Africa. First, they were symbolic opposites to the ritual meats preferred by Muslims, like mutton, and to which lamb, in particular, has a ritual status in some Jewish rituals, such as Passover. Second, beef is a meat valued by that French middle class into which emancipating North African Jews wished to be integrated. Finally, and I should say fortunately, bovine flesh is the ultimate kosher meat, since chapter 11 of Leviticus, the book of the Bible that regulates Jewish dietary laws, allows the consumption of the flesh of ruminates equipped with cloven hooves, that is, the archetype of domestic herbivorous animals.

In the modernizing and Frenchifying of the North African Jewish diet, beef has been introduced into ritual menus, although in an overvalued way, as a representation of the very concept of kosher. In my view, this change constitutes a process of symbolic concentration of the structural schemes organizing the religious regulation of the laws of Kashrut, so central in the social identification of Jews in any Gentile society. Beef is a friendly factor of Frenchification because it allows identification with the French middle class, even as it also allows the preservation of religious boundaries and observance. It is the perfect "boundary keeper," allowing the protection of the religious order while reforming it and permitting cultural dialogue with the entity on the other side of the boundary—in this case, French cuisine and culture.

Another implication of this symbolic and practical system was the preservation of the family and of its role in religious practice. The ritual table was an imperative family setting, and the family was instrumental in the quotidian elaboration of ethnic and religious identity in colonial society. The frontiers of religious identity withdrew behind the bastion of kinship interactions and domestic privacy. This has until this day had extremely dramatic implications for the status and role of women in the process of decolonization and Jewish ethnicization in France. I shall return to this discussion in the last part of this essay.

These ethnographic observations call for the following two conclusions. First, the changes introduced in the North African Jewish diet as a result of their integration into an European cultural register have been most dramatic in the consumption of meat. I argue this is because it is a carnivorous consumption primarily regulated by Jewish dietary laws. In other words, some-one can be considered to be following a perfectly kosher regimen by main-taining a vegetarian diet. But in our day and age, the same Jewish person can also obtain a similar status by observing the new valuation of beef, since it al-lows the preservation of "purity" with minimal "danger."[14] Second, the the-oretical implication of this ethnographic datum, in terms of global history, is that the universalization of some food patterns is actually integrated into local and particular practices by the emphasis on practical and symbolic *boundaries*, a process that, in my view, constitutes a form of "particulariza-tion" of the "universal," as I have indicated in the introduction of this essay. In other words, the global is definitely not some mighty machine of stan-dardization, domination, and destruction to which individual groups remain impotent. Instead, I am arguing that, in fact, individual groups are integrat-ing universal patterns into their particular schemes of thought and social practice by treating them on the level of the particular. Global history is a matter of defining a constellation of boundaries.

But let us now return to ethnographic considerations. In a striking para-dox regarding the process of distinction elaborated in meat consumption, North African regional custom, or 'ada, is observed through the foods featured on local recipes, including vegetables and fruits characteristic of the local marketplace shared by Jews and Moslem Arabs. So in Eastern North Africa, spinach or Swiss chard is served on the Jewish New Year's table, a practice similar to that of the Moslem tradition, in which green veg-etables are featured on the most important ritual menus of the *A'yid el-k'bir*.[15] Thus, the Jewish religious code of food habits brought the Jews closer to the indigenous Arab population, even as a collective memory of their pre-colonial socio-cultural status was used to distinguish them from their Moslem neighbors. During the colonial period, the politics of interreli-gious relationships reached in a complex but dramatic manner to the table, which was organized as a regional history in a practical microcosm, a sym-bolic battlefield.

The Limits of Frenchification: Keeping the Social "Body" Intact

The core of ethnic food symbolism is that it inscribes the duality of otherness and identity on (in) the body. It is the incorporation of Otherness and iden-tity that is at stake here. In almost all world cultures, the other is defined in vernacular discourse through the use of physiological terms[16]; and the poli-tics of ethnic identity and interethnic relationships are most strikingly elabo-rated in food. Here, they are a form of daily and sensual education. Thus, the vernacular North African Jewish discourse has it that in North Africa, the Jewish holidays could be seen, felt, and smelled in the street. It was on this sensual terrain that identity in colonial society was most evidently dramatized and communicated. It was in the same arena of the senses that it was also fought for and submitted to profound changes. It was there that North African Jews strove to elaborate their own agenda of Frenchification: They were going to be full-fledged French citizens, but to achieve that goal, they had not reached a point where they would symbolically insult their religious tradition.[17] Jews may have interpreted the nineteenth-century Napoleonic ideology of citizenship as requiring them to give up their religious particularism, but this perception was manipulated by the food they put on the table. Jews were indeed going to become Frenchified but remain Jewish. At stake in this ambitious plan to overcome all the handicaps facing them in preserving their ethnic diet was the formulation in private life of the Jews' own interpretation of the French Republican tradition, their own vision of emancipation and social advancement: The table was set as a discourse of resistance and self-control addressed to colonial power.

The ways that people formulated this agenda in their plates involved three major principles. Non-kosher foods inspired by French gastronomy would be cooked and consumed outside the family circle with non-Jewish friends and colleagues, outside the religious calendar and only in secular settings of food consumption, outside the home and traditional dishes. The traditional pot was thus not a "melting pot" but one that underlines marked cultural and political boundaries.

This exclusion of French and European influence from the private world of the self—as it is represented by the trilogy composed of the family, the home, and Jewish religion—had a major implication: The register of European culture was profane, one in which non-sacred gestures and exchanges develop. By contrast, this meant that the trilogy was represented as the ultimate sacred register. The boundary between the colonized Jewish identity and the French colonizer's world stood between sacred and profane, even in practical settings involving secular forms of social processes. It was as if the world of the Other constituted the ultimate of the impure, while the world of the Self was the ultimate of the pure.[18] Indeed, that aspect of the Jewish response to colonialism has evolved in most post-colonial societies of the Moslem world in particular. The register of the sacred self has been erected as a weapon of the weak against what is perceived as the secular nature of the mighty colonizer. The recent development of this symbolic system in the political relationships between Middle Eastern modern nation-states and developed Western nations is another terrain for the articulation of this modern manipulation of the symbolic opposition between sacred and profane in global politics and national identity. The cuisine of North African Jews, though elaborated on a much smaller scale, is also impregnated with this political signification. This politics of taste is another expression of the perception of social, economic, and political domination.

The Migration and Transplantation of Dishes

Once established in French society, the cuisine of North African Jews has been exposed to a new social and cultural context, to a new ethnic game, to new socio-cultural barriers and boundaries. Nevertheless, some aspects of the former markers of identity survived migration, in a form of collective memory and as a new formulation of identity within French society. In one way or another, the self and the other have remained the same. Here, there are still French and Arab-Moslem cultural worlds to confront, though in very different political terms. The new situation,though, holds that these Jews are completely integrated in French society inasmuch as French society is now aware of its post-colonial multicultural nature. The French no longer represent a colonial power to struggle against privately and a socio-cultural world to integrate into. The immigrants are definitely integrated, and their children and grandchildren do not even regard Frenchness as a goal to pursue, since they have already achieved it. Intermarriage rates have increased in these later generations. As a result, dietary laws and the religious dimension of food practice have been downplayed, especially at the upper levels of the social ladder.[19]

The new factor introduced in this landscape is an additional Other: a non-Mediterranean Jewish culture. The previous religious formulation of identity and difference has been retained in the same dual opposition between the world of the pure home and family and the ruleless world of workplace and non-Jewish social networks. In confronting the non-Mediterranean Jewish world, the North-African Jewish cuisine has imposed itself as an authoritative Jewish one with the kosher food distribution trade,[20] markedly dominated by North-African merchants. One need merely walk in a characteristically Jewish neighborhood, such as the few streets surrounding the Saint Paul neighborhood in Paris, to see that among the dozen kosher butchers located in this limited area, almost all are of North African descent, except for one noticeable Ashkenazic butcher long established in the area. The neighborhood is demonstrably Jewish because of its many businesses catering to the demand for Jewish food: kosher or kosher-style restaurants, groceries, delicatessens, butcher shops, bakeries and *salons de thé* closed on the sabbath, while the clothing stores—including those owned by Jewish merchants—remain open on Saturdays. The large majority of these kosher or kosher-style food stores are owned by North African Jews,[21] while the neighborhood's merchants of European descent (the "Ashkenazic" component) take pride in saying that almost all are in the business of selling books. The distinction in this Jewish scene between Mediterranean-North African and European is formulated in terms of the opposition between food and book in the self-representation of Jewishness. The symbolic and practical paradox in this discursive statement is that most of the Saint Paul's kosher

food merchants have in the last few years made a noticeable return to an orthodox, if not ultra-orthodox, observance of kosher practices. The influence
in the area of the orthodox Hasidic movement of the Lubavitchers is profound among the North African Jewish food caterers. To the innocent eye,
the succession of owners, all wearing long beards and orthodox garments
while displaying the photograph of the Lubavitchers' defunct rabbi, is a
striking representation of the Jewish world as one that conveys the image of
the traditional Jewishness as it is usually imagined in European consciousness. Similarly, the food produced by these businesses is certainly not devoid
of any references to a book, even if these literary references are exclusively
religious.[22] The largest portion of the menus found in most strictly kosher
restaurants features North African food, including of course the famous
couscous in its Jewish version.

An interesting element of the modifications included in the immigrant diet
is the symbolic rearrangement in France of the 'ada, the original North
African local custom. The observance of this custom of arranging festive
menus makes the consumption of certain dishes of traditional North African
gastronomy almost exclusively ritualistic. The grilled unleavened bread
made of semolina flour is now prepared only for consumption the day before Passover. Remembrance of North African origins has been associated,
in the French context, with celebration of the major Jewish religious holidays. Thus, North African local custom has acquired a further religious significance in France through these procedures, which evoked gustatory memory. Remembering one's North African cultural origins has become a
statement of self-representation, and eating these customary dishes is now a
strategy to shape identity and collective memory. This not only addresses
the dominant world of French culture but also a Jewish scene characterized
by diverse associations and geographical origins.

Another new factor introduced in the food symbolism and practice of
this North African immigrant population in France is the relation of Jews to
Israel. The trend now making kosher foods imported from Israel so much
more a part of the dietary supply and in the last decade the observance of dietary laws so much stricter in some families is politically related to the support accorded to the Israeli nation. In the rue des Rosiers, a street in the
Parisian neighborhood of Saint Paul, most of the restaurants sell *falafel* at
take-out counters. Many visitors to the neighborhood admit that they come
regularly on Sunday afternoons to eat their weekly falafel here. The kosher
grocery stores supply a number of other food ingredients imported from Israel that could otherwise be produced by the French food industry, such as
some types of Middle Eastern pasta, pickles processed in the kibbutz,
kosher Israeli wines, kosher commercial candy and pastries. The noticeable
return to a stricter orthodox religious practice among North African Jews
in France definitely has something to do with the wider distribution of
kosher foodstuffs imported from Israel. Paradoxically (in its early manifesta-

tions, Zionism was a secular Jewish national ideology), the development of popular Zionism has brought some Jews back to more orthodox religious practice. Many a historian of immigration has asserted that immigrants often "vote with their feet." Similarly, one can say that people "vote with what they put on their plates," providing evidence that the latter are deeply involved in global history, if not in global politics.

Gender and Identity in Immigrant Food Practices

In a symbolic landscape including the cook, the stove, God, and His people, one has to notice a primary dimension when dealing with North African immigrant food. The cook is a woman and has always been, with few historical and practical exceptions.[23] The discussion of this aspect of the immigrants' food practices will be my conclusion, not because I assign it a diminished status but because I view it as an ultimate factor. Methodologically, it is the patient ethnography of kitchens that provide this striking evidence to the observer. Indeed, my primary informants on immigrant food practices throughout my twenty years of field work have been women, interviewed in the intimacy established around their stoves.

When correlating the gender factor to the political and cultural implications of these practices, one is struck by the instrumental role played by women in the processes of identity formulation and the daily politics of symbolic and practical integration. In their quotidian interpretation and manipulation of the global changes occurring around them, women are the primary agents for the particularization of global experiences. They do this in the area of food preparation, just as they do in other areas of domestic or physiological practice. In this immigrant community of North African Jews, as in other communities of formerly colonized populations around the world, the dimension of gender in this global experience is essential in the formation, evolution and preservation of sensual experience, whether taste, sexuality, sight, or even emotions. I do not mean here to say that women are particularly good in the area of senses as opposed to ideas. I intend to demonstrate that they play an essential role in the production of symbols and practical ideologies out of sensual experiences and changes occurring on a global scale. My field-work data found that folk narratives translated this process into a recurrent discourse about the experience of change and deracination. These female cooks expressed more than nostalgia about their former cultural world and the necessity of modifying the scale of their cultural affiliations through the following expression: "We are now in France, so we need to be French, we need to be modern!" Thus, at least in terms of narrative, women were preoccupied with opening up their traditional world to make it comply with changes occurring in other places and among other peoples with similar experiences. The goal is to enlarge the scope of practical and private experiences and yet to maintain symbolic boundaries that identify and distinguish the different cultural orders involved in the syncretic product.

As evidence of this quotidian social and cultural invention, I would like to provide two ethnographic vignettes that are two recipes of the traditional ritual menu, as they have been modified after being transplanted in the French cultural context. The first is a vegetable stew composed of tomatoes, onions, peppers, paprika and some hot sauce, traditionally called *tshukt-shuka* in Arabic. Served as an appetizer in most festival meals, the dish is almost exclusively ritualistic because of the way it is featured. After immigrating to France, some cooks added eggplants and zucchinis, then started to call it the Jewish version of ratatouille. This has been particularly observed among families established in the southeastern Mediterranean regions of France, where ratatouille has its origins. The process translates a form of the dialectical incorporation of French regional cuisine into traditional North African gastronomy and marks a desire to integrate North African cuisine into French gastronomy. The second recipe provides an illustration of a similar cultural invention: *m'hatsar*, a soup of lamb seasoned with garlic and pepper, with fresh mint and beaten eggs added just before it is eaten and traditionally served in Passover meals or in meals that are part of the Jewish ritual of the New Year. Once settled in France, some women started to replace lamb with veal and to call the modified version a *blanquette de veau* to signify the white color of the soup that the beaten eggs supplied. This linguistic modification exhibits a desire for cultural integration similar to that involved in Jewish ratatouille, but the presence of veal in the process also indicates the social rise achieved after migration. The blanquette is one of the dishes that most significantly represents contemporary Frenchness.

In response to the efforts of the North African immigrants to integrate French culinary categories into their traditional cuisines, French gastronomy has fostered a relatively similar process of integration with defined symbolic boundaries. As an ethnographic example, in most large French cities today one can find a panoply of different, and especially North African, immigrant cuisines. It is as if no city in France can claim gastronomic status in the French urban landscape without at least one *resto-couscous*. Yet in the restaurants classified as offering typical French cuisine, one does not yet find (or very rarely) menus combining blanquette de veau or *croque-monsieur* with lamb *tajines*. So the process of integrating the immigrants' cuisines has, here too, maintained strict symbolic boundaries and categories. The geographical distribution of ethnic restaurants in Paris is a significant ethnographic representation of a similar process. Although they are found in almost every neighborhood, couscous restaurants dominate the food industry in neighborhoods where immigrant populations are large, or in the Latin Quarter. The latter locale displays restaurants from a variety of international origins: Greek and Middle Eastern, North African, Vietnamese and Chinese, Southeast Asian, as well as French provincial restaurants. This multicultural climate in the Latin Quarter, historically identified as an academic and intellectual progressive locale, is not without cultural significance. Because it is strongly oriented towards serving tourists, the area constitutes an official display of the French politics of identity and Otherness, at least in the domain of the food industry.

Notes

1. R. Barthes, "Towards a Psychosociology of Contemporary Food Comsumption," in E. and R. Forster, eds., *European Diet from Pre-Industrial to Modern Times* (New York: Harper Torchbooks, 1975), 47–59; M. Douglas, ed., *Food in the Social Order* (New York: Russell Sage Foundation, 1984); J. Goody, *Cooking, Cuisine, and Class: A Study in Comparative Sociology* (Cambridge: Cambridge University Press, 1982); C. Lévi-Strauss, *The Origins of Table Manners* (New York: Harper and Row, 1978); J-F. Revel, *Culture and Cuisine: A Journey Through the History of Food* (New York: Doubleday, 1982); F.J. Simoons, *Eat Not This Flesh: Food Avoidances from Prehistory to the Present*, 2nd ed (Madison: University of Wisconsin Press, 1994); D. N. Walcher et al., eds., *Food, Man, and Society* (New York: Plenum, 1976).

2. C. Lévi-Strauss, *Structural Anthropology* (New York: Basic Books, 1963).

3. C. Lévi-Strauss, *Séminaire sur l'identité* (Paris: Grasset, 1977).

4. Derrida, J. *The Other Heading: Reflections on Today's Europe* (Bloomington: Indiana University Press, 1992).

5. F. Braudel, *The Identity of France* (New York: Harper and Row, 1988–90).

6. The current political climate of hostility against immigrants from the Southern Mediterranean, especially as it is formulated in the National Front's agenda, has stigmatized these immigrant cuisines as a threat to the authentic French gastronomy. One particular ingredient category severely attacked in this debate has been a specific gamut of spices (cumin in particular), presented as an agent of alteration of the taste characteristic of the French "Terroir" (see C. Ripe, "Chauvinist Chefs' Reign of Terroir," in *Wall Street Journal*, 11/8/96).

7. J. Bahloul, "Palais d'Amérique," in *La Gourmandize* (*Autrement*, no. 140 [November 1993], 101–05).

8. This term is not used here in a general "functionalist" perspective.

9. The terminology of "ethnicity" is not employed in French official language to characterize the cultures of the immigrants. Typically, these cultures are referred to through their geographical origins.

10. J. Bahloul, *The Architecture of Memory* (New York: Cambridge University Press, 1996); J. Bahloul, "Noms et prénoms juifs nord-africains" (*Terrain*, 4 [1985], 62–69).

11. See J. Bahloul, "Les barrières coloniales," in *Les Juifs d'Algérie, images et textes* (Paris: Editions du Scribe, 1987), 24–25; R. Ayoun and Bernard Cohen, *Les Juifs d'Algérie: deux mille ans d'histoire* (Paris: J.C. Lattès, 1982).

12. M. Douglas, "The Abominations of Leviticus," 41–57, in *Purity and Danger: An Analysis of the Concepts of Pollution and Taboo* (London: Routledge and Kegan Paul, 1966).

13. For further consideration of this approach, see the psychoanalytical analysis of Gérard Haddad in *Manger le livre* (Paris: Editions, 1983).

14. I am obviously referring to the work of Mary Douglas on dietary laws. In her chapter on "the Abominations of Leviticus," she specifically mentions the category of "bovine" as the archetypical representation of purity in Jewish dietary laws, as structurally articulated in the Old Testament.

15. This tradition has its origin in the valuation of the green color in Moslem folk representations, and its presence in the ritual beginning of the year, among both Jews and Moslems of the region, refers to a popular conception of the yearly cycle as an agrarian and cosmological one (see J. Bahloul, *Le culte de la Table Dressée*, 97–98 (Paris: Editions A.M. Métailié, 1983).

16. See for example how folk discourse on racial difference is elaborated in terms of "blood" ancestry, of essential "odors", and of "epidermical" intolerance (a symbolic trilogy of skin, blood, senses).

17. Yet this point was reached in some upper-middle-class families ready to make this sacrifice in order to be treated as Frenchmen. It was also in these families that intermarriage had become more accepted. The vernacular agenda of emancipation did have a variable formulation depending on class and socio-economic status.

18. Douglas, *Purity and Danger*.

19. A similar process is at work in the later generations of Arab Moslem North African immigrants in France, who have now reached high levels of secular education, similar to that of the Jews (F. Sechaud, "Sociologie religieuse ou anthropologie politique de l'alimentation? Une enquête sur l'alimentation musulmane à Marseille en 1989," in *L'Islam en France*, sous la dir. de B. Etienne [Paris: Ed. du C.N.R.S., 1990], 312–30).

20. This includes kosher butcher shops and delicatessen stores, as well as kosher caterers providing the food entertainment for weddings and bar-mitzvahs.

21. Some businesses demonstrate their affiliation with North Africa by including it in their trade name, such as "Les délices de Tunis."

22. To give some further evidence of this process, I would like to provide here an ethnographic anecdote that I experienced two years ago while doing field work in this Parisian neighborhood. As I was interviewing one of the owners of a kosher restaurant with a front entrance that displays the name "Café des Psaumes" (The Book of Psalms Cafe), my interviewee, while preparing *falafel* for the lunch customers, bypassed my questions even as he tried to "proselytize" me and gave me a poster printed with a list of the Rebbe's spiritual sayings. Although I would not say that these kosher food catering businesses supply literature as their primary trade, I argue that they are at least claiming to provide "food for thought" when they provide literary support along with their nutritional services.

23. I certainly do not mean to present this as a specificity of North African culture. With some circumstantial exceptions, this factor is strikingly universal, as documented in ethnographic observation (M.Z. Rosaldo, "Woman, Culture, and Society: A Theoretical Overview," in *Woman, Culture, and Society*, Michelle Zimbalist Rosaldo and Louise Lamphere, eds. [Stanford University Press, 1974], 17–42.)

Part Two

Public Policy and Global Science

Chapter Six

Food Policies, Nutrition Policies, and Their Influence on Processes of Change: European Examples

Elisabet Helsing

Food Policies in Human History

Shopping in the supermarket, with tens of thousands of foods available to choose, is a very new way for the human race to find its food. Our pre-agricultural foremothers and forefathers, who gathered and hunted in their immediate environment, had their food choice limited by forces which were beyond their capacity to influence, however much they tried. With agriculture came choice, but a limited one again constrained by limits of the natural environment. Even today we have not quite overcome the forces of nature, although in parts of the world we have managed to increase our food supplies and provide so well for ourselves that the choice of foods may seem unlimited.

It can be argued that when some 10,000 years ago hunting and gathering gave way to agriculture, food supplies began to be regulated, more or less successfully, by those who had the power to do so through various forms of food policies, out of a desire and ability to plan tomorrow's food supply. Over time, food policies thus defined have been dictated by a variety of motives on the part of the powers that be, such as the need to keep people alive, peasants quiet, traders prosperous, and armies fit for fighting. The commercial value of food has of course always been a strong pressure in food policies. Increasingly, and primarily in the present century, a new factor has emerged with force: the possibility for food manufacturers to add value, and hence profit, by processing of farmers' primary food products at the factory level. All of these considerations, some of which may comprise mutually exclusive elements, have always had to compete for a place on the crowded agenda of food policy-makers.

Diet and Health: A Contested Concern

Considering the health effects of different foods, especially in the context of disease prevention, is of course not new. The emergence of health promotion as a food policy objective is, however, a relatively recent phenomenon. Subsequent recent successes and failures in obtaining a place for health considerations on food policy agendas, thus making them what we choose to call "food and nutrition policies," are closely linked to the development of nutrition science as a discipline in its own right.

The development of nutrition-related sciences has proceeded, in leaps and bounds, mainly in the twentieth century. During this period, these sciences have been in a more or less explicit, continuous interaction with the vast food industry, one of the largest, if not *the* largest, commercial sector in the world. The relationship of nutrition science with what could easily be a rather intimidating associate has had a subtle influence on the development of priorities for research in, and action on, the policy arena of food and nutrition.

In this essay, I will examine some aspects of this interaction between nutrition science, food and nutrition policy and related political and economic forces, seeking to show how in parts of the globe commercial interests have set the priorities for research and action in nutrition science. I will also try to show that food and nutrition policies do work. Policymakers have the power to change food patterns in a population, and I will also discuss how this power may have had a negative effect upon health when used in a system that for two generations was closed to the influences of a developing nutrition science.

Recent History of the Nutrition Sciences: The Nutrient Deficiency Paradigm

Scientific work in nutrition, when it emerged in the nineteenth century, focused on the identification of nutrients in foods and on understanding their nature and function. Some associations had been known for centuries. Among these are Eber's papyrus, an ancient Egyptian treatise of about 1500 BC, which describes how the lack of ascorbic acid produces scurvy and which very sensibly prescribes taking ox liver to avoid the night blindness caused by a deficiency of vitamin A.[1] This also illustrates the fact that knowledge once acquired, can be lost, and has to be developed all over again.

The earliest scientific confirmation of the existence of special nutrients promoting health resulted from diseases caused by their absence. In the late nineteenth century and the first three decades of the twentieth, nutrient-related scourges such as pellagra, rickets, and beri-beri were described; the deficient nutrients, isolated and identified; and human requirements, quantified. Somewhat later, from the 1950s on, amino acids, the basic elements of proteins, were identified and described and human requirements determined for those that are "essential", that is, those that must be provided through diet because the human body needs them but cannot itself synthesize them. This was often a slow, step-by-step exploration to find new ground and successfully and ever more precisely to discover which nutrients human bodies require and how they get them from food. This research often employed quite cumbersome but meticulous methods of study. This research might, for example, imply eliminating the nutrient in question from the diet of their subjects for prolonged periods of time, months and sometimes years, waiting for symptoms of deficiency to become manifest (today's ethics committees would hardly have permitted these investigations!).

Sometimes researchers even seem to have been somewhat carried away by the spirit of pioneering and the importance of their findings for humankind. Dr. Casimir Funk is credited with having coined in 1912 the slightly misleading term "vitamines" for a heterogeneous group of substances, combining the chemical term "amine" with "vital," that is, pertaining to life.[2] He later admitted that "when I chose the name 'vitamine' I was well aware that these substances might later prove not all to be of an amine nature. However, it was necessary for me to use a name that would sound well and serve as a catch word." [3]

These initial scientific investigations into the lower limits of nutrient intake did not threaten any commercial interests. To the contrary; quite apart from their usefulness to military caterers and the shipping industry, these investigations also had commercial value for the pharmaceutical industry, which began to see the potential in producing both single and combined formulae of essential nutrients. The commercial value of vitamins, minerals and essential amino acids also soon became apparent to food producers, who began to use modern scientific nutrition concepts in marketing their products. The food-producing sectors in the best position to make advantageous use of this new information were those who were well-organized, resourceful, and rich, such as the meat and the dairy industries. This argument was increasingly used by the dairy industry from 1930 onwards and in Europe after 1945 even took on the proportions of propaganda. In this, the dairy industry was enthusiastically supported by scientists. Producers of other kinds of foods, such as fruit and vegetable producers or those working in the fishing industry, were less active in using the comparative advantage offered by the science of nutrition as an argument for increasing sales volume. This may have been because they were less well organized, less aware of the need for aggressive marketing of their produce, or had less to spend on marketing and advertising as the result of their slimmer profit margin.

In the 1960s there were no perceived conflicts of interest between nutrition scientists and those selling food and food products. After all, their interests coincided. Convinced of the importance of their findings on the public health, scientists would exhort people to consume enough of the nutrients in question, which then made it possible for the food industry to profit by providing them.

The 1970s Sees the Limits of Magical Bullets

In the 1970s , a new interest emerged in what was called "applied nutrition." This branch of nutrition science applied a public health perspective to the findings in basic and clinical nutrition and often employed social science analysis to better understand eating behavior. In this way, a more realistic awareness emerged among nutritionists about the relative importance of nutrient deficiencies in normal dietary practice, one somewhat at odds with the foregoing recent assumptions. In most societies, ordinary foods commonly provided in most food cultures would supply enough of all the nutrients needed, essential as well as non-essential, provided people had enough of them. In the case of protein, a downward revision of recommendations and norms for the intake of this class of nutrients eventually followed in 1972.[4] The popular slogan which very accurately summarized this new understanding was that if people get enough food, protein will usually take care of itself.

The case of vitamins and minerals is slightly less straightforward. In the 1970s a similar slogan was applied to vitamins and minerals: with enough food the vitamin and mineral intake would "take care of itself" in populations with a reasonably balanced dietary pattern. The emerging understanding in the late 1980s of the negative role of the oxidative process in the development of cardiovascular lesions and possibly also in the etiology of some cancers, as well as the potential importance of the antioxidant properties of some vitamins and minerals, made this problematic, however. Should recommendations for these antioxidant nutrients be set so high that they not only made deficiency unlikely but also result in a discernible antioxidant effect within the human organism? This would in many cases mean that the normal level of vitamins and minerals found in foods were not high enough and that supplementation or fortification of foods would be necessary. This line of discussion, investigation, and speculation continues; and the process has by no means concluded. The 1990s has seen the concepts of "designer foods," "functional foods" and "nutraceuticals"—quasi-scientific and often commercially driven attempts to raise public concern over nutrient deficiencies.

The New Nutrition Paradigm: Nutrient Excesses or Imbalances

The other end of the spectrum of nutrient intake concerns "unbalanced overnutrition," or what happens to the organism when it is supplied with too much, rather than too little, of a nutrient. This was not initially the concern of modern nutritionists, although in many cultures, philosophers, and medical officials concerned with public health issues have for centuries discussed the need to avoid gluttony and to strive for "moderation in all things."[5]

One of the first representatives of the modern Western medical school of epidemiology, Ancel Keys of the United States, explored the relationship between potentially excessive intakes of nutrients and consequent ill health. Having observed the epidemic of heart disease in the United States, which started to emerge well before the Second World War, Keys was struck by the low prevalence of circulatory diseases in the European Mediterranean area in the early post-war period. He further observed that in Northern Europe the prevalence of dietary restrictions enforced during World War II had resulted in a transient beneficial effect on heart disease. As these effects wore off after the war, the epidemic of heart disease continued to rise along its pre-war trend. When examining heart disease and dietary patterns of populations of middle-aged men in seven countries around the world, Keys and his associates identified for the first time an excessive intake of one class of nutrients, in this case saturated fatty acids, as the main suspects in the etiology of this epidemic of circulatory diseases.[6]

The Commercial Agenda: Do Not Tread on Our Circles

A line of research of this nature, which might point to some foods as containing more than others of a less desirable component, could not be expected to be received enthusiastically by all food producers and manufacturers. Those manufacturers whose commodities were singled out as not conducive to good health were particularly cool toward this new research. This included the mighty dairy and meat industries, which had earlier embraced nutrition science, especially research findings about the merits of animal protein but now decided that it might rather be in their interest not to have this new line of investigations in nutrition pursued too enthusiastically.

A Global View: Nutrition and the Young United Nations

The history of nutrition within the specialised agencies of the United Nations provides evidence of how difficult it was for the concept of "unbalanced over-nutrition" and its relation to chronic diseases to make its way to the public health and agriculture policy agendas. After the Second World War, nutrition was a shared responsibility among such agencies as the Food and Agriculture Organisation (FAO) and the World Health Organisation (WHO). The two organisations divided the areas of this responsibility thus:

In FAO the emphasis is on nutrition in relation to the production, distribution and consumption of food,; in WHO it is on nutrition in relation to the maintenance of health and the prevention of disease.[7]

The relationship between nutrition and what was then called "chronic degenerative diseases" was on the agenda of these young agencies from the beginning. The first four reports of the meetings of their joint Expert Committee on Nutrition show that "nutrition and degenerative diseases" were indeed of concern to the Committee. The report from their 1951 Second Session stated that:

> There is also reason to suppose that excessive consumption of carbohydrates and fats, quite apart from calories, may produce serious forms of malnutrition. While these are rare in many parts of the world, they may be of outstanding importance in regions in which food supplies are abundant and economic levels high. The association of obesity with a high incidence of "degenerative" diseases, e.g. certain cardiovascular and metabolic disorders, suggests that in these regions malnutrition from the over-consumption of food is a problem of major significance.[8]

During the period from 1955 to 1962, the reports from these meetings show a slow change of emphasis away from the uncomfortable link between fat and disease toward the need to "bridge the world's protein gap" and to increase the production of high-protein foods. This shift away from the connection between diet and chronic diseases accelerated in 1962, when WHO, in its role of being responsible for the health-related aspects of nutrition, called for an expert consultation on prevention of ischemic heart disease, which *inter alia* stated that:

> It must be reported that at the present time there are no effective means by which the occurrence of ischaemic heart disease can be prevented. Such therapeutic measures as are available must therefore be applied to the disease itself in the hope of delaying its progression or preventing late complications..... Nevertheless, much further research is needed before public health authorities can recommend major alterations in the diet, or are justified in advising that more or less of any particular kind of fat would be beneficial.[9]

The committee consisted solely of cardiologists, but its conclusions were not refuted by nutrition scientists. Instead these conclusions had the effect, at least in many European countries, of turning many scientists away from any preoccupation with nutrition and chronic diseases for the next few decades. It also consolidated the direction of nutrition work in UN agencies for many decades to come. For four years the Joint FAO/WHO Expert Committee for Nutrition was not even convened. When it finally reconvened in 1966, Committee members seem to have taken the position that their concern was to be nutrient deficiencies and undernutrition. All they had to say about nutrition and degenerative diseases was that "the relationship between nutrition and atherosclerosis" was "currently an area of intensive inquiry."[10] It might thus be inferred that the statement by the WHO Committee in 1962 discouraged these U.N. Agencies from further pursuing the relationship between dietary patterns and heart health. Nevertheless, in this essay we will focus on some examples from Europe that serve to illustrate elements of the processes that change food behaviour and give some examples of the consequences for health under the very different conditions that pertain within the heterogeneous European region.

Europe: No Dietary Melting Pot!

Europe is a rather special continent when it comes to the comparison of different diets and disease patterns, since its food cultures are—and remain—diverse, based on the variety of geographic and climatic conditions that set the European peoples apart. Europe has food systems in different stages of development, including those in more-or-less-rapid transition from centralized to market economies. Periods of political isolation in some European countries have contributed to the preservation of this heterogeneity, and the end result is a striking difference in documented mortality rates from nutrition-related, non communicable diseases.

Europe: Nutrition Science with a Limited Scope

Ancel Keys included five European countries in his pathbreaking study of the relationship between diet and non-communicable diseases. Following Keys' lead, it would have been relevant to continue to map the health effects of the different European dietary experiences during and after the Second World War. However, after WHO renounced the link between diet and chronic diseases in 1962 mentioned above, scientific interest in taking up research in this area waned in Europe. It is of course impossible to provide specific and clear proof of interference by commercial interests with nutrition research agendas. It may have been just coincidental that the uncomfortable links between chronic diseases and nutrition which nutrition scientists had begun to explore in many parts of Europe in the early 1950s, were not pursued after the 1962 WHO "verdict," except for the work in the Nordic countries, discussed below. The majority of European nutritionists were instead continuing to concentrate on the much-less controversial area of nutrient deficiencies. There is nothing really surprising in this. Few scientists are ready to work in areas of investigation where political resistance and professional conflict can be anticipated.

When in the 1980s European consumer interest groups such as heart and cancer associations forcefully presented the case for a linkage between diet and chronic disease, they were eventually able to overcome the resistance and to put the subject back on the political agenda. Overcoming such political resistance and professional conflict was not easy, however, and turned out to be an—often trying—learning process for many of those scientists who were working on this. The intensity of the resistance inspired by parts of the food industry demonstrated to those involved the magnitude of the commercial interests at stake.[11]

The United States Takes a Different Direction

Over the years, the United States has often tended not to take the cues of the United Nations and its organizations too literally. So, while nutritionists in Europe agonized over WHO's verdict of 1962, nutritionists in the United States, who received the enthusiastic support of the American Heart Association, simply continued to go about their business of exploring the relationship between dietary factors and chronic diseases with large-scale intervention trials and a variety of epidemiological studies.

An example illustrates the difference in direction between Europe and the United States: In the United Kingdom, early in the 1980s a committee of nutrition scientists nominated by the Department of Health tried, in a carefully guarded report, to raise among national nutritional educators the issue of chronic diseases and nutrition. They found themselves quietly suppressed [11] by health administrators. [12] At the same time, their counterparts in the United States were busy preparing, with the assistance of the federal health administration and the National Academy of Sciences, two voluminous presentations of existing evidence [13] for the relationship between diet and chronic diseases.[14] This difference in attitude and development may perhaps also serve to explain why nutrition in the United States during the second half of this century seems to have commanded much more public attention than it does in Europe. The preoccupation of nutrition scientists with chronic diseases may have contributed to keeping the U.S. public interested in the results of nutrition research, since it corresponded to public health concerns at the time. The emphasis of European nutritionists on deficiency diseases was not matched by a corresponding concern among members of the European public — after all, the overt nutrient deficiency diseases such as rickets or scurvy had ceased to be a threat to European public health quite some time ago.

Nutrition Policy Development:
Early Stage, 1930s to 1970s

Nutrition policy as a distinct, multi-sectoral type of food policy[15] emerged even before the Second World War and was described, for example, in a document published in 1937 by the League of Nations.[16] In the course of the Second World War, food-supply policies with explicit health-related objectives were actually in operation in many of the countries where governments were concerned about the food-supply situation and sought to provide food security through the instruments at their disposal, such as planning food production, rationing food, and planning purchases through Governmental catering entities.

In the 1960s and 1970s, the United Nations, in particular the FAO, initiated much of the thinking and discussion[17] around nutrition policies. [18] A handbook on the subject was published in 1969. [19] By remarkable oversight, such policies were regarded as only relevant to developing countries. In the 1970s, as the concept was further elaborated in FAO, it was explicitly linked to "development policy"; and food and nutrition planning was seen as an important element in the overall "development planning" that was being encouraged[20] in poor countries. [21] Nutrition policies—or "nutrition planning"—were indeed tried for longer or shorter periods of time in a limited number of countries, such as Tanzania, some Latin American countries, the Philippines, India, and Thailand. It was a complex, ideally multisectoral procedure, based on the assumption that the basic causes of malnutrition, inequity, and poverty, could be remedied through public education and by the manipulation of the food supply. This approach, even though it was supported by international assistance agencies, tended eventually to scare off politicians and policy-makers and thus to have limited impact[21].

Nutrition Policies for Rich and Poor Countries Alike

When delegates at FAO's World Food Conference in 1974 introduced a resolution[22] that emphasized the need to improve nutrition in all countries and recommended that all governments formulate and integrate concerted food and nutritional plans and policies, this was, at the time, an innovative idea.[23] The Norwegian delegation at the Conference underlined this departure from the past when observing that nutrition policies were seen as relevant to poor countries only, declaring that work was already under way to present a national food and nutrition policy in their country, directed not at deficiency diseases but at nutrition-related chronic diseases.

Nordic Countries: Health Gets on the Agenda on Food Supply Policy

It may not have been coincidental that eventually this development emerged from the Nordic countries—Iceland, Denmark, Norway, Sweden and Finland—which had a history of strong Governmental activism in health policy matters and were the first to try to extend health-policy objectives to agriculture. The extent to which the agricultural sector in these countries responded to this invitation varied according to the advantage they saw in its association. So, while the rest of Europe swung away from preoccupation with diet and chronic diseases, nutritionists in the Nordic countries persisted—perhaps in the light of their war-time experiences—to pursue the link between diet and chronic diseases.

The food patterns in the five countries are not identical, although foreigners would probably have some difficulty in seeing much of a difference among these Nordic diets. All are based on the potato and bread as traditional staple foods, although people in Iceland and Norway consume a relatively large amount of fish and those in Denmark prefer meat. For historical and political reasons, the public availability of alcohol is regulated in all these countries except Denmark, where alcohol consumption is twice as high as in the other four.[24] At the risk of oversimplification, one might say that the dietary trend in all the Nordic countries in the post-war period was away from a diet very high in staple foods like cereals and potatoes toward one in which meat was readily available, a trend shown by the near doubling of meat consumption in many Nordic countries during the period from 1945 to 1975. It is worth noticing that Iceland and Norway are to this day not self-sufficient in food, while Sweden and Finland are; and in Denmark food production is a very important export industry.

Nordic Rebels: Nutrition Policies Lead the Way from Fat to Lean Diets

In 1975, the Norwegian Parliament was the first political body in an industrialized country to adopt a comprehensive food supply and nutrition policy. [25] The Norwegian agricultural sector, which received considerable state subsidies that were not always popular with non-agricultural tax payers, needed to demonstrate agriculture's important contribution to public health and hence supported the new policy initiative. In Sweden, an official paper on nutrition policy had, at the request of the government, been prepared in the early 1980s[26]; but the Swedish Parliament eventually, in 1985, adopted only a very general recommendation proposing that agriculture policy should help the population obtain nutrients as recommended,[27] with education as the main tool. Apparently the Swedish agricultural sector did not see the need to court public opinion the way the Norwegian sector did. Finland adopted a reasonably comprehensive nutrition policy in 1986.[28] Although it was succinctly stated, the decision to have such a policy led to considerable dietary changes in Finland in a number of areas, notably fat intake (see below). In Denmark, a Parliamentary resolution was passed in 1984 that listed certain measures to be taken toward establishing a nutrition policy, such as forming an academic institution for nutrition research and carrying out a national dietary survey.[29] These were relatively short-term measures that did not directly address food supply matters. Iceland's parliament, the Allthinget, adopted a modest but well-meaning nutrition policy.[30] Here, too, the interaction between agriculture and health interests was important.

In all the Nordic countries, possibly as a result of political attention, food-supply policies during the 1980s became more focused on health. In Finland and Norway, the main and explicit objective of such policies was to reduce the overall intake of fat, especially saturated fat, as a way to reduce premature mortality from circulatory diseases. In both countries, the proportion of dietary energy from fat subsequently decreased, from over 40 percent around 1975 to less than 35 percent in 1991, and have stayed at this level ever since.[31] All the Nordic countries have established publicly funded Nutrition Councils or similar institutions charged with the responsibility of educating or informing the public; their structures vary considerably, however. In all of the Nordic countries, the overall changes in dietary patterns have moved in the direction advocated since the 1970s by their Nutrition Councils or nutrition educators.

All of these activities may have resulted in people being kept aware of nutrition issues and, through nutrition-oriented food policies, at times giving them easy access to options for changing their diet in line with the best knowledge of nutrition science at the time. It is perhaps not too surprising, however, that in Denmark, with its relatively stronger agricultural sector, especially in dairy farming and meat production, the changes were less remarkable. This is a not a new development. As early as 1965, a published international account noted contemporary Nordic dietary guidelines recommending lowered consumption of fat to combat chronic diseases. [32] This account explicitly emphasized that in Denmark these guidelines had been only provisionally adopted.

In Finland, where in the 1960s mortality from chronic disease was the highest in Europe, the situation in the 1990s has improved quite a lot. As in all the Nordic countries, the heart disease epidemic among middle-aged men, which had reached an apex in the early 1970s, was almost back to pre-war levels by 1995. Cerebrovascular diseases—mainly stroke—also steadily decreased in the Nordic countries, as in all European countries except those of the former Eastern block. Premature mortality from cancer also decreased or remained stable in the Nordic countries, the only exception being Denmark, where the prevalence of smoking among women has resulted in ever-increasing rates of lung cancer.

Average life expectancy rose among men forty-five years of age, as seen in Table 6.1, in all these Scandinavian countries. This indirectly indicates that the overall impact of chronic non-communicable diseases on life expectancy decreased considerably in this period. The table also demonstrates that Finnish men have made great strides, while Danish men lag behind in increasing life expectancy. It would be foolish to suggest direct relationships between this table and the intensity and success of food and nutrition policy

TABLE 6.1   Average Increase in Life Expectancy Among Men, Age 45, from
1981–1985 to 1993–1994

Country	1981–1985 [percentages]	1993–1994 [percentages]	Increase [years]
Denmark	29.3	30.1	0.8
Finland	28.0	30.6	2.6
Iceland	31.8	34.1	2.3
Norway	30.4	32.0	1.6
Sweden	30.9	33.0	2.1

SOURCE: Health Statistics in the Nordic Countries, 1994 (NOMESCO47:1996).

endeavors—such a relationship would at best be indirect. Further, given the
many causes of chronic non-communicable diseases, dietary changes have to
be considered together with lifestyle changes such as decreasing the use of
tobacco and alcohol and increasing physical activity, as well as improving the
effectiveness and the efficiency of emergency health care.

Bearing this caveat in mind, one could perhaps speculate that Finland,
which had a long way to go to improve health, has succeeded, possibly assisted by rather strong public policies in the area of food. Denmark, with its
reticence towards employing policy measures that might "disturb" the agriculture sector, has, on the other hand, seen a less-pronounced improvement
in mortality from chronic disease during the last decade.

The Soviet Union: What Happened Behind the Iron Curtain — or the Effect of Global Isolation

The many countries belonging to what was formerly described as the com-
munist bloc are, of course, not a homogeneous cluster but very different
countries, most with several distinctly different cultures within their borders. A fuller picture, underpinned by carefully evaluated statistical and epidemiological data, has emerged only recently. That picture shows a certain
difference between what is now commonly termed Central Europe, the former buffer states between the Soviet Union and Western Europe, and the
countries in the former Soviet Union, sometimes called the Newly Independent States. For the sake of brevity, we will concentrate on the latter.

Food and Nutrition Policies in the Soviet Union, 1919–89

The history of public health policies in the former Soviet Union provides a
very valuable study. In the young Union of the early nineteen twenties,
ideals were high and the field for action was wide open. In every area of ac-

tivity society was restructured, as ruthlessly as necessary, to create what was envisaged as a brave new world. Whatever Moscow believed needed to be done could be done: A series of five-year plans ensured that what was envisaged would be achieved, not merely for a short period, but far into the future. Since one of the fundamental needs was to feed a large, diverse and growing population reliably and well, a planned and orderly development of the food supply became a major component of those plans. Horticulture, agriculture, food manufacturing and distribution were all taken as matters that must be systematically and scientifically tackled in the interests of building a strong and healthy nation.

Although it was never explicitly stated, the Soviet Union in these years carried out a centrally planned nutrition policy on a vast scale, without historical precedent. Unlike in the West, the commercial sector with its economic imperatives was notably absent. Consumer demand was also non-existent, since consumers' demands were by definition taken care of by the planners. In retrospect, what that meant was that nutrition and food science in the early 1920s was taken as the basis for long-term policies which became engraved, as it were, in stone. The nutritional recommendations of the 1920s thus came to dictate not only the goals set for the agricultural and other sectors but also the infrastructure on which these were to be built, the facilities with which they were provided, and the training given their workers. And so these policies remained for nearly seventy years, little influenced by changes in scientific thinking and knowledge in the world outside, until the end of the eighties, when the entire Soviet Union collapsed.

Once that Union disintegrated, a fascinating process of study began. Here was a society which to an important extent had chosen to go its own way for three generations. Here, for the first time, data were slowly becoming accessible on that society, ready for analysis and for international comparison. What had the results of that vast social experiment been? Here we will examine only a few of the issues pertaining to the food chain, the feeding of the population, and the ultimate effect upon its nutritional well-being and health.

It is clear, from what is known of food supply policies in the early years of the former Soviet Union, that two factors were dominant in political thinking and in planning. One was the evident need to provide sufficient food overall for a population that in the past had suffered much from food insecurity. The other, dictated by the common nutrition concerns of the period before World War II, was to provide sufficient animal protein. Agriculture and animal husbandry in the Soviet Union as in the West were attuned to that latter goal, resulting in a heavy emphasis on the production of meat. Indeed, World Bank figures show that in the late 1980s over half of the Soviet Union's total annual grain production went to feed animals for meat production. [33] Still, mainly because of an inefficient distribution system, the supply of meat never seemed to catch up with demand and never reached the level of supplies in the United States, an implicit, if not admitted, goal of many Soviet endeavors at the time. The provision of fresh vegetables and fruit was even less well developed, especially for the cities, because of the failure to provide refrigerated transportation that could ensure their arrival in good condition. Perishable commodities are obviously especially difficult to manage within a tightly controlled command-economy system.

We have very little reliable data on the actual food situation, as it was called, since this was classified information in the Soviet Union; studies of food intake consequently were few and methodologically weak. From the best figures available on the food supply in the former Soviet Union, the following conclusions about the pre-transition nutrition situation emerge.[34] The centrally planned food and nutrition policy of the old system seems to have succeeded in its primary goal, namely to secure enough food for all Soviet citizens. Yet, while none starved, the stern monotony of the food supply made people feel that they were deprived. When times got more difficult toward the end of the 1980s, people would often claim that "there was no food to be had," even when it could be shown that some foods—such as noodles and coarse vegetables: turnip, beet root, carrot and onion, and potatoes— were widely available. The traditional Russian bread, of excellent quality, was also usually available; and the patient customer usually had access to meat of highly variable quality. Yet the lack of variety made people overlook these foods.

Nutrition Problems in the Soviet Union

Those officials concerned with Soviet nutrition would claim, without much evidence, that the most precarious nutrient in the Union was protein. In fact, whereas in 1992 it could be calculated that in the countries of the European Union the proportion of total energy available from protein generally ranged between 10–12 percent, the corresponding figure for Russia was over 14 percent, indicating that protein deficiency was hardly the problem there that it was made out to be.[35] More problematic was the lack of choice and variety in the food supply.

One might add that educating the public about nutrition, an effort that in the West over a long period led to a progressively more informed public, hardly developed nor gained any momentum further East. Indeed, since the options for nutrition there were so limited and were not on the political agenda as items to be linked with the issue of health, it would indeed have been almost pointless to develop consumer education in this area anyway. The only choices involved were those made for consumers by the many people who planned menus for feeding millions of citizens in public spaces every day. These state-employed nutritionists based the menus they designed according to the Soviet requirements for "rational nutrition," the preferred normative term.

The science of nutrition had not been among those disciplines that Soviet leaders selected for contacts with the West (in contrast, for example, to cardiology, where the Kremlin gerontocracy could not afford to take any chances and saw to it that contacts with the best of Western science were frequent and unimpeded). Soviet scientists were infrequently represented in meetings of international experts on nutrition, in which standards and norms in the post-war period were determined and guidelines for education of the public were discussed. This is perhaps not surprising, given the introspective and static state of nutrition science in the Soviet Union at that time.

The Public Health Picture in the Soviet Union

Once reasonably reliable figures on premature cardiovascular mortality in the former Soviet republics became available for study, it was more than evident that something was gravely wrong.

Figure 6.1 shows the annual standardized death rates from ischaemic heart disease as they became available, including some retrospective figures cover-

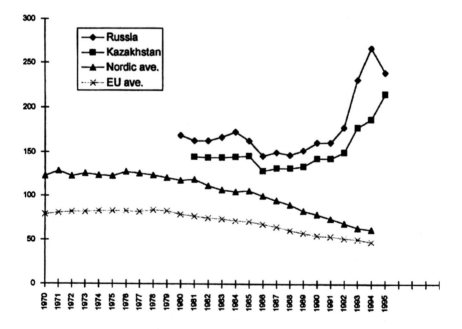

FIGURE 6.1 Mortality from Ischaemic Heart Diseases Among Men Aged 0–64 in Russia and Kazakhstan Seen Against Averages from the European Union and the Nordic Countries.

NOTE: Data represents standardized death rates (SDR) per 100,000.

SOURCE: Health for all 2000, a Database of the Unit of Statistics and Epidemiology, WHO Regional Office for Europe, Copenhagen 1997.

ing the final years of the USSR's existence.[36] The upper three curves represent the situation in Russia and Kazakhstan; in 1981 premature mortality (before age 64) among men were 145 and 163 per 100,000. By contrast, as the lower two curves show, the average annual mortality from this cause in 1981 among men in the countries of the European Union (EU) was only 77 per 100,000, while in the five Nordic countries taken together, three of which are geographically very close to the former Soviet Union, mortality in 1981 was rather higher than the EU average but still only 119 per 100,000 and with a downward trend.

Figure 6.2 shows an even greater contrast with Western countries where cerebrovascular disease is concerned. Annual premature mortality rates among men in the two ex-Soviet Republics ranged between 69 and 73 in 1981. The EU average figure was only 22, and the Nordic countries showed an average mortality as low as 18 per 100,000, with both cases demonstrating a well-established and continuing decline. These are only examples, but the

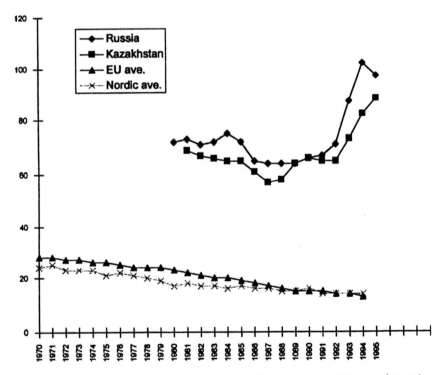

FIGURE 6.2   Mortality from Cerebrovascular Diseases Among Men Aged 0–64 in Russia, Kazakhstan, Seen Against Averages from the European Union (EU) and the Nordic Countries, in Standardized Death Rates (SDR) per 100,000.

SOURCE: Health for All 2000 Database from the Unit of Statistics and Epidemiology, WHO Regional Office for Europe, Copenhagen 1997.

astonishing picture which they present essentially remains when other measures of circulatory mortality are examined, using figures broken down by
sex or age and those of other countries within or beyond the borders of the
former Soviet Union. For one reason or another, the figures for mortality
from these causes in this medical field are some two and one-half times
higher than in Western countries, even in those countries in close proximity
to the former USSR. These differences between East and West are highly significant.

The Post-Soviet Era

From the end of the 1980s onward, the old course of the former Soviet
Union no longer dictated policies; but it would also be fair to say that no
other and better policy emerged to take its place. The breakdown of services
and supplies and the derangement of the economy has led to an aggravation
of social problems reflected in many health variables as well as the few cited
in Figures 6.1 and 6.2 that have still not found a solution, including those in
the production and supply of food. Far from emulating the decline in premature mortality which has long been in progress in the West, the republics in
the former Soviet Union have seen a most serious worsening of the situation.
In 1992, to quote only a single figure, annual premature mortality (before
the age of 65) from ischaemic heart disease among men in Russia has report-
edly risen to 150 per 100,000, compared with a level of 52 in the European
Union. The Russian situation continued to worsen rapidly, with mortality
attaining 215 in 1995; while the mortality figures in the west continued their
long decline and are currently well below 50 per 100,000. This does not tally
with the reports on food shortages, which in European history has commonly led to an improvement in cardiovascular mortality. Consequently, the
data from the former Soviet countries have been the object of intense
scrutiny, for it seemed almost improbable that such an explosive increase in
circulatory disease mortality could be real. The analysis thus far has, however, concluded that the data[37] are robust enough[38] even though the discussion about causality is impeded by lack of good supplementary data on possible contributing causes. Even if it is not possible to be precise about the
relative contribution of each lifestyle factor, there is agreement that heavy
consumption of alcohol, increased smoking, along with archaic dietary patterns, are all likely to have played a part, together with the lack of therapeutic facilities in the poorly functioning health-care system.

The Contemporary Situation — From Bad to Worse?

It is, thus, entirely clear that factors other than food intake could and did influence the rate of cardiovascular mortality in the latter years of the former
Soviet Union. In addition poverty, despite everything, has become and

remained a widespread problem, especially in the cities. Nevertheless, there is so much evidence of the negative role played by unhealthy or unbalanced nutrition in the state of health that it cannot be ignored. In Russian food rankings, there were only two categories of meat—prime and second, with the former containing a much higher level of fat.[39] Fat meat is expensive, yet popular and in great demand; lard, somewhat more available, is also in great demand. No better illustration could be given of the failure to teach the population modern concepts of sound nutrition.

Policy making is the art of the possible. What is possible depends on the situation, which therefore must be objectively assessed. There was scant attention to the actual development of the dietary patterns in the Soviet era. Perhaps the leadership intuitively reckoned that sleeping dogs were best left lying and that this was a potentially very mean dog. The dietary surveys that were undertaken were few, unrepresentative, and poorly designed, and kept under close wraps. This made adjustments impossible and stopped any discussion.

Can Nutrition Policies Influence Processes of Change?

Several international conferences in the early 1990s had as their theme food and nutrition policy and strategy or nutrition action plans.[40] The attention thus given to this policy area seems to have made a difference in the perception about food and nutrition policies and their applicability. While in the 1970s apparently only one European country had a nutrition policy, the number in the 1980s rose to six Nordic countries plus the Netherlands and Malta. When WHO's Regional Office for Europe undertook a survey in 1994 on how nutrition policy was formulated among the 50 European countries, out of the 33 respondents, 29 claimed to have or to be close to having, such policies, strategies or plans of action. While[41] it is doubtful that all of these countries are fully aware of the potential or even the workings of a nutrition policy, the fact that these countries were in the process of adopting them seems to demonstrate concern on the part of politicians.

The re-emergence of this interest may have several explanations. The simplest would be that the series of meetings, reports, and other events drew the attention of national policymakers to the potential benefits of, possibilities for, a systematic, comprehensive, and multisectoral approach to governmental action in the area of nutrition. More complex explanations are also possible. In Europe, as in most of the world, popular awareness about diet and health is certainly growing, albeit not at the rate that it does in the United States. Changes in health-care systems favoring decentralized care and increased privatization provoke a justified fear that health care costs for the individual will increase. This in turn means that the prevention of disease takes on a new urgency for individual citizens in many countries around the world, and particularly in Europe, although not in the United States.

Concern about the costs of health-care services and the difficulties of changing lifestyles may therefore have led politicians to be more attentive to policy options that might prove effective in reducing the burden of chronic disease. The falling rates of chronic diseases in some countries may have helped convince policymakers that it might be possible after all to influence the development through measures at their disposal , such as increasing public awareness of the benefits of healthy eating.

The developments that took place behind the Iron Curtain, where there was a notable absence of public awareness about diet and health, and in particular about healthy patterns of eating, shows in a striking way what may happen if the formation of policies on nutrition is left to itself. The Soviet example also illustrates the dangerous power of nutrition policies: The goals of a policy based on nutrition science must be constantly adjusted to incorporate the best of contemporary scientific evidence. For example, when nutrition scientists realized that protein deficiency was not as overwhelming a problem as originally suspected, most countries quietly dropped references to the need for attention to this problem in their dietary guidelines and action plans. The rigidly constructed and centrally planned Soviet system did not allow such flexibility and continued to push for protein awareness and increased consumption, resulting in possibly unnecessarily high levels and in concomitantly and detrimentally high animal fat intakes.

In conclusion, the history of nutrition policy in Europe may teach us a lesson. Policymaking is still the art of the possible, but it is also a very powerful tool that should not be misused. The negative attitude of commercial enterprises toward action on nutrition policy when they fear that their interests would be negatively affected may stem from an intuitive understanding of how powerful nutrition policies can be in influencing the food supply. Yet there are many examples to show that industries may benefit from collaborating with those who make nutrition policy, thus making these choices easier for the consumer to make. Used wisely, and with care, nutrition policy may be of benefit to all.

Notes

1. "Papyrus Ebers—Medical Writings ca 1550 BC" (quoted in *Encyclopedia Britannica*, Chicago, 1964).

2. C. J. Funk, *Journal of State Medicine* (1912), 20:31.

3. "The Vitamine Theory," in G. F. Combs, *The Vitamins*, 22 (San Diego:Academic Press Inc, 1992).

4. FAO and WHO, *Energy and Protein Requirements.* Report of a Joint FAO/WHO Ad Hoc Expert Committee. WHO Technical Report Series, no. 522 (Geneva:WHO, 1973).

5. G. Benham Sr., *Benham's Book of Quotations, Proverbs and Household Words* (London: Harrap and Company, 1948), 1118.

6. A. Keys et al., "Epidemiological Studies Related to Coronary Heart Disease: Characteristics of Men Aged 40–59 in Seven Countries," *Acta Medica Scandinavia*, 460 (1967; or Finland: Tampere, 1966).

7. World Health Organization, *Technical Report Series*, no. 16 (Geneva:WHO, 1950).

8. FAO/WHO, "Joint FAO/WHO Expert Committee on Nutrition, April 1951. Report on the Second Session," WHO *Technical Report Series*, no. 44 (Geneva: World Health Organization, 1951).

9. World Health Organization Expert Committee, "Arterial Hypertension and Ischaemic Heart Disease. Preventive Aspects," *WHO Technical Report Series*, no. 231 (Geneva: World Health Organization, 1962).

10. Joint FAO/WHO Expert Committee on Nutrition, *1967. Seventh Report* (Rome: Food and Agriculture Organisation of the United Nations, 1966).

11. G. Cannon, *Food and Health: the Experts Agree. An Analysis of One Hundred Authoritative Scientific Reports on Food, Nutrition and Public Health Published throughout the World in Thirty Years, between 1961 and 1991* (London: Consumers' Association, 1992).

12. The Health Education Council, *A Discussion Paper on Proposals for Nutritional Guidelines for Health Education in Britain* (London: National Advisory Committee on Nutrition Education (NACNE), 1983).

13. Committee on Diet and Health, Food and Nutrition Board, Commission on Life Sciences, National Research Council, *Diet and Health. Implications for Reducing Chronic Disease Risk* (Washington DC: National Academy Press, 1989).

14. U.S, Surgeon General, *The Surgeon General's Report on Diet and Health* (Washington DC: U.S. Department of Health and Human Services, Public Health Service. DHHS (PHS) Publication no. 88–50210, 1988).

15. Nutrition policy is defined here as politically mandated multisectoral action to achieve health objectives through agriculture and food policies, and nutrition objectives through health policies, using those instruments for policy implementation normally at the disposal of governments, and including continuous outcome monitoring.

16. League of Nations, "Final report of the Mixed Committee of the League of Nations on the Relation of Nutrition to Health, Agriculture and Economic Policy," *Nutrition*, ch. 3, pars. 10–17 (Geneva, 1937).

17. M. Ganzin, J. Perisse, P. François, "Need for Food and Nutrition Policies," in *Man, Food and Nutrition* (Cleveland: CRC Press, 1973).

18. P. Lunven, D.L. Bocobo, "Food and Nutrition Policy and Planning in Asia and the Far East Region," *FAO Nutrition Newsletter,* 12:2 (1974), 12–18.

19. B. F. Johnston, J.P. Greaves, "Manual on Food and Nutrition Policy," *FAO Nutritional Studies,* no. 22 (Rome: FAO, 1969).

20. L. Joy, "The Concept of Nutrition Planning," in *Nutrition Planning, the State of the Art* (Guilford, England: I.P.S. Science and Technology Press, Ltd., 1978).

21. J. Osgood Field, "Multisectoral Nutrition Planning: A Post-Mortem," *Food Policy,* 12:1 (1987), 15–28.

22. World Food Conference 1974, "Resolution V (by the First Committee)," *Food and Nutrition,* 1:1 (1975), 15–16.

23. E. Helsing, *The Initiation of National Nutrition Policies. A Comparative Study of Norway and Greece* (Groningen, the Netherlands: Styx Publications, 1990).

24. FAO/WHO, *Food and Health Indicators in Europe, Nutrition and Health 1961–1990. A Computerised Presentation* (Copenhagen: WHO Regional Office for Europe, Nutrition Unit, 1993).

25. The Royal Norwegian Ministry of Agriculture, *Report No.32 to the Storting (1975–76) on Norwegian Nutrition and Food Policy* (Oslo, Norway: Approved by Royal Decree November, 1975; published, 1976).

26. Expert Group for Diet and Health, Food Committee of 1983, *Report on Agriculture and Food Policy* (Stockholm: Ministry of Agriculture, 1985).

27. *The Swedish National Food Administration's Programme of Action in the Area of Diet and Health* (Uppsala, Sweden: Approved by the Board 3 April 1987; published, 1987).

28. Ministry of Social Affairs and Health, *Health for all by the year 2000. The Finnish National Strategy* (Helsinki, Finland, 1987).

29. National Food Agency, *Proposal for a Parliamentary Resolution regarding the Implementation of a Nutrition Policy in Denmark,* English version of the Parliament Document translated by the National Food Agency (Søborg, Denmark, 1984).

30. Ministry of Health and Social Security, *A Parliamentary Resolution on an Icelandic Nutrition Policy* (Reykjavik, Iceland, 1989).

31. Norwegian Nutrition Council, *Utviklingen i norsk kostold 1995 (Development of the Norwegian Diet 1995)* (In Norwegian; Oslo, 1996).

32. A. Keys, "Official Collective Recommendation on Diet in the Scandinavian Countries," *Nutrition Review,* 9 (1968), 259–63.

33. World Bank, Food and Agricultural Policy Reforms in the Former USSR," *Studies of Economies in Transformation,* no. 1 (Washington DC:IBRD/World Bank, 1992).

34. E. Helsing, "Health Promoting Policies: Strong, Weak, . . . , and Sometimes Harmful?" [Editorial], *International Journal of Risk and Safety in Medicine,* 9 (1996), 1–6.

35. "Protein Requirements and Recommendations in the former USSR" [Study commissioned by the World Bank, Nutrition Unit] (Copenhagen: WHO, 1993).

36. Figures 6.1 and 6.2, based on data supplied to the World Health Organisation by the countries concerned, have been incorporated into the World Health Organisation's Health For all Data Base (1997).

37. D.A. Leon, L. Chenet, V.M. Shkolnikov, S. Zakharov, J. Shapiro, G. Rakhmanova, S. Vassin, M. McKee, "Huge Variation in Russian Mortality Rates 1984–94: Artefact, Alcohol or What?," *Lancet,* 350 (1997), 383–8.

38. D. Kromhout, B. Bloemberg, G. Doornbos, "Reversibility of Rise in Russian Mortality Rates," *Lancet,* 350 (1997), 379.

39. Skurikhin et al., *Chemical composition of food* (In Russian; Moscow: Agroproniz dat, 1987).

40. These included three conferences in 1990, 1992, and 1996. In 1990 was the First European Conference on Food and Nutrition Policies (Budapest: WHO Regional Office for Europe, 1992). In 1992, two conferences were held: the Second European Conference on Food and Nutrition Policies (The Hague: WHO Regional Office for Europe and the Netherlands Ministry of Health, 1992) and The International Nutrition

Conference (Rome: WHO and FAO, 1992). In 1996 was The Food Summit (Rome: FAO, 1996).

41. WHO Regional Office for Europe, *Nutrition Policy in WHO European Member States- Progress Report following the 1992 International Conference on Nutrition* (Copenhagen: WHO, Nutrition Unit, Document EUR/ICP/LVNG 94 01/PB04, 1995).

Chapter Seven

Food Policy Research in a Global Context: The West African Sahel

Della McMillan and Thomas Reardon

Think of research as one of many inputs, including political and natural factors, that gives rise to decisions by policy makers, in a manner similar to a production function; these effects can be complex and take a long time; one may have an interesting research insight (such as ours on the effect of head taxes in rural Mali) that may not affect policy making until the time is right, until all factors come together to give weight to the insight.

— Dione (1993)

Food policy research takes place in a rapidly evolving political, economic, and physical context. This context determines both the type of research that is undertaken as well as the extent to which the results of research influence government policy. This chapter provides a brief overview of the complex interrelationship between research and the three major shifts in food policy that have occurred since World War II in the West African Sahel. This historical analysis describes the critical role of research in reevaluating many of the core assumptions that have undergirded these major policy shifts. The same analysis shows that the wider impact of research was seldom direct. Rather, it tended to redirect or strengthen trends that were already under way due to:

1. the long-term structural economic, social and political characteristics and problems of the region (highly seasonal and variable rainfall, trade deficits, poverty, expanding urban clients) acting in concert;

2. the evolving "conventional image" of the food system and the behavior of its actors (consumers, producers, and traders);
3. the shifts in the development ideologies of the major regional and international actors, such as the Organization of African Unity (OAU), the World Bank, and the International Monetary Fund (IMF);
4. the short-term shocks (such as physical shocks from droughts and shocks from external policies such as regional currency devaluation) that force governments to respond to high profile urgent problems; and
5. the government's perception both of its political best interest and of its people's best interest.

The final section of this essay includes a list of practical suggestions for how the link between research and food policy might be clarified and strengthened within this global context.

Background Issues to Which Food Policies Were Addressed

Asante (1986: 12) defines food policy as "an integrative policy approach to food production, distribution, and consumption, encompassing the broad economic and social policies and reforms that affect the wider distribution of income and people's access to food." In other words, it is a set of policies that attempt to "influence the decision making environment of food producers, food consumers, and food marketing agents in order to further social objectives" (Timmer et al. 1983: 9).

National food policy in most societies is designed to achieve four basic objectives: efficient growth in the food and agricultural sectors, job creation, a decent minimum standard of living, and security against famine or extreme food shortages (Timmer et al. 1983: 14–15). The emphasis placed on each objective varies by country and over time and is invariably linked to complex political decisions about how each objective contributes to the nation's health and welfare and, implicitly, to its political stability. One of the key contributions of global history is to discern some of the important global trends that affect this decision-making process. Since 1970, a significant portion of all bilateral and multilateral aid to Sub-Saharan Africa has focused on strengthening national food policies. The reasons are complex but have essentially to do with the fact that Sub-Saharan Africa is the only developing region in the world in which the per capita food production declined throughout most of the 1970s and 1980s (Figure 7.1). The issue is especially serious for the semi-arid countries considered to belong to the West African Sahel.

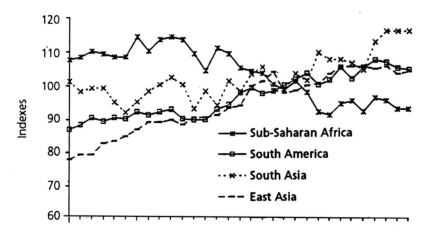

FIGURE 7.1   Indexes of Food Production, Developing Countries, 1961–1994

SOURCE: J. Sanders et al. (1996:3). Reprinted by permission.

The term Sahel refers to the agroclimatic "shore" of semi-arid steppe and savanna (average rainfall, 150 to 900 millimeters) that lies between the Sahara Desert and the coastal forests of West Africa. Since the early 1970s, the term has most frequently been used to identify all or parts of six to eight West African nations that include the large Sahelian zones most severely affected by the drought from 1968 to 1974. These countries include two coastal states, Mauritania and Senegal; and four land-locked states, Mali, Niger, Burkina Faso, and Chad. The coastal state of Gambia and island country of Cape Verde are sometimes also included.[1] As a group, these Sahelian countries appeared on almost all the major lists of chronically underdeveloped countries compiled in the mid–1970s (Berg 1975: 5). Their poverty can still be measured in terms of per-capita income, food production per capita, and most leading indicators of development (World Bank 1995; Sanders, Shapiro, and Ramaswamy 1996).

The Sahelian countries are not only poor but also extremely dependent (Berg 1975: 7–9). The annual crop production cycle is dictated by a short three- to four-month rainy season followed by a much longer dry period. The area is also subject to extreme variation between years and within single years in the seasonal patterns of rainfall (Nicholson 1986; Rasmussen 1987). Opportunities to use irrigation to level out the ups and downs of this environmental variation are limited by the highly seasonal flow of the internal river system.

The Sahelian countries import all of their petroleum, and even before the 1968–74 drought most of them imported significant amounts of food. A substantial percentage of this imported food is wheat and rice, which tends to be consumed by the swelling urban population. Between 1965 and 1983, the Sahel population doubled; but the urban population more than quintupled (Reardon 1993: 19).

Because most countries obtained their independence at a time when there were only a few university-trained agricultural specialists, these countries have had to rely significantly on imported skills and foreign training. They have also had an early and persistent dependence on outside donors for almost all development investment and, in many cases, for current government budget support. Because of their long, uncontrolled frontiers and old tradition of moving goods and people between north and south, the Sahel economies have limited control over trade flows, so smuggling accounts for a major proportion of food and non-food imports and exports. Berg (1975: 9) notes that this high rate of smuggling put "serious limits on the autonomy of internal economic policies. . . . [since] no Sahel country can have an independent price policy or an independent commercial policy." Autonomous economic policies are further constrained by virtue of a majority of the countries' membership in the French-managed Franc Zone. Member countries agree to some explicit restrictions on their fiscal and monetary independence in return for a line of credit at the French treasury and for other benefits in trade and aid (Berg 1975; IMF 1994).

Food Policy Research and the Major Shifts in Public Policy from the Colonial Period through Early Independence

Despite strong similarities over time in the Sahel's principal economic and environmental problems, there have been three important shifts in food policy as well as the underlying "conventional images" of the area's food problems.

A key factor in food policy in the late colonial period was that the average recorded rainfall was one standard deviation above the norm. One result was to encourage people to occupy more marginal lands in drier areas than had previously been primarily used by pastoralists. Another consequence was to set in motion the notion that the area enjoyed enough land to support food self-sufficiency if extensive techniques were used in crop production. Indeed, residents often argued that any overt investment in crop technology or supports would only contribute to a collapse of prices. These perceptions help explain why there was almost no investment in basic infrastructure or support for basic food crops during the late colonial period or the first decade after independence.

To generate revenues for colonial administration or subsequent govern-ments, agricultural policymakers have focused on cash crops, mainly cotton and peanuts and later, in some areas, green beans (Sanders, Shapiro, and Ra-maswamy 1996: 54). One consequence of the colonial government's sus-tained investment in research—some of which has continued in association with cotton parastatals after independence—has been a steady increase in the production per unit of land and the use of inputs. To facilitate the foreign marketing of these crops, the colonial governments created grain marketing boards that provided farmers with guaranteed transportation subsidies and fixed prices for their products. The difference between the purchase price and the price of sales abroad became a "tax," a portion of which was recycled into further investments in research, extension services, and infrastructure development. Although officials focused less attention on rice, the crop never enjoyed the sustained attention in research as the more popular crops of cotton and peanuts. The French were also actively involved in promoting veterinarian services and developing water sources as strategies to increase smallholder livestock production, which was the major source of tax revenue outside of migrant remittances.

Buoyed up by an above-average rainfall and the persistent alliances forged during the preceding decade of liberation movements, most countries en-joyed modest increases in per-capita growth rates and food production in the first decade after independence. France continued a strong relationship with her colonies, which included her continued willingness to underwrite the area's currency, the Franc CFA (FCFA). This policy, which included a fixed exchange rate geared to the French franc, facilitated France's strong trade linkages with her former colonies. The same policies imposed a degree of currency activity unmatched in Anglophone West African countries like Ghana (not usually classified as being in the Sahel) and Gambia (some times classified as being in the Sahel) that were forced to develop their own cur-rency. Outside the persistent influence of their former colonial masters, there was relatively little bilateral or multilateral foreign donor interest in the Sahel until recently (see Berg 1975; Christensen et al. 1981).

From the 1968 Drought to 1980

Short-Term Shocks. The 1968–74 drought was the first of three short-term shocks that galvanized a radical reorientation of food policy through-out the Sahel in the mid–1970s. Quantitatively the drought consisted of six years of below-average rainfall and a substantial drop in per-capita food pro-duction (especially sorghum and millet). The Centers for Disease Control and Prevention (CDC) estimated that in 1973 alone about 100,000 deaths were attributable to famine in Mali, Burkina, Mauritania, and Niger (CDC 1973, cited in Sen 1981 and Sheets and Morris 1994).[2] The animal loss alone was estimated to be as high as 40 to 60 percent (Sen 1981: 115). Total cereal imports in Mali rose nine-fold between 1972 and 1974, representing almost 60 percent of Mali's total imports (Berg 1975: 73). In Mauritania, cereals imports doubled from 5 to 8 percent of total imports; in Senegal cereals moved from 10 to 16 percent of total imports during the same years. Although food production improved slightly in the late 1970s, the period continued to be characterized by much lower rainfall than the previous three decades (Figure 7.2).

The economic impact of the drought was exacerbated by the global shocks ensuing from, first, a substantial increase in the price of oil after 1973 in all African countries except the five oil-producing states and, second, a sharp increase in the world price of food.

Global Development Ideology.   These triple shocks, which increased the Sahel's need for foreign aid, coincided with a number of global trends that increased the supply of foreign aid. The first trend was a dramatic shift in international development ideology toward viewing agriculture as the motive force in economic growth (Staatz and Eicher 1986: 46). Earlier models advocated industrial investment as the key to stimulating long-term economic growth. Conventional wisdom based on the European experience suggested that the process of pulling excess labor out of agriculture would create labor shortages and create a need for agricultural innovation. Early experiences with development in Latin America identified technology as an important limiting variable. One result was a new emphasis on targeted investment in crop technology research. The Rockefeller Foundation led the way with its early investment in crop research to develop higher yielding rice varieties in Asia. The World Bank and other donors followed with their support of an international system of agricultural research centers supported by the Consultative Group on International Agricultural Research (CGIAR). The goal of the CGIAR centers was to stimulate the international exchange of knowledge, thus creating new technologies and varieties for higher-yielding crop production. One result was the Green Revolution, which substantially increased maize yields in Latin America and rice yields in Asia. The spectacular impact of the CGIAR research institutions in Latin America and Asia led to their expansion into West Africa in the early 1970s. By 1986 the CGIAR centers were devoting 40 percent of their resources to Africa in a concerted effort to improve food production on the continent (Plucknett, Smith and Herdt 1986: 292). As in other parts of the world, the early focus of the CGIAR institutions in Africa was on developing new crop varieties (often introduced from other countries) that would create higher and more stable yields (Sanders, Shapiro, and Ramaswamy 1996: 37; Matlon 1987, 1990).

The same shift in international development ideology increased the total number of bilateral and multilateral donors active in West Africa and the Sahel. Especially important was the addition of the United States as a major donor, a development resulting from the demise of U.S. interests in south-

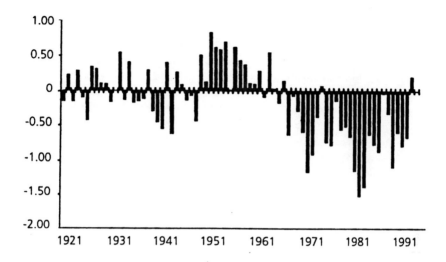

FIGURE 7.2   Rainfall in the Sahel, 1921–1994.

SOURCE: J. Sanders et al. (1996:3). Reprinted by permission of the USAID/FEW Project, Tulane/Pragma Group.

east Asia, the rising power of the Black Caucus in Congress, and the need to leverage anti-Soviet support during the Cold War. A third important global trend was the massive accumulation of "petrodollars" in the international banking system, which made borrowing cheaper and thus paved the way for incurring debt to fund an expanded array of agricultural investments.

These three trends increased total funding levels for agricultural development in the Sahelian regions. They were also a catalyst for a new perception of shared economic interests between the countries that included large Sahelian zones and those vulnerable to drought, resulting in the formation in 1976 of the Permanent Inter-State Committee for the Fight Against the Drought in the Sahel (CILSS) (Giri 1983: 9–14; Christensen et al. 1981: 133).[3] Although CILSS has played a role in sharing best practice for technological innovations and policy reform, its primary role has been to stimulate international donor interest in funding research and assistance. A similar concept was behind the creation of the United Nations Sudano-Sahelian Office.

Governmental Reaction.   One consequence of these global trends and short-term shocks was a major shift in the national governments' perception of their political interest in food policy. The first shift was a steady increase in these governments' interest and investment in agricultural research and extension services during the 1970s and early 1980s, which was designed to increase yields and raise living standards.

When world food prices increased sharply after 1973, most Sahelian governments responded with a series of costly attempts to shield their consumers from higher prices by granting subsidies and imposing price ceilings on staple urban foods such as cereals, sugar, and cooking oil (Berg 1975: 101). The mechanism for achieving this price regulation was the governments' creation of a series of financially autonomous (parastatal) marketing boards. Most boards had an official mandate to redistribute cereals from areas of surplus to those of scarcity and to enforce official producer and consumer prices in most Sahelian countries (Christensen 1981: 137).

The decisions of national governments to support parastatal marketing boards were based on three widely held beliefs. First, leaders feared that if local prices were to rise in line with world prices, the cost of living in towns would rise sharply and political and social grievances might be generated or exacerbated (Berg 1975: 102). The second was the widespread urban perception that private merchants would exploit food shortages by hoarding food and raising prices. The third was the widespread belief that state-operated marketing boards built on the model of the marketing boards for export crops could stabilize the huge price swings in cereal prices between years of good and bad amounts of rainfall.[4]

To pay for these food subsidies, the governments taxed the rural sector by reducing the prices paid for export crops such as cotton and peanuts, which gave farmers little incentive to expand production. This caused price distortions, rising urban incomes, and deteriorating terms of trade as urban preferences shifted to imported cereals, wheat and rice, and away from the domestically produced staples of sorghum and millet in the semi-arid regions and maize and root crops in the areas of higher rainfall. To offset these distortions, which reduced the profitability of agriculture, many countries subsidized imported chemical inputs, especially inorganic fertilizers and fuel, as well as pesticides (McMillan, Sanders, Koenig, Akwabi-Ameyaw, and Painter 1998: 190).

Research.   The same infusion of government and donor aid to develop agriculture resulted in a rapid increase in survey-based studies of crop production, marketing and consumption, mainly in rural areas. This research played an important role in drawing attention to the potential pitfalls of many of the governments' newly initiated strategies. By the late 1970s, this research had shown that livestock and cereal markets were more competitive than previously assumed but were plagued by wretched transport infrastructure, high transaction costs, and inefficient regulation (Ariza-Nino, Herman, Makinen, and Steedman 1980; Sherman, Shapiro, and Gilbert 1987; Moussie 1985; Sherman 1984). Many of the same studies showed that the official prices had been (in practice) difficult to administer and that parallel market prices had been more important to farmers than those set by the parastatal marketing boards.

Another key research finding revealed that some of the ways that the price ceilings on cereals and overvaluation of the FCFA were creating a host of macro-economic policy distortions that were undermining the profitability of cereal production (Berg 1975). This over-valuation of FCFA currency was facilitated by the generous global environment for foreign aid in the 1970s, which enabled Sahelian countries to cover the growing deficit between the supply and demand for foreign exchange as a result of their macro-economic policies, which discouraged exports and encouraged imports of food and goods. The advantage of the overvalued exchange rate acted as a hidden tax on exports and reduced the cost of imports. This hidden tax benefited urban consumers and industrialists but depressed the prices paid to rural and sub-urban farmers and reduced exports (Sanders, Shapiro, and Ramaswamy 1996: 18–19).

A key contribution to research came with the provision of better descriptions of the semi-arid farming systems, especially the critical role of labor and soil constraints in explaining why the new higher-yielding cultivars developed by the International Agricultural Research Centers were not adopted (Matlon 1987). In light of these difficulties, researchers recommended that food crop development programs should be designed within a "systems" framework that would be better able to take into account the complex social and economic risk-aversion strategies of farmers in the semi-arid zones.

Early 1980s to the Present

Short-term Shocks. By the late 1970s, food imports in the Sahel had exacerbated the trade deficit, and consumption subsidies had inflated the fiscal deficit of most countries (Christensen et al. 1981; Sanders, Shapiro, and Ramaswamy 1996: 18). These deficits were exacerbated by the global hike in oil prices in 1979 and the 1981 Mexican economic crisis, which brought many private and international banks to the brink of insolvency (Little, Cooper, Corden, and Rajapatirana 1993:74–96). The Mexican bank crisis precipitated an abrupt increase in international interest rates in the early 1980s and put pressure on the private banking sector to recover some of their previous investments (Sanders, Shapiro, and Ramaswamy 1996: 18).

Global Development Ideology. Since very little of the Sahelian countries' debt was privately held, they were only marginally affected by the sudden jump in interest rates. They were, nonetheless, very much affected by the resulting shift in international development ideology, which called into question the earlier degree of state intervention in third-world development. Almost overnight the pendulum swung from advocating government intervention in institution building to "getting the price right" and getting the government out of the national economy in general and food policy in particular (Sanders and Masters 1995: 5). This, combined with the world-wide recession, made the OECD governments much less willing to pay for the basic operating costs of the Sahelian governments (including cereal marketing parastatals) or to invest in rural infrastructure (Sanders, Shapiro, and Ramaswamy 1996: 18).

In the 1980s, most World Bank lending became tied to the execution of "structural adjustment programs" sanctioned by the World Bank and International Monetary Fund (IMF), which included the dismantling of public rural credit institutions and cereal marketing parastatals, elimination of fertilizer and rice subsidies, liberalization of domestic markets, and the reduction of export controls. Any country that resisted these changes was faced with the prospect of reduced capital flows from the IMF and World Bank and even from bilateral donors like the United States and Germany (Sanders, Shapiro, and Ramaswamy 1996: 18).

Government Reactions. Most governments reacted by freezing civil service hiring and proceeded to lay off large numbers of employees from the heretofore subsidized, semi-autonomous government businesses or parastatals. These same policies pressed Sahelian governments to eliminate input subsidies. The most visible short-term impact of these policies was a dramatic increase in the prices paid for fertilizer in the 1990s that outstripped the increase in food prices and the administered price for exports such as cotton.

Alarm over the extremely rapid increase in imports of food crops, especially rice and wheat, and of livestock products started a heated debate in the Sahel, Europe, and North America about whether or not the Sahelian countries should impose a common tariff on rice imports (Reardon 1993: 17). This tariff was intended to protect the Sahels agricultural economies from the cheaper imports of Asian and American rice.

The same structural adjustment policies reduced internal funds for the fledgling national systems of agricultural research. Unfortunately, these cuts coincided with the large-scale return of the first generation of agricultural scientists who had been trained abroad as part of the previous ideology's emphasis on the deveopment of human capital through education and training.

Research: Structural Adjustment and Protection. Food policy research played a role in testing the validity of underlying assumptions that the Sahel economy could easily respond either to structural adjustment or to protection. Research on urban consumption patterns predicted that it would be hard to reduce imports merely by raising the price of imported cereals (through protection or devaluation), since rice and wheat consumption was closely tied to changes in basic food habits brought on by urbanization (Delgado and Reardon 1992; Reardon 1993; Kennedy and Reardon 1994). There was growing evidence that poor urbanites and some rural households were consuming imported cereals. Although it was generally believed that this shift was occurring because prices were kept low, it became increasingly clear that other factors were at work as well, including the changing structure of the economy associated with high rates of immigration into urban areas. Urbanization was associated with the increasing opportunity costs of women's labor due to their entry into the urban work force and with the number of men in the city working away from home (Reardon 1993; Kennedy and Reardon 1994). The higher rates of urban settlement also resulted in an increased amount of time spent commuting and a gradual shift from the long three-hour lunch break to continuous work days.

Moreover, research on consumption in the Sahel in the 1980s called into question, as it had, for instance, in India in the 1970s, the simplistic assumption that raising crop prices would be an unmitigated blessing for rural households (Delgado and Reardon 1992). In particular, it was shown that many rural households bought an important part of the food they consumed, especially in years of poor rainfall (Reardon and Peters 1991). Raising food prices would hurt them (Reardon 1993), a realization linked to the fact that farm households not only took part in the monetized economy but also diversified by receiving income from the nonfarm sector.

Extending earlier studies of farming systems, the research confirmed the importance of policy-created restraints on increased agricultural profitability and of structural constraints within the food system. These included the high cost in cash and labor of food processing and transportation that would hinder or delay positive consumer response to the policy reforms advocated by structural adjustment (Reardon 1993; Kennedy and Reardon 1994; Dibley, Boughton and Reardon 1995).

These research results went against the assumptions underlying the prevailing government policies that relied on protectionism to have the desired effect of restricting imports by increasing prices. The same research raised real questions about the political feasibility of higher food prices, given the governments' critical dependence on low food prices to please their constituent base. Antiprotectionists also used the evidence of imported rice consumption among the Sahel poor to attack rice tariffs as potentially inequitable. In most cases these antiprotectionists tended to neglect one of the main implications of the research: the need to address the longer-term structural problems such as inadequate rural infrastructure and food processing technologies and facilities. To be specific, women and commercial food establishments in urban areas place a higher value on their time, so they prefer cereals or cereal products that are more easily prepared and incur lower fuel costs than the traditional cereals. This underemphasis on the region's deep-rooted structural problems continues to plague the post-devaluation debate.

Research: Devaluation. The FCFA was devalued in January 1994 as part of a structural adjustment that had been delayed due to political resistance (Sanders and Masters 1995: 6). Planners' models predicted that the short-term impact of such a devaluation, which cut the value of the FCFA in half, would increase the price of imported food and inputs but that the long-term impact would increase the prices that farmers receive for their products by raising the prices of imported grains. Recent analyses of price data from Mali since devaluation (covering the agricultural seasons of 1994–95 and 1995–96) shows that the nominal price of cereal is in fact rising, as is the price of cereal relative to fertilizer (Coulibaly 1995; Sanders and Vitale 1996; Vitale, Coulibaly, and Sanders 1996). Sanders and Vitale (1996) estimate that the percentage increase in price relative to fertilizer since the 1994 devaluation in Mali is 20 percent for sorghum and 80 percent for maize. The short-term impact of these trends in rising prices is to make it more profitable for farmers to use intensive technologies such as inorganic fertilizer (Savadogo, Reardon, and Pietola 1995; Sanders and Vitale 1996; Vitale, Coulibaly, and Sanders 1996; Sanders, Southgate, and Lee 1995; Kelly, Reardon, Diagana, and Fall 1995: 312). These research findings—if verified on a larger scale for other countries—have important policy implications, since recent farming systems research has shown that there are real limits to the production increases that can be obtained from alternative soil fertility measures that do not depend on imports (Sanders, Shapiro, and Ramaswamy 1996; Sanders and Vitale 1996: 4, 14). It is especially important to note that this information is likely to encourage governments and international aid donors to support the development of modern input markets that provide supplies and credit, especially for seeds and inorganic fertilizer.

Other data suggest that the positive impact of devaluation resulting in income increases is not evenly distributed across rural areas. Indeed Kelly, Reardon, Diagana, and Fall's simulation model (1996) of the impact of devaluation on Senegalese households, based on pre-devaluation data (1988–91), found that devaluation had relatively strong positive effects on incomes, with a 14 to 16 percent increase in real income, in only two zones where peanuts account for a large share of revenues (about 50 percent). From this analysis, as well as other evidence of strongly negative effects on rural households in urban areas and those not producing peanuts, these researchers argue that particular attention needs to be given to policies that protect vulnerable groups (and thereby maintain political stability).

Researchers note that "structural constraints" continue to exist in the Sahelian economies (rural as well as urban), since they were not removed by merely changing relative prices (devaluation) in ways that stimulate farmers to produce (Savadogo, Reardon, and Pietola 1995). Governments and researchers need to be concerned with expanding not only the supply of the traditional cereals through the use of new technologies but also expanding markets through alternative uses for agricultural products that can reduce or eliminate the price collapse from good rainfall years and from the long-term effects of improved distribution and higher incomes (Sanders and Vitale 1996: 13; Kelly et al. 1996). Deficient roads, inadequate grain-processing facilities, degraded land, inadequate access to organic matter, and the disappearance of programs providing equipment for animal traction are examples of longer-term problems likely to hamper farmers' response to price incentives (Kelly et al. 1996:312). This means that many of the same structural problems that researchers found limiting the effectiveness of simple protectionism (with regard to import prices) also plague simple, unreinforced devaluation as a total, all-purpose panacea affecting both import and export prices.

Conclusions

In this chapter, we have explored the role of food policy research in a global context by examining the specific case of the West African Sahel. In doing so, we have presented a brief overview of the complex interrelationship between food policy research and the three major shifts in food policy that have occurred in the West African Sahel since World War II. This historical perspective shows several instances in which national and international research played a key role in re-evaluating some of the key assumptions that undergirded these policy shifts. To be realistic, one should note that seldom did these research results turn policy in a direction opposite to the dominant ideology or the national political economy. Rather, the main effect of this research was that it eventually resulted in sufficient evidence to change the conventional images held by policy makers about how the food system works and how different actors would be affected by a particular policy or action. This roundabout influence can be contrasted with the pressure for accountability by donors funding research, who expect that direct and sure lines can be drawn from research to changed policy (Sanders and Masters 1995). The occasions when such lines can be drawn are few, not because of the unusual quality of this research but because of the requirement that it coincide with the other factors that influence policy makers.

Although this analysis focuses specifically on the Sahel, the trends highlighted here apply to the continent as a whole. If anything, the extreme poverty of the Sahelian region and the area's high levels of dependence on foreign aid, food, and oil imports means that the Sahel is especially vulnerable to global shifts in development ideology and world trade.

Within the global context, food researchers need to be cognizant of four important factors that affect the way research results are interpreted:

First, of primary concern for both national and international policy makers has been and continues to be the search for ways by which they can resolve the concrete, prominent problems (like drought, food shortages, financial crises) that they are forced to attend to. The ability of an individual or a group of policy makers to advance a policy is linked to their discovery of solutions that address these problems in ways that are acceptable to the powers in charge.

Second, these groups of policy makers, both national and international, are almost always split into factions, usually along the lines of ministries such as the Ministry of Trade, the Ministry of Agriculture, and the Ministry of Finance that incorporate different currents of economic ideology. These global ideologies represent different approaches to policy and concerns such as reliance on structural adjustment versus reliance on protectionism, coupled with developing food self-sufficiency. Each ideology has policy implications attached to it.

Third, the ideologies of these different factions are based on shared ideas or conventional images about how different groups of people (rural and urban marketers, transporters, producers, and consumers) are going to behave and why. Policy makers base their policies on these assumptions.

Fourth, researchers do not create dominant economic ideologies, nor can they directly change structural facts or problems. What researchers do affect are the conventional images about behavior, and in doing so they can give the upper hand to politicians and policy makers who support different ideologies. Sometimes competing ideological factions will use the same data to support opposing recommendations, as in the earlier debate over the evidence of consumer surveys that the urban poor consume imported rice.

If researchers in the area of global food history hope to have any impact on the conventional images that undergird food policy decisions, then they have to understand how those adhering to different ideological groups are likely to use the information available to them to suggest practical policy solutions to current global and national food policy concerns. For researchers to do this, they need to:

- increase their understanding of and ability to work within the major food policy debates;
- spell out the different interrelationships (past and projected) between their research and the five factors listed at the beginning of this chapter: long-term structural characteristics of the region, conventional images of the food economy and its actors, international development ideologies, urgent problems, and the government's perception of its political interest and the peoples' best interest); and
- clarify some of the alternative interpretations that can be given to all or portions of the results of their research.
- More attention must also be paid to how research can be designed to create a more effective demand for it by policy makers (Weber, Staatz, Holtzman, Crawford, and Bernstein 1988).

That is, researchers must address the question of how to make research more acceptable to policy makers and thus be more likely to change their perceptions.

This chapter focuses on food policy research. The same argument can be used for other types of development research that are guided by scientific visions of what types of incentives and development structures will be needed to bring out sustainable increases in income and living standards that we refer to as development. Food policy problems in developing countries are complex and unlikely to respond to any single ideology or vision of development. A more successful approach is likely to result from a healthy debate that reassesses the conventional images undergirding ideologies that shape the policy of foreign donors and domestic officials. For research to lose its critical capacity, and its funding, would be a loss—slowing processes that will undoubtedly become priorities again when another "shock" brings the chronic underdevelopment of one or more of these countries and regions to the forefront of food policy concerns.

Notes

1. Sen (1981: 114) does not include Gambia or Cape Verde in his definition although these countries are considered to be part of CILSS.

2. There is a great deal of controversy about the impact of the drought on human mortality. Berg (1975:25–66) and Caldwell (1975) argue that the actual impact in terms of increased mortality was negligible, due in large part to the population's "self-insurance" (migration and income diversification that allowed for the purchase of food), to rapidly implemented emergency food aid and food imports and to population shifts away from the most affected zones.

3. Comité Inter-Etats pour la Lutte Contre la Sécheresse dans le Sahel.

4. In 1984, the price of sorghum and millet was between 100 to 120 FCFAs per kilogram in Burkina. In 1986, the price plunged as low as 25 CFAs per kilogram.

References

Ariza-Nino, E.; L. Herman; M. Makinen, C. Steedman. 1980. *Synthesis Upper Volta, Livestock and Meat Marketing in West Africa*, vol. 1. Ann Arbor, MI: the Center for Research on Economic Development.

Asante, S.K.B. 1986. "Food as a Focus of National and Regional Policies in Contemporary Africa," in A. Hansen and D. McMillan, eds., *Food in Sub-Saharan Africa*, 11–24. Boulder, CO: Lynne Rienner Publishers, Inc.

Berg, E. 1975. *The Recent Economic Evolution of the Sahel.* Ann Arbor, MI: The Center for Research on Economic Development.

Caldwell, J.C. 1075. *The Sahelian Drought and Its Demographic Implications.* Overseas Liaison Committee, Paper No. 8. Washington, D.C.: American Council on Education.

Christensen, C.; A. Dommen; N. Horenstein; S. Pryor; P. Riley; S. Shapouri; H. Steiner. 1981. *Food Problems and Prospects in Sub-Saharan Africa: The Decade of the 1980s.* Foreign Agricultural Economic Report No. 166. Washington, D.C.: U.S. Department of Agriculture, Africa and Middle East Branch, International Economics Division.

Coulibaly, O. N. 1995. "Devaluation, New Technologies, and Agricultural Policies in the Sudanian and Sudano-Guinean Zones of Mali." Unpublished Ph.D. dissertation. West Lafayette, IN: Purdue University Department of Agricultural Economics.

Delgado, C.; and T. Reardon. 1992. "Cereal Consumption Shifts and Policy Changes in Developing Countries: General Trends and Case Studies from the West African Tropics," in *1991 International Sorghum and Millet CRSP Conference Proceedings.*" *INTSORMIL*, 92:1 (May 1992).

Dibley, D; D. Boughton; and T. Reardon. 1995. "Processing and Preparation Costs for Rice and Coarse Grains in Urban Mali: Subjecting and *Ipse Dixit* to Empirical Scrutiny." *Food Policy*, 20:1 (1995).

Dione, J. 1993. Institut du Sahel [INSAH]. Bamako, Mali. May, June. Personal Communication.

FEWS (Famine Early Warning System). 1995. "Bulletin" SH.11. Nov. 30. USAID/FEWS. Tulane: Pragma Group, Arlington, Va.

Giri, J. 1983. *Le Sahel Demain: catastrophe ou renaissance?* Paris: Editions Karthala.

Kelly, V.; T. Reardon; B. Diagana; A.A. Fall. 1995. "Impacts of Devaluation on Senegalese Households: Policy Implications." *Food Policy*, 20: 4 (1995), 299–313.

Kennedy, E.; and T. Reardon. 1994. "Non-traditional Grains in the Diet of East and West Africa: A Comparison of Kenya and Burkina Faso." *Food Policy*, 19:1 (1994), 45–56.

Little, I.; R. Cooper; W. Corden; and S. Rajapatirana. 1993. *Boom, Crisis and Adjustment: The Macroeconomic Experience of Developing Countries.* New York: Oxford University Press, for the World Bank.

Matlon, P. 1987. "The West African Semi-Arid Tropics," in J. Mellor, C. Delgado, and M. Blackie, eds., *Accelerating Food Production in Sub-Saharan Africa.* Baltimore: Johns Hopkins University Press.

Matlon, P. 1990. "Improving Productivity in Sorghum and Pearl Millet in Semi-Arid Africa." *Food Research Institute Studies*, 22:1 (1990), 1–44.

McMillan, D.; J. Sanders; D. Koenig; K. Akwabi-Ameyaw; T. Painter. 1998. "New Land is Not Enough: Agricultural Performance of New Lands Settlement in West Africa." *World Development*, 26:2 (1998), 187–211.

Moussie, M. 1985. *An Assessment of Grain Marketing in the Sahel: The Case of Burkina Faso.* Jefferson City MO: Lincoln University, Department of Agriculture and Office of International Programs.

Nicholson, S. 1986. "Climate, Drought, and Famine in Africa," in A. Hansen and D. McMillan, eds., *Food in Sub-Saharan Africa.* Boulder, CO: Lynne Rienner Publishers, Inc.

Plucknett, D; N. Smith; and R. Herdt. 1986. "The Role of International Agricultural Research Centers in Africa," in A. Hansen and Della McMillan, eds., *Food in Sub-Saharan Africa*, 292–304. Boulder CO: Lynne Rienner Publishers, Inc.

Rasmussen, E. M. 1987. "Global Climate Change and Variability: Effects on Drought and Desertification in Africa," in M. Glantz, ed., *Drought and Hunger in Africa*, 3–22. Cambridge: Cambridge University Press.

Reardon, T. 1993. "Cereals Demand in the Sahel and Potential Impacts of Regional Cereals Protection." *World Development*, 21:1 (1993), 17–35.

Reardon, T.; and M. Peters. 1991. "Self-Financing of Rural Household Cas Expenditures in Burkina Faso: The Case of Net Cereal Buyers," in C. Benoit-Cattin and A. Griffon, eds., *Finance and Development in West Africa*. Proceedings of an International Conference sponsored by CIRAD, Ohio State University and University of Ouagadougou, held in Ouagadougou, October 21–15.

Sanders, J.; and W. Masters. 1995. "Economic Impact Studies of Agricultural Research: Lessons from Sub-Saharan Africa." Unpublished manuscript. West Lafayette IN: Purdue University, Department of Agricultural Economics. October.

Sanders, J.; B. Shapiro; and S. Ramaswamy. 1996. *The Economics of Agricultural Technology in Semiarid Sub-Saharan Africa*. Baltimore, The Johns Hopkins University Press.

Sanders, J.; D. Southgate; and J. Lee. 1995. *The Economics of Soil Degradation: Technological Change and Policy Alternatives*. Soil Management Support Services (SMSS) Technical Monograph, no. 22. West Lafayette IN: Department of Agricultural Economics, Purdue University. December.

Sanders, J.; and J. Vitale. 1996. "Technology Development for Traditional Cereals in the Sahelian Countries." Invited paper presented at the African Farming Systems Symposium, Ouagadougou, Burkina Faso. August 21.

Savadogo, K.; T. Reardon; and K. Pietola. 1995. "Mechanization and Agricultural Supply Response in the Sahel: A Farm-Level Profit Function Analysis." *Journal of African Economies*, 4:3 (December 1995), 336–77.

Sen, A. 1981 [1984]. *Poverty and Famines: An Essay on Entitlement and Deprivation*. Oxford: Clarendon Press, 1984. First ed.

Sherman, J. 1984. "Grains Markets and the Marketing Behavior of Farmers: A Case Study of Manga, Upper Volta." Ph.D. dissertation, University of Michigan. Available from CRED as Project Report no. 29.

Sherman, J.; K. Shapiro; and E. Gilbert. 1987. *The Dynamics of Grain Marketing in Burkina Faso , vol. 1: of An Economic Analysis of Grain Marketing*, Ann Arbor MI: The Center for Research on Economic Development.

Sheets, H.; and R. Morris, 1974, *Disaster in the Desert: Failures of International Relief in the West African Drought*. Washington, D.C.: Carnegie Endowment for International Peace.

Staatz, J.M.; and C.K. Eicher, 1986. "Agricultural Development Ideas in Historical Perspective," in A. Hansen and Della McMillan, eds., *Food in Sub-Saharan Africa*, 43–63. Boulder CO: Lynne Rienner Publishers, Inc.

Timmer, C. P; W.P. Falcon; and S. R. Pearson. 1983. *Food Policy Analysis*. Baltimore: The Johns Hopkins University Press for the World Bank.

Vitale, J.; O. Coulibaly; and J. Sanders. 1996. "Technological Change in a Semiarid Zone of the Sahel: The Sudanian Region of Southern Mali." Unpublished manuscript, West Lafayette IN: Department of Agricultural Economics, Purdue University. August 11.

Weber, M.; J. Staatz; J. Holtzman; E. Crawford; and R. H. Bernstein. 1988, "Informing Food Policy Security Decisions in Africa: Empirical Analysis and Policy Dialogue," *American Journal of Agricultural Economics*, 70:5 (December).

World Bank. 1995. *African Development Indicators: 1994–95*. Washington, D.C.: The
  World Bank.
Source: J. Sanders et al. (1996:3). Reprinted by permission.
Source: J. Sanders et al. (1996:3). Reprinted with permission of USAID/FEWS Pro-
  ject, Tulane/Pragna group.

Chapter Eight

Child Nutrition in Developing Countries and Its Policy Consequences

Noel W. Solomons, M.D.

The Historical Background

Focus and Definitions

The first task of analysis and interpretation may be to analyze and interpret the meaning (operational definitions) of certain terms and concepts to be used and addressed. The term developing country is a euphemism. It is the successor to the term less-developed country, (or LDC), which was in the lexicon of the United Nations' agencies and the bilateral development assistance community until the 1970s. With the emergence of political correctness, it came to be considered pejorative when juxtaposed against its antonym, the more-developed country. Other contrasts that will be used interchangeably for variety's sake include South (as contrasted to North) and third world (as contrasted to first world). The bottom-line in this designation is primarily economic and secondarily geographical. The developing countries we are talking about are nations in which the majority of the populace is poor and cannot easily satisfy basic necessities; this is independent of both the intrinsic resource base of the country and the net worth of the elite monied class, and the ruling aristocracies. Poverty is accompanied by high rates of illiteracy and morbidity and low rates of child survival. Expressed political instability and overt social unrest alternate with political repression and authoritarian rule. Most of the world's population, 75 to 80 percent, lives in the developing world. Most of these nations lie in the band circumscribed by the Tropics of Cancer and Capricorn. However, areas farther south in the Southern Cone of South America and in southern Africa and farther north in China, Tibet and North Korea, also constitute less-developed countries.

The breadth of the definition of child nutrition—whether broader or narrower—is the crux of the matter being addressed here. In terms of this volume on food in global history, one would be tempted to focus on the narrower topic of food and to restrict the discussion to dietary intake. Doing this would embrace only the issues of the availability and accessibility of food, its selection in terms of preferences and taboos, its microbiological quality, and the content of its nutrients and anti-nutritional substances. However, nutrition can also have the connotation of nutritional status, or *nutriture*, the state of nutrient supplies in the body. The intake of food is only part of the equation determining nutritional status (Herbert 1968). The utilization and retention of nutrients once consumed, along with variations in nutrient requirements, are all co-determinants of nutritional status. In the present discussion, we shall use this broader definition of nutrition in referring to child nutrition. By policy, we shall mean the decisions taken (or not taken) that characterize the array of programs and projects that are implemented to impact—directly or indirectly—on child nutrition. Given the existence of the United Nations and its agencies, global history embraces the policy concerns influencing the nutritional status of the third-world's children.

Global History and Child Nutrition

The fingerprints of global history can be found on the issues of child nutrition in many dimensions. The heritage from the pre-modern era relates to the development of agriculture and of food cultures through the millennia, their interaction with climatic changes and national disasters, with human migration and changing political hegemonies, and with the demographics of population expansion. How the background of food, diet and cuisine set the stage for considerations of "nutrition" is covered in many of the other chapters of this book.

The concept of nutrition cannot exist without its elemental units, the *nutrients*. From the time of Priestley and Lavoisier, we have known the chemical nature of at least two essential chemical substances: oxygen and water. However, it was in the first half of the twentieth century that the chemical and physiological bases of the roster of macronutrients (protein, carbohydrates, fats, alcohol) and micronutrients (vitamins, minerals) were established. Only then could a science of nutrition come into existence. This chemical and biochemical basis of nutrition is essentially Western in origin, but it is incontrovertibly universal and essential in nature.

Less universal, and distinctly more Eurocentric, has been the definition of what is normal and what is problematic in human nutrition. This had its origins in the clinical description of diseases related to foods and to choices of foods in diets, dating to the identification of scurvy, pellagra, and beri-beri.

Once the manifestations of these syndromes were linked to their biochemical bases, the essentials for nutritional pathology were in place. Subsequently, issues of what is ideal in terms of nutritional health, related not only to anatomical and clinical but also to functional and behavioral norms, have come to dominate the discussion. Again, it is largely through the paradigms and prisms of Western medicine that the operational definitions of normative nutrition have been created. As such, the travel and communications revolution of the last fifty years has created a globalization of child nutrition issues for developing countries that is, ironically, dependent on diagnostic criteria based on Western biomedical sciences. We have all heard the folklore surrounding goiter in the sixteenth century, in which swelling of the neck was considered to be a component of beauty in European society. Where else but in a world with endemic iodine deficiency, might some positive or normative cultural definitions embrace goiter? This question is secondary to the demonstrations, within the framework of the nutritional sciences, that goiter-belt regions promote the risk for cretinism (a disease) and reduce the cognitive function of children in school. The dominance of the paradigm of negative effects from low nutrient intakes, over and against any positive or normative ones, has become absolute, largely due to a globalization of definitions of nutritional normality and abnormality promulgated by the scientific literature and adopted by the international public health community.

Moreover, in a rather direct way, the advent of concepts of national development (and underdevelopment) in themselves accelerated a public health and research focus on the nutrition of third-world children. Until World War II, children in tropical countries were born in great numbers but died in early life in almost equal numbers. If underdevelopment were characterized by poor health and high rates of child mortality, then development involved the elimination of these conditions. Hence, a focus on maternal and child health became the fulcrum to establish a more developed pattern of health and survival. However, beyond vital statistics, development meant tapping the human resources of previously colonial nations. In both the physical capacity to build the infrastructure and the intellectual capacity to create sustainable institutions, a nutritionally sound population (as defined by Western milestones for good nutrition) would be needed. As discussed below, Alan Berg (1968) convinced one of the most powerful sectors of efforts for international development, namely the World Bank, that investing in improved nutrition was a precursor to (rather than a result of) national development.

Child Nutrition: The Chronology

Once upon a time, however, perhaps only two centuries ago, no distinction was made between developed and developing countries; there were only countries. And in fact there were not so many countries but, rather, small states and tribal aggregates. Before the industrial age, all parts of the world were primarily agricultural with many, unincorporated populations subsisting with a hunter-gatherer lifestyle. It is often postulated that a state of adequate nutrition occurred at some times in the past when human populations were dispersed, when forage and game were abundant, and when human food systems incorporated the entire diversity of edible species. Conditions for the nutrition of hunter-gatherers and nomadic tribes such as Eskimos and Great Plains Indians are cited widely as providing ideal diets. These groups might indeed have been meeting or exceeding the intake requirements for all of the nutrients, but the environmental stresses of climate, along with parasitic and infectious diseases (specifically those that were endemic *before* the encounter with Europeans) were likely taking their toll on nutrient reserves. Biological anthropology provides fossil evidence of small body size, suggesting failure to achieve genetic potential for stature and of hypoplasia of dental enamel, indicating stress. Thus, the Garden of Eden and the Elysian Fields on Earth have probably never existed with respect to child nutrition.

Nevertheless, the formulation of my topic could not have been made in the times described above but only *after* the social and economic differentiation of nations. *Developing* countries only became identifiable as in a second (inferior) tier when technology allowed for a first (superior) tier of nations to become affluent and *developed*. Industrialization and trade were the motors for this differentiation. Then it took a war and its aftermath to bring the present topic of child nutrition into its infancy. The crucial spark that ignited the breath of life for any subsequent discussion of "child nutrition in developing countries" actually occurred in the early 1930s. Dr. Cecily Williams, a British physician working in the Gold Coast, discovered the nutritional basis of the lethal syndrome of child edema, skin changes, apathy and organ failure, called *kwashiorkor* in the local Ga dialect. In 1933, she published a paper in *Archives of Diseases in Childhood* entitled, "A nutritional disease of childhood associates with a maize diet," which introduced the world to the concept of a protein deficiency of an endemic nature (Williams 1933).

The end of the Second World War brought renewed interest. Firstly, there was a rediscovery of Dr. Williams' observations of a dozen years earlier. The pediatric community became interested—if not obsessed—with the extent and epidemiology of kwashiorkor and its companion syndrome, nutritional marasmus. Surveys were conducted by a commission of the Food and Agriculture Organization in the United Nations (FAO) in Africa, Asia and Central America to determine the extent of the "kwashiorkor epidemic"). In turn, this search and the mapping of protein deficiency syndromes would not have occurred, had it not been for the founding of the United Nations with its derivative agencies, the FAO and the World Health Organization (WHO). These agencies had the effect of extending the concerns and emerging scientific understanding around the world. They also supported subregional institutions such as the Institute of Nutrition of Central America and Panama in Guatemala and the Caribbean Food and Nutrition Institute in Jamaica. Regional centers for the study of various staple crop foods have emerged on the agricultural and food-production side.

Second, the end of the war initiated the process that brought about the final decolonization of Africa and Asia. This occurred early on in the Philippines, Indonesia and the Indian subcontinent, and later in Africa. Independence from colonial rule meant the loss of the expatriate talent that had made advances in tropical medicine, but it also democratized its concern. Classical tropical medicine focused on the diseases troublesome to members of the expatriate European population who migrated to the tropics, not necessarily those that were most important to the indigenous populations. The end of World War II brought resources and attention to the widely endemic issues of child health, and malnutrition was—and continues to be—high on that list.

The Undernutrition Paradigm

Undernutrition is the cornerstone of concern for child nutrition in developing countries. In its

> essence it is the concern that a child (or a population of children) has insufficient intakes, body reserves, or both of a given nutrient or nutrients to meet the "needs" of the developing child for growth, health and function. It is estimated that, although the cause of mortality on death certificates is not listed as malnutrition, deficiencies of macro- and micronutrients contribute to the eventual demise of up to half of all children who die in Third World countries before their fifth birthday (Pelletier 1993).

Protein-Energy Malnutrition and the "Protein Gap"

Protein (the building block of body structures and the functional elements in tissues) and carbohydrates plus fat (nutrients that provide fuel for bodily functions) are the concerns of the consolidated area known initially as protein-calorie malnutrition and subsequently as protein-*energy* malnutrition (PEM). The momentum that led to a foray of nutrition concerns, namely those related to the discovery of kwashiorkor, into the developing world carried over to establish the major area of scientific and public health interest that was to reign for the three decades of the 1950s, 1960s, and 1970s.

The discussion of nutrition for the populations of developing countries was dominated from the late 1940s by two imposing figures. Both were physicians who spoke English and were from outside of the third world, one being from the United Kingdom and the other from the United States. John Waterlow, the professor emeritus of Human Nutrition at the London School of Tropical Medicine and Hygiene, began his career in Jamaica in 1947 at the

Tropical Metabolism Research Unit sponsored by the Medical Research Council of Great Britain. Nevin Scrimshaw, two years his junior and professor emeritus and former head of the Department of Nutrition and Food Science of the Massachusetts Institute of Nutrition in Cambridge, was the founding director of the Institute of Nutrition of Central America and Panama (INCAP) in Guatemala City in 1949. The latter was a subgroup of the Pan American Health Organization in Washington. The combined influence of these nutritionists was dominant, and their primary pursuits were protein metabolism and clinical protein-energy malnutrition. The Protein-Advisory Group was founded within the agency structure of the United Nations and served for several decades as a forum for the discussion of international nutrition, both in terms of science and policy. The dominant paradigm was that of the Protein Gap, the supposed deficit of protein in the food supply in relation to mouths to feed. Concerns about PEM ranged from its influence on overall mortality to its effects on growth and cognitive development (Scrimshaw 1976)

Then suddenly, in the late 1970s, the Protein Gap shrank, not so much because of greater supplies or higher quality of protein, but because of a recalculation with pencil and paper of how various staple foods support minimal protein needs. Any diet with a density of protein greater than about 10 percent would provide an adequate basis for nutrition (Payne 1975). Most staple cereal grains met this criterion. Only some root crops and tubers, notably cassava and yams, would contribute to a truly protein-deficient diet unless supplemented by more concentrated protein sources.

Because protein-energy malnutrition was so prevalent, a revisionist trend took place. Anthropometric data such as the adequacy of one's weight-for-age, and height-for-age, as well as the adequacy of one's weight-for-height, had been used for survey purposes to map the extent of what were called malnourished populations. No one doubts that a person who is underweight, in terms of his or her *stature*, has a nutritional problem. But, if the person is underweight in relation to standards for his or her *age*, then a logical question arises. The reference population, that is, that of the United States, is much taller than that of a population in a developing country. Thus, for a shorter child of a given age, a lesser weight may be totally appropriate. Short-stature (or stunting) has often been equated to chronic malnutrition, but it has not been established exactly how much of this is due to dietary pattern or nutrient deficiency. The accumulation of the deficit in linear growth occurs before three years of age, and growth generally proceeds normally thereafter. Recurrent infection (Brown and Solomons 1991) and possibly chronic stimulation of the immune system by the teeming burden of microbes in the environment (Solomons et al. 1993) are more responsible for height deficit than a lack of nutrient intake.

So, the first thirty years of the post-war period were interesting in their monolithic dedication to protein-energy deficiency. The legacies of this period are manifold. Detailed knowledge of protein metabolism was gained as well as ingenious new techniques to explore it. However, the premise that the intake of protein and its quality were a major problem had been proven to be false. The fancy had been fed by fashion. Moreover, the indicators used to diagnose the prevalence of protein-energy malnutrition, such as low weight, are also of doubtful validity. Within the undernutrition paradigm, by the close of the 1970s, it was time for a new focus.

Specific Micronutrient Nutrient Deficiency and Its Consequences

The 1980s produced the paradigm-shift within the area of undernutrition of children. The intellectual vacuum left by the end of the Protein-Gap Era was filled by the mid–1980s by a new concern which has taken the picturesque name of "hidden hunger" (Scrimshaw 1993–94). This refers to its basis in the *micro*nutrients (vitamins, minerals) which are such small molecules they cannot be seen in the food. This is not a new concern. In fact, from its very inception, the World Health Organization has listed a Big Four of childhood nutrition problems. Protein-Energy Malnutrition (PEM) headed the list but was followed by nutritional anemias, hypovitaminosis A, and endemic goiter. What hidden hunger represented was a new *priority* (or set of priorities) in the paradigm of child undernutrition.

Just as the impetus for the Protein-Gap era can be attributed to specific individuals, the present concerns with micronutrients are the product of the work and influence of another major professional, Alfred Sommer, Dean of the Johns Hopkins School of Hygiene and Public Health in Baltimore. Prof. Sommer is an ophthalmologist with training in public health nutrition and epidemiology. His initial work in Indonesia was to better characterize the ocular problems that led to xerophthalmia and keratomalacia, the causes of "nutritional blindness" resulting from vitamin A deficiency. However, he and his colleagues found that marginal deficiency of this vitamin A made children 34 percent more susceptible to death from infectious childhood illnesses (Sommer et al. 1986; Solomons 1995). This finding has been confirmed in studies in Nepal, Ghana, and India (Beaton et al. 1993). It is estimated that between 1 to 2 million deaths in children could be prevented by paying more attention to their vitamin A deficiency (Humphrey et al. 1992).

Nutritional anemias are conditions in which the circulating red blood cells are insufficient because their production is limited by the deficiency of one (or several) nutrients. The deficiency of iron, by far the major contributor on a world-wide basis, occurs when the intake of meat is too low (for economic or cultural-religious reasons) in most parts of the developing world and the iron in plants is not easily absorbed. Some would argue that moving away from iron cooking pots and infestations with parasites such as hookworm are also major determinants. Folic acid and vitamin B_{12} deficiencies are causes of nutritional anemia as well, although this is confined to a few ecosystems of Africa and Asia. In terms of the number of affected individuals on a world-wide basis, nutritional anemias are the most widespread condition of undernutrition. Children, however, have high rates only at certain ages—infancy and preschool years (Yip 1994): School-age children are relatively resistant to anemia, except in adolescence, when the occurrence of anemia increases once again. Anemia reduces physical endurance and makes children less productive both in work and at play. However, what has troubled nutritionists in recent years has been the demonstration that even a single episode of anemia in early life can lead to a permanent loss of intellectual and cognitive capacity (Walter et al. 1989).

Endemic goiter (renamed Iodine Deficiency Disorders, or IDD) is unique insofar as there are no natural, reliable food sources of iodine in most food systems of the world. Widespread low environmental iodine leads to endemic IDD (Hetzel et al. 1987). Cretinism was traditionally the major concern in child health, but the effects of restricted iodine on cognitive development in school children have emerged as the major contemporary concern. Other nutrients deficient in certain sectors of populations of developing countries are riboflavin (worldwide) and selenium (parts of China). A great curiosity has arisen as to whether or not a *zinc* deficiency poses an endemic problem in developing countries and possibly is a contributing determinant to the short stature of third-world people (Shrimpton 1993). One of the manifestations of zinc deficiency in experimental animals and pediatric patients with metabolic or gastrointestinal problems is poor growth.

Ironically, fad and fashion (scientific correctness), expressed on a global basis, are both push-and-pull factors in setting the agenda. Within a year of my arrival in Guatemala in 1975, I was working on issues of zinc nutrition and its availability from the typical Guatemalan diet of maize, corn, squash and coffee. Around 1980, a new Director of INCAP expressed his disapproval of my working in such an "irrelevant" domain of human nutrition when the problems were in protein malnutrition and perhaps in iron and vitamin A. He even ridiculed any claim that zinc was important. Yet, within the next decade, the pendulum of concern as to the nutritional importance of zinc shifted. Perhaps he should have held his judgment for another decade, when the hegemony of hidden hunger in public-health thinking would have brought that "orphaned" trace metal into the mainstream fold.

Life-Stage and Life-Style Issues

Enmeshed with undernutrition in all of its specific dimensions is the question of the feeding practices for children. These, in turn, can be related to the life-*stage* of the child (his or her age related to the needs for growth and development related to the capacity to assimilate food), and the lifestyle issues of the family (related to their environmental and economic circumstances). Herbert's synthesis (1968) of the mechanisms by which a body can be deprived of an adequate supply of nutrients included low intake, poor absorption, and increased losses. The way a child eats can provide or deprive him or her of the array in diversity and quantity of nutrients needed and can set up situations (through food-borne infections) that will produce nutrient wastage. Breast-feeding, the process of weaning to the household diet, and the issues of adolescent pregnancies can be classified in this category of life-stage and lifestyle issues.

In the 1970s, there was an investigative explosion regarding human lactation in terms of its physiology and regulation, the nutrient composition of the milk, its immunological constituents, and the demographic variance in the prevalence, intensity, and duration of breast feeding. It was found that the concentrations of many micronutrients were quite modest in maternal milk but that nutrient requirements for infants are, by definition, what the breast milk delivers. Rich assortments of immune protective factors were discovered in colostrum and milk, but it has been shown that the major anti-infective property of breast milk is that it excludes the contamination from formula and weaning foods. Most important in this history, however, was the demonstration of declining rates of breast-feeding among third-world mothers, especially in urban areas. The promotion of infant formulas was signaled as a cause for the decline. The Nestle Company of Switzerland became the symbol of adverse industry practices (Sai 1991). A Code of Good Practice was adopted and imposed on the marketing practices of the multinational food industry.

In a global history context, the evolutionary nature of lactation and maternal feeding of the infant must be addressed. Lactation biology and breast milk composition, like most other adaptations, make for a *compromise* among infinite possibilities, a compromise defined and constrained by the survival of the human species. Since a mother and her nursing child must essentially survive on the same (maternal) diet, mechanisms evolved to ration the nutrients between the mother and the infant. Perhaps the compromise was not ideal for maximal nutriture for either, but it was "adequate" for the symbiotic maintenance of both and allowed the survival not only of both persons in the dyad but also of the tribe. In the technological age, the evolutionary forces that formulated breast milk have been superseded by rapid changes in maternal diet as well as in techniques for feeding infants.

Another problem of child nutrition that has received tardy recognition is the complex nutritional balance exhibited in adolescent pregnancy. In the phenomenon characterized as "children having children," the nutrient demands to sustain a pregnancy and subsequent lactation are superimposed on the already high nutrient requirements needed to complete a young mother's growth, including the development of her pelvis. This is also complicated by the fact that in many parts of the developing world, early marriage has been traditional in rural populations. With urbanization, equally early conception is occurring in the third world, although perhaps with reduced association with the notion of a stable marriage or support from an extended family.

Insufficient attention on both the scientific and the programmatic level has been given as to how best to nourish the adolescent mother during the gestation of her child.

Non-Food Issues: Interaction of Nutrition and Infection

Since this essay is a chapter in a volume on food in global history, the inclusion of non-food issues might be considered out of place. Nature, however, has placed non-food issues at the center of the discussion on nutrient undernutrition. However, only one of Herbert's mechanisms (1968) for determining nutriture relates to food intake. Experience in the tropics modifies and conditions the assumptions that "we are what we eat." For children in developing countries, it might better be stated that: "We are what we eat, plus what is sharing what we eat (parasitism), plus what is eating *us* (infections)."

The classical monograph by Scrimshaw, Taylor and Gordon (1968) was a watershed in the overall understanding of how nutritional status is determined in developing countries and how undernutrition influences health and survival beyond the strict domain of nutritional pathology. Scrimshaw et al. (1968) demonstrated the synergistic nature of the relationships between infections and nutritional status. Infections produce a deterioration in nutritional status, that is, they make us more undernourished; and malnutrition conditions a poorer response to infectious illnesses. Much of what is characterized as poor nutritional status in the third world can be directly attributed to the inhabitants' experience with parasites and infections. As a corollary of this, changes in diet will not provide any universal solutions (see below) to the problematic aspects of undernutrition in children of developing countries.

As history catches up to today, the AIDS pandemic, which began in the 1980s, looms as a significant mediator of child nutrition. It must be remembered that infection with the human immunodeficiency virus (HIV) in children is overwhelmingly the result of contracting the virus from an infected mother, the so-called "vertical" transmission. HIV infection accompanies the child from birth or the neonatal period. Becoming an orphan is a virtual certainty. The combined issues of child care and impaired nutrient utilization and catabolic losses imposed by the advancing disease lead to nutrient depletion. Tomkins (1994) has suggested that protein-energy malnutrition in children with AIDS will again be a major feature of the public health scenario in Africa and parts of Asia. But, it will have a different context and epidemiology from the patterns of PEM ascribed in the past to the "Protein Gap." AIDS will force us to revise and re-learn all that was outlined on PEM in the classical era of international nutrition.

Imbalanced Nutrition Paradigm

Emerging and co-existing—but not yet replacing—the undernutrition (deficiency) paradigm for children in the developing world is the "imbalanced nutrition" paradigm. Rather than being cast in the broad and deep deficiencies of essential nutrients, the concern of this latter paradigm is an imbalance in which some dietary constituents are relatively excessive when compared to the relative deficits of others. In fact, since massive poverty has been eliminated in the first world, imbalanced nutrition has been the primary concern in the North for at least the past fifty years. As similarities with, and analogies to, the living conditions and lifestyles of more-developed countries emerge in the less-developed ones, the imbalanced nutrition paradigm becomes more useful and universal.

Our popular image of developing countries is that of their being poor and rural. This could be the result of these facts: First, these countries traditionally have more poor people and more severe poverty in the countryside; and, second, most nutritional scientists and public health professionals have concentrated on rural issues (Solomons 1987). Further, when general tourists visit a tropical country on vacation, they are not searching for museums and cathedrals but, rather, are exposed to the rural populace when exploring beaches, forests, volcanoes and archeological sites. Thus, we have created the myth that that which is tropical is rural. Increasingly, however, developing countries are becoming poor and *urbanized*.

Popkin (1995) defines a term called "nutrition transition" as "the rapid shift in the structure of diet in low-income countries and the coexisting problems of under- and overnutrition." He adds that "an increasing number and proportion of people [in low-income nations] consume the types of diets associated with chronic diseases." Thus, being poor and less developed also exposes one to the risk of excessive burdens of nutrients. The liabilities from excess are diverse. Excess storage of energy (calories) is the cause of (in fact, the definition of) obesity. It may be that short-stature, common in these societies, is a risk factor for being obese when nutrient-dense foods replace the traditional high-fiber diets or rural foodways. Hence, if one is born and reared in conditions that lead to stunting, and then is exposed in childhood and adulthood to a more abundant fare, one's chances of becoming obese are greater than they are for people of normal stature (Popkin et al. 1996).

Aligned with this concern, is a related one regarding low birth weight and chronic disease risk. David Barker (1996) has shown in the British population that being small at birth and in infancy predisposes one to greater incidences of diabetes, obesity, hypertension, cardiovascular disease, stroke and premature demise. A similar added risk of chronic disease could arise through a combination of early life deprivation with the changing diets and lifestyles accompanying the urbanization of developing countries, under increasingly prevalent circumstances. It is precisely in an urbanizing and economically developing setting, as in much of South America and the so-called "Tiger" nations among the peninsulas and archipelagoes of Southeast Asia, that public health officials may potentially have a tiger by the tail in terms of chronic disease epidemics.

Although iron deficiency is endemic, iron excess is a latent problem. For third-world countries, abundant iron stores may support increased susceptibility to infection with certain bacteria, amoebas, and malarial organisms. Excess intake of iron protects against lead accumulation but can prejudice zinc status. Finally, selenium excess is not widespread, but certain regions of China and Venezuela provide hyperseleniferous soils with endemic selenotoxicosis in child populations. This excess leads to abnormalities of dentition and cutaneous manifestations, with a strong suspicion that long-term exposure can lead to increased rates of neoplasmia.

Diseases of excess and chronic diseases are well recognized, and their expansion has been documented as populations become older and more sedentary. They have traditionally not been a concern for the public health of tropical nations. The globalization of concerns about health probably spurred an initial inquiry as to whether the risk factors—or the diseases themselves—were appearing in developing countries. Global trends in export economics may accelerate the introduction to children in developing countries of the dietary patterns associated with chronic disease.

Policy and Programmatic Implications

Having developed diagnostic standards and judgmental landmarks, nutrition scientists have generally found nutritional health in the third world to be impaired and in need of improvement. The desire for redress is often a blend of two distinct motivations—a humanitarian one and another pragmatic or practical one. The humanitarian one is based on the notion that adequate dietary intake and nutritional status for children, no matter where they live, is a basic human right (Eide et al. 1984). The logical consequence is that eventually there should be some uniformity among all children worldwide in their nutrient intake and their nutrient status. The pragmatic one is related to "investing in human capital" based on the concepts espoused in Alan Berg's *The Nutrition Factor* (1968). Saving the children and improving their nutrition is the underpinning for the social and economic development of a less-developed country.

The Generic Nature of Public Health Interventions in Nutrition

As defined above, policy consists of "decisions taken (or not taken) that characterize the array of programs and projects that are implemented to impact—directly or indirectly—on child nutrition." Those that impact more indirectly are clearly a derivative of global history, since they relate to the agricultural and food production and the food importation policies of a given country, region, or trading bloc of nations. The contribution by McMillan and Reardon in the previous chapter treats an example of these concerns in the context of Africa. These macro-economic issues, however, are relatively unrelated to child nutrition as conceived of in nutritional science or public health. The discussion in this chapter is more concerned with direct, intentional interventions at the national, community, or individual level.

When a policy decision is made to do something positive—either proactively or reactively—it sets into motion a series of programs composed of projects. In the aggregate, these programs and projects are made up of interventions. In the domain of nutrition, Table 8.1 outlines the loci that can be addressed for programs and projects to address childhood nutrition problems. Table 8.2 illustrates a series of only a few of the contrasting options that are debated in the formulation of such intervention policy. In practice, interventions have been part of *tactics,* rather than strategy. The policy begins not with a holistic focus on the child's status but usually on a given nutrient or set of nutrients in excess or in deficiency. As a result, interventions have generally been very vertical in nature, overtly trying to target a specific geographic region and a specific age-group and to correct the deficiency of a single nutrient.

If we examine the two tables in terms of what would be required to implement a given action, there is some unevenness. The options for intervention fall into two general categories: first, those aimed at changing voluntary behavior so that persons and households act in ways that improve the nutritional situation; and, second, those in which the food, nutrient, or nutrient-sparing agent is delivered directly to the target population. For instance, of the options listed in Table 8.1, changes in behavior would seem to be needed if food selection, lifestyle issues, and to some extent, infection control are to be effected. The presumption of nutritional education needs to be examined. It implies that cultural evolution has failed to maximize the efficacious use of resources. The educational messages can derive either from western academia or from the successful practices observed in the community. The concept of "positive deviance" (Zeitlin 1991) is interesting. Zeitlin argues that in any poor community some families are doing well in protecting the growth, health and development of their children. By identifying the coping strategies used in these more "successful" households and generalizing them throughout the whole community, a relatively "endogenous" and low-cost approach can be developed. However one conveys the message for change,

TABLE 8.1   The Loci of Interventions to Address Child Nutrition Issues

Loci of Interventions	
Dietary Actions	*Non-Dietary Actions*
Supplementation	Infection control
Fortification	Life-style change
Food selection and diversity	

TABLE 8.2 Formulating Child Nutrition Policy Tactics and Strategies: Contrasting Options

- Individual nutrients versus a combination of nutrients
- Supplementation versus fortification versus natural foods
- Targeting the most vulnerable populations or general distribution
- Government action versus community initiative
- Address selective issues or operate on a broad front

basing it on education is a sequential issue. Social marketing of nutrition-promoting ideas, analogous to advertising commercial products (Griffiths 1993–94), is the vehicle in vogue. Once put into place, the sustainability of the change in behavior is the perpetual unknown in the nutrition education equation.

The options of supplementation, fortification, and some aspects of infection control can be delivered in a direct manner. The alternatives for direct delivery range from the surreptitious to the visible. In the former category are interventions such as the fluoridation of water, universal iodination of salt, and the fortification of flour in bread. These can be high on efficiency and efficacy but low on attributable visibility, hence they have low public relations spin-offs. Combining nutritional ends to immunization campaigns and school-feeding programs can also be considered direct delivery, since the only behaviors required are attendance and compliance. Their higher visibility may make them more attractive to the agencies and governments. Only rarely have interventions been part of integrated and horizontal health and well-being initiatives, and only recently, for instance, have combinations of micronutrients been addressed simultaneously and interactively. An evolutionary focus in which a truly strategic approach is taken to form a holistic vision—an assessment of the child in his or her family, the diet in terms of culture, the environment, and its perspective over time—has never been realized. Policy decisions, however, also add to, and subtract from, programs and projects. Policies can institute and maintain (apply) projects that are expected to be positive and beneficial, but they can also eliminate (delete) those that are ineffective, not cost-effective, or even injurious and counterproductive. A programmatic consequence is the possibility that disruption of the equilibrium among diet, nutrition, and ecology can produce undesirable consequences. This would be true especially if an intervention were transitory and not sustainable.

Historical Perspectives on Child Nutrition Policy and Programs

The response since World War II to dysnutrition in childhood has been activist, rather than reflective. Governments and assistance agencies have taken the posture that they must do something to relieve the situation. The pragmatic argument that redressing the incapacity resulting from malnutrition can favor overall national development (Berg 1968) has overshadowed the idea that diet and nutritional status are basic human rights. It has also resulted in an elusive search for a "magic bullet" to solve complex problems of poverty and underdevelopment through superficial solutions rather than those seeking to probe the depths of root causes.

In the half-decade considered in the previous sections, policy for child nutrition can be characterized as "highly visible" in its presentation, "fashionable and conformist" in its conception and "limited and piecemeal" in its scope. The currency of policy response has been programs and projects, namely interventions. The agencies of interventions have been the national ministries (Health, Agriculture, Development, and Welfare) and international bilateral or multilateral assistance agencies such as WHO, FAO, UNICEF of the United Nations, the U.S. Agency for International Development (USAID); and the various analogous organizations in other industrialized countries. Finally, a host of non-governmental organizations (NGOs) such as CARE, Catholic Relief Services, and Project HOPE have taken part in addressing child nutrition issues around the world.

The more visible the action, the better for the public relations of the intervening parties. The idea that the situations of growth, nutrient status and health encountered in poor communities constitutes a balanced adaptation to the circumstances is rarely expressed. Rather, the humanitarian and Hippocratic impulse to preserve all lives at risk and roll back all treatable illness and provide prophylaxis for all preventable conditions has been dominant. Interventions have been guided in broadest terms by the scientific discussions of the day, although at the technical level the products of academia and industry have not always guided the response. However, it is clear that, once rolling, a snowball of conformity ensues. This is exemplified by the era of the Protein Gap, when the emphasis was on agriculture and food technology. For example, the high-lysine corn, Opaque II, was developed to give a higher quality amino acid mix. Direct addition of lysine at the mill was attempted in other countries. High protein mixtures based on vegetable proteins, such as Incaparina in Guatemala, and fish protein concentrate, are products of the ingenuity of the Protein-Gap era. Presently, all is virtually quiet on the protein-quantity and protein-quality fronts.

Isolated and piecemeal micronutrient interventions have surged, however, in the demise of protein issues. For instance, in the wake of evidence of excess mortality due to marginal deficiency (Sommer et al. 1986), a world-wide attack on hypovitaminosis A has been engaged over the last decade. An intense debate goes on between the medical approach of giving periodic, high-dose capsule supplements to the vulnerable age-groups (a direct delivery intervention) and the food-based model, which sees increasing the amount in the diet as the long-term, sustainable solution (a behavior-modification solution).

With respect to the latter strategy, the animal-product sources of that vitamin, such as butter, liver, milk, cod liver oil, and so forth are expensive; however, the ability of our bodies to convert plant sources of provitamin A (carotenes) into the active vitamin may be much less efficient than currently estimated (Solomons and Bulux 1994). An intermediary strategy of fortifying some common vehicle such as sugar or flour with vitamin A is also undertaken in some countries, with positive results.

Iodine deficiency is not so much a cause of mortality as of morbidity (in terms of disfiguring goiters) and reduced cognitive capacity. It has been argued that universal iodization of salt (Venkatash-Mannar 1987) would lead to an eradication of IDD as complete as that which we have seen for smallpox. However, at the present time, coverage is incomplete even where legislation for iodine fortification of table salt is in effect. Alternative options such as the periodic distribution of oral iodinated-lipid capsules, adding iodine to water sources (analogous to fluoridation), or iodine fortification of foods targeted to vulnerable groups must all be considered, given the failure of salt iodination to meet its promise.

Iron deficiency is the most widespread of these conditions, although with a selective age distribution in children, and the most challenging to address. Unlike vitamin A or iodine, iron cannot be absorbed efficiently in large supplemental doses. Iron must be given on a daily (or at the most, weekly) basis. As a reactive metal, it presents problems in food technology for fortification. As an intrinsically poorly absorbed nutrient, its absorption is limited when incorporated into typical meals of developing countries. When taken on an empty stomach, iron supplements produce gastrointestinal side-effects that reduce compliance. Given the co-existing danger of excess accumulation of iron for some sectors of the population, even where anemias are endemic in others, the logistics of any mass approach to enriching diets with iron are problematic. Iron-fortified candies and chewing gum are currently being explored as a way to reach at least the toddler and preschool child as well as the adolescent.

In the hidden hunger era, the efforts of UNICEF have often been mobilized to address selective issues that are not aimed at the most dramatic and damaging problem of the day but rather at accomplishing the most *doable* task. Currently, the universal iodination of salt is the priority micronutrient issue. Arguably, vitamin A deficiency produces much more mortality and iron deficiency interferes more with cognitive development than IDD; but it is widely believed that a simple, direct solution (salt iodination) can virtually eradicate the public health problem.

With respect to the lifestyle issues, the promotion of breastfeeding through social marketing and workplace strategies to reduce barriers to it are now in place, although with less fanfare and enthusiasm than in the 1970s. The baby formula industry is judged largely to be in good voluntary compliance with the Code of Good Practice with respect to the manufacture and promotion of substitutes for breast milk. Complementary feeding and weaning foods are a current subject of applied research. The use of fermentation to increase the nutrient density is one of the favored strategies. As important as the nutrient content and balance, however, is the microbiological safety of foods for infants and toddlers in the weaning process. Resources have not always been abundant, and the current economic crises and fiscal policies have restricted the means by which states and NGOs can provide an activist response. Historically, the agribusiness and the food industries have been regarded with great suspicion and have only recently been engaged as partners in the solution to juvenile nutritional problems.

The Debate on Training of Applied Nutrition Professionals

The making of policy and the designing and implementation of programs and projects requires professional personnel. One of the theories advanced to explain the limited success and coverage of nutrition interventions has been the lack of human resources devoted to applied nutrition in developing countries. The present era has seen a vigorous discussion on the training of professionals to work in nutritional operation at agency and community levels. The debate was joined by Alan Berg (1993), who accused the academic nutrition research community of having spent resources over decades without contributing to the solution of the nutritional problem. He called for the creation of "nutritional engineers" who would not ask the fundamental "why" questions but rather the practical "how" questions at the ministry and grassroots levels.

Berg's notion of providing "nutritional engineers" did not receive an enthusiastic reception but has evolved into the proposal to create a multidisciplinary training area called "public nutrition" (ACC/SCN, 1995; Mason et al. 1996). Both of these propositions have two precepts: that health is too narrow a focus for that training and aspects of agriculture, communication, food science, social science need to be blended; and that the scientific method is more of a distraction than an asset. Clearly, public nutrition looks with suspicion on academia and investment through traditional academic programs. On their face, the precepts of these proposals speak to a more integral, horizontal, and holistic approach. The disciplines involved range from policy and anthropology to agricultural and food technology to clinical and public health nutrition. Children and mothers (MCH) are the explicit and almost exclusive concern. However, there is a certain ideological bias in favor of an almost exclusive concern with undernutrition. On the other side of the argument are the demonstrations in which existing formats, namely those involving "community nutrition," can combine the scientific method and research experience into integral components of training (Gross et al. 1995). A number of global forces are shaping—and will continue to shape—the argument about the setting and curriculum for training of the practitioners of child nutrition interventions in developing countries. These will range from the electronic communications media (to permit long-range courses) to the philosophical trends in state versus private financing to the ideological debates about the relative priority of undernutrition versus imbalanced nutrition as the dominant paradigm for the Third World.

Conclusions

Because they compose about half of the total population of rapidly expanding populations in developing countries, children consume about half of all food. In the critical early period of a child's life, however, the extreme example of non-commercial food, human milk, is the focus of concern. Later, with the transition to a solid diet, concerns run the gauntlet between under- and overnutrition. With an increasingly urbanized population, the co-existence of nutrient deficits and excesses pose both scientific and programmatic challenges. But, we are *not* exclusively what we eat: The role of non-food factors such as infections and exposure to ubiquitous microbes may explain the variance in poor growth and diminished nutrient utilization in early life.

The sequential foci of research and public health concern–protein-energy malnutrition, breast-feeding, micronutrient malnutrition (hidden hunger), complementary feeding—can be outlined. Overnutrition of urban children and a new breed of PEM related to HIV would seem to be the next horizons. Intellectual concerns in child nutrition can be shaped by dominant individuals and obey a fluctuation based on discussions fashionable at the moment.

Although the causes of these problems may not be exclusively related to the scarcity or availability of foods and nutrients, the conception of the interventions to provide solutions almost invariably is. They seek either to change customary behavior or to deliver additional nutrients to the child's diet. The priorities of the day follow, in large measure, the topics in discussion on the academic side. They are picked up by the development agencies and become a fashion *du jour*. In a rather vertical and isolated manner, the fashionable interventions are implemented. Limited resources, the inertia of culture, and the intrinsic limitation of technology will inherently modulate the real impact of such interventions on child nutriture. Not often considered, moreover, is the fact that the redress of a specific deficiency in one nutrient may exacerbate an overall imbalance or undo an evolutionary adaptation to the ecological situation of deprivation. What is taught, and how it is taught, to the field workers who will conceive of, design, implement, and evaluate policy, programs, and projects of child nutrition also becomes a polarizing topic of discussion. One should not discount the influence on educational strategies of the reality that they are also part of global history. Obviously, few attempts have heretofore been made to place in the context of global history this topic of child nutrition or the steps taken to improve it for nations with low-incomes and in transition. The issues raised here will hopefully serve to extend and broaden this focus in a field which is almost exclusively devoted to the day-to-day implementation of the cluster of ideas that have captured the attention of intellectuals and donor agencies in any given period along a changing continuum of tactics and priorities.

References

Administrative Committee on Coordination/SubCommittee on Nutrition. 1995. *Training and Research Needs in Nutrition.* Summary of Proceedings of a Bellagio Conference on "Addressing the 'How' Questions in Nutrition: Unmet Training and Research Needs." Geneva: ACC/SCN.

Barker, D. 1996. "Growth in Utero and Coronary Heart Disease." *Nutrition Reviews,* 54:S1-S7.

Beaton, G.H.; R. Martorell; K.J. Aronson; B. Edmonston; G. McCabe; A.C. Ross; and B. Harvey. 1993. "Effectiveness of Vitamin A Supplementation in the Control of Young Child Morbidity and Mortality in Developing Countries." ACC/SCN State-of-the-art Series Nutrition Policy Discussion Paper no. 13.

Berg, A. 1968. *The Nutrition Factor.* Cambridge: MIT Press.

_____. 1993. "Sliding toward Nutrition Malpractice: Time to Reconsider and Redeploy." *Annual Review of Nutrition,* 13:1–15.

Brown, K.H.; N.W. Solomons. 1991. "Nutritional Problems of Developing Countries," in A.M. Velji, ed., *International Health. Infectious Disease Clinics of North America,* 297–317. New York: W.B. Saunders.

Eide, A.; W.B. Eide; S. Goonatilake; J. Gussow, eds. 1984. *Food as a Human Right.* Tokyo: United Nations University Press.

Griffiths, M. 1993–94. "Social Marketing: Achieving Changes in Nutrition Behavior, from Household Practices to National Policies." *Food and Nutrition Bulletin,* 15:25–31.

Gross, R.; S. Sastroamidjojo; W. Schultink; A.D. Sediaoetama. 1995. "Academic Action-Oriented Nutrition Training in Developing Countries: A Southeast Asia Experience." *South African Journal of Clinical Nutrition,* 8:12–16.

Herbert, V. 1968. "The Vitamins," in R.S. Goodhart, M.E. Shils, *Modern Nutrition in Health and Disease,* 5th ed., 221–44. Philadephia: Lea and Febiger.

Hetzel, B.S.; J.T. Dunn; J.B.Stanbury, eds. 1987. *The Prevention and Control of Iodine Deficiency Disorders.* Amsterdam: Elsevier Science Publishers.

Humphrey, J.H.; K.P. West; A. Sommer. 1992. "Vitamin A Deficiency and Attributable Mortality among under 5-Year-Olds." *Bulletin of the World Health Organization,* 70:225–231.

Mason, J.B.; J-P. Habicht; J.P. Greaves; U. Jonsson; J. Kevany; R. Rogers; B. Martorell. 1996. "Public Nutrition" (letter to the editor) *American Journal of Clinical Nutrition,* 63.

McMillan, D.; T. Reardon. 1998. " U.S. Food Policy in Africa," in Raymond Grew, ed., *Food in Global History.* Boulder: Westview.

Payne, P.R. 1975. "Safe Protein-Calorie Ratios in Diets. The Relative Importance of Protein and Energy Intake as Causal Factors in Malnutrition." *American Journal Clinical Nutrition,* 28:281–86.

Pelletier, D. L.; E.A. Frongillo; J-P Habicht. 1993. "Epidemiologic Evidence for a Potentiating Effect of Malnutrition on Child Mortality." *American Journal of Public Health,* 83: 1130–1138.

Popkin, B.M. 1995. "The Nutrition Transition in Low-Income Countries: An Emerging Crisis." *Nutrition Reviews,* 52: 285–98.

Popkin, B.M.; M.K. Richards; C.A. Monteiro. 1996. "Stunting Is Associated with Overweight in Children of Four Nations That Are Undergoing the Nutrition Transition." *Journal of Nutrition,* 126: 3009–16.

Sai, F.T. 1991. "The Infant Food Industry as a Partner in Health," in F. Falkner, ed., *Infant and Child Nutrition Worldwide: Issues and Perspectives,* 245–60. Orlando: CRC Press.

Scrimshaw, N.S. 1976. "Stattuck Lecture—Strengths and Weaknesses of the Committee Approach. An Analysis of Past and Present Recommended Dietary Allowances for Protein in Health and Disease." *New England Journal of Medicine,* 294:136–42, 198–203.

_____. 1993–94. "The Consequences of Hidden Hunger for Individuals and Societies." *Food and Nutrition Bulletin,* 15:3–24.

Scrimshaw, N.S.; C.E. Taylor; J.E. Gordon. 1968. *Interactions of Nutrition and Infection.* Geneva: World Health Organization.

Shrimpton, R. 1993. " Zinc Deficiency —Is It Widespread But Under-Recognized?" *SCN Notes,* 9:24–27.

Solomons, N.W. 1995. "Vitamin A and Developing Countries." *International Child Health: A Digest of Current Information,* 6:33–47.

Solomons, N.W.; J. Bulux. 1993. "Plant Sources of Provitamin A and Human Nutriture." *Nutrition Reviews,* 51:199–204.

Solomons, N.W.; M. Mazariegos; K.H. Brown; K. Klasing. 1993. "The Underprivileged, Developing Country Child: Environmental Contamination and Growth Revisited." *Nutrition Reviews,* 51:327–32.

Sommer, A.; I. Tarwotjo; E. Djunaedi; K.P. West, Jr.; A.A. Loeden; R. Tilden; L. Mele; The Aceh Study Group. 1986. "Impact of Vitamin A Supplementation on Childhood Mortality. A Randomised Controlled Community Trial." *Lancet,* 1:1169–73.

Tomkins, A. 1994. "Malnutrition and Risk of Infection," in M.L. Wahlqvist, A.S. Truswell, R. Smith, P.J. Nestel, eds., *Nutrition in a Sustainable Environment. Proceedings of the XV International Congress of Nutrition,* 665–58. London: Smith-Gordon.

Venkatesh-Mannar, M.G. 1987. " Control of Iodine Deficiency Disorders by Iodination of Salt: Strategy for Developing Countries," in B.S. Hetzel, J.T. Dunn, J.B. Stanbudy, eds., *The Prevention and Control of Iodine Deficiency Disorders,* 111–26. Amsterdam: Elsevier Science Publishers.

Williams, C.E. 1933. "A Nutritional Disease of Childhood Associates with a Maize Diet." *Archives of Diseases of Childhood,* 8:423–33.

Yip, R. 1994. "Iron Deficiency: Contemporary Scientific Issues and International Programmatic Approaches." *Journal of Nutrition,* 124:1479S–90S.

Zeitlin, M. 1991. "Resilience in a Hostile Environment: Positive Deviance in Child Nutrition." *Nutrition Reviews,* 49:259–68.

Part Three

---

*Global Systems and
Human Diet*

Chapter Nine

Food System Globalization, Eating Transformations, and Nutrition Transitions

Jeffery Sobal

In contemporary global history (Mazlish and Buultjens 1993), globalization is one of the most significant processes that will shape future historical developments. Globalization is the world-wide linkage and integration of previously local, national, and regional phenomena into organizational arrangements on a global scale. This process is more than simply internationalization because it involves global institutions and organizations that operate beyond the jurisdiction of national boundaries—and often outside the control of nation states (Robertson 1990). A variety of new global actors has emerged as a result, including global government bodies, nongovernmental organizations, corporate entities, media systems, and other institutions. An example of such an institution is the transnational corporation, which may originate or be headquartered in a particular nation state but which operates in the global system (Dicken 1992; Friedmann 1990; Wimberly 1991).

This chapter[1] will discuss the globalization of the food system and its relationship to eating transformations, nutrition transitions, and subsequent health outcomes. Many phenomena are involved in globalization, and multiple approaches to the topic exist (Featherstone 1990; McMichael 1996; Mittelman 1996; Schaeffer 1996; Sklar 1991). Several perspectives on globalization will be differentiated and applied in this chapter to issues surrounding food, eating, nutrition, and health. This presentation will use broad conceptualizations as analytical tools to portray large-scale patterns, recognizing that much variation and diversity occurs within overall trends and changes.

Most work on globalization has not considered food, eating, or nutrition, with little attention given to globalization and health (McMichael 1993). Global analyses of this topic have tended to focus on producing and supplying foods and on the political, economic, and environmental impacts of the globalization of food production (McMichael 1994), although some work has considered the globalization of food consumption as an exemplar for wider consumption patterns (Ritzer 1993). The nutritional and health aspects of the globalization of agriculture and food have been ignored, partly because scholars have not thought about the full scope of the linkages between agriculture, food, eating, nutrition, and health. Conceptualizing the food and nutrition system in its entirety provides a model for examining connections between these areas.

The Food and Nutrition System as a Conceptual Framework

The scope of the links between food production and nutritional status can be examined by a broad conceptualization of the food and nutrition system (summarized in Figure 1), based on an analytical examination of the concept and integration of existing models (Sobal, Khan, and Bisogni 1998). The food and nutrition system is a set of transformations that begins with resource inputs and moves through a series of stages that ultimately lead to health outcomes. The focus of this system moves from crops to foodstuffs to foods to nutrients and finally to diseases. Agriculture and food processing have social, economic, psychological, and other outcomes closely linked to nutrition and health.

The food and nutrition system has three major subsystems: a producer subsystem with production, processing, and distribution stages; a consumer subsystem with acquisition, preparation, and consumption stages; and a nutrition subsystem with digestion, transport, and metabolism stages. Storage of various materials occurs at every stage, including those of silage during production, cooking oil at preparation, and iron at metabolism.

The food and nutrition system operates within two major contexts: the biophysical and the sociocultural. The biophysical context includes the physical and biological environments of ecosystems, gene pools, geological areas, hydrological systems, and so forth. The sociocultural context includes cultural, economic, political, and other human systems that interact with the food and nutrition system. Inputs and outputs occur at all stages as the food and nutrition system interacts with its environments, providing resources for the system and accepting products (and byproducts).

Smaller units within larger food and nutrition systems have been conceptualized as foodsheds (Hedden 1929; Getz 1991; Kloppenburg et al. 1996). Foodsheds draw upon the concept of watersheds in the larger hydrological system but move beyond a physical perspective to be seen as geo-social units with structural and symbolic dimensions. Foodsheds are source areas for categories of foods or particular foods such as milk in milksheds (Durand 1964).

Foodsheds have increasingly moved from being local to regional to global in size, scope, variety, and volume. Traditional hunting and gathering cultures tended to have very local foodsheds that provided seasonal foods based on natural ecological cycles specific to that culture's environment. The globalization of the food system has expanded food sources into a world-wide foodshed for increasing numbers and amounts of foods and, consequently, a world-wide source of nutrients. The current global foodshed can supply foods, even highly perishable foods like strawberries, at all times of year anywhere on earth. The actual movement of foods is contingent upon the social, cultural, economic, and political structures and processes operating in a specific food and nutrition system.

The Globalization of the Food and Nutrition System

The globalization of food is not a new process, but the emergence of widespread interlinkages of producers and consumers throughout the world and of exchanges of large amounts of commodities and foods is a recent historical development. Early cases that began movement toward globalization included the transportation of pigs thousands of miles by ancient Polynesians (Oliver 1989), spice trade between Asia and Europe (Schievelbusch 1991), and the exchange of foods such as maize and potatoes between the Americas and Europe (Foster and Cordell 1992; Salaman 1985; Verrill 1937).

Preindustrial food systems exchanged some food information but relatively few food materials. Knowledge about food production, preservation, or preparation could be widely communicated through contact among cultures. However, relatively small amounts of actual food commodities could be globalized on a large scale because of the great costs of energy and effort in transportation. Agricultural plants and domesticated animals diffused widely in the forms of cultivars and breeding stock rather than crops and meats as commodities. Spices were early food ingredients that were widely traded because of their portability and the small amounts needed in cooking (Schievelbusch 1991), but core foods (Bennett et al. 1942; Jerome 1975, 1980) such as grains and even secondary core or peripheral foods like meats were produced and consumed locally. The burden of transport and competition for space required preindustrial food and nutrition systems to be based in local foodsheds of limited scale and scope.

The widespread globalization of the food supply and other phenomena is a new historical occurrence made possible by social and technological changes that began after industrialization (Robertson 1990). Industrial and post-industrial revolutions permitted the escalation and intensification of globalization as technologies in the food system and in the transportation and communication systems that transformed food production, processing, and distribution, with consequent transformations of food consumption.

Increasing the durability of crops, foodstuffs, and foods was a necessary factor in the globalization of all parts of the food and nutrition system (Friedmann 1992; Thompson and Cowan 1995). Durable foods are more transportable and storable and can therefore overcome limitations of time and space. Foods that have been made durable can be preserved for long periods of time and be transported to virtually any place. Making foods durable began with ancient food technologies such as drying, smoking, salting, and spicing (Sefa-Dedeh 1993)—methods that continue to be used. Both canning and tinning of foods were industrial developments that extended durability into new realms, increased the shelf life of foods, and permitted new, larger scales of mass food processing (Thompson and Cowan 1995). Procedures like freeze drying and irradiation are more recent examples of processes that further extend the life of foods by making them more durable. Durability can be conceptualized as a continuum from preserved to processed to manufactured foods (Thompson and Cowan 1995), with progression along the continuum increasing the capacity to make foods global commodities that contribute to the globalization of the food and nutrition system.

Both durable and fresh foods can now be transported anywhere in the world (Friedland 1994) as a result of efficiencies in transportation, especially in trucking and air transport. These efficiencies have greatly extended the penetration of perishables into foodsheds from which they were previously excluded. For example, fresh fish are increasingly likely to be transported by airplane rather than ground transportation; and saltwater fish can be harvested on a coastline and eaten far away in the interior of a continent on the same day.

Historical Transitions and Trajectories of Food and Nutrition Systems

Each of the earth's populations has existed on earth in several periods, each of which has had its own trajectory for developing the relationship between food and society, and transitions between these periods marked by inflection points often characterized as social revolutions. These periods have included the hunting and gathering, agricultural, and industrial phases.

Hunting and Gathering. Thousands of hunting and gathering cultures have existed (Murdock 1983, Otterbein 1976). Early cultures each developed their own particular cultural foodways and adapted their own food and nutrition system to the local environment. Traditional subsistence patterns emerged that were based on hunting, gathering, and scavenging but did not include any significant agricultural production. Diets for these early phases were based on a variety of foods extracted from local foodsheds, typically in seasonal patterns (Eaton et al. 1985, 1988, 1997). Transportation of foodstuffs was minimized because of the limited energy expenditure required to move foods across space. The human population during this period remained relatively small. The food and nutrition systems of hunters and gatherers were diverse but organizationally simple (Kelley 1995), until that trajectory underwent a transition brought on by the agricultural revolution (Howell 1986).

The Agricultural Revolution. The domestication of animals and plants that occurred in the Neolithic period over 10,000 years ago provided an increasing surplus in the amount of food and a stability of food sources compared to hunting and gathering subsistence techniques (Howell 1986). Because it also decreased the variety of foods used in a culture, agricultural production narrowed the number of species used as sources of food and consequently the diversity of nutrients consumed (Howell 1986). The domestication of plants and animals led to even greater spatial ties to farming and pasturing settings, since the vast majority of the population was involved in agricultural production. Although large-scale transportation of foodstuffs was minimal for early agriculturalists because of energy costs, it could increase to levels higher than those of hunting and gathering, if domesticated beasts of burden were used.

The transition to agriculture is typically assumed to have led to improved health through a stable food supply that produced surpluses to guard against famine. However, some analysts argue that the emergence of agriculture decreased the quality of health (Cohen 1989; Cohen and Armelagos 1984) or that agriculturalization had complex short- and long-term impacts on health for different segments of the population (Brown and Whitaker 1994). Subsistence agriculture generally could support a larger population than hunting and gathering. With the transition involved in the development of more formally organized agriculture, human populations established trajectories that included the less-diverse food systems than those involved in hunting and gathering but generated greater security in the amount of food available through surplus agricultural production. The subsistence agriculture period maintained its trajectory for about 10,000 years until the industrial revolution provided the impetus for a transition to new forms of food systems.

The Industrial Revolution. The industrialization of Europe and other areas in the 1800s harnessed the energy of water and fossil fuel sources and led to massive increases in the levels of food production, the ability to process foods, and the capability for transporting food over long distances. The tractor, mill, and train transformed the food system by increasing capacity and centralizing production and processing.

The food and nutrition system had occasionally operated in a global manner for a few foods, selected places, and restricted periods before industrialization. The scope and scale of globalization accelerated and expanded when European societies industrialized and incorporated portions of industrialized agriculture so that food systems were broadened across increasingly distant places. Industrial and post-industrial technological developments led to a fundamental shift towards the globalization of the food system because it permitted world-wide transport both of less perishable durable foods and, later, even highly perishable foods (Thompson and Cowan 1995).

Changes that resulted from the agricultural and industrial revolutions also produced substantial changes in the production and processing of food, a topic that has been extensively examined (McMichael 1994,1995). These changes in the earlier stages of the food system also produced changes further down the system, leading to important eating transformations as well as dietary, nutrition, and health transitions.

Eating Transformations

Transformations in eating practices occurred as changes in the consumer subsystem involved food acquisition, preparation, and consumption (Marshall 1995). The transition to new trajectories in food production, processing, and distribution resulted in a cascade of effects further down the food and nutrition system. Consumers experienced eating transformations because of changes in the origins and sources of their foods.

Historical changes in the food system dealt with some persistent eating problems of earlier periods, but new ones also emerged. For example, the development of agriculture overcame the vicissitudes of hunting and gathering but sacrificed diverse and uncertain traditional diets in exchange for stable but monotonous agricultural diets. The rapidity of recent changes led to lags in the ability of cultures to adapt to changes (Ogburn 1923).

The techniques used by hunters and gatherers and subsistence agriculturalists to acquire foodstuffs varied greatly. However, a common feature was that most traditional food was self-produced, grown, and eaten by the same household. As agriculture and transportation changed, increasing amounts of food were acquired from others, at first in local foodsheds and later from distant reaches of the earth. The development and expansion of industrialized food systems led to increasing acquisition of foodstuffs from non-local sources (Pelto and Pelto 1983). With globalization, food acquisition draws upon world-wide sources, with many foods transported thousands of miles from different origins and passing through several processing points before the foods reach the people who will consume them.

Food preparation methods were also transformed as the system supplying food changed. A major shift was the institutional substitution of commercial food preparation for what had formerly been done by consumers themselves. In most traditional food systems, households cooked most of the food consumed by household members, often from basic, less-processed ingredients. For example, a century ago most households baked their own bread by necessity; but in post-industrial societies, most bread is baked commercially (except for ceremonial and recreational home baking). Post-industrial food systems have an increasing amount of cooking performed by food-service enterprises. This is evidenced by the increased frequency of eating at restaurants as well as in the growing movement towards "take-out" foods that are commercially prepared for people to eat at home. In the contemporary United States, almost half of the food budget is spent eating away from home (Dumagan and Hackett 1995).

Food consumption has undergone parallel transformations in its acquisition and preparation. Food consumption in many traditional societies was a collective activity that occurred in households, while in post-industrial societies an increasing amount of food is eaten away from home and often alone. The globalization of eating occurs as manners and meals homogenize in the spread of cuisines across the world. Eating transformations vary by the type of meals, with the traditional midday meal in many Western societies being the dominant food event of the day, a time when the entire family eats together. More recently, commensality shifted from the family to co-workers or friends as professional identities displace family ties as the overriding allegiances that determine mealtime partners. Dietary individualization also occurs as people within a household eat separate meals, facilitated by the availability of commercial foods that are easy and quick to prepare or ready to eat. Dietary individualism is also facilitated in restaurants, where selections are diverse and not contingent upon the more traditional efficiency requirements for preparing common foods for the entire household.

Many eating transformations reflect broader cultural and social changes, such as increasing social stratification, smaller families, and rising labor force participation by women (Senauer et al. 1991). These eating transformations have reciprocal relationships with production and processing, since consumer demands have increasingly shaped the operation of prior stages in the food system as well as shifts in production, processing, and distribution that also simultaneously modify eating patterns. An important underlying factor is the perception that a globalized society has increasing demands on time, making it a scarcer commodity than money (Senauer et al. 1991). Time shortages have led to greater emphasis on convenience, which encouraged food processors to develop products that have increasingly included preparation steps formerly done by consumers themselves.

An important aspect of eating transformations is the increasing separation of activities in the various stages in the food and nutrition system. Global food production and processing has become detached from acquisition, and food preparation is increasingly segregated from consumption. Much of this is driven by cultural values and structural arrangements that are grounded in time demands and the search for convenience.

Dietary Transition

Dietary transitions involve shifts in the foods consumed in a society and are driven by agricultural and industrial revolutions (Grigg 1995; Khor et al. 1998). Dietary behaviors are shaped by social structure and social processes. As global influences change, so do the diets of global societies. Industrialized Western nations, the first cohort of societies involved in the transition from local to global diets, have initiated changes that led to globalization. Other societies experienced dietary transitions when they began to be incorporated in larger foodsheds and when their diets were delocalized (Pelto and Pelto 1983) with increases in food production, attempts to increase its durability, and the exportation of local foods, as well as the importation of durable foods from other localities. Other changes in diet occurred when eating patterns were altered by fundamental changes in social institutions, such as the increasing penetration of the mass media into everyday life (Senauer et al. 1991).

The overall patterns involved in dietary transitions included the consumption of fewer locally produced plant foods and of more imported and processed animal foods (although a considerable local variation occurs in these trends). This has been described by economists as Bennett's Law, whereby the consumption of starchy staples in the diet is inversely related to the level of industrialization (Bennett 1941,1954). With the increasing technological and energy resources of industrialized societies, the consumption of a variety of foods increased, along with the consumption of meat, dairy, seafood, alcoholic beverages, and processed foods, but that of staple grains and tuber consumption decreased (Grigg 1993, 1995, 1996).

Nutrition Transitions

Nutrition transitions occur when food choices within a society provide different mixes of nutrients (Drewnowski and Popkin 1997; Monteiro et al. 1995; Popkin 1993, 1994, 1998; Popkin et al. 1993). Considerable variation exists among the traditional diets of various cultures because the variety of foodways that evolved adapt to the multitude of ecosystems in which human beings have lived (Eaton et al. 1997). Some cultures, a classic example being the Inuit of the Arctic, consume predominantly animal foods; while others, such as the Miwok of the California forests, who rely on acorns as the staple calorie source in their diets, eat primarily plant foods.

With the development and diffusion of agriculture, including the displacement of hunting and gathering cultures by rapidly growing agricultural cultures, many cultural foodways became extinct and dietary diversity decreased to take advantage of the more stable and plentiful supplies of agriculturally produced foods. Low-technology agriculture increased the consumption of plant foods, particularly grains such as rice, wheat, oats, barley, millet, sorghum, and root crops such as potatoes, cassava, and yams. Industrialized agriculture became linked with industrialized food manufacturing in cultivation through the use of monocropping agricultural systems and the production of processed durable foods on a large scale.

Nutrition transitions occurred as a consequence of changes in the stages of the food and nutrition system: production, processing, distribution, acquisition, preparation, and consumption. Transformation from traditional to industrialized agriculture led to changes in the proportion of macronutrients consumed (Howell 1986). The intake of fiber and complex carbohydrates as plant food consumption was displaced and replaced by the increased consumption of animal foods, refined carbohydrates from industrialized food processing, and plant oils used to make processed foods more durable. As the intake of animal products rose, more fats were consumed. This shifted the sources of protein from plants to animals, whose proteins contained more of the eight amino acids necessary for human beings and therefore had a greater biological value for maintaining health. More plant oils and simple carbohydrates were consumed as more durable and processed foods were ingested. The greater variety and volume of food available in industrialized food systems facilitates the opportunity for overall energy intake. In the world today, the composition of macronutrients in a diet is directly associated with Gross National Product (GNP) because it reflects these trends (Perisse et al. 1969; Posner et al. 1994).

Micronutrient consumption also changed when nutrition transitions caused the shift from diverse to monotonous diets (Howell 1986; Eaton et al. 1997). Local deficiencies in micronutrient availability from an ecosystem could be overcome when foods from a larger foodshed were consumed. However, the sedentarization accompanying agriculture meant an increased reliance on fewer species grown in fewer places. This further limited local options for diversity of crops and food. Micronutrient deficiencies became problems in industrialized societies, since large numbers of people there relied on food systems that provided diets based on grains with micronutrient deficiencies, such as niacin deficiencies that occur when diets primarily based on corn are adopted (Roe 1973). The recent globalization of food systems has often overcome such micronutrient deficiencies by adding nutrients, vitamins, and minerals during manufacturing to fortify and enrich food and to prevent micronutrient deficiencies in consumers. More consistent provision of food supplies also makes it possible to provide particular nutrients despite the constraints of seasonal variations.

Transformations of food systems that produce more abundant and more stable food supplies also led to nutrition transitions in the overall caloric intake available per person (Sobal 1991; Sobal and Stunkard 1989). Such increases in the volume, caloric density, and constancy of food supplies have led to larger food energy supplies as a result of agricultural and industrial transformations in food production, processing, distribution, acquisition, preparation, and consumption (Howell 1986). This is reflected in less wasting and stunting among children, greater attained stature among adults, and rising levels of obesity in industrialized populations, even though this has also resulted in a growing number of people discarding food (Sobal 1991).

Health Transitions

Health transitions (Caldwell et al.1990) include epidemiological transitions in morbidity, changes in causes of death as mortality shifts, and modifications in the performance of health behaviors (Frenk et al. 1991). Transitions in morbidity and mortality occur as the relative prevalence of acute infectious diseases and accidents declines and as the prevalence of chronic, degenerative diseases increases. Diet and nutrition are important, and some argue, central, factors in these transitions (McKeown 1976).

Epidemiological Transitions. Epidemiological transitions (Omran 1971, 1977a, 1977b) occurred in the shift from frequent undernutrition, where famine plays a major role in acute illnesses, to overnutrition, where excess fat and protein consumption constitute major risk factors for chronic diseases (Campbell et al. 1992). Currently, many societies are seen as being at a new stage in the epidemiological transition, where people are attempting to prevent degenerative diseases such as coronary heart disease and cancer by eating low-fat and high-fiber foods that their ancestors once subsisted on (Olshansky and Ault 1986; Bah 1992, 1995; Bah and Fernando 1991; Rogers and Hackenberg 1987). This shift has led to interesting reversals in health patterns. Royalty once suffered from gout while peasants starved, while today elites struggle with anorexia nervosa, and the working masses consume excess cholesterol.

Mortality Transitions. Mortality transitions occurred as people survived infancy and childhood infectious and accidental deaths that in large part occurred because of improved nutrition and hygiene rather than advances in medicine (McKeown 1976; McKinlay and McKinlay 1977). The population increasingly began to suffer from chronic diseases in adulthood, partly as the result of the excess consumption of high-fat, low-fiber durable foods that operated as risk factors for initiating and enhancing the progression of pathologies that led to coronary heart disease, cancer, stroke, diabetes, and hypertension (McGinnis and Foege 1993). The transition patterns for global mortality show a secular decline in mortality (Caldwell et al. 1990), in which changes in morbidity shifted from acute conditions to chronic degenerative factors and the age at death increased (although such patterns are unevenly distributed across places and population groups). The overall globalization of health and mortality is occurring rapidly as diseases leading to infant deaths decline, only to be replaced by the diseases associated with later adult mortality. Overall life expectancy has increased dramatically since the industrial revolution, so that the expected life spans have doubled from the 40 years common in earlier historical periods to average life expectancies of 80 years in some nations at the close of the twentieth century.

Transformations Involved in Food System Globalization

Analysis of the food and nutrition system makes qualitative distinctions based on the scale of the processes operating on the local, national or regional, and global levels. These levels are not mutually exclusive, and no clear boundaries exist among them. The processes involved in the food and nutrition system are also multifactorial, since different traits may predominate at different scales. A particular food may have local preparation but national processing and global production and distribution.

Transformations in food systems tend to proceed as they are delocalized and denationalized to become globalized, although they do not have to be nationalized nor is this step or stage between local and global always required. Delocalization may involve simple trade between local foodsheds or preparing for the market a local food system from subsistence food production by commodifying cash crop production for national or global food systems (Pelto and Pelto 1983). The industrialization of food systems may involve relatively simple harnessing of energy sources and more efficient mechanical techniques or Fordist mass production of foods (Friedmann 1991). The globalization of food systems occurs when multiple sources and outputs are organized vertically and horizontally as parts of integrated global food systems that comprise agri-food complexes and food regimes operated by transnational corporations (Friedmann 1991; McMichael 1992; Pritchard 1998).

Similar to population transitions (Beaver 1975; Caldwell 1987), two types of globalization—emergent and conversion—are occurring: Emergent globalization occurred when the current world agri-industrial complex was developed as part of the industrialization of European nations and their close descendants. Conversion globalization occurs when local, traditional foodsheds lose their autonomy and are subsumed as parts of already established global food systems. In this way, globalization diffuses into previously more isolated cultures. The patterns and consequences of each type differ: Emergent globalization offers the privileges of priority, and conversion globalization includes the opportunity to gain from the experience of earlier global changes.

Urbanization occurs in a process parallel to that of globalization, since an increasing proportion of the world's population resides in metropolitan areas. The concentrated, high-density urban food systems offer different eating and nutrition problems than those dispersed, low-density rural food systems (Solomons and Gross 1995; Popkin and Bisgrove 1988). The problems of transportation between rural food production sites and those of urban distribution areas pose important dilemmas that influence food, eating, and nutrition patterns.

Perspectives on Globalization

Many perspectives on globalization are currently being employed, and each provides a different way to frame the topic of food-system globalization, eating transformations, and nutrition transitions. For analytical purposes, the major lenses for viewing globalization can be broadly focused in terms of those emphasizing the economic, political, and cultural aspects of globalization, only three of many possible lenses. There is considerable variation within them and overlap between them. The three perspectives are not exhaustive nor mutually exclusive but capture some of the most salient perspectives in thinking about globalization. The three perspectives provide one analytical strategy to untangle the many intertwined themes involved in globalization. Central ideas from each perspective will be applied here to food, eating, and nutrition.

Each of the economic, political, and cultural perspectives employs different styles of discourse to weigh economic development, political dependency, or cultural diversity in forming its own primary interpretation of globalization. The different perspectives on globalization tend to differ little in their description of what has actually happened in the past with respect to globalization of food, eating, and nutrition; but these perspectives do apply different rationales for explaining these past events. These perspectives also offer very different versions of what may occur in the future as the result of globalization.

Several key questions exist in thinking about globalization. First is the scale and scope of globalization, along with differing interpretations of whether it is currently extensive or trivial. Second is whether the rate or pace of globalization is slow or rapid. Third is whether globalization is leading to world-wide homogeneity or whether heterogeneity will persist or even increase. Fourth is determining the realm of life most important in global processes, with differing emphasis on economic, political, or cultural arenas. The following sections describe how the three perspectives on globalization offer varying views on these issues as for food, eating, and nutrition.

Economic Perspectives on Globalization. Economic paradigms deal with globalization by using a rational choice perspective that focuses on economic development (as industrialization and modernization) and uses nations as units of analysis (Chenery and Srinivasn 1988). Nations are typically seen as moving relatively slowly through evolutionary progressions or stages, so that economies rely first on primary production to extract resources from the environment, then secondary production to transform resources into consumer products, and finally on tertiary production to offer services to consumers (Harrison 1988; Timmer 1988). More consensus exists in economic thinking about globalization than in political or cultural perspectives on globalization.

Much economic work on globalization is grounded in developmental economics, which examines how societies form markets and develop industries to create links to international markets and their food systems. Nation states are seen as relatively autonomous food systems, with each reproducing the production, processing, distribution, and other food system processes largely independently of other nations. Contemporary Western societies are used as models for such economic development.

Economic development models are compatible (and often linked) with medical and public health thinking about epidemiological transition perspectives that emphasize the spread of Western diseases to developing societies as they modernize (Campbell et al. 1992; Temple and Burkitt 1994; Trowell and Burkitt 1981). The materialist, rational assumptions of economic thinking fit well with the biological thinking of medical models.

Developing national food production and free international food trade shapes the emphasis of an economic perspective on globalization, and there is some evidence that these patterns are occurring. For example, in the late eighteenth century, only 1 percent of grain produced in Europe crossed national boundaries, while currently 12 percent of the food that is produced is involved in world trade, more so among developed than developing nations (Grigg 1995). An economic perspective also emphasizes the processing of food into durable goods, encouraging the inclusion of "value added" steps in the food system to increase economic profit. Economies of scale and scope are emphasized in economic thinking, with mass production and consumption leading to an increasing homogeneity of dietary intake (and consequently nutrient intake and health outcomes). Such economic approaches recast eaters into consumers. Economic perspectives tend to see globalization increasing as nations participate in a world-wide food market that makes foods available to all people, with adequate and optimal nutrition according to their ability to pay in the marketplace.

Political Perspectives on Globalization.   Focus on unequal power relationships between nations is the hallmark of political perspectives on globalization, although much diversity exists in political approaches. Such thinking is grounded in dependency and world systems theories which posit interdependent and unequal relationships among nations. World systems theory analyzes such global activities as comprising a stratified world system of core, semi-periphery, and periphery nations (Wallerstein 1974,1979,1980) that operates as an independent unit of analysis to explain historical and contemporary global processes based on a theory of dependency (Chirot and Hall 1982; Shannon 1989; Chase-Dunn 1989). World systems formed with the development of capitalism and the emergence of colonialism and the creation of settler colonies. In their search for crops and foodstuffs as raw materials, European countries colonized the "carbohydrate frontier" of other nations (Hugill 1993).

Food has become an important topic of work related to world systems because of the notion that core countries create and maintain a chronic state of underdevelopment of the countries in the periphery (McIntosh 1996). These peripheral countries supply raw food commodities, which the agri-industrial complex of the core nations process and sell back to developing nations as manufactured food products. From this perspective, an unequal division of labor resulting from this specialization of various areas occurs in a global food and nutrition system, instead of each nation developing a complete and more local system of food and nutrition.

Moving beyond dependency and world systems perspectives, other analyses that emphasize power differences have revealed additional complexity in the political organization of agriculture, food processing, and consumption. Scholars who focus on the entire world as a unit of analysis have made it possible to examine the formation of international food regimes and transnational corporations that operate on a global level, independent of nation states. Friedmann (1982,1991), Friedmann and McMichael (1992), and McMichael (1994) have examined how at a particular historical period the world system aligned into a set of global food regimes for specific commodities controlled by transnational corporations, including a global complex of wheat and another of livestock. Such food regimes structure the food supply on a global basis, influencing the world-wide division of labor between countries for specific commodities. An example can be seen in the consolidation and integration of the chicken broiler industry (Kim and Curry, 1993), when it standardized inputs, consolidated production, integrated processing, and unified distribution.

With the globalization and development of food regimes, diets become increasingly standardized and homogeneous within nations and the world as a whole. Class differences are based on price, not culture (Friedmann 1991). A hegemony of taste developed that used power and influence as the basis for interpreting food. Those interested in political perspectives expect that globalization will lead to nutrition and health consequences by perpetuating and exacerbating inequalities across the world and that undernutrition and overnutrition will occur among disadvantaged groups in the global system according to their level of political power.

Cultural Perspectives on Globalization. Focusing on the cultural aspects of globalization emphasizes a relativist perspective like that expressed by postmodernism and related culturally based theories (Featherstone 1990, 1995; Sklar 1991), although a great diversity exists in cultural approaches to globalization. The common emphasis on cultural perspectives has tended to focus more on consumption than production, with the appreciation of cultural diversity a key underlying theme. Analysts in the cultural studies tradition regard taste and identity as important forces in consumer consumption (Corrigan 1997; Edgell et al. 1996; Warde 1997). The meaning of food is stressed over its cost, availability, or nutritional outcome. Those interested in cultural perspectives on globalization express concern about the de-emphasis on, or even loss of, cultures when economic or political globalization processes are homogenized and when an emphasis is placed on the unique forms that globalization may take as the homogeneity of global food systems is contested and opposed. These cultural perspectives tend to consider values and autonomy, instead of an economic emphasis on costs and a political emphasis on power. A nostalgia for past cuisines often exists along with a discourse about losing cultural identities drawn from food and eating.

Examples of global consumerism in food include the marketing of infant formula by the Nestle corporation and cola marketing wars in the third world (Sklar 1991). Exporting the rationality of American culture into the food systems of other cultures has been described as the "McDonaldization" of society (Ritzer 1993), a process of globalization that is primarily one of Americanization because it promotes the cultural dominance of the United States in most new global forms (Ritzer 1995). In this way, culturally dominant societies like the United States spread their culture throughout the world by creating a cultural dependency based upon processed fast foods (Sklar 1991).

Cultural analyses have often focused on the reactions and resistance to globalization of the food and nutrition system by dichotomizing the issue into one of global versus local interests. Direct challenges to globalization may contest the economic assumptions of global food systems and oppose those strategies that view the complete commodification of food. The re-emergence of food riots has occurred when some nations were asked to engage in economic programs to fit the needs of the world food economy (Walton and Seddon 1994). Quiet changes rather than open opposition to global forces can also occur when mass, global food systems valorize self-production of foods and re-emphasize the craft of food production, preservation, and preparation. The relocalization of the food system can take place in some places in the forms of consumer supported agriculture (CSA), farmers' markets, consumer food cooperatives, and other relatively new institutional forms are used under the ideological banner of the sustainability of the food system. The preservation and resurrection of traditional food cultures is another example of this perspective, such as in native food movements promoting a culture's return to producing and consuming ancestral foods.

Still, those interested in cultural perspectives emphasize the meaning of foods in terms of cuisines that include specific foods, preparation methods, flavor principles, and rules for meal behavior, and meal patterns and structures (Farb and Armelagos 1980; Fieldhouse 1996; Rozin 1983). Other less nutritionally important aspects of cuisines are the ingredients and preparation involved in creating the cultural format characteristic of dishes for that cuisine. For example, approximately the same amount of beef, wheat, and vegetables can produce a hamburger, burrito, dish of spaghetti, or Chinese noodles, depending on the cultural orientation of the cook, the use of food preparation techniques, spicing, presentation, and consumption. Because each of these dishes has the same ingredients, all have similar nutritional consequences. Globalization may matter greatly for the symbolism and identity of cultural cuisines but may be less crucial to the health outcomes of cuisine development, change, and extinction.

Those concerned with culture primarily focus on food consumption rather than production. This leads to an emphasis on cultural form (especially critiques of global homogenization of foodstyles) and a de-emphasis on biological function in the consequences for nutrition and health. Fears of disconnection in the food and nutrition system is an important cultural theme, with a tension about the separation of eating from production. With globalization, cultural analysts project a loss of food and eating identity that could potentially lead to "gastro-anomie" (Fischler 1988). The culturalists' thinking about globalization and food is more symbolic than structural in its attention. They tend to expect globalization to have significant consequences for cuisine and eating, but these may or may not influence the physiological intake of nutrients nor promote good health.

Conclusions

This chapter examined the relationship between globalization of the food system and transitions in nutrient consumption through the use of a conceptual model of the food and nutrition system to establish linkages across the categories of agriculture, food, eating, nutrition, and health. It is important to deal with issues across the entire scope of the food and nutrition system, a focus that past analyses lacked, since they concentrated only on parts of the system. Partly because they lacked an integrative model and partly because they observed a disciplinary isolation, previous analysts focused on the globalization of food production and ignored the consequences on a global basis of extending eating, nutrition, and health practices and systems. This chapter attempted to link several diverse literatures by using the food and nutrition system as a framework to connect perspectives on globalization.

The historical progress of the globalization of the food and nutrition system has been uneven, with the agricultural and industrial revolutions providing inflection points in trajectories that eventually moved towards globalization. Increases in the durability of foods resulting from social, political, economic, and cultural changes as well as technological advances in food manufacturing was a necessary step in the current globalization of the food and nutrition system. Technological shifts in food processing also changed the types of foods and the ingredients in foods. This led to dietary and nutritional transitions from plant-based high-fiber, low-fat diets to animal- and vegetable-oil based, low-fiber, high-fat, high-protein diets. The globalization of the agri-industrial complex is bringing dietary and nutritional transitions to an increasing proportion of the world's population.

Three perspectives are commonly used to interpret globalization: economic, political, and cultural. Each offers a different focus. These three perspectives can be viewed as multilayered vantage points for explaining, interpreting, and predicting patterns of globalization and their nutritional consequences. The scale and scope of globalization does not tend to be seen as a large or a significant problem from an economic perspective. Indeed, it is likely to be framed as a growing problem, causing difficulties from a political perspective, and often a massive and major threat from a cultural perspective. The homogenization of the food and nutrition system tends to not be viewed as problematic from an economic perspective, is often perceived as an imperialistic force from a political perspective, and is regarded from many cultural perspectives as a dangerous process that can result in the extinction of local cultural foodways.

Understanding the current status and future course of the globalization of food systems, as well as its impact on eating transformations and nutritional transitions, depends on which perspective is supported by future developments. Debate about how the relative influence of global compression will lead to the homogenization of food, eating, and nutrition and how global diversification will lead to the heterogenization of the food and nutrition system will continue to be a crucial problem that will be enacted and interpreted in many ways in the future. However that debate is resolved, it should provide some interesting global history of food.

Note

1. Acknowledgements: The author thanks Philip McMichael, Frank Young, and Julie Locker for helpful comments.

References

Bah, S.M. 1992. "Epidemiologic and Health Transition in Mauritius." *Journal of Population Studies*, 15:137–59.

_____. 1995. "Quantitative Approaches to Detect the Fourth Stage of the Epidemiological Transition." *Social Biology*, 42:143–48.

Bah, S.M.; and R. Fernando. 1991. "Has Canadian Mortality Entered the Fourth Stage of the Epidemiological Transition?" *Canadian Studies of Population*, 18:18–41.

Beaver, S.E. 1975. *Demographic Transition Theory Reinterpreted*. Lexington, Mass.: Lexington Books. 1975.

Bennett, J.W.; H.L. Smith; and H. Passin. 1942. "Food and Culture in Southern Illinois – A Preliminary Report." *American Sociological Review*, 7:645–60.

Bennett, M.K. 1941. "International Contrasts in Food Consumption." *Geographical Review*, 31:365–76.

_____. 1954. *The World's Food: A Study of the Interrelations of World Populations, National Diets, and Food Potentials*. New York: Harper.

Brown, P.J.; and E. D. Whitaker. 1994. "Health Implications of Modern Agricultural Transformations: Malaria and pellagra in Italy." *Human Organization*, 53:4, 346–51.

Caldwell, J.C. 1987. "Toward a Restatement of Demographic Transition Theory," in S.W.Menard and E.W. Moen, eds. *Perspectives on Population*, 42–69. New York: Oxford University Press.

Caldwell, J.C.; S. Findley; G. Santow; W. Cosford; J. Brai; and D. Browers-Freeman, eds. 1990. *What We Know about Health Transition: The Cultural, Social, and Behavioral Determinants of Health*. Proceedings of an International Workshop. Canberra: Australian National University.

Campbell, T.C.; J. Chen; T. Brun; B. Parpia; Y. Qu; C. Chen; and C. Gerssler. 1992. "China: From Diseases of Poverty to Diseases of Affluence. Policy Implications of the Epidemiological Transition." *Ecology of Food and Nutrition*, 27:133–44.

Chase-Dunn, C. 1989. *Global Formation: Structures of the World-Economy*. New York: Blackwell.

Chenery, H.; and T. N. Srinivasan, eds. 1988. *Handbook of Developmental Economics*. New York: Elsevier Science.

Chirot, D.; and T.D. Hall. 1982. "World-System Theory." *Annual Review of Sociology*, 8:81–106.

Cohen, M.N. 1989. *Health and the Rise of Civilization*. New Haven, CT: Yale University Press.

Cohen, M.N.; and G. J. Armelagos, eds. 1984. *Paleopathology at the Origins of Agriculture*. New York: Academic Press.

Corrigan, P. 1997. *The Sociology of Consumption*. Thousand Oaks, CA: Sage.

Dicken, P. 1992. *Global Shift: Industrial Change in a Turnabout World*, 2nd ed. London: Harper and Row.

Drewnowski, A.; and B. M. Popkin. 1997. "The Nutrition Transition: New Trends in the Global Diet." *Nutrition Reviews*, 55:31–43.

Dumagan, J.C.; and J. W. Hackett. 1995. "Almost Half of the Food Budget Is Spent Eating Out." *Food Review*; January-April, pp 37–39.

Durand, L. 1964. "The Major Milksheds of the Northeastern Quarter of the United States." *Economic Geography*, 40:9–33.

Eaton, S.B.; and M. Konner. 1985. "Paleolithic Nutrition: A Consideration of Its Nature and Current Implications." *New England Journal of Medicine*, 312:283–89.

Eaton, S.B.; M. Shostak; and M. Konner. 1988. *The Paleolithic Prescription*. New York: Harper and Row.

Eaton, S.B., and M. J. Konner. 1997. "Paleolithic Nutrition Revisited: A Twelve-Year Retrospective on Its Nature and Implications." *European Journal of Clinical Nutrition*, 51:207–16.

Edgell, S.; K. Hetherington; and A. Warde. 1996. *Consumption Matters: The Production and Experience of Consumption*. Cambridge, MA: Blackwell.

Farb, P.; and G. Armelagos. 1980. *Consuming Passions: The Anthropology of Eating*. Boston: Houghton Mifflin.

Featherstone, M., ed. 1990. *Global Culture: Nationalism, Globalization, and Modernity*. Newbury Park, CA: Sage.

———. 1995. *Undoing Culture: Globalization, Postmodernism, and Identity*. Thousand Oaks, CA: Sage.

Fieldhouse, P. 1996. *Food and Nutrition: Customs and Culture*, 2nd ed. New York: Chapman and Hall.

Fischler, C. 1988. "Food, Self, and Identity." *Social Science Information*, 17:275–92.

Foster, N.; and L. S. Cordell. 1992. *Chilis to Chocolate: Food the Americas Gave the World*. Tucson, AZ: University of Arizona Press.

Frenk, J.; J. L. Bobadilla; C. Stern; T. Frejka; and R. Lozano. 1991. "Elements for a Theory of the Health Transition." *Health Transition Review*, 1:1, 21–38.

Friedland, W.H. 1994. "The Global Fresh Fruit and Vegetable System: An Industrial Organization Analysis," in P. McMichael, ed., *The Global Restructuring of Agro-Food Systems*, 173–89. Ithaca, NY: Cornell University Press.

Friedmann, H. 1982. "The Political Economy of Food: The Rise and Fall of the Postwar International Food Order." *American Journal of Sociology*, 8 (supplement), S248–86.

———. 1990. "The Origins of Third World Food Dependence," in H. Bernstein, B. Crow, M. Mackintosh, and C. Martin, eds., *The Food Question: Profits versus People*, 13–31. New York: Monthly Review Press.

———. 1991. "Changes in the International Division of Labor: Agri-Food Complexes and Export Agriculture," in W.H. Friedland, L. Busch, F.H. Buttel, and A.P. Rudy, eds., *Towards a New Political Economy of Agriculture*, 65–93. Boulder: Westview Press.

———. 1992. "Distance and Durability: Shaky Foundations of a World Food Economy." *Third World Quarterly*, 13:2, 371–83.

Friedmann, H.; and P. McMichael. 1989. "Agriculture and the State System: The Rise and Decline of National Agricultures, 1870 to the Present." *Sociologia Ruralis*, 29:2, 93–117.

Getz, A. 1991. "Urban Foodsheds." *Permaculture Activist*, 8:3, 26–27.

Grigg, D. 1993. "International Variations in Food Consumption in the 1980's." *Geography*, 78:251–66.

———. 1995a. "The Nutritional Transition in Western Europe." *Journal of Historical Geography*, 21:3, 247–61.

———. 1995b. "The Pattern of World Protein Consumption." *Geoforum*, 26:1, 1–17.

———. 1996. "The Starchy Staples in World Food Consumption." *Annals of the Association of American Geographers*, 86:412–31.

Harrison, D. 1988. *The Sociology of Modernization and Development*. London: Unwin Hyman.

Hedden, W.P. 1929. *How Great Cities Are Fed*. Boston: D.C. Heath.

Howell, N. 1986. "Feedbacks and Buffers in Relation to Scarcity and Abundance: Studies of Hunter-Gatherer Populations," in D. Coleman and R. Schofield, eds., *The State of Population Theory: Forward from Malthus*, 156–87. New York: Basil Blackwell.

Hugill, P.J. 1993. *World Trade since 1431: Geography, Technology, and Capitalism*. Baltimore, MD: Johns Hopkins University Press.

Jerome, N.W. 1975. "On Determining Food Patterns of Urban Dwellers in Contemporary United States Society," in M. L. Arnott, ed., *Gastronomy: The Anthropology of Food Habits*, 91–111. The Hague: Mouton.

_____. 1980. "Diet and Acculturation: The Case of Black-American In-Migrants," in N.W. Jerome, R.F. Kandel, and G.H. Pelto, eds., *Nutritional Anthropology: Contemporary Approaches to Diet and Culture*, 275–325. Pleasantville, NY: Redgrave Publishing Company.

Kelley, R.L. 1995. *The Foraging Spectrum: Diversity in Hunter-Gatherer Lifeways*. Washington: Smithsonian Institution Press.

Khor, G.L.; B. H. Hsu-Hage; and M. L. Wahlqvist. 1998. "Dietary Practices in Nutritional Transition: The Case of Malaysian Urban Chinese." *Ecology of Food and Nutrition*, 36:463–89.

Kim, C-K.; and J. Curry. 1993. "Fordism, Flexible Specialization and Agri-Industrial Restructuring: The Case of the U.S. broiler Industry." *Sociologia Ruralis*, 33:1, 61–80.

Kloppenburg, J.; J. Hendrickson; and G. W. Stevenson. 1996. "Coming in to the Foodshed." *Agriculture and Human Values*, 13:3, 33–42.

Marshall, D., ed. 1995. *Food Choice and the Consumer*. London: Blackie Academic and Professional.

Mazlish, B.; and R. Buultjens, eds. 1993. *Conceptualizing Global History*. Boulder, CO: Westview Press.

McGinnis, J.M.; and W. H. Foege. 1993. "Actual Causes of Death in the United States." *Journal of the American Medical Association*, 270:2207–12.

McIntosh, W.A. 1996. *Sociologies of Food and Nutrition*. New York: Plenum Press.

McKeown, T. 1976. *The Rise of Modern Population*. London: Edward Arnold.

McKinlay, J.B.; and S. M. McKinlay. 1977. "The Questionable Contribution of Medical Measures to the Decline in Mortality in the United States in the Twentieth Century." *Milbank Memorial Fund Quarterly*, 55:405–28.

McMichael, A.J. 1993. *Planetary Overload: Global Environmental Change and the Health of the Human Species*. New York: Cambridge University Press.

McMichael, P. 1992. "Tensions between National and International Control of the World Food Order: Contours of a New Food Regime." *Sociological Perspectives*, 35:2, 343–65.

_____, ed. 1994. *The Global Restructuring of Agro-Food Systems*. Ithaca, NY: Cornell University Press.

_____, ed. 1995. *Food and Agrarian Orders in the World-Economy*. Westport, CT: Praeger.

_____. 1996. "Globalization: Myths and Realities." *Rural Sociology*, 61:1, 25–55.

Mittelman, J. , ed. 1996. *Globalization: Critical Reflections.* Boulder: Lynne Renner.

Monteiro, C.A.; L. Mondini; A. L. M. de Souza; and B. M. Popkin. 1995. "The Nutrition Transition in Brazil." *European Journal of Clinical Nutrition*, 49:105–13.

Murdock, G.P. 1983. *Outline of World Cultures,* 6th ed. New Haven, CT: Human Relations Area Files.

Ogburn, W.F. 1923. *Social Change: With Respect to Culture and Original Nature.* New York: W.B. Huebsch.

Oliver, D.L. 1989. *Oceana: The Native Cultures of Australia and the Pacific Islands.* Honolulu: University of Hawaii Press.

Olshansky, S.J.; and A. B. Ault. 1986. "The Fourth Stage of the Epidemiological Transition: The Age of Delayed Degenerative Diseases." *Milbank Memorial Quarterly*, 49:509–38.

Omran, A.R. 1971. "The Epidemiologic Transition: A Theory of the Epidemiology of Population Change." *Milbank Memorial Fund Quarterly*, 49:509–38.

_____. 1977a. "Epidemiologic Transition in the United States: The Health Factor in Population Change." *Population Bulletin*, 32:2, 1–42.

_____. 1977b. "A Century of Epidemiological Transition in the United States." *Preventive Medicine*, 6:1, 30–51.

Otterbein, K.F. 1976. "Sampling and Samples in Cross-Cultural Studies." *Behavior Science Research*, 11:2, 107–21.

Pelto, G.H.; and P. J. Pelto. 1983. "Diet and Delocalization: Dietary Change since 1750," in R.I. Rothberg, and T.K. Rabb, eds., *Hunger and History: The Impact of Changing Food Production and Consumption Patterns on Society*, 309–30. Cambridge: Cambridge University Press.

Perisse, J.; F. Sizaret; and P. Francois. 1969. "The Effect of Income and the Structure of the Diet." *FAO Nutrition Newsletter*, 7:1–9.

Popkin, B.M. 1993. "Nutritional Patterns and Transitions." *Population and Development Review*, 19:138–57.

_____. 1994. "The Nutrition Transition in Low Income Countries: An Emerging Crisis." *Nutrition Reviews*, 52:285–98.

_____. 1998. "The Nutrition Transition and Its Health Implications in Lower-Income Countries." *Public Health Nutrition*, 1:1–21.

Popkin, B.M.; and E. Z. Bisgrove. 1988. "Urbanization and Nutrition in Low Income Countries." *Food and Nutrition Bulletin*, 10:3–23.

Popkin, B.M.; K. Ge; F. Zhai; X. Guo; H. Ma; and N. Zhoori. 1993. "The Nutrition Transition in China: A Cross-Sectional Analysis." *European Journal of Clinical Nutrition*, 47:333–46.

Popkin, B.M.; M. K. Richards; and C. A. Monteiro. 1996. "Stunting is associated with Overweight in Children of Four Nations That Are Undergoing the Nutrition Transition." *Journal of Nutrition*, 126:3009–16.

Posner, B.M.; M. Franz; and P. Quatromoni. 1994. "Nutrition And the Global Risk for Chronic Diseases: The INTERHEALTH Nutrition Initiative." *Nutrition Reviews*, 52:201–07.

Pritchard, W.N. 1998. "The Emerging Contours of the Third Food Regime: Evidence from Australian Dairy and Wheat Sectors." *Economic Geography*, 74:64–74.

Ritzer, G. 1993. *The McDonaldization of Society.* Thousand Oaks, CA: Pine Forge Press.

_____. 1995. *Expressing America: A Critique of the Global Credit Card Society*. Thousand Oaks, CA: Pine Forge Press.

Robertson, R. 1990. "Mapping the Global Condition: Globalization as a Central Concept." *Theory, Culture and Society*, 7:15–30.

Roe, D. 1973. *A Plague of Corn: The Social History of Pellagra*. Ithaca, NY: Cornell University Press.

Rogers, R.; and R. Hackenberg. 1987. "Extending Epidemiologic Transition Theory: A New Stage." *Social Biology*, 34:234–43.

Rozin, E. 1983. *Ethnic Cuisine: The Flavor-Principle Cookbook*. Brattleboro, VT: Stephen Greene Press.

Salaman, R. 1985. *The History and Social Influence of the Potato*. London: Cambridge University Press.

Sefa-Dedeh, S. 1993. "Traditional Food Technology," in R. Macrae, R.K. Robinson, and M.J. Sadler, eds., *Encyclopedia of Food Science, Food Technology, and Nutrition*, 4600–06. New York: Academic Press.

Schaeffer, R. 1996. *Understanding Globalization: The Social Consequences of Political and Economic Change*. Lanham, MD: Rowman and Littlefield Publishers.

Schievelbusch, W. 1991 [1980]. *Tastes of Paradise: A Social History of Spices, Stimulants, and Intoxicants*, David Jacobson, trans. New York: Pantheon.

Senauer, B.; E. Asp; and J. Kinsey. 1991. *Food Trends and the Changing Consumer*. St. Paul, MN: Eagan Press.

Shannon, T.R. 1989. *An Introduction to the World-System Perspective*. Boulder: Westview Press.

Sklar, L. 1991. *Sociology of the global system*. Baltimore: Johns Hopkins University Press.

Sobal, J. 1991. "Obesity and Socioeconomic Status: A Framework for Examining Relationships between Physical and Social Variables." *Medical Anthropology*, 13:3, 231–47.

Sobal J.; L. K. Khan; and C. A. Bisogni. 1998. "A Conceptual Model of the Food and Nutrition System." *Social Science and Medicine*, 47:7, 853–863.

Sobal, J.; and A. J. Stunkard. 1989. "Socioeconomic Status and Obesity: A Review of the Literature." *Psychological Bulletin*, 105:2, 260–75.

Solomons, N.W.; and R. Gross. 1995. "Urban Nutrition in Developing Countries." *Nutrition Reviews*, 53:90–95.

Temple, N.J.; and D. P.Burkitt, eds. 1994. *Western Diseases: Their Dietary Prevention and Reversibility*. Totowa, NJ: Humana Press.

Thompson, S.J.; and J. T. Cowan. 1995. "Durable Food Production and Consumption in the World Economy," in P. McMichael, *Food and Agrarian Orders in the World Economy*, 35–52. Westport, CT: Praeger.

Timmer, C.P. 1988. "The Agricultural Transformation," in H. Chenery, and T.N. Srinivasan, eds., *Handbook of Developmental Economics*, 276–331. New York: Elsevier Science.

Trowell, H.C.; and D. P. Burkitt. 1981. *Western Diseases: Their Emergence and Prevention*. London: Edward Arnold.

Verrill, A.H. 1937. *Foods America Gave the World*. Boston: L.C. Page.

Wallerstein, I. 1974. *Capitalist Agriculture and the Origins of the European World-Economy in the Sixteenth Century*, vol. 1 of *The Modern World System*. New York: Academic Press.

_____. 1979. *The Capitalist World Economy.* Cambridge: Cambridge University Press.

_____. 1980. *Mercantilism and the Consolidation of the European World-Economy, 1600–1750*, vol. 2 of *The Modern World System*. New York: Academic Press.

Walton, J.; and D. Seddon. 1994. *Free Markets and Food Riots: The Politics of Global Adjustment.* New York: Cambridge University Press.

Warde, A. 1997. *Consumption, Food, and Taste: Culinary Antinomies and Commodity Culture.* Thousand Oaks, CA: Sage.

Wimberly, D.W. 1991. "Transnational Corporate Investment and Food Consumption in the Third World." *Rural Sociology*, 56:406–31.

Chapter Ten

Fat and Sugar in the Global Diet: Dietary Diversity in the Nutrition Transition

Adam Drewnowski

Chronic undernutrition is mostly a consequence of widespread poverty (World Development Report 1993). World economic development has been associated with both an improvement in and a progressive globalization of the human diet. As countries develop and populations become more urban, societies enter different stages of what has been called the nutrition and demographic transitions. As incomes grow, grain-based diets rich in complex carbohydrates and fiber are being gradually abandoned in favor of diets that contain more animal products, sugars, and vegetable fats. The nutrition gap between rich and poor countries grows narrower, as all nations converge on a global diet higher in meat, milk and sweeteners and deriving 30 to 35 percent of its energy from fat.

Such diets are often superior to what had gone on before. Yet changing dietary habits are regarded by many nutritionists as a deplorable by-product of global economic growth (Gopalan 1992). Nutritionists have warned that the nutrition transition in developing nations has been associated with a shift in disease patterns away from malnutrition and nutrient deficiency diseases and toward increased risk of cardiovascular disease, non-insulin dependent diabetes, and cancer (World Development Report 1993). A world-wide epidemic of childhood obesity is another potential consequence of changing lifestyles and changing diets. Childhood obesity is an intermediate health marker that can serve as a predictor of more diet-related chronic diseases to come (Popkin 1992). However, it must be noted that diet-related chronic diseases are still, for many nations, an indication of longevity. Higher life expectancy is another characteristic of the nutrition transition.

With relief efforts still focused on global malnutrition, international agencies dealing with developing nations have paid comparatively less attention to issues of overnutrition and nutritional imbalance (Popkin 1992). However, under- and overnutrition can coexist within the same society (Solomons and Gross 1995). One dilemma facing the World Bank and other agencies for international development is how to promote economic growth while preventing or delaying the more undesirable effects of the associated nutrition transition. The 1990 WHO Study Group recommended that developing countries begin formulating a nutrition and food policy more appropriate to the prevention of chronic diseases observed in the industrialized world (WHO 1990). Other writers have noted the need for effective nutrition education and intervention programs that would delay the pace of nutrition transition and postpone or reduce the growing risks of chronic disease (Popkin 1992; World Development Report 1993). These are all appropriate public health nutrition measures now being undertaken on a global scale.

A more extreme approach has been to resist economic development in the name of protecting public health. Indeed, some nutrition experts in developing nations openly dare hope that affluence never comes, at least not to the poor. Fearful that the nutrition transition in South East Asia is heading in the wrong direction, Gopalan (1992:15) pointed to the beneficial health effects of dire poverty, poor diets, and strenuous manual labor. "Fortunately," he wrote, "fast foods and soft drinks are beyond the reach of the poor, who, for this reason, will be spared." In this view, economic development is undesirable from the public health standpoint. He also argued that "fortunately, diets of the poorer segments of the population are low in fat and high in fiber. Development and affluence could alter this situation in an undesirable direction" (Gopalan 1992:92–93). He makes this point despite the fact that development and affluence have been generally associated with improved nutrition and improved public health.

Not surprisingly then, the general public sees the nutrition transition in Asia as a clash of cultures or a hostile encounter between East and West. Conventional wisdom has blamed the agriculture and food industries for the creeping Westernization of the Asian diet. Traditional ethnic foods—hot and freshly made—are said to be no match for ready-to-eat fast foods, junk foods, and soft drinks of little nutritional value that are finding increasing use, especially among urban middle class youth (Gopalan, 1992:15). Even the WHO Study Group noted that although food companies could develop nutritious foods, if they so wished, they continued to advertise foods rich in fat, sugar, and salt because the company could then maintain its profitability (WHO 1990:129). The observer is left with the impression that hamburgers, confectionery, and soft drinks—all products of multinational corporations—

are replacing vibrant ethnic cuisines and destroying unique food habits. In this imagined cultural encounter, foreign invaders win, and native populations lose.

The nutrition transition in developing countries has thus been presented as a form of alien invasion. Food imports, notably meat, milk and eggs, the advent of fast-food chains, and food consumption away from home have been singled out for special blame. The food industry has been held responsible for the globalization of the human diet and the reputed decline of native cultures and ethnic food habits. This has led to a certain nostalgia for dietary things past. Forgetting sometimes the very real disadvantages of rural poverty, some nutritionists in the United States and elsewhere have focused on the healthful aspects of diets of poverty, composed as they are of tubers, pulses, and grains.

As a result, there is a major global paradox in the making. As developing nations, particularly those in East and South East Asia, embrace a more diverse diet with a higher proportion of meat, milk, dairy products, fresh vegetables and fruits, the already affluent countries devote major educational resources to promoting simpler, plant-based diets rich in complex carbohydrates and fiber but low in fat. Whether affluent nations will ever voluntarily adopt diets of poverty is, of course, an open question. Current evidence suggests that global economic development and the nutrition transition are inextricably linked. Arguably (and this is a hotly contested point), the worldwide trend toward increased consumption of dietary fats will be difficult, if not impossible, to reverse. One reason is that diets higher in sugar and fat are typically more diverse and more varied. A search for dietary variety appears to be an innate human trait.

Global Transitions

The different typologies of change all apply to Asian nations (Popkin 1992). Countries move through demographic, epidemiological, and nutrition transitions at different rates of speed (World Development Report 1993). Demographic transition involves a shift from high fertility and high mortality to low fertility and lower mortality. Epidemiological transition involves the shift from infectious disease and malnutrition to a different pattern of chronic and degenerative diseases in later life, including obesity, diabetes, coronary heart disease, and cancer. Contemporary nutrition transition involves the elimination of systematic famine and the gradual replacement of staple grain crops with a higher fat diet that includes vegetable oils and animal fats (Popkin 1992). These trends, currently observed in Asian nations and elsewhere, can be tied directly to the level of economic development.

The changing diets of Japan and China, examined in relation to different stages of economic growth, provide a good example of how diets and incomes are tied. Japan went through a process of accelerated change from the

1940s through the 1970s, and its 1994 Gross National Product (GNP) exceeded that of the United States. China, with its still-low GNP, is at this point the most rapidly growing economy in the world. It will be interesting to see whether the dietary shifts and changes observed during the rapid economic growth of Japan will also occur in China. Patterns of dietary change following economic development in one country may predict the trajectory of future dietary trends in another.

Whereas China is entering the early stages of the nutrition transition, the United States is thought to be at its final stage (Popkin 1992). The typical American diet is rich in animal products and derives close to 60 percent of its energy from only two nutrients: sugars and fats. Nutrition policy efforts have been directed at getting the public to consume a plant-based diet rich in whole grains that is more typical of low-income countries. Whether such nutrition initiatives have led to major dietary changes is a debatable point. Despite major efforts at nutrition education and intervention, U.S. consumption of sugar and fat hit record highs in 1995, with even higher levels projected for 1996 (Putnam 1995). Nutritionists still disagree as to whether fat consumption has declined as a result of nutrition policy efforts. Though the proportion of energy from fat has declined from 37 to 34 percent, total energy intakes rose substantially; and the consumption in fat in grams per day has, in fact, increased from 1976–80 to 1989–91. The prevalence of obesity among U.S. adults during that period has also increased from 25 to 33 percent. Genetic predisposition, physical inactivity, and high energy density of the diet are typically mentioned as the chief causes of obesity in the industrialized world.

Why We Like Sugar and Fat

All children love sweets. Preferences for sweet taste are present at birth, serving to orient the infant toward sources of nutrients and energy. Children quickly learn to prefer those tastes and flavors that are associated with high-energy density and so thereafter tend to select foods that are sweet, rich in fat, or both. Not only is fat the most concentrated source of energy in the foods supply but the key ingredient that makes a diet flavorful, varied, and rich. Fat is responsible for the characteristic texture, flavor and aroma of many foods, and makes a major contribution to the overall quality of the diet. Preferences for sugar and fat appear to be universal, and mixtures of sugar and fat, such as chocolate, are among the most preferred of foods.

Nutritionists have long argued as to whether the desire for fat in the diet is physiologically determined. Studies in neuroscience, largely based on animal models, have focused on the role of brain peptides and neurotransmitters in determining the fat consumption. Fat consumption, at least in rats, may be under internal control. In human studies, opiate peptides, or endorphins, have been implicated in binge eating and eating disorders. Clinical studies

have explored the physiological nature of preferences and cravings for sweet
and high-fat foods. Developing drugs to curb such cravings has been the
long-term goal of the pharmaceutical industry. Existing medications for
weight loss are reputed to reduce the consumption of sweet, carbohydrate-
rich snacks but trigger sensations of satiety and well-being.

While the appetite for sugar and fat appears to be a universal human trait,
the amount of fat in the human diet is largely determined by socioeconomic
factors. The major factor influencing fat consumption is income. Although
references to the desirability of sugar and fat are scattered thoughout history
(starting with biblical references to the land of milk and honey), the consumption of high levels of meat and sugar by all strata of society is a relatively recent phenomenon. Diets of preindustrial societies were largely composed of starchy roots and coarse grains, with minimal amounts of animal
protein and animal fat. The nutrition transition has always involved a shift to
meat, milk, sugar, and vegetable oil. The present trends in Asia parallel,
within a much shorter time period, the more gradual evolution of diets in
Europe and the United States.

As the proportion of fats, saturated fats, and sugar in the diet increases in
proportion to growing incomes, the proportion of total dietary protein remains constant. The only change is the replacement of vegetable proteins
with animal proteins derived from milk and meat. Animal proteins are of
higher quality and have a full complement of amino acids. These data, show-
ing that protein consumption is independent of social and economic factors,
suggest that only protein intakes are likely to be regulated by internal physiological mechanisms. In contrast, the consumption of fats and saturated fats
may be governed simply by the availability of fats in the food supply.

Dietary Diversity and the Nutrition Transition

Changes in eating patterns that occur in the course of nutrition transition
have sometimes been presented in terms of an unaccountable shift towards a
small number of imported fast foods, rich in fat, sugar, or salt. Hamburgers,
ice cream and soft drinks are said to have replaced a broader variety of native
foods. That view is incorrect. In reality, the diets of poor societies are based
on a limited number of foods and are largely restricted to starchy roots,
pulses, and coarse grains. Though low in fat and high in fiber, these foods
neither offer much in the way of diversity or variety, nor contain the essential components of good nutrition, nor even offer much eating pleasure. Insofar as new foods are being introduced, they often include meat, milk, and
eggs, and other sources of animal protein and animal fat, as well as fresh vegetables and fruit. These foods are generally richer in fat, sugar, or both. Dietary variety, more accessible to increasing segments of the population, may
be the primary vehicle for increasing the proportion of fat and sugar in the
total diet.

Increasing fat and sugar consumption can therefore be viewed as indicative of a more varied diet that incorporates a higher level of animal protein and fat. Yet the conventional view (WHO Study Group 1990) has been that the proportion of fat in the diet, independent of any other food consumed, can threaten or promote health. The overwhelming priority in epidemiological studies has been given to tracking total fat, since animal fat (as proxy for saturated fat) and the intake of complex carbohydrates are markers of chronic disease worldwide. Using fat content as the sole measure of diet quality, some experts have concluded that global nutrition trends are unfavorable with respect to coronary heart disease (CHD) morbidity and mortality (Posner et al. 1994). However, fat consumption is only one aspect of diet quality—dietary diversity and variety are another.

Greater dietary diversity, coupled with the desire for more energy-dense foods, may be at the core of the nutrition transition. For such foods to be integrated into an everyday diet, some technological resources are needed; and these too depend on economic growth. These may include refrigeration, in other words power supply, and efficient systems of mass distribution and storage. Greater urbanization, that is a population shift from rural to urban areas, may in fact be an accelerating factor in promoting a nutrition transition.

Dietary Trends in Japan and China

The role of dietary diversity in the nutrition transition is illustrated by the example of the changing Japanese diet. In 1910 the daily per-capita intake in Japan consisted of 430 grams of carbohydrate (rice and beans), 13 grams of fat, and only 3 grams of animal protein. In 1989, the daily intake of carbohydrates dropped to 190 grams per day; but fat intake rose to 59 grams per day, and intake of animal protein rose to 42 grams per day. At the same time, the consumption of salt, the principal condiment for bland carbohydrates dropped from an estimated 30 grams per day to 12 grams per day.

During that time, traditional habits of eating rice (with salt) accompanied by soybean soup and preserved (pickled) vegetables with some fish and shellfish has been replaced by what the Ministry of Agriculture, Food and Fisheries (MAFF) calls the "new Japanese type eating habits": small servings of boiled rice, with the addition of meat, fish, vegetables, and milk. The Japanese diet now includes red meat, poultry, milk and other dairy products, eggs, fruit and fresh vegetables, all of which had been inaccessible to the average consumer. MAFF spokespeople specifically credit the economic revolution and provision of lunch to school children for these improvements in Japanese eating habits.

Although fat consumption in Japan has almost tripled between 1946 and 1987 (from 9 to 25 percent of daily energy), fat content of the diet is not the only criterion for diet quality. Changes in the Japanese diet are illustrated in Table 1. As recently as 1955, the Japanese diet was based on cereals (66

TABLE 10.1   Japanese Food Consumption (Kilograms per Capita per Year) from 1955 to 1994

Item	1955	1970	1975	1980	1985	1990	1993	1994
Cereals	156.1	128.5	121.5	112.9	107.9	103.5	103.0	100.9
Rice	111.0	95.3	88.0	78.9	74.6	70.0	69.2	66.3
Wheat	25.1	30.9	31.5	32.2	31.7	31.7	32.2	33.1
Other	20.0	2.2	2.0	1.4	1.6	1.8	1.6	1.5
Meats	3.3	13.4	17.9	22.5	25.1	28.5	29.9	30.6
Beef, Veal	1.1	2.1	2.5	3.5	4.4	6.1	7.4	8.0
Pork	0.8	5.3	7.3	9.6	10.3	11.5	11.4	11.5
Poultry	0.3	3.8	5.3	7.7	9.1	10.2	10.4	10.5
Whale	0.9	1.5	0.9	0.4	0.3	0.0	0.0	0.0
Fish, Shellfish	26.4	31.7	34.9	34.8	35.8	37.1	36.7	36.1
Eggs	3.4	14.8	13.7	14.3	14.9	16.5	17.9	17.8
Milk and Dairy	12.1	50.2	53.6	65.3	70.6	83.2	83.6	89.2
Fruit	12.3	37.7	42.5	38.8	36.8	37.4	39.3	42.8
Vegetables	82.6	115.9	109.4	112.0	110.2	107.2	102.6	102.9
Potatoes	46.2	16.1	16.0	17.3	18.6	20.6	19.8	20.4
Starches	4.6	8.1	7.5	11.6	14.1	15.9	15.1	15.7
Pulses (Soy)	9.4	10.1	9.4	8.5	9.1	9.3	9.2	9.2
Sugars	12.3	27	25.1	23.3	21.7	21.0	19.3	19.7
Fats, Oils	2.7	9	10.9	12.6	14.0	14.2	14.4	14.4

SOURCE: Japan's MAFF (1990–1991), Previous Issues, and (1996).

percent of daily energy), predominantly rice. This has now declined to 39 percent. In contrast, there were major increases in meat consumption (7.3 to 63.1 pounds per year), a huge increase in chicken consumption (35-fold), and major increase in the consumption of milk (6-fold) and eggs (5-fold). Although fish consumption is high, there has been a shift from cheap sardines, mackerel, and herring to more expensive salmon, tuna, shrimp, and lobster. The consumption of vegetable fats and oils increased from 6 to 31.5 pounds per year. The consumption of fruit and vegetables increased initially until 1970 but has stayed at about that level since. Most of the transition was accomplished through growth in domestic production, rather than imports.

Western observers, including WHO officials, commenting on the Japanese diet have invariably focused on the undesirable aspects of high fat consumption (WHO 1990). However, not all Japanese nutrition experts have shared this view. Although they all agree that "Western habits [have] penetrated Japanese life to an enormous extent, bringing important changes in dietary and eating practices" (Fujita 1994), these changes are viewed as beneficial. Some (like Matsuzaki 1994) note the benefits of the "excellently balanced ratio of animal to vegetable protein; retaining rice as main dish and adding more meat." Others are even more pointed, stating that "intake of animal foods, such as meat, eggs, milk, and dairy products, has markedly increased, resulting in expanded intakes of animal protein and fasts and total fats. This change has greatly improved the nutritional status of the Japanese people" (Fujita 1994).

The trend toward greater dietary diversity, previously observed in Japan, is also occurring in China. As in Japan, nutrition transition in China has been associated with rapid decrease in fertility, decline in mortality, and with increasing education and affluence (Popkin 1991). The new Chinese diet is more diverse and more varied, as well as being higher in both sugar and fat.

The major source of data regarding the Chinese diet is the 1989 China Health and Nutrition Survey (CHNS), based on household food-consumption data over three consecutive days and on individual dietary intake data (Drewnowski interview). Diet of the poor was clearly based on rice, millet, sorghum, cabbage, salted vegetables, pastes, soybean sauce and salt, with some red meat (pork). CHNS data show a substantial income-dependent increase in dietary diversity (Popkin et al. 1993: Table 2). Instead of millet, sorghum, and corn, higher-income respondents consumed rice and wheat. Vegetables and pickled vegetables were also replaced with more meat, poultry, eggs and dairy products, and fresh fruit. Perhaps most importantly, a greater proportion of high-income respondents consumed a greater variety of foods from all food categories. Only the consumption of coarse grains and starchy tubers (arguably healthy but undesirable foods) dropped

TABLE 10.2   Nutrition Transition in China: Changing Patterns of Food Consumption between 1970 and 1994 (Data in Kilograms per Capita Each Year)

Item	1970	1975	1980	1985	1990	1994
Cereals	168.9	177.9	201.6	230.0	226.7	222.3
Rice	90.9	92.8	98.1	115.0	110.2	108.6
Wheat	33.7	43.8	61.7	79.2	82.0	81.2
Other	44.3	41.3	41.8	35.8	34.5	32.5
Meats						
Beef, veal	0.2	0.3	0.3	0.4	0.9	2.7
Pork	6.8	8.1	11.4	15.5	19.9	26.8
Poultry	1.0	1.1	1.3	1.5	2.8	6.3
Eggs	2.0	2.2	2.5	4.6	6.3	11.3
Milk, Dairy	2.0	2.1	2.4	3.8	5.3	6.3
Fruit	7.6	8.8	10.3	14.5	21.2	31.8
Vegetables	56.1	59.7	68.5	73.4	81.2	86.6
Potatoes	13.4	13.3	11.1	10.8	11.2	15.4
Starches	116.1	107.7	92.8	66.5	58.3	59.3
Pulses (Soy)	5.8	5.0	4.9	4.6	2.8	2.9
Sugars (Raw)	2.4	3.0	4.3	6.5	7.4	7.4
Fats, Oils	1.7	1.7	2.9	4.0	5.1	6.0

SOURCE: FAO food balance sheets

sharply as a function of income. As people consumed more different foods, portion sizes dropped. As a result, mean number of grams consumed per person each day declined for all foods except meat, fresh fruit and alcohol.

Food balance sheets obtained from the Food and Agriculture Organization (FAO) in Rome provide another glimpse of the changing Chinese diet from 1961 to 1994. FAOSTAT data (1961–94) show an increase in cereal and vegetable consumption up to 1984. After that time, there was an increase in the consumption of meat, edible oils, sugar, eggs, fish, and to a lesser extent fruit. As a result, the proportion of energy from fat has increased as well.

Dietary Diversity and Economic Growth

Though nutrition transition has been conventionally described in terms of increased fat and sugar content, it also involves greater dietary diversity and variety. Higher incomes are generally associated with the consumption of a more varied diet. However, the quality of the total diet is typically judged by its sugar and fat content. By this measure, diets composed exclusively of rice and vegetables are "better" than more diverse diets that also contain meat, milk and eggs.

Differences in macronutrient composition of the diet between developed and developing nations has been documented by Perisse et al. (1962). A correlation based on some eighty-five nations demonstrated a direct relationship between the logarithm of the Gross National Product (GNP) in U.S. dollars, and the proportion of fat, saturated fat and sugar in the diet. This classic relationship is shown in Figure 1. A similar pattern of results was observed in the more recent INTERHEALTH study (Posner et al. 1994).

However, it must be noted that important differences exist among countries, culture tradition and cuisine, not to mention any genetic predispositions to disease. In addition, the consumption of a more diverse diet is inextricably tied to a higher GNP and other indices of economic development. For this reason, the net increase in fat consumption in Japan has actually been associated with better health, as measured by greatly increased life expectancy.

Sources of Dietary Fats

Descriptions of changing diets in Asia have tended to overstate the impact of Big Macs. In reality, vegetable oils contribute far more to global consumption than do meat or animal fats, and their production (and consumption) are growing. Between 1991–92 and 1996–97, the forecast of the global production of vegetable fats and oils rose from 60 to 71 million metric tons. In contrast, the production of visible animal fats (butter and tallow) has remained steady at approximately 12 million metric tons (11.9 versus 12.3). Principal oils include soybean, sunflower, rapeseed, palm oil, and peanut oil.

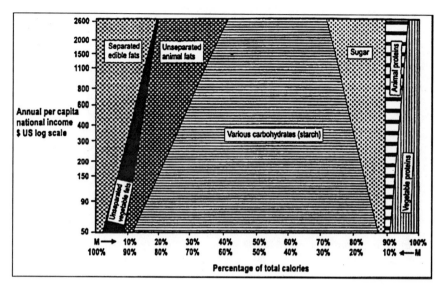

FIGURE 10.1   Structure of the Diet in Relation to GNP. Correlation Based on 85 Nations.

SOURCE: Perisse and Sizaret (1962).

With the exception of peanut oil, the global availability of each has approximately tripled between 1961 and 1990.

U.S. Department of Agriculture estimates (FAS Online 1996) show that China's production of oilseeds has gone up by 50 percent since 1991. At the same time oil imports more than tripled. Palm oil doubled; rapeseed oil tripled; and soybean oil went up 15 times (0.1 to 1.5 million metric tons). China now imports more soybean oil than it produces. However, China's vegetable oil imports are slowing down, perhaps in anticipation of growing consumption of meat.

Dietary Diversity Is an Irreversible Phenomenon

It has been generally accepted that nutrition change follows economic growth. However, it is also assumed that the two can be dissociated at will. Nutrition education and intervention programs in developed nations are geared to promote diets of poverty, high in fiber and low in fat. The approach suggested for developing nations has been to promote growth but formulate public health nutrition and food policies to delay the associated nutrition transition. It has been argued that the adoption of new dietary habits is slow and that sufficient time exists to put the necessary policies and programs in place. Yet available data strongly suggest that once a certain level of dietary variety (and therefore fat consumption) has been achieved, it may be irreversible. In reality, the consumption of a varied diet may be inseparable from other indices of economic development, such as motorized transport, improved sanitation, number of telephones, childhood immunizations and so forth. It may be naïve to think that we may revert to diets of poverty while retaining many other features of wealth.

What evidence supports this view? Examination of FAO food balance sheets and GNP data obtained from the World Bank clearly demonstrates that transient decreases in GNP (in Mexico, Venezuela and Chile in the 1980s) were not in fact accompanied by a corresponding decline in fat consumption (UN 1992:65). The proportion of fats in their diet continued to increase even though GNP per capita fell. It appears that once a certain level of fat in the diet is adopted by a population, if incomes fall, dietary patterns do not revert to the previous state. It will be interesting to see whether the trend can be reversed or slowed down through nutrition education and intervention strategies.

Globalization of the Human Diet

As the world economy grows, the nutrition gap between developed and developing nations continues to narrow. The new global diet is characterized by greater diversity and variety and a greater proportion of sugars and fat. These changing dietary patterns are the combined outcome of innate individual preferences coupled with the greater availability and accessibility of foods in the global economy. Whether this global trend is detrimental to public health is another issue. For their part, nutrition experts in developed nations have used fat consumption as the exclusive measure of diet quality. In the view of some, we should develop policies for education and intervention that would avert nutrition transition, steering the population toward a more healthy vegetarian-style diet.

The question is whether affluent nations will ever voluntarily adopt a diet of poverty. It is somewhat paradoxical that calls for a widespread adoption of a "Chinese-style" diet, rich in complex carbohydrates and fiber, with meat used only as a condiment, are more likely to originate in Boston than in Beijing. For their part, Chinese nutrition experts acknowledge that people who still consume such diets do so not because they are concerned about their health or because they like to but simply because they have no other choice. Residents of Asia are more in a position to appreciate newly won wealth and the improved nutritional quality of the diet. Even the American public, while often paying lip service to the principles of nutrition and good health, has come to appreciate the advantages of dietary diversity, variety, and eating pleasure, as demonstrated in this recent quotation from the USDA Food Report:

It may be chic in the current milieu of diet-health mania to say that one has cut back on meat and refined sugars, and people report as much in numerous consumer surveys. However, U.S. per capita food supply data indicate that Americans consumed record-high levels of caloric sweeteners and total meat in 1994. And, forecasters predict still higher consumption in 1995 and 1996 (Putnam 1995).

This is a global trend in food consumption that countries in East Asia and elsewhere will most likely follow.

References

Chevassus, Agnes S. 1994. "Disponibilites des lipides alimentaires dans le monde." *Food, Nutrition and Agriculture*, 11:15–22.

Drewnowski, A. 1989. "Sensory Preferences for Fat and Sugar in Adolescence and in Adult Life," in *Nutrition and the Chemical Senses in Aging*, C. Murphy, W.S.Cain, D.M. Hegsted, eds. Ann Arbor: New York Academy of Science, 561:243–9.

_____. 1992. "Linking Taste Perception and Eating Behavior to Obesity," in *A Trimmer Generation: Meeting the Challenge. Proceedings of the Seminar on Healthy Weight Management in Children and Adolescents.* Washington DC:ILSI Press.

_____. 1995. "Energy Intake and Sensory Properties of Food." *American Journal of Clinical Nutrition*, 62 (supplement),1081S–5S.

FAOSTAT.PC. 1961–94. *Food Balance Sheets 1961–94*. Rome: Food and Agriculture Organization.

Fujita, Y. 1992. "Nutritional Requirements of the Elderly: a Japanese View." *Nutrition Review*, 50:449–453.

Ge, K. 1995. "The Dietary and Nutritional status of the Chinese Population." *National Nutrition Survey*. Beijing: Chinese Academy of Preventive Medicine.

Chen, C; Z. Shao. 1990. *Food, Nutrition and Health Status of Chinese in Seven Provinces*, Beijing: China Statistical Publishing House.

Gopalan, G. 1992. "Nutrition in Developmental Transition in South East Asia." *Regional Health Paper SEARO*, 21:1–130. New Delhi: World Health Organization.

Lands, W. E. M; T. Hamazaki; K. Yamazaki; et al. 1990. "Changing Dietary Patterns." *American Journal of Clinical Nutrition*, 51:991–3.

Ling, T. W. 1992. "Food Consumption Trends in Singapore," in *A Trimmer Generation: Meeting the Challenge. Proceedings of the Seminar on Healthy Weight Management in Children and Adolescents*. Washington D.C.:ILSI Press.

MAFF (Ministry of Agriculture Food and Fisheries). 1994. Japan. *Food Balance Sheets*.

Matsuzaki, T. 1992. "Longevity, Diet and Nutrition in Japan: Epidemiological Studies." *Nutrition Review*, 50:355–59.

Perisse, J.; F. Sizaret; P. Francois. 1969. "The Effect of Income and the Structure of the Diet." *FAO Nutrition Newsletter*, 7:1–9.

Popkin, B. M. 1994. "The Nutrition Transition in Low-Income Countries: an Emerging Crisis." *Nutrition Review*, 52:285–98.

Popkin, B. M.; K. Ge; F. Zhai; X. Guo; H. Ma; N. Zohori. 1993. "The Nutrition Transition in China: a Cross-Sectional Analysis." *European Journal of Clinical Nutrition*, 47:333–46.

Popkin, B. M.; S. Paeratakul; F. Zhai; K. Ge. 1995. "A Review of Dietary and Environmental Correlates of Obesity with Emphasis on Developing Countries." *Obesity Research*, 3 (supplement 2),145s–153s.

Popkin, B. M.; S. Paeratakul; F. Zhai; K. Ge. 1995. "Dietary and Environmental Correlates of Obesity in a Population Study in China." *Obesity Research*, 3 (supplement 2), 135s–143s.

Posner, B. M.; M. Franz; P. Quatromoni; et al. 1994. "Nutrition and the Global Risk for Chronic Disease: the INTERHEALTH Nutrition Initiative." *Nutrition Review*, 52:201–07.

Putnam, J. J.; L. A. Duewer. 1995. "U.S. Per Capita Food Consumption: Record-High Meat and Sugars in 1994." *Food Review*, 18:2, 2–11.

Scott, L.; S. Shapouri. 1995. "World Food Consumption Up, But Not Everywhere." *Food Review*, 18:2, 48–54.

Solomons, N. W.; R. Gross. 1995. "Urban Nutrition in Developing Countries." *Nutrition Review*, 53:90–95.

Taha, F. A. 1993. "Japan Adds Western Flavor to Its Traditional Diet." *Food Review*, 16:30–37.

United States Department of Agriculture, World Agricultural Supply and Demand Estimates (WASDE–315), 1996. "FAS Online." July.

United Nations, ACC/SCN. 1992. *Second Report on the World Nutrition Situation*, 1–80, Geneva: United Nations.

World Bank. 1993. *World Development Report 1993. Investing in Health: World Development Indicators.* New York: Oxford University Press.

World Health Organization. 1990. "Diet, Nutrition, and the Prevention of Chronic Diseases." *Technical Report* series, 797:1–203. Geneva: World Health Organization.

Chapter Eleven

The 'Mad Cow' Crisis: A Global Perspective

Claude Fischler

The mad cow crisis has been described as an irrational, collective scare; a lethal epidemic with potential casualties in the thousands or hundreds of thousands; a criminal or quasi-criminal cover-up; an epitome of government negligence and bureaucratic incompetence; a tragic outcome of Conservative, laissez-faire policy and capitalist greed; as well as a pitiable failure of veterinary medicine and science. As the crisis unfolded, the only safe statement that could be made was that none of these characterizations was established but that none could be clearly and totally ruled out. The most striking feature of the crisis was that the risk involved could be assessed with no better accuracy than being within a range from zero to infinity.

The BSE crisis

A bit of background might help the American reader at this point, although I realize that there was rather extensive media coverage of the crisis in the United States and around the world. The disease, Bovine Spongiform Encephalopathy (BSE), was first identified in November 1986 in Britain. This degenerative neural disease has slow incubation (about five years) and is always fatal. It belongs to a category of diseases known as Transmissible Spongiform Encephalopathies (TSE). The most common TSE disease is scrapie, which has been recognized in sheep since the early eighteenth century and in humans as kuru or Creutzfeldt-Jakob Disease (CJD), a rare disease (about 1 case per 1 million) that is also always fatal. Kuru was studied in the 1950s by Victor Zigas and Carleton Gajdusek in the Fore tribe of Papua-New Guinea, who practiced endocannibalism, since they ate the bodies of deceased members of the tribe. Zigas and Gajdusek (who was later to receive a Nobel prize for his findings) observed that kuru was particularly prevalent in women and children. It turned out that the disease was transmitted through neural tissue absorbed in the course of cannibalistic rituals and that during these rituals women and children consumed the brains and various organs, while tribal men mostly devoured muscle. Apparently, infectivity was at its highest in neural tissues, and almost nonexistent in muscle, so the women and children were the most affected.

For a long time it was believed that these TSE diseases are transmitted by a virus of some particular type. Although the viral hypothesis has not been entirely abandoned, the consensus today is that the agent is of a non-conventional nature. Stanley Prusiner, a neurologist at the University of California, San Francisco, purified brain tissue from CJD victims and found that no genetic material (viruses are made of DNA or RNA) was present, only a protein. When laboratory animals were injected with the protein, some of them developed a spongiform encephalopathy. Prusiner named the protein "prion" and proposed a theory regarding TSEs that at first encountered considerable skepticism, to put it mildly. At. this point, there is still no consensus on the transmission of TSEs, but most of the scientific community accepts the premise that prions play at least a part in the process. Prusiner's prion theory has one major merit: It accounts for the otherwise inexplicable fact that TSEs are transmitted both genetically and by infection. The prion is, according to the theory, the pathogenic form (PrPsc) of a protein that is normally present in organisms (PrPc). The gene coding for the normal protein can be altered by a mutation, thus resulting in the coding for prions instead and the "sporadic" form of the disease. Yet prions seem to have the property of turning normal PrP proteins into pathogenic prions by contact through a mechanism that is still hypothetical. As a consequence, an animal can in turn develop the illness if fed tissue containing prions.

In the case of BSE, it became accepted, after two years of investigation by British epidemiologists, that the likely source for the disease was meat and bone meal fed to dairy cows to improve their production of milk. Meat and bone meal (MBM) is made by the rendering industry from slaughterhouse by-products and dead animals collected from farms. It was hypothesized that the initial source for BSE was the presence in the MBM of neural tissue from scrapie-affected sheep or from cattle that might have developed an undiagnosed, sporadic case of the disease.

A 1988 ban on MBM for ruminants failed to bring about the eradication of the disease for lack of sufficient enforcement. Only after 1993, when additional measures were taken, did the number of new cases begin to decrease. As of 1996, however, a total of 160,000 animals had been diagnosed with BSE in Britain. The export of MBMs to other countries is the most likely cause for the spread of BSE abroad, although it occurred much less frequently. The second most affected country is Switzerland, with about 230 cases. Ireland has declared about 150; Portugal, around 40; France, 22; and Germany, 4.

The big question, of course, was and still is: Can BSE be transmitted to humans? If it can, does it take the form of CJD? For the better part of ten years, it was widely believed and asserted that prions were prevented from jumping from one species to the next by a "species barrier." This dogma had already been eroded by various episodes, most particularly by the contamination of British cats, probably through pet food that included bovine offal.

The "meltdown" of March 20, 1996, occurred when the British government solemnly announced in the House of Commons that scientists closely following the epidemiology of Creutzfeldt-Jakob Disease had identified 10 cases (later to become 12) of what seemed to be a new form of the illness. The new variant (V-CJD) was different in that it affected young people and post-mortem examination of the brain tissues showed a specific type of lesion. According to these scientists, the most likely cause for this variant of CJD was contamination by the BSE agent before 1989.

From a Problem to a Crisis and from British to Global

The Bovine Spongiform Encephalopathy (BSE) crisis, after what was called the meltdown of that March in 1996 almost immediately exploded into a truly global dimension. France, Germany, and then the whole of the European Union embargoed British beef and beef-derived products in a matter of days. Other countries around the world followed suit. What had so far been a mostly British veterinary problem turned into a full-blown public health crisis.

The Oxford Dictionary defines "crisis," in a pathological sense, as "a point in the progression of a disease when an important development or change takes place which is decisive of recovery or death." The Greek verb "krisein" actually means "to decide." The central notion in the concept of crisis is thus precisely that of an eventually decisive stage marked by conflict and indecision. A crisis involves a situation of disorder, of *hubris*, with complex, multidimensional effects, often in opposite directions. A crisis can emphasize and accelerate existing trends or reverse them or trigger paradoxical countertrends. It does result in a different order of things. All this applies quite appropriately to the BSE case.

The official British statement and the ensuing embargo had repercussions around the world, even in remote areas and improbable segments of various markets. Governments, including those in developing or newly developed countries of the world, were forced to make decisions about the BSE risk even though their populations traditionally ate no beef to speak of. In the days following meltdown, Thailand announced that any imports of non-authorized beef or beef-derived products would be destroyed. In the Shenzhen area of Southern China, significant amounts of suspected meat were seized and destroyed. In Canton province, in early April, police even searched food factories, stores, markets, hotels and restaurants. About 2,000 foreign vessels were also searched while in port.

From the very first days of the meltdown, retail consumption of meat was affected, not only in Britain and Europe but all over the world. It fell by about 20 percent in France; by about twice this proportion in Germany, Britain, Italy; and by almost 70 percent in Greece at the peak of the crisis. But the consequences were also notable as far away as Korea and Japan (where the decline in consumption was accelerated by a massive, unrelated, food poisoning in the meat industry, particularly in those businesses involved in exporting, which were hit very severely).

The prices of livestock were also affected almost all over the world. For example, in central France, an area mostly devoted to prime-quality cattle farming, the price of a young steer went down about 40 percent compared to the prices in the year before. About the same drop was observed in Austria, Portugal, and other countries, not to mention Great Britain. Simultaneously, the price of pork went up by 30 or 40 percent in many European countries. At the Chicago Commodity Exchange, pork belly prices were very bullish. At the other end of the world, in China, there was a similar decline in consumption, along with a similar drop in cattle prices. New Zealand was hit as well, with livestock prices declining about 14 percent.

The Japanese and Korean manifestations of the crisis had very serious consequences for the Australian cattle industry, which competes with American beef in these rapidly emerging markets. According to members of the Australian industry, the Americans were more adept at distancing themselves from the mad-cow crisis and, as a consequence, actually gained market share, even though the global market was shrinking. The same thing was observed in Argentina, which apparently took some advantage of the crisis to assert itself as one of the leading producers of "safe" beef.

National Territories versus International Networks

Thus, the crisis clearly affected markets in livestock, meat and meat products all over the world. But it also became clear, at a very early stage, that other markets were to be affected as well. The complexity of modern industry and trade became increasingly obvious as the big scare emerged and began to involve products that no one in the public had previously thought came from beef. Such was the case, for instance, with gelatin (derived in part from bovine bones), which is used in innumerable products, such as pharmaceuticals, candy, yogurt, processed foods and cosmetics. (Even lipstick came under suspicion from consumers.) Governments tried to protect such products but had nevertheless not thought of everything. In France, for instance, surgical thread made of bovine tissue was overlooked and was still authorized.

The crisis revealed one very important feature of modern societies: that they are enmeshed in increasingly complex networks of trade, exchange, and general interaction. Any local government can, with adequate organizing and management, control what happens at its more limited level. However, it is much more difficult, if not impossible, to achieve control over complex, international networks.

Global Trends and Local Features

As noted earlier, the BSE crisis accelerated trends that had been dormant or already apparent in various countries. This was the case with the perception and consumption of beef in particular and meat in general. For much of the twentieth century, meat consumption had been increasing all over the developed world. In fact, for centuries, people have consistently increased the rate of their consumption of meat as their incomes rise, which is why historians have been using levels of meat consumption as a reliable indicator for prosperity. This was no longer so after the 1980s. For the first time, in the Western world, the trend seemed to reverse itself, first in the United States, then in Europe. In France, this became apparent in the middle of the 1980s, when it was not only a matter of price and affordability but also the young and the affluent's shunning of red meat, particularly the cheaper cuts, in favor of such other sources of proteins as chicken, turkey, and fish.

Another world-wide trend was the turn against processed foods and modern technology in general. The history of food consumption since the rise of the great food processors has been ridden with bursts of anxiety and distrust, if not panic, regarding processed foods. Rumors and urban legends about problems with fast foods or various products have abounded. There have been recurring "scares." In Germany, a 1987 prime-time television program showed in great detail dangerous parasitical worms in fish from the North Sea, creating an almost fatal crisis in the German fishing industry. Earlier on, in France, high levels of synthetic hormones in veal (a then highly popular meat) caused a scare that resulted in a long-term decline in consumption and increased substitution of chicken and turkey (a newcomer on the French market) for veal.   •

Such distrust can be ascribed to the fact that modern consumers of increasingly processed foods experience a disturbing sense of distance and mystery in relation to those elaborate products they are supposed to take into their bodies. They have no sense of what these foods are made of nor how they have been produced. This clashes with the very basic, universal perception that "you are what you eat," the notion that the identity and integrity of the self are constructed by what is consumed. To a certain extent, not knowing what one eats results in not knowing who one is. At any rate, it produces anxiety.

While distrust of processed foods produced frequent tension in the form of rumors, panics, and other crises, the mad cow scare seems to surpass them all in terms of the tensions it created and its sheer scale. Although the bases for the prejudice against beef before the mad cow scare were global, it is interesting to note that they seemed to vary with local culture. In Britain, America, and Northern Europe, the health factor was crucial. Beef was indicted for the saturated fat it contained, its role in the etiology of coronary heart disease, and—if contained in processed foods—also suspected of being detrimental to one's health because of pesticides, additives, and so forth, in such foods. In addition, consumers in America and Northern Europe supported the opposition to eating beef because of increasing concerns for the rights of animals and for the popularity of various forms of vegetarianism often associated with anti-capitalist and feminist stances. In southern Europe, in contrast, particularly in France, the motivations were not nearly so oriented to health and ethics. Interviews and surveys showed that the main concern was taste and quality. Beef had first slipped out of fashion in haute cuisine when top chefs used beef only on occasion and then only the best cuts of prime quality beef. When the mad cow crisis started in France, the same logic prevailed, so that sales of ordinary beef sold in the supermarket were the most severely hit; while upmarket products, which could provide guarantees of origin (*labels de qualité*), absorbed the shock best. This is consistent with general features of food markets across Europe and the world: Southern, Latin, Catholic Europe is more concerned with quality than the best nutrition. Southern Europe values the dimensions of enjoyment and sociability associated with food, while North America, Britain, Northern Europe, predominantly Protestant cultures, have a more moralistic, anxiety- and guilt-ridden approach to eating.

The BSE Crisis as a Global Rorschach Test

The global aspects of the BSE crisis are many, yet one of them is particularly striking: The fact is that the mad cow works like a giant, global perception test that seems to invite everyone to supply his or her own explanation. Alas, understanding and explaining the crisis and extracting meaning from it are indeed not easy tasks by any means.

The political and economic dimensions of the BSE crisis are lost to few people. The British cattle farmers tend to blame Europe, its regulations as well as its protectionism. Continental farmers, in contrast, blame Great Britain, its government, and its isolationism. French farmers and their unions tend to rationalize the crisis in terms of a conspiracy manipulated by the United States in retaliation for a previous European ban on cattle treated with synthetic hormones. Rumors and interpretations, such as those discussed in this essay, which reflect political and national biases and interests abound. Yet one type of reaction—that of regarding this crisis as the kind of threat reminiscent of archaic, very basic responses to catastrophes like plagues and disasters—seems to be universal.

The mad cow epidemic is perceived as punishment for some human misbehavior that caused it in the first place by attracting some sort of a sanction, the most common description of this misbehavior being the conversion of herbivores into carnivores or even into cannibals. In this sense, there is a religious or a covertly religious dimension in the perception of this crisis that crossed national boundaries. And the culling of hundreds of thousands of cattle, in this light, takes on an entirely different dimension. In ancient Greece, a hecatomb was the offering of a hundred oxen. In the BSE crisis, one could speak in kilohecatombs or even megahecatombs—quantities of truly global proportions.

Part Four

Eating Together Globally

Chapter Twelve

The Family Meal and Its Significance in Global Times

Alex McIntosh

Families and the meals they eat vary in nature over time and space. Were researchers able to observe these during the Roman Empire or the early Middle Ages, they might find the view quite alien. Similarly, a look at families and the meals they eat across the cultures of today's world would also yield a number of surprises. Presently, the family as an institution is undergoing what many consider to be fundamental and perhaps fatal changes. This is occurring at a time in which much of the world's cultural diversity has diminished as a result of the last several centuries of colonialism and the increase in international connections, particularly in this century. Both families and meals have altered because of these forces. Today, the world is confronted by even greater homogenizing processes through what is called globalization. This major turning point has fundamentally altered production and labor practices, consumption patterns, and cultural traditions. There is some concern that globalization will further weaken the family and its meals. Part of the attraction of families is the role they play in the socialization of children. The concern expressed over the disappearing family meal lies in its perceived role in promoting family solidarity and contributing to the socialization of children.

In order to address globalization and its possible impacts on families and meals, it is necessary to understand the importance of the family as a social institution and the role the family meal plays in it. After a brief discussion of these, I move to an abbreviated history of the Western family's meal patterns and child-rearing practices and the part that meals play in these, then to those of the present-day third world. A brief discussion of globalization follows before concluding with an examination of the possible effects of globalization on families and family meals. For my purposes here, I will assume that despite differences, a kinship unit, somewhat similar to what we refer to as the family, is a universal institution. Likewise, I assume that such units engage in collective eating practices of some sort and will refer to these as meals, fully cognizant that since great diversity exists in family structure and the norms and values that govern it, similar variety in the structural and normative aspects of meals also exists.

The Importance of the Family

Historically, the family's importance lay in its basic role in production. For most of their existence, human beings have survived through the collective efforts of family members (Lenski et al. 1991). Food production at the subsistence level, for example, has almost always involved family labor and management. Even in more recent times, during which corporate farming has increased, family members form these economic structures (McIntosh 1996).

The family has proved a significant social institution in other ways. Because of its connection to production, it remains the mechanism for the intergenerational transfer of wealth. Furthermore, the family's involvement in the production and control of wealth has made it a source of political power. Families also sustained the earliest forms of religion and these in turn have provided the family with ideological support. At the present time, many religious institutions continue to sanctify the family.

One important role that the family continues to play is in the socialization of children as new members of society. This enables their participation in social activities and makes possible their eventual contribution as productive members of society. Furthermore, socialization has a bearing on the kind of person the child becomes in adulthood. Developmental psychology argues that many dysfunctions of adulthood result from childhood experiences, particularly those that involve the family.

Functional analyses of the family indicate that the meal has several functions, including the integration of the family unit and the socialization of children by providing instruction in social practices. Others have argued that family meals may instead be battlefields readily available to continue family hostilities and develop family pathologies. Despite evidence that supports these claims, the family meal is considered by many to represent a final bulwark against the destructive forces of the market and modern hedonistic culture.

The Importance of the Family Meal

Many believe that the family meal represents a cornerstone of family viability. Social critics and theorists alike have argued that the family meal has a history as long as the family itself and has served as a basic mechanism of family integration and solidarity. Some would claim that, unlike other social entities, families cannot continue to exist without some degree of solidarity. The basic argument suggests that human beings have needs and corollary drives that must be satisfied and that, for social stability, these must be accommodated in an orderly, predictable fashion. Furthermore, social order depends on the accommodation of these needs and drives with available resources; and families continue to be the site at which most basic human needs are met (McIntosh 1996).

Analysis of the family meal has resulted in the identification of a number of functions that are obtained by first positing the functions that families provide society and then deducing the functions of the meal from these. The first is, of course, integration. Sharing food as a group promotes group identification. This process begins with the provision of food to infants, primarily by the mother. It is reinforced not only by communal seating but also by the use of common serving plates and bowls. This sharing routine contributes greatly to the sense of a shared fate and history. Solidarity, in turn, provides motivational energy, so the participant willingly takes on family and community responsibilities. The motivation to fulfill family goals is assisted by the focusing of physical and mental energy that can occur in settings in which the whole family is present. Part of this comes as the result of the information that is typically shared during a meal (Lewis and Feiring 1982). Finally, the socialization that takes place during family meals inculcates food knowledge and preferences as well as the norms that govern behavior while eating. It is through interaction at meal time that children learn food-related emotions, the most profound of which is disgust (Rozin 1988). More generally, the routinized context provides a medium for social interaction through which personality and concept of self are formed (DeGarine 1972), but we have no guarantee that families and family meals have always functioned in similar ways.

Functionalists base their analysis on the observation of modern and traditional societies, although only for limited periods of time. In fact there is some evidence that not all families in either modern or traditional societies consume their food as a group (Visser 1991; MacClancy 1995). There are class and ethnic differences both in the act of eating with others and in the social importance attributed to group food consumption. There is also the suggestion that a fundamental break in the meal patterns and their importance for human sociality occurs when making the transition to modernity.

Pasi Falk (1994) has developed a neo-structuralist view of the meal that focuses primarily on integration and social solidarity. His analysis begins with the dichotomy found in much of classical sociology: the distinction between mechanical and organic societies. The former is based on tight social bonds and a low level of individuation. In such societies, the division of labor is minimal. The latter, the organic sort, is based on a complex division of labor, looser social bonds, and greater individuation. Meals in mechanical societies have tremendous integrative importance, for the experience of shared eating is the experience of sharing society. It is to eat society itself. This experience is far more important than the interaction that goes on during such events. Interaction during meals has superseded the importance of eating in modern, organic societies. Because of greater individuation, this interaction does not require the meal per se and, in fact, individual choice now gives a person the freedom to eat what he or she wants with whom he or she wants.

In fact, the contemporary notion that family meal is the important social ritual seems to have been the invention of the nineteenth century, when the idea first developed of the compassionate family in a home as a sanctuary (Gillis 1996). I think that if families do indeed perform universal functions, then many of these are in fact accomplished through a myriad of activities, not just meals. As a unit of production, family members are brought into frequent contact during the waking hours of the day. Meals, in fact, are often woven into other activities. Thus, meals are often taken at the site of the work itself. Surely socialization and other family functions take place as a part of these activities as well, a phenomenon suggested during my observation of the work days of peasants in Laos in the late 1960s.

The History of Meals

What observers know of the history of meals depends on the written record; what is known of contemporary meals in both traditional and modern societies results from observational studies of various sorts. The historical record tends to be incomplete for a number of reasons. First, the meal is perhaps sufficiently mundane that observers and diarists failed to record it. Much of the historical record regarding food discusses feasts and banquets rather than ordinary, everyday family meals. Second, much of what has been written has to do with comportment at meals, primarily in the form of advice about proper behavior. Something about eating habits and perhaps everyday norms governing them can be inferred from this literature, but this provides a very incomplete picture.

Most of the historical work on European families that contains extended discussions of meals and mealtimes begins with the period just prior to the Victorian Age. Gillis (1996) would likely argue that this lack reflects the relative unimportance of these events. Yet this disparity may result from a simple absence of information, for others have indicated that at least among some classes, meals were important social events governed by precise rules of conduct (Jeanneret 1987). Furthermore, Aymard et al. (1996) assert that from the thirteenth century to the present, laborers regularly claimed the right to regular mealtimes and for many years resisted the three-meal-a-day schedule favored by industry. In addition, meals were important in non-European cultures as well. The Chinese, for example, purposely scheduled meals in order to differentiate themselves from animals (Aymard et al. 1996).

Writing about the period between the Black Death and the Industrial Age, Gottleib (1993: 43) suggests that meals served as "a source of some pleasure, but they were often rudimentary and bleak for the poor and a reminder of hierarchical arrangements for everyone." Furthermore, "sitting down together [as a family] for a formal meal may have been almost as rare as eating meat" (Gottleib 1993: 44). While Gottleib may have it right, I choose to quibble with several parts of her remark. First, some have claimed that after the Black Death, Europeans ate meat with some degree of regularity (Livi-Bacci 1991). Second, Gottleib's use of the word formal may leave open the possibility that families ate informally but together. Gottleib (1993) also suggests that peasants ate in silence, a description often used in commentaries about mealtime norms in present-day, lower-class households of the West; similarly, some have claimed that not all cultures of the third world place high value on conversation during meals. Like Gottleib, O'Day (1994) provides little detail regarding meals before industrialization but notes that peasants began the day with "a meal and a prayer." However, some of the household members had already departed for fields and pastures when this occurred. In some families, members would not gather together again until the evening meal; in others, a few would return home for lunch. Some families practiced sex segregation at mealtime, but others were so inclusive that servants sat at the same table and ate the same fare as the family (O'Day 1994). Gillis (1996) argues that the earlier conception of family and household differed significantly from both those of the Victorian Age and those of the present. People ate together in households but did so as a matter of convenience instead of as an opportunity to develop and maintain family solidarity. As recently as the early nineteenth century, according to his account, women and children ate at no special time in no special place. At the same time, there is evidence that family mealtime in present-day, third-world countries is more than a matter of convenience or efficiency.

When they examined periods for which more information is available, researchers have found that families in the eighteenth century differentiated eating little from other activities at least in one sense: Families took their meals in the same room in which the parents slept (Perrot 1991). The seating arrangement reflected the authority structure of the family itself, in that the husband sat in a place from which he could not only monitor other family members but also the street, the courtyard and the corner of the house in which the family papers were stored. The wife sat to the right of her husband; sons sat on his left; and daughters were seated next to their mother (Perrot 1991: 514). O'Day's account (1994) argues that in middle-class families, hierarchical seating patterns at meals were absent. In many households, however, the mother spent little time in her seat, since it was her task to serve the meal; the father sliced the bread and distributed food to the rest of the family. There is some suggestion that the seating assignments and interaction patterns served to instill proper manners, including appropriate behavior and respect for elders. These descriptions, however, cannot be taken as universal, since they may be a product of particular cultures and classes during particular periods of history.

By the nineteenth century, the home in France had come to be viewed as a haven from work for men (Perrot 1991), in which women were expected to make meals contribute to this ambiance. Advice books stressed the importance of creating an "agreeable atmosphere." In writing about the middle class in Victorian America, Kasson (1987: 135) cited advice manuals that argued the meal should be "civilized; it should bestow pleasure and dignity on the satisfaction of our needs." Gentle conversation was recommended. However, mealtimes represented an opportunity for molding young minds and were not without some unpleasantness, as we shall see. In many Victorian households, children ate separately until they could adhere to rigid behavioral prescriptions and proscriptions regarding eating and speaking. Even in middle- and lower-class households at the end of the century, American parents excluded their children from teatime (Jamieson 1994). Re-emphasis on the importance of the family in the molding of character and on family activities appeared early in the twentieth century and then again after the Second World War (Matthews 1987; Margolis 1984).

Family meals today tend to be far less formal affairs than those of the Victorian middle and upper classes. Formality may, of course, vary to some degree with social class as is the case in present-day France (Bourdieu 1984). In fact formality is one of the means by which classes in the past have distinguished themselves from others (Grignon 1996; Mennell 1985). Lamont's comparison (1992) of the upper-middle classes in France and the United States indicates that while Americans make little use of culinary distinctions to distinguish themselves from other classes, the French continue to do so. Americans do, however, distinguish between wine and beer drinkers in class terms. Their chief means of distinction, however, is the possession of audiovisual equipment and automobiles (Lamont 1992).

Meals, Manners, and Child Development

While it seems clear that parents loved their children in colonial America, belief in the inherent evil of children justified the parents' use of beating and whipping as punishment and as a means of building character. Fear of this punishment was felt to be a strong motivator (Coontz 1992: 213). Europeans held similar beliefs about childhood and child rearing. Nineteenth-century advice manuals were written during a period when children were thought to be more malleable. No longer were children considered intrinsically bad; instead, they represented blank slates upon which parents could inscribe good character. During this period in Europe and to a lesser degree in the United

States, manners served not only as a means for distinguishing oneself from the lower classes but also as a mechanism to prevent rough, rude habits from forming. Children and home life in general were to be shielded from a corrupting world. Social conservatives, for example, applauded middle-class efforts to dine privately and to admit only a few carefully chosen friends to their tables (Kasson 1990). It was during this period that the separate dining room became a standard in new homes. Advice books suggested that along with the parlor, the dining room should receive the greatest amount of investment in furnishings because of its importance as a quiet place where all the family could congregate (Green 1983). At the same time, reformers in the United States directed some of their efforts so that immigrants could be taught American ways of eating (Levenstein 1988).

Education of children was to begin with weaning, which commenced shortly after the first birthday. The use of aversive stimuli served as the chief means of bringing this about as it continues to do in some third world countries today (Morton 1996). Mealtimes served as a major training ground in these efforts. Children were to see their fathers as the king, their mothers as the queen, and themselves and family servants as subjects (Green 1983). Parents could thus expect absolute obedience. Children would not only be properly shaped by obedience and self denial, but also their happiness was seen to hinge on it. To create a sense of responsibility, children were assigned a place at the table as well as a set of dishes and silverware of their own.

Guilt rather than fear was the preferred motivational response parents believed most salient and the use of punishment by example was employed. This might have included banishment from the dinner table for an infraction, either to eat by oneself in the kitchen or not eat at all. During this period, however, the notion prevailed that a rebellious child had to be broken. Such resistance was to be put down swiftly and strongly. Physical punishment was not unusual and could involve whipping or beating; children carried into adulthood memories of the pain inflicted by such punishment (Greven 1990). An example of such harshness is provided by the case of the Reverend Frank Stafford, who reacted to his son's refusal to obey a command by keeping the six-year-old locked in his room for seventy-two hours without food or water.

Child-rearing manuals not only provided advice about comportment but also made recommendations regarding the use of foods for character development. "Food for children was to be plain, dull, and heavy. Victorians justified starving the taste buds of their offspring in this way because they thought that the youngsters' digestive systems feeble and imperfect. . . Parents' reasons for imposing this rigorous regime were not just alimentary. In the late nineteenth century, authority was everything and children were to be the puppets of their masters" (MacClancy 1992: 47). Some even held that, if children showed dislike for a food, this was proof that the food was good for them. Apparently, American parents permitted their children to eat what they liked from what was placed in front of them and, despite similar concerns regarding spiciness and character development, provided them with less bland food.

In descriptions of various types of nineteenth-century households, mealtime was to feature talk but only if it was highly constrained by the mores of restraint and comportment. These rules were aimed at adults; children were to be seen and not heard. The fact that in many households children stood rather than sat indicated the limited range of actions open to them relative to the seated adults. Treatment of children at meals and other places and events reflected the prevalent parenting styles of the period.

Child Rearing and Parenting Style

Baumrind (1967) developed a classification scheme of parenting that accounts for the methods of punishment, participation by children in decisions that affect them, and emotional responsiveness. In the authoritarian-autocratic pattern, parents make greater demands on their children than their children are able to make on them. Parents recognize that their children have needs but allow no expression of these needs by their children (Macoby and Martin 1987). In the extreme, the child may not speak unless given permission to do so. Rules governing behavior are never negotiated, much less discussed. Proper behavior is maintained through punishment rather than expectations for maturity. The emotional environment of the home is likely to be cold and inexpressive. Behavioral infractions result in severe punishment. Families of this sort are referred to as parent-centered. Children reared in such homes are found to be obedient, lacking in creativity, and emotionally starved (Macoby and Martin 1987).

Both indulgent and permissive parents generally tolerate the impulses of their children, use little punishment, assert little authority, expect little maturity, and make few rules. Most indulgent parents are emotionally responsive while permissive parents tend to be emotionally disconnected. Children from such families tend to remain immature, lack self-control, act non-aggressively, and take little independent, responsible action (Macoby and Martin 1987). Authoritative-reciprocal patterns of parenting involve expectations of mature behavior, based on clear standards of conduct, firm enforcement of rules without the use of harsh punishment for infractions, open communication, and recognition of the rights of both parents and children. Children raised in such homes tend to exhibit greater competence, social responsibility, and greater independence than children raised with other styles of parenting (Macoby and Martin 1987). The goals of authoritative parenting generally involve raising children who are respectful of others but capable of independent, responsible action.

The variety of parenting styles extant in the present and their relationship to social class and ethnicity should alert us to the possibility that parenting techniques and ideologies of the past may differ from those of today and that these styles may have varied across region, by class, and other salient features of family background in the past. Greven's work (1977, 1991) on parenting in America from the seventeenth to the twentieth century demonstrates this is indeed the case. He found three types of parenting that parallel closely those identified by Baumrind. Authoritarian styles predominated in the seventeenth century, and rural and frontier families continued to emphasize a strict upbringing bolstered by physical punishment. Authoritative parents emphasizing "love and duty" rather than "love and fear" outnumbered authoritarian parents by the eighteenth century. Ferguson (1997) also describes family types that conform to the Baumrind scheme. Most families raised their children with an eye toward both independence and obedience as well as responsiveness to the needs of kin and neighbors. Part of the movement toward more authoritative styles of parenting may have had something to do with the movement away from an agrarian way of life toward one in which family labor was less vital to family survival and prosperity.

Parenting in the Third World

LeVine et al. (1994), Berry et al. (1992), and Whiting and Edwards (1982), among others, have sought to identify universal insights with regard to child rearing. They conclude that these vary with economic circumstances. In societies in which family-produced food security is paramount to survival, children are raised with the goal of developing character traits consistent with persons who, at an early age, will become entry-level workers in a family-based, hierarchical work unit. In such places, children are raised to be obedient and respectful in dealing with elders and to be responsible for subsistence and taking care of siblings (LeVine et al. 1994; Berry et al. 1992). Children are also taught to think in terms of group survival rather than individual gain. In some places, care and concern for others is stressed as well (Morton 1996; Bhanthumnavin 1985; Jansen 1997). Ethnic differences in parenting thus reflect differences in economic advancement. For example, Chinese immigrants in the United States are found to be more controlling and not as warm as Chinese-American parents (Lin and Fu 1990). Greek children are raised under more authoritarian patterns, although this tendency occurs less in urban than in rural homes (Georgas 1989).

Parents in subsistent-dependent societies tend to make greater use of shame, ridicule, and physical punishment in dealing with children than do Western households. In Okinawa, children are ridiculed after one year of age if they ask to be carried (Maretzki and Maretzki 1966). Morton (1996) reports that parents are excessively indulgent and punitive of their children. Both Thai and Tonganese children are sometimes punished for no apparent reason (Bhanthumnavin 1985; Morton 1996). Japanese mothers apply guilt in some situations by implying that to disobey is to threaten the bond between child and parent (Azuma 1986).

Altruism is a trait not mentioned in the literature on parenting. Children in Western societies are taught to respect and help others, but these qualities are not given the same emphasis as more individualistic traits. In a number of third-world countries, altruism is taught beginning at an early age. Tongans associate the provision of sufficient food as a sign of love; both Tongan and Jordanian children are taught to share their food with younger children (Morton 1996; Jansen 1997). Similarly, Fijians' personal bodily state (weight) is perceived as an indicator of how well the person's family cares for her or him (Becker 1995) and of the person's ability to make significant contributions to the community.

Modern Families, Modern Meals

Despite claims regarding the importance of family meals in contemporary life, little research on the topic exists. Among the first U.S. researchers to take the family meal seriously as a social event of some importance was William Bossard. One study of the American family that he conducted with Eleanor Boll involved the identification of family rituals which provided many functions for the family (Bossard and Boll, 1950). These rituals, defined as fairly rigid patterns of behavior that develop over time in a group, helped families develop a sense of identity and social integration. They eventually become habitual and infused with emotion. Some are passed down from one generation to the next. These rituals included dinner, Sunday lunch, and Saturday night recreation, to name only a few (Bossard and Boll 1950). Rituals appeared to be more prevalent in the middle than lower classes. Finally, they suggested that family rituals would likely increase as leisure time increased, but this was a prediction made during the 1950s.

Bossard's *The Sociology of Childhood* (1948), in which an entire chapter is devoted to the family meal, was based on data obtained through an unspecified number of observations of families as they ate meals together. From these observations, he concluded that meals represented one of many family activities that served indirectly to socialize children. At the table children learned about culture and how to interact with others, sharing information with other family members. DeGarine (1972) had made much the same observation about the functions of meals in the third world. More recently, analysts have begun to argue that family rituals such as meals promote family stability and shelter them from some of the worst consequences of stressful life events (Boyce et al. 1986; Bennett et al. 1987; Wolin and Bennett 1984).

Other, non-functionalist accounts of family meals exist but, again, are few in number. Gullestad (1984) provides considerable detail about meal patterns in suburban Norway. Four meals with little ritual are the daily norm. Most families do not possess a dining room but eat in the kitchen instead. Food at the table is served directly from pots and pans. An effort is made to schedule dinner at a time at which all family members can be present; the dinner hour and the complexity of the meal varies with the work schedules of both parents (Gullestad 1984). Goode et al.'s description (1984) of Italian-American family meals relates much the same picture regarding work and meal scheduling. These accounts say little about mealtime interaction or its role in child socialization.

The extant literature on family meals of the past several decades hints at socialization practices. Implicit in many of these accounts is the authoritative model of parenting. Other accounts, however, explicitly demonstrate more authoritarian patterns. Many women in England and the United States appear to subscribe to the view that meals provide both a time for family togetherness and child socialization. DeVault (1991) describes the amount of invisible work that mothers devote to constructing meals. This means that mothers acquire knowledge of the likes and dislikes of each family member and then incorporate this when they shop and cook. She asserts, in fact, that women develop the notion of family among family members by means of successful meals. Other scholars who focus on low-income mothers have found that the sociability during mealtime ranked highest among the values they placed on meals, followed by concerns for the health of family members and the cost of the meal (Suitor and Barbor 1982). Charles and Kerr (1988) found, however, that while lower-class women in England attempted to prepare meals that would create harmony in the home, they were more constrained by insufficient resources than were their middle-class counterparts. American women relied on childhood memories in their attempts to construct happy homes (DeVault 1992), and many of Lupton's (1995) Australian respondents reported a strong sense of nostalgia for the meals and foods of their childhood, although many admitted, when pressed, that family meals were often rife with conflict.

Middle-class parents in particular also view the meal as a proper means of child socialization. Most also claim that persuasion rather than coercion is the method of choice when attempting to teach from the dinner table not only the principles of proper eating but of proper behavior in general. Many would consider a dinner, for example, ruined if conflict or the exchange of harsh words took place. This describes well the behavior of authoritative parents; yet research on families in the United States demonstrates that families adhere to multiple parenting styles rather than to just the authoritative. These styles ought to be apparent in mealtime interaction.

Observational studies of family meals have not, however, reported evidence of authoritative parenting during meals, and interviews with women regarding their efforts to "construct" families through meals tend to portray little serious conflict. Some studies, like Lupton's (1995), elicit reports of conflict only after the respondents are pressed in this direction. Morrison's article (1994) begins with a quote from one of her respondents whose childhood memories of family meals were so "horrible" that even at the time of the interview, she still could not enjoy either preparing or eating a meal. The extremes that some families take with regard to meals is described by Ellis (1983), whose sample of lower-class women reported physical abuse by husbands angered because a hot meal was not ready and waiting for them when they returned from either work or bars at unpredictable times at night.

A handful of studies have attempted to measure the effects of parental efforts to influence their children's eating habits while at the dinner table. Several studies indicate that the more forcefully a parent attempts to gain compliance in eating, the more likely children are to eat what they are told (Elvera-Ezzell 1990; Kleges et al. 1983). Better-educated mothers were more likely to use persuasion rather than directive strategies of behavioral change.

Meals in the Third World

Anthropologists sometimes describe meals in studies that deal with issues such as child socialization and gender differences. Jansen (1997), who conducted field work in Jordan, describes not only the socialization that occurs during meals but also the gender roles played in the production of the meal. As in a number of societies, midday represented the preferred time for the main meal. However, the main meal had to include the father, so if his work schedule did not permit his coming home at noon, the main meal was postponed until evening. Status, age, and gender had no effect on seating arrangements during Jordanian meals. Finally, while interaction was permitted, enjoyment of the food was thought to be more important. Thus, the family might eat with little conversation.

Because of their work schedules, agriculturists in Okinawa ate their main meal after dark. The corner of the room next to the kitchen was set aside for meals (Maretzki and Maretzki 1966). The family head sat near the elevated hearth with little other differentiation made in seating. The amount of interaction that took place varied by family. Europeanized Ecuadorians observed a schedule of three meals per day, beginning with coffee and a roll, then having their main family meal in the early afternoon. The Zumbaguan Indians of Ecuador, however, have gone to great lengths to maintain their traditional routine of four meals each day (Weismantel 1996). Not all accounts of third-world peoples suggest that families and their mealtimes are similar to those found in modern, Western societies. The Bakairi of the Amazon basin prefer to eat alone, and in northern Vanuatu, men form age-grade societies for cooking and eating (MacClancy 1993; Visser 1991). However, these groups appear to be more the exception than the rule.

Meals and Their Constraints

Meal patterns become a part of culture, and tremendous ideological support develops to support their continuance. Meal patterns likely result from the material pressures of work and school. Aymard et al. (1996) argue that the traditional European pattern grew out of a compromise between the demands of work and the necessity of maintaining class distinctions. It should also be apparent, however, that the demands of work, among the first constraints on meals, developed only later, when a class system emerged. It was not until some societies had surplus to distribute that the need to distinguish one's family became a constraint.

Meal patterns initially followed the agricultural work day. As Europe began to industrialize, pressures from employers grew to restrict the number of meal breaks allowed during the work day. Even so, for many years the traditional European pattern of four meals per day resisted pressures to change. Similarly, this pattern, also practiced in a number of third-world countries, has managed to escape change. As family members obtained work in urban areas and as more children were permitted to attend school, women found it more difficult to sustain this tradition (Weismantel 1996).

Constraints in the more modern of today's societies are usually defined in terms of time. Much has been made of notions of the second shift for those women who participate in the labor force and then return home for a full shift of housework. Others complain that children are involved in so many after-school activities that family schedules are disrupted. However, Goldschieder and Waite (1991) assert that women no longer settle for the traditional division of labor between work and home, choosing to have no family if their husbands were not willing to share more of the household burdens. Some observers claim that the increased time pressures reported by Americans are more apparent than real. Robinson and Godbey (1997) analyzed the time diaries of 10,000 people and found that, when compared with similar data collected in 1965, Americans had more leisure time than ever before. However, certain kinds of personal care activities such as meals did decline for some adults, with the amount of time that adult Americans spent eating meals decreasing at home from 58 minutes per day in 1965 to 50 minutes per day in 1985. Time spent on meals outside the home increased from 11 to 19 minutes during this same period (Robinson and Godbey 1997: 322). Those who work longer hours away from home spend less time on child care and on eating meals. However, these data do not, by themselves, persuade me that the family meal and its functions will soon disappear.

Data from the National Survey of Families and Households indicate that the frequency of eating breakfast and dinner together as a family is the same in dual-headed households, regardless of the working status of the head of the family, as in single-headed households (MacLanahan and Sandefur 1995). These same data, however, describe a different kind of constraint on the family meal: In households in which a step-father was present, the frequency with which mothers ate breakfast and dinner with their children was significantly lower.

Much has been made of the substitution of convenience or fast foods for more traditional fare, but there is little evidence that these labor-saving devices have an impact on the social quality of the family meal. Commentators like Ritzer (1996a), who claim that the efficient McDonald's meal reduces the amount of time that families have to interact during meals, also subscribe to the notion that the microwave and convenience foods have made it possible for the individual members of the household to prepare their own meals at times convenient to them, thus driving yet another stake into the heart of the family meal. But no one seems to produce any evidence that this is so.

Third World Constraints

Families in the third world have their own constraints to overcome. Some authors have attempted to demonstrate that children's nutrition depends a great deal on the amount of time and help available to mothers (McIntosh and Evers 1982; Popkin and Solon 1976). Labor force participation is only one of a number of potential demands on time. However, a number of studies have shown that the income from this work is generally spent on improving the children's physical well-being. The integrity of the family meal is usually not an issue in these studies. However, it should be recalled that many such households rely on the labor of other family members to maintain household stability. This additional labor may be sufficient to insure that family meal patterns continue.

Seasonality is less of a concern in more developed countries because foods that were once eaten with the rhythm of the seasons are usually available year round. In less-developed countries, however, many people remain tied to the seasons associated with food production. Thus, some seasons are leaner than others in terms of the quantity of food available. There is some evidence which suggests that during the lean season, fewer meals are normally scheduled (DeGarine and Koppert 1990: 261).

Constraints on families and their meals are basically matters of the limitations either of time or money. Economic and social changes alter the nature of these constraints over time and may either increase or decrease their effects. Globalization is a source of social change that many believe will bring both opportunities and new restrictions to families. Some of these restrictions may apply to family meals.

Globalization

Globalization is defined in many ways. For some, its defining characteristic is represented by the "new international division of labor" (Bonanno 1994: 1). This is associated with a greatly increased degree and amount of international trade. Like others, Bonanno (1994) asserts that globalization has permeated the main features of everyday life. Barnet and Cavanaugh (1996) make even stronger assertions, claiming that globalization has feminized the labor force to a far greater degree than ever before, since flexible labor schemes have replaced the promise of full-time work. Barnet and Cavanaugh (1996) argue that certain aspects of production and marketing have transformed consumption in less-developed countries. For example, the fast food industry is said to globalize tastes. Coke and Pepsi represent the food products most exported from the United States, and these products are said to have destroyed the indigenous beverage market in the Philippines (Barnet and Cavanaugh 1996). Children in Mexico City beg for money in order to buy Frito-Lay products; families in Malaysia have succumbed to watching television during their meals (Barnet and Cavanaugh 1996). Indigenous versions of fast food have sprung up in France, India, and Lebanon, to cite just a few examples (Fantasia 1995; Ritzer 1996a, 1996b). Conversation during Russian family meals has remained undisturbed even with television on (Lempert 1995).

Like Bonanno (1994), Dicken (1992) and Barnet and Cavanaugh (1996) base much of their discussion on the transnational corporation (TNC) as the driving force behind globalization. Countries were once bound together by trade, treaty, and tourism, much of which was regulated by nation-states. The global economy of today involves production processes that take place in multiple firms located in two or more countries. By 1991, for example, McDonald's had 760 operations in Japan and 51 in Hong Kong (Barnet and Cavanaugh 1996). Most of McDonald's recent growth, in fact, occurred outside the United States (Berstein 1997), and half its profits derive from these (Ritzer 1996: 298). Friedmann (1990) notes that a small number of TNCs increasingly control food from the point of production, through processing, to its final destination as a finished product. Senauer et al. (1990) find trends toward concentration in both food processing and food retailing. The impact of these changes on third-world families include the loss of self-sufficiency, forced migration out of rural areas, and the disruption of family life.

Some patterns of family life appearing in countries like Norway, where both parents are likely to be employed, include the re-allocation of portions of household chores to children (Solberg 1995). Children perform some of the house cleaning, cooking, and dish washing in a substantial number of families. This suggests a return to nineteenth-century patterns in which children were responsible for helping maintain the household and a movement toward the experience of children in the third world who discharge a great number of household tasks. Such shifts toward promoting greater interdependence in families may result in a return toward more authoritarian child socialization. This in turn, might move families away from more democratic mealtime norms toward a re-emergence of the "seen, not heard" dictum, but I admit to wild speculation as well as pessimism on this point.

The concern here is how changes in production and consumption might affect the family meal. Numbers concerning the global expansion of firms such as McDonald's are not difficult to find. What these reports are unable to tell, however, is the frequency with which people eat fast foods and how this consumption is distributed across class and ethnic groups. How deeply has McDonald's penetrated various groups in places like Russia or Thailand? Fantasia's (1995) account of fast food in France notes that age and occupation determine the market for such products. A recent survey conducted for *Restaurants & Institutions* indicated that ethnic groups in the United States consume fast foods at quite different rates (Rousseau 1997). Furthermore, some ethnic groups are more likely than others to eat in fast food restaurants as a family.

Mass media and its effects are described as global. Global culture is said to be the consequence of the spread of mass media. But a number of sociologists and anthropologists have parted company with this interpretation. Appadurai (1996: 42) asserts that "the globalization of culture is not the same as its homogenization, but globalization involves the use of a variety of instruments of homogenization (armaments, advertising techniques, language hegemonies, and clothing styles) that are absorbed into local political and cultural economies only to be repatriated as heterogeneous dialogues of national sovereignty, free enterprise." Featherstone (1995) makes much the same observation, arguing that global culture is multicultural. He believes that the mass media becomes indigenized and fluid. Kahn (1995: 125) asserts that "we live in a world characterized by not just difference, but by a consuming and erotic passion for it." Gewertz and Errington (1996), based on their field work in Papua, New Guinea, report that the Pepsi ads accompanying the popular music video show, "Pepsi Fizz," combined Western with traditional themes. The monopoly of Western TNC mass media has been challenged by TV Globo, a major Brazilian company, which exports Brazilian programs to 128 countries (Sreberny-Mohammadi 1991: 121). However, Brazilian television itself remains dominated by old American shows.

Inkeles (1986) and others who promote the universalistic themes of modernization have argued that exposure to the mass media leads to more modern (Western) world views and behavior. Kazan (1993) found that despite access to Western videos, television and radio programming, as well as a great variety of Western print media, well-educated citizens of the Gulf States devoted the majority of their media consumption to local products. Foreign media preferences were, furthermore, largely restricted to materials produced in Egypt; but in Egypt itself, the Bedouin preferred either local programming that reflected their traditions or international programming that supported Islamic values (Abu-Lugod 1990). The Balinese have taken advantage of VCR technology to preserve traditional music and dance (Kahn 1995).

Part of a culture's ability to resist change is how much of its practices are bound up in the habits of the body. As Appadurai notes (1996:67), "But even where hedonistic and antinomian consumption practices have taken deep hold, there remains a tendency for those practices that remain closest to the body to acquire uniformity through habituation: food, dress, hairstyling," It would be, however, a mistake to assume that mass-media-driven messages regarding life style alternatives have had no impact. Youth appear most prone to suggestion and experimentation. Weismantel (1996) reports, for example, that Zumbanguan young adults bring home from the city the European notion that the pattern of three meals per day is superior to that of the traditional four per day. It is also the young adults who have embraced McDonald's hamburgers in France and Russia, precisely because these objects have come to represent, more than any other product, that which is American (Fantasia 1995; Ritzer 1996). Localism has received a boost from global tourism: in order to make themselves attractive to outsiders, groups like the Ainu of Japan have consciously revived their traditional culture, including its food and food festivals (Friedman 1990).

Globalization of the Family Meal

How does globalization affect the family meal? Much remains unknown, so I must speculate for lack of data. To begin with, globalization has to do with a changing international division of labor. In the third world, this has led in some cases to the migration of family members or whole families to urban areas of their own country or others. Many have been pulled toward jobs offered by TNCs. These migrations expose at least some family members to new ideas, new lifestyles. These might be fast food restaurants or processed foods. According to Wehrfritz and Bogert (1997), the new frozen wonton rolls now available in China permit many more Chinese families to eat them. Exposure to the mass media means exposure to Western products or to non-Western products which use a Western frame of reference, as well as the Western lifestyle seen on old Western television programs sold to television stations in the third world. How might these things affect the family meal? In France, those who consider fast food restaurants appropriate places to eat are the young and unattached, not families. In the United States, among the customers of these restaurants are the members and families of some ethnic groups. Is there any real evidence that families interact in a restaurant in a manner that differs from that they would observe at their own dining table? In many European countries such as Germany, Belgium, and Italy, less than 40 percent of the households own a microwave oven (U.S. Department of Commerce 1995: 857). Do these lower ownership figures for European countries mean they are less at risk of losing the family meal than a country, like the U.S., where over 80 percent of the households possess a microwave?

The real threats of change historically have always come from the changing material constraints imposed by work. Changing demands of the work day have led families to alter their meal patterns, but the family meal did not disappear, despite the major wrenching that family routines received as industrialization separated work and home. In fact, while the family meal became restructured, its importance increased as both an event and a symbol of family unity. As families respond to changes in the world of work today, they have adjusted meals accordingly. Family dinners have not disappeared, although what is served may increasingly be based on the amount of time available. Material circumstances imposed by the seasons and perhaps by extreme poverty may make it very difficult to maintain the family meal, but no real evidence exists to suggest that it completely disappears among the very poor. The use of take-out food, for example, may simply mean that families continue to perform the evening meal and all its functions but use food prepared by someone else.

It is by no means clear that the spread of Western lifestyle messages and products have changed families or family meals in the third world. Some evidence exists that parenting styles appear more Western in urbanized segments of third-world populations, but any suggestion that this will ultimately lead to global parenting styles is to ignore the continued differences in those styles that exist across classes and ethnic groups in what supposedly is the most modern of all countries, the United States.

The transition of family types, associated living patterns such as gathering to eat meals, and views of children and how they ought be socialized underwent major changes in European societies as they moved from agrarian to industrial conditions. The mode of production makes a major impact on the structure of families and family activities and how family members are viewed. What researchers must begin to examine is how globalization changes work and how these changes affect, in turn, family structure, activities, and views of family members and appropriate ways of treating those members.

Very little is known about family meals anyway. Historical materials contain little by way of description, and it is difficult to determine just what these meals meant to those that participated in them. Data on meals in third-world countries is equally scant, and little more is known about them in countries like the United States, France, or Japan. Recent interest in studying family meal patterns, interaction patterns during these events, and the importance that family members place on participation in them may begin to provide answers to some of these questions. Such research will also have to be conducted in a number of third-world countries as well if we ever hope to be able to make claims safely about family meals as universal practices or otherwise. The effects of globalization on meals will remain undetected until researchers gain a clearer understanding of the general consequences of globalization.

References

Abu-Lugod, Lila. 1990. "Bedouins, Cassettes, and Technologies of Public Culture." *Middle East Report*, 59 :4, 7–12.

Allen, Donald E.; Zella J. Patterson; and Glenda L. Warren. 1981. "Nutrition, Family Commensality, and Academic Performance Among High School Youth." *Journal of Home Economics*, 62 :5, 333–337.

Appadurai, Arjun. 1996. *Modernity at Large: Cultural Dimensions of Globalization.* Minneapolis: University of Minnesota Press.

Aymard, Maurice; Claude Grignon; and Francoise Sabban. "Introduction." *Food and Foodways*, 12:3–4, 161–85.

Azuma, H. 1986. "Why Study Child Development in Japan?," 3–12, in H. Stephenson, H.

Azuma, and K. Hakuta, eds., *Child Development and Education in Japan.* New York: Freeman.

Barnet, Richard; and John Cavanaugh.1996. *Global Dreams: Imperial Corporations and the New World Order.* New York: Simon and Schuster.

Baumrind, Diane. 1967. "Child Care Practices Anteceding 3 Patterns of Preschool Behavior." *Genetic Psychology Monographs*, 75:1, 43–88.

———— 1971. "Current Patterns of Parental Authority." *Developmental Psychology Monograph*, 4 :1, Pt. 2.

Becker, Anne E. 1995. *Body, Self, and Society: The View from Fiji.* Philadelphia: University of Pennsylvania Press.

Bennett, L. A.; S. J. Wolin; and K. J. McAvity. 1988. "Family Identity, Ritual, and Myth," 211–34, in *Family Transitions*, C. J. Falicow, ed. New York: Guilford Press.

Bernstein, Charles. 1997. "Chain Champions and Contenders." *Restaurants & Institutions*, 1 (February), 52–60.

Berry, John W.; Ype H. Poortinga; Marshall H. Segall; and Pierce R. Dasen. 1992. *Cross-Cultural Psychology: Research and Applications.* New York: Cambridge University Press.

Blaxter, Mildred; and Elizabeth Paterson. 1983. "The Goodness Out of It: The Meaning of Food to Two Generations," 95–105, in *The Sociology of Food and Eating: Essays on the Sociological Significance of Food*, Ann Murcott, ed. Aldershot: Gower.

Bhanthumnavin, Duangduen. 1985. "Moral Development and Child Rearing," 195–211, in *Handbook of Asian Child Development and Child Rearing Practices*, Chancha Suvannathat, Duangduen Bhanthumnavin, Ladtongbai Bhuapirom, and Daphne M. Keats, eds. Bangkok: Behavioral Research Institute, Srinakharinwirot University.

Bonanno, Alessandro. 1994. "Introduction" 1–28, in *From Columbus to ConAgra: The Globalization of Agriculture and Food*, Alessandro Bonanno, Lawrence Busch, William Friedland, Lourdes Gouveia, and Enzo Mingione, eds. Lawrence: University Press of Kansas.

Bossard, James. H. 1948. *The Sociology of Child Development.* New York: Harper and Brothers.

Bossard, James H.; and Eleanor S. Boll. 1950. *Ritual in Family Living: A Contemporary Study.* Philadelphia: University of Pennsylvania Press.

Bourdieu, Pierre. 1984. *Distinction: A Social Critique of the Judgment of Taste.* Cambridge: Harvard University Press.

Boyce, W. Thomas; Eric Jensen; Sherman A. James; and James L. Peacock. 1983. "The Family Routines Inventory: Theoretical Origins." *Social Science and Medicine*, 17:6, 193–200.

Charles, Nickie; and Marion Kerr. 1988. *Women, Food and Families: Power, Status, Love, and Anger.* New York: Manchester University Press.

Coontz, Stephanie. 1992. *The Way We Never Were: American Families and the Nostalgia Trap.* New York: Basic Books.

DeGarine, Igor. 1972. "The Sociocultural Aspects of Nutrition." *Ecology of Food and Nutrition,* 1:3,143–63.

DeGarine, Igor; and Sjors Koppert. 1990. "Social Adaptation to Season and Uncertainty in Food Supply," 240–89, in *Diet and Disease in Traditional and Developing Societies,* G.A. Harrison and J.C. Waterlow, eds. New York: Cambridge University Press.

DeVault, Marjorie L. 1991. *Feeding the Family: The Social Organization of Caring as Gendered Work.* Chicago: University of Chicago Press.

Dickin, Peter. 1992. *Global Shift: Industrial Change in a Turnabout World,* 2nd ed. New York: Harper and Row.

Ellis, Rhian. 1983. "The Way to a Man's Heart: Food in the Violent Home," 164–71, in *The Sociology of Food and Eating: Essays on the Sociological Significance of Food,* Ann Murcott, ed. Aldershot: Gower.

Falk, Pasi. 1994. *The Consuming Body.* Thousand Oaks: Sage.

Fantasia, Rick. 1995. "Fast Food in France." *Theory and Society,* 24:2, 201–43.

Featherstone, Mike. *Undoing Culture: Globalization, Postmodernism, and Identity.* Thousand Oaks: Sage.

Ferguson, Priscilla. 1997. *Growing Pains: Children in the Industrial Age, 1850–1890.* New York: Twayne.

Fiske, John. 1991. "Postmodernism and Television," 55–67, in *Mass Media and Society,* James Curran and Michael Gurevitch, eds. New York: Edward Arnold.

Flandrin, Jean-Louis. 1996. "Mealtimes in France before the Nineteenth Century." *Food & Foodways,* 6:3–4, 261–82.

Friedmann, Harriet. 1990. "The Origins of Third World Food Dependence," 13–31, in *The Food Question: Profits vs. People,* Harry Bernstein, Bernard Crow, Mary Mackintosh, and Charles Martin, eds. New York: Monthly Review Press.

Gewertz, Deborah; and Frederick Errington. 1996. "On PepsiCo and Piety in a Papua New Guinea 'Modernity'." *American Ethnologist,* 23 :3, 476–93.

Gillis, John. 1996. *A World of Their Own Making: Myth, Ritual, and the Quest for Family Values.* New York: Basic Books.

Goldschieder, Francis K.; and Linda J. Waite. *New Families, No Families?: The Transformation of the American Home.* Berkeley: University of California Press.

Goode, Judith G.; Karen Curtis; and Janet Theopano. 1984. "Meal Formats, Meal Cycles, and Menu Negotiation in the Maintenance of an Italian-American Community," 143–218, in *Food in the Social Order: Studies of Food in Three American Communities,* Mary Douglas, ed. New York: Russell Sage Foundation.

Gottlieb, Beatrice. 1993. *The Family in the Western World from the Black Death to the Industrial Age.* New York: Oxford University Press.

Green, Harvey. 1983. *The Light of Home: An Intimate View of the Lives of Women in Victorian America.* New York: Pantheon.

Greven, Philip J., Jr. 1977. *The Protestant Temperament: Patterns of Child-Rearing, Religious Experience, and the Self in Early America.* New York: Alfred A. Knopf.

_____ 1991. *Spare the Child: The Religious Roots of Punishment and the Psychological Impact of Physical Abuse*. New York: Alfred A. Knopf.

Griffin, Michael; K. Viswanath; and Dona Schwartz. 1994. "Gender Advertising in the U.S. and India: Exporting Cultural Stereotypes." *Media, Culture & Society*, 16 (July), 487–507.

Grignon, Claude. 1996. "Rule, Fashion, Work: The Social Genesis of the Contemporary French Pattern of Meals." *Food and Foodways*, 6:3–4, 205–42.

Gullestad, Marianne. 1984. *Kitchen-Table Society: A Case Study of Family Life and Friendships among Working Class Mothers in Urban Norway*. New York: Columbia University Press.

Gurevitch, Michael. 1991. "The Globalization of Electronic Media," 178–93, in *Mass Media and Society*, James Curran and Michael Gurevitch, eds. New York: Edward Arnold.

Inkeles, Alex. 1984. *Exploring Individual Modernity*. New York: Columbia University Press.

Jamieson, Lynn. 1994. "Theories of Family Development and the Experience of Being Brought Up," 127–46, in *Time, Family, and Community: Perspectives on Family and Community History*, Polly Wiessner and Wulf Schiefenhoevel, eds. Cambridge: The Open University, in association with Blackwell.

Jansen, Willy. 1997. "Gender Identity and the Rituals of Food in a Jordanian Community." *Food & Foodways*, 7:2, 87–118.

Jeanneret, Michel. 1987. *A Feast of Words: Banquets and Table Talk in the Renaissance*. Chicago: University of Chicago Press.

Kahn, Joel S. 1995. *Culture, Multiculture, Postculture*. Thousand Oaks: Sage.

Kasson, John F. 1987. "The Rituals of Dining: Table Manners in Victorian America," 114-41, in *Dining in America, 1850–1900*, Kathryn Grover, ed. Amherst: University of Massachusetts Press and the Margret Woodbury Strong Museum.

Kasson, John F. 1990. *Rudeness and Civility: Manners in the Nineteenth-Century Urban America*. New York: Wang and Hill.

Kazan, Fayad E. 1993. *Mass Media, Modernity, and Development: Arab States of the Gulf*. Westport: Praeger.

Kraehmer, Steffen. 1994. *Quantity Time: Moving Beyond the Quality Time Myth*. New York: Deaconess Press.

Lamont, Michele. 1992. *Money, Morals, and Manners: The Culture of the French and American Upper-Middle Class*. Chicago: University of Chicago Press.

Lempert, David H. 1995. *Daily Life in a Crumbling Empire: The Absorption of Russia into the World Economy*. New York: Columbia University Press.

Lenski, Gerhard; Ann Lenski; and Patrick Nolan. 1991. *Human Societies*, 6th ed. New York: McGraw-Hill.

Levenstein, Harvey. 1988. *Revolution at the Table: Transformations of the American Diet*. New York: Oxford University Press.

LeVine, Robert A.; Suzanne Dixon; Sarah LeVine; Amy Richman; P. Herbert Leiderman; Constance H. Keefer; and T. Berry Brazelton. 1994. *Child Care and Culture: Lessons from Africa*. New York: Cambridge University Press.

Lewis, Michael; and C. Feiring. 1982. "Some American Families at Dinner," 115–45, in *Families as Learning Environments for Children*, Luis M. Lasoa and Irving E. Sigel, eds. New York: Plenum.

Lin, Chin-Yau Cindy; and Victoria R. Fu. 1990. " A Comparison of Child-Rearing Practices among Chinese, Immigrant Chinese, and Caucasian-American Parents." *Child Development*, 61 (April), 429–33.

Livi-Bacci, M. 1991. *Population and Nutrition: An Essay on European Demographic History*. New York: Oxford University Press.

Lupton, Deborah. 1996. *Food, the Body, and the Self*. Thousand Oaks: Sage.

MacClancy, Jeremy. 1992. *Consuming Culture: Why You Eat What You Eat*. New York: Henry Holt.

Maccoby, Eleanor E.; and John A. Martin. 1987. "Socialization in the Context of the Family: Parent-Child Interaction," 1–101, in *Socialization, Personality, and Social Development*, vol. 4 of *Handbook of Child Psychology*, 4th ed., Paul Mussen, ed. New York: John Wiley and Sons.

McIntosh, Wm. Alex. 1996. *Sociologies of Food and Nutrition*. New York: Plenum.

McIntosh, Wm. Alex; and Susan Evers. 1982. "The Role of Women in the Production of Food and Nutrition in Less Developed Countries," 27–51, in *Women in International Development*, Pamela S. Horn, ed. College Station: Texas A&M University President's World University Series No. 2.

McLanahan, Sara; and Garay Sandefur. 1994. *Growing up with a Single Parent: What Hurts, What Helps*. Cambridge: Harvard University Press.

Martin-Fugier, Anne. 1991. "Bourgeois Rituals," 261–337, in *A History of Private Life. IV. From the Fires of Revolution to the Great War*, Phillippe Aries and Georges Duby, eds. Cambridge: Belknap Press.

Maretzki, Thomas; and Hatsumi Maretzki. 1966. *Taria: An Okinawan Village*. New York: John Wiley and Sons.

Margolis, Maxine L. 1984. *Mothers and Such: Views of American Women and Why They Changed*. Berkeley: University of California Press.

Matthews, Glenna. 1987. *"Just a Housewife": The Rise and Fall of Domesticity in the United States*. New York: Oxford University Press.

Mennell, Stephen. 1985. *All Manners of Food: Eating and Taste in England and France from the Middle Ages to the Present*. New York: Blackwell.

Morton, Helen. 1996. *Becoming Tongan: An Ethnography of Childhood*. Honolulu: University of Hawaii Press.

Morrison, Marlene. 1996. "Sharing Food at Home and at School: Perspectives on Commensality." *Sociological Review*, 44:4, 648–74.

Murcott, Ann. 1982. "On the Sociological Significance of the 'Cooked Dinner' in South Wales." *Social Science Information*, 21:4–5, 677–96.

O'Day, Rosemary. 1994. *The Family and Family Relationships, 1500–1900: England, France, and the United States of America*. New York: St. Martin's Press.

Olvera-Ezzell, Thomas G. Power; Jennifer H. Cousins; Ana Maria Guerra; and Marisela Trujillio. 1994. "The Development of Health Knowledge in Low-Income Mexican-American Children." *Child Development*, 65 (April), 416–27.

Perrot, Michelle. 1991. "The Family Triumphant" 99–259, in *A History of Private Life*, vol. 4 of *From the Fires of Revolution to the Great War*, Phillippe Aries and Georges Duby, eds. Cambridge: Harvard University Press.

Popkin, Barry; and Francis F. Solon. 1976. "Time, Income, the Working Mother, and Child Nutrition." *Environmental Health*, 22:2, 156–66.

Ritzer, George. 1996a. *The McDonaldization of Society: An Investigation into the Changing Character of Contemporary Social Life*, rev. ed. London: Sage.

———. 1996b. "The McDonaldization Thesis: Is Expansion Inevitable?" *International Sociology*, 11:3, 291–308.

Robinson, John P.; and Geoffrey Godbey. 1997. *Time for Life: The Surprising Ways Americans Use Their Time*. State College: Pennsylvania State University Press.

Rousseau, Rita. 1997. "Feeding the New America, Part I: Customers." *Restaurants & Institutions*, February 15, 28–42.

Rozin, Paul; and April E. Fallon. 1987. "A Perspective on Disgust." *Psychological Review*, 94 (January), 23–41.

Senauer, Ben; Elaine Asp; and Jean Kinsey. 1991. *Food Trends and the Changing Consumer*. St. Paul: Eagan Press.

Solberg, Anne. 1995. "Negotiating Childhood: Changing Constructions of Age for Norwegian Children," 118–37, in *Constructing and Reconstructing Childhood: Contemporary Issues in the Sociological Study of Childhood*, Allison James and Alan Prout, eds. New York: The Falmer Press.

Sreberny-Mohammadi, Annabelle. 1991. "The Global and the Local in International Communications," 118–37, in *Mass Media and Society*, James Curran and Michael Gurevitch, eds. New York: Edward Arnold.

Sutor, Carol B.; and Helen F. Barbour. 1975. "Identifying Food-Related Values of Low-Income Mothers." *Home Economics Research Journal*, 3:3, 198–204.

Touliatos, J. B.; W. Lindholm; M. F. Weinberg; and R. Melbagene. 1984. "Family and Child Correlates of Nutrition Knowledge and Dietary Quality in 10–13 Year Olds." *Journal of School Health*, 54 (May), 247–49.

Tucker, K.; and Diva Sanjur. 1988. "Maternal Employment and Child Nutrition in Panama." *Social Science and Medicine*, 26:6, 605–612.

United Nations Development Programme. 1995. *Human Development Report*. New York: Oxford University Press.

U.S. Bureau of the Census. 1995. *Statistical Abstract of the United States 1995*. Washington, DC: U.S. Government Printing Office.

Visser, Margaret. 1991. *The Rituals of Dinner*. New York: Grove Weidenfeld.

Wandel, Margareta; and Gerd Holmboe-Otterson. 1992. "Maternal Work, Child Feeding and Nutrition in Rural Tanzania." *Food and Nutrition Bulletin*, 14:1, 49–54.

Wehrfritz, George; and Carroll Bogert. 1997. "Soap Operas, Frozen Food and Convertibles." *Newsweek*, March 3, 30.

Weismantel, M. J. 1996. "Children and Soup, Men and Bulls: Meals and Time for Zumbagua Women." *Food and Foodways*, 6:3–4, 307–28.

Whiting, Beatrice Blyth; and Carolyn Pope Edwards. 1988. *Children of Different Worlds: The Formation of Social Behavior*. Cambridge: Harvard University Press.

Wolin, Steven J.; and Linda. A. Bennett. 1988. "Family Rituals." *Family Process*, 23:3, 401–20.

Chapter Thirteen

We Eat Each Other's Food to Nourish Our Body: The Global and the Local as Mutually Constituent Forces

Emiko Ohnuki-Tierney

Given the dual emphases on global dynamics and on food in this volume, this chapter starts with a very brief review of approaches to understanding global forces, past and present, primarily in anthropology, in order to situate my discussion of food as a symbol. Then I use a major portion of this essay to argue that "the global and the local" are mutually constituent forces and that in order to understand the complex dynamics of these interacting forces we must examine the role of global dynamics as historical processes. I do that by exploring the representation of three food items introduced to Japan at different times in its history. These include the introduction of rice from somewhere in Asia and the subsequent uses of rice as a metaphor of the Japanese self as it changes over time; the introduction of meat in the context of Japanese reassessment of self at the end of the nineteenth century; and the introduction of the McDonald's restaurants in this global era.

The Debates

In terms of quantitative flow, the current evidence of globalization is imposing. Examples range from Coca Cola, McDonald's, and the television program "Dallas" to the spread of democratization, the human rights movement, feminism, minority rights, international agencies such as the United Nations (UN) and the World Health Organization (WHO), various environmental movements, the transplantation of human organs, the notion of brain death, and global forms of communication like e-mail and the use of the world-wide web, transnational corporations and trading companies, global competitions like the Olympics, international lawyers, tax accountants, financial advisers, and management consultants. Not only the black market sale of human organs for transplantation but also the traffic in drugs and weapons operates on a global scale. The diffusion of food and foodways on a global basis is likewise overwhelming. The golden arches of McDonald's and most kinds of fast foods are ubiquitous, coming from the United States and elsewhere, to reach even into relatively remote areas, while most major cities enjoy foods and cuisine from around the world.

Does globalization, then, present the Carlylian "Signs of the Times" for today? While scholars in many disciplines, including the social sciences but also medicine and the humanities, have joined the debate, their opinions differ on the question of whether the phenomenon is of an entirely different nature and order from the past. We have seen a healthy debate among three distinguished historians participating in the conference that resulted in this book. Historian Bruce Mazlish (1993: 1) believes that "Global History" must "start from our present position, where new factors building on the old have given a different intensity and synchronicity to the process of globalization." He believes that the quantitative differences constitute a quantum leap in quality. Mazlish's position is not a radical denial of the local, but Schäfer (1993) emphasizes the multiplicities of global histories anchored in specifically localized histories with, nonetheless, cross-cultural, multinational and interdisciplinary connections. Schäfer accuses the "world history" of McNeill and others of being too totalizing. Both Mazlish and Schäfer are concerned with temporality and converge in viewing global history as a problem of periodization. Schäfer reminds us that the Renaissance was defined *post facto* some 300 years later, whereas historians are now trying to define the global era while living in it. Grew (1993), on the other hand, views current global trends as part of historical processes that operated in the past as well. What is new is the way our perception is brought into the foreground of our thinking: "And it may be that what marks our new era is not the fact of global consciousness but a particular set of beliefs about it (including the view that this era is unique)" (1993:223).

In Anthropology, I discern three major approaches. Associated with the term global are a series of recent works by anthropologists who belong to the generation that espouses "postmodernism," a notion that has swept through Anthropology, which used to have a vision of primitive societies isolated and insulated from the flows of world history, with each culture having a coherent structure. There are many reactions to this older view, the global approach being one of them, for it does not want to see the world as consisting of discrete cultures.

Perhaps the majority of new publications by anthropologists interested in global issues is on either consumerism or aspects of pop culture, such as the spread of jazz, reggae, Coca-Cola, or McDonald's. The implicit vision is of humanity, now including youth, across the globe, obsessed with capitalistic consumption. For example, Friedman (1990: 316) observes that, for the Congolese, "Consumption is a life and death struggle for psychic and social survival" and that for them "identity is very much outside of the body, outside of the society" (1990: 324). A quest for similarity also led to Appadurai's idea of cosmopolitanism and "ethnoscape." Cosmopolitanism also has long roots that reach back to Diogenes the Cynic, the Stoics, and the Epicureans, as well as Voltaire (cited in Mazlish 1993: 14–15), all, however, in the ethnocentric equation of the Greek, the French, or the Ainu, associated with humanity in general.[1] Not so with the cosmopolitans of Hannerz, for whom "the occupational subcultures as well as the general life styles of certain groups of peoples" are as "at home in metropolitan culture as any European or American" (Hannerz 1987:549). He proposes Creolization as a root metaphor for this world of movement and mixture (Hannerz 1987:551, 1996). Appadurai's own cosmopolitanism (1991; see also 1996) is close to home, within his nuclear family—a Tamil Brahmin in the United States, his white American wife, and their part-Indian son, all of whom visit Madurai only to find out that the priest his wife particularly wanted to see was in Houston. He uses the term ethnoscape to characterize these constant movements of people. Sociologist Michael Featherstone (1990:1) proposes the concept of "third cultures," however, with an emphasis on the plural, which "are conduits for all sorts of diverse cultural flows that cannot be merely understood as the product of bilateral exchanges between nation states."

These anthropologists are attempting to create a new "space" within our discipline. In other words, they see the current global flow as not the sum total of multiple bilateral exchange, but something more, although at this point they have not proposed new methods or theories. They are decisively ahistorical. They do not treat the current situation of globalization as a process with a temporal dimension. Hannerz, for example, is even anti-historical, when he declares that "the study of culture in a global framework" should not be "a *retreat into history* " (Hannerz 1992:228, emphasis added).

In contrast to these approaches, Marc Augé's most recent works (1992, 1994, 1995, 1997a, 1997b) are attempts to examine change in the basic concepts of space, time, and self in response to the forces of what he calls *surmodernité*. He does not concentrate on the global diffusion of specific objects and phenomena, such as a particular technology or business technique. His approach is historical in that he is interested in change and sees the present situation as a palimpsest on which both changes and continuities are ceaselessly rewritten.

The third approach, which in fact antedates the above approaches, is decisively historical. Like historian Raymond Grew, these anthropologists maintain that globalization has been going on for a long time. Earlier forms of globalization have reflected the spread of such notions as so-called world religions, industrialization, imperialism and colonialism, capitalism, biomedicine (Western medicine), the Western scale of measurement of time and space, the universal proletarian movement, and the notion of citizenship. For these scholars, the *urtext* is historian Fernand Braudel's *The Mediterranean and the Mediterranean World in the Age of Philip II* (1972 [1949]), which points to the enormous movements across the Mediterranean whose tentacles of commerce reached not only the Ottoman empire but also China, Africa, and the New World.[2] In anthropology, Eric Wolf (1982) made an enduring contribution to our knowledge by charting the global flow of the effect of European mercantile expansion and the subsequent "laws of motion" of the capitalistic mode, which contributed to the subjugation of the peoples at the periphery. Sidney Mintz's (1985) work pointed to a dazzling series of examples of the impact from "mere sugar"—from slavery and colonization on a massive scale to the taste and life style of working-class English people. Marshall Sahlins (especially 1988, see also 1985) portrayed the effect of the sandalwood trade that engulfed the Pacific islanders, the Northwest coast Indians, the Chinese, and others, as well as various European populations. Sahlins's work also offers a model, using Lévi-Strauss's tradition of viewing conceptual forms as generating economic and political practices and other spheres of culture. While his 1981 and 1985 publications emphasize the local in the context of the global, Sahlins focused his British Academy lecture (1988) on the global as the local responded to it. Richard Fox (1997) offers an erudite exposition of globalization in the opposite direction. He examines how Gandhi's non-violent mode of protest became "natural" for American movements—Martin Luther King's civil rights movement, CORE (Congress of Racial Equality, 1942), MOWM (the March on Washington Movement, in the fall of 1942), and the civil-rights protest of the 1960s, including such American protestors as the Berrigans, Dellinger, and many other anti-Vietnam activists in the 1970s, plus Cesar Chavez and Mitch Snyder in the 1980s, and contemporary advocates concerned with issues centering on ecology, animals, human reproduction, and gender identity. In the context of our discussion, it is important to recognize that instead of reducing Mahatma Gandhi (1869–1948) to some sort of a quintessential Indian, Fox argues that his notion of non-violent protest was a result of his own experience in England and South Africa, as well as in India (Fox 1997). In other words, Gandhi was a "cosmopolitan" during the first half of this century.

Historians in this project on food in global history raised three questions. First, should we emphasize a discontinuity with the past and recognize a new global era. Second, if so, how precisely can we identify the watershed

between the past and the present (since World War II, according to Schäfer).
Third, do we recognize that there are global histories and cultures, apart
from local cultures, even if they do not reveal to us everything that is going
on. Debates among anthropologists suggest that they may not totally deny
the presence of a global culture, even if ours is not a global village.

This cursory review of opinions and approaches, primarily in Anthropology, is only meant to locate my chapter within a burgeoning field. I will use
examples from Japan to illustrate how culture has always been Creolized,
something that anthropologists have failed to see only because we were
trapped in a false vision of culture as a coherent entity which "assimilates"
foreign elements selectively. Here, I aim only to provide a simple description. I do not even begin to address the issues I raised with regard to the assessment of new global forces in comparison with those of the past.

Our Food, Our Body, Our Selves: Food in "Global and Local"

There are many symbols for a social group. Animals, flowers, and flags are
fairly common symbols that people consciously use as a metaphor of the
group, as in the case of the eagle and the Stars and Stripes on the flag of the
United States. Various food items also act as symbols for social groups, although they seldom become official emblems. Thus, apple pie represents, informally, the American way of life, though it does not function as an official
icon. In ordinary times, people cherish what they call their traditional food
without much thought for its symbolic value, something especially true for
staple foods. In fact, the notion that food is what fills the stomach has somehow prevented us from looking at its enormous symbolic value, which sur-
faces at times of crises, such as those times when the existence of a social
group is threatened.

Yet food can serve as a unique metaphor of the self of a social group. As a
result, food can have a power that no other symbol can surpass. There are
two powerful symbolic mechanisms that assign power to food items, enabling them to act as symbols. First, as the metaphor of a social group, an
important food involves interlocking dimensions: When each member of the
social group consumes the food, it becomes a part of his or her body. Thus,
this important food becomes *embodied* in each individual and functions as a
metonym by being part of the self. In addition, when individual members of
the social group eat food together, they are participating in a communal action that bonds them as a group. In Japan, the communal consumption of
food leads to rice as a *metaphor* for us, our social group and, often, the people as a whole. The double linkage in which the metaphor is underscored by
metonym provides food with added symbolic power. Whether a food represents an individual self, a social group, or a people as a whole, this symbolic
process renders foods powerful symbols not only conceptually but also, we
might say, at the level of the most basic emotions.

The second mechanism that enables food to accrue power as a symbol is its close linkage to space and time. Made from plants and animals, food is intimately linked to the earth where they grow or roam. From this perspective, it is important to note that agriculture symbolizes the primordial self of the highly urbanized and industrialized. This is demonstrated by French art, such as Millet's peasants or Monet's wheat stack series (1840–1926) and a series of Japanese woodblock prints by Hokusai and Hiroshige produced as Edo (Tokyo) became rapidly urbanized (for details, see Ohnuki-Tierney 1993). In the now-notorious Cultural Revolution, Mao's attempt to recapture the Chinese self was a return to the rural, agricultural and peasants' world, renouncing the urban and the intellectual. Agriculture symbolizes *our space*. It also represents our history because in this construction, agriculture represents the pristine self before it was contaminated by urbanization or industrialization.

In sum, food is enormously powerful as a symbol of self because, first, as a metonym turned metaphor, food is simultaneously a symbol of self at the individual and the collective level; and, second, it also has the capacity to represent our land and our history, that is, the primordial self. Folk wisdom in many societies captures this. Jonathan Parry (1985: 613) notes of Hindu culture, "A man *is* what he eats. Not only is his bodily substance created out of food, but so is his moral disposition"; and Braudel (1973:66) tells of similar sayings in Europe: "Tell me what you eat, and I will tell you who you are" is similar to the German proverb, *"Der Mensch ist was er isst"* (*a man is what he eats*).

Our Food versus Their Food

The basic ontological premise of the self is that without the Other, the concept of the self does not articulate in the mind of the people, individually or collectively. The self is predicated upon the presence of the Other. At a very basic level, the Others are non-human animals, as opposed to us, who are human beings. In the United States, where pets are not only allowed in the house but on items of furniture like couches and beds, pet foods are still placed in a separate section in supermarkets. In Japan not only are pets not allowed in the house, but being beasts they are marked by their foodways, for they eat while standing, whereas human beings eat while seated.

Within social groups, food symbolically expresses and reproduces important distinctions. As Bourdieu concludes, "The body is the most indisputable materialization of class taste" (Bourdieu 1984:190). An intriguing aspect of food symbolism is the use of different culturally inscribed qualities to serve as markers of distinction. If those who eat rice insist that there are subtle differences among rices, bread eaters are equally fussy. In the past, the dark bread of European peasants distinguished them from the upper classes who ate white bread. In Ann Arbor, Zingerman's bread is the only bread considered adequate for the students and faculty of a mid-Western school with Ivy League status. Thick asparagus is not served at the Harvard Faculty Club, where the liberals of Harvard do much of their patrician networking. Similar distinctions separate members of dominant groups from members of minorities, ethnic groups, and groups based on age or gender.[3]

Similarly, an important food item, such as a staple food, often plays a powerful role as a mark distinguishing one people from another. Peoples are in fact classified and represented by their staple food: rice-eating Asians, bread-eating Euro-Americans, and corn tortilla-eating Latin Americans.[4] The distinction between our food versus their food is often extended to table manners. Food and table manners are psychologically potent means of expressing not only distinctions but also prejudices.

Global Diffusion of Food and Foodways

Yet, people do adopt other people's foods and do so quite easily. In many urban areas of the world today, ethnic foods are enormously popular; and food has become globalized.[5] If the contemporary scene of the global flow of food and of foodways seems dazzling, one must remember that it has been going on for a long time. In Japan, even before the recent introduction of fast-food restaurants like pizza parlors, McDonald's, A & W, and Kentucky Fried Chicken, a large number of foreign foods had been adopted and domesticated, including a Chinese noodle dish (*rāmen*) and Indian curry. These two items, so dear to the Japanese, are not only staples at university cafeterias, but whenever the Japanese form overseas colonies and establish Japanese restaurants, there are *rāmen* and curry shops, as I witnessed in Waikiki. While these two are the best-known adopted dishes in Japan, there are numerous examples whose foreign origins are no longer remembered. In a famous Japanese restaurant on the chic Ginza Street in Tokyo, women in kimono serve an exquisite "Japanese" dish using seabream. A brochure for the store explains that this hybrid dish was devised by a sixteenth-century feudal lord impressed by Portuguese cuisine.

While the internationalization of cuisine has occurred in many parts of the world, today we simultaneously witness the revival of an interest in ethnic festivals and foodways. These ethnic revivals often take the form of "the retrospective invention" of tradition (Hobsbawm and Ranger 1986).[6] This is happening in contemporary Japan, where traditional Japanese cuisine (*washoku*) has made a tremendous comeback precisely because of what Japan is undergoing as the result of the dynamics of global geopolitics that have created an urgent need to redefine its national identity. The world-wide phenomenon of ethnic or cultural revivals must be seen as the presentation and representation of the self, using food as a metaphor of self, when social identity must be reinforced or redefined.[7] The resultant cuisine is always a hybrid, like all "traditional" Japanese dishes.[8]

Rice, Meat and McDonald's in Japanese History and Culture

Rice as Self. Wet-rice agriculture was introduced into Japan around 400 B.C. and gradually supplanted the previous hunting-gathering subsistence economy that began with the first occupation of the archipelago around 200,000 B.C. Wet-rice agriculture provided the economic foundation for the Yamato state and what later became the imperial family.[9] Japan's written history starts with the appropriation of imported rice and rice agriculture as Japan's own. The eighth-century historical myths of the *Kojiki* and the *Nihongi*, the first written documents of Japan, were commissioned by the Tenmu Emperor, who sought to establish a Japanese identity distinct from that of Tang China, whose influence was engulfing Japan. These myth histories are replete with references to rice as deities. In one version in the *Kojiki*, Amaterasu (the Sun Goddess) is the mother of a grain soul whose name refers to rice stalks. The legendary Jinmu Emperor, the so-called "first" emperor, is the son of the grain soul or the grandson of Amaterasu, who sends him to rule the earth. At the time of his descent, Amaterasu gives her grandson the original rice grains that she has grown in two fields in Heaven (Takamagahara) from the seeds of various types of grains given to her by Ukemochi no Kami, the deity in charge of food. The grandson's mission is to transform a wilderness into a land of succulent ears of rice (*mizuho*) nurtured by the rays of the Sun Goddess.

Unlike the creation myths of other peoples, this version of the myth is not about the creation of the universe but about the transformation of a wilderness into a land of abundant rice at the command of Amaterasu, whose descendants, the emperors, rule the country by officiating at rice-harvest rituals. The myth history is an attempt to appropriate rice, introduced from outside Japan as being Japanese and grown by Japanese deities. This myth establishes a symbolic equation between rice and deities, and rice paddies and Japanese land.

Further, by consuming rice, the Japanese internalized the divine power embodied in each grain. Rice and rice products, therefore, are the single most important food for commensality between human beings and deities, on the one hand, and among humans, on the other. During agricultural rituals for farmers and during nation-wide New Year's celebrations, rice wine is consumed and rice cakes are offered to the deities and then shared among humans. Also, in the daily lives of the Japanese, rice and rice products play a crucial role in commensal activities, as an offering in the family ancestral alcove and as the only food shared at meals and served by the female head of the household, while other dishes are placed in individual containers. Rice stands for us, that is, for whatever social group one belongs to, as in a common expression, "to eat from the same rice-cooking pan," which connotes a strong sense of fellowship from sharing meals. In contrast, expressions such as "to eat cold rice (rice is usually served hot)" and "to eat someone else's rice" suggest the opposite—social isolation.

Sake (rice wine) is the most important item of commensality, especially among men, and a basic rule is that one never pours sake for oneself. Instead, people take turns in pouring sake into each other's cup in a never-ending series. The phrase drinking alone (*hitorizake*) emphasizes that there is nothing lonelier than having to pour one's own sake—an act portraying a lone individual on the verge of socially becoming a non-person.

During the Edo period (1603–1868), seigniorial power was expressed through the image of golden ears of rice stretching across the lord's domain, where his people identified themselves with his rice paddies. In rural Japan today, the notion of ancestral land serves as a spatial symbol of family. If rice is a symbol of a "we" expressed through the act of commensality, rice paddies are the spatial symbolic equivalent of the social group, whether family, local community, or the nation at large. Although the valorization of the countryside by intellectuals and artists, as epitomized in rice paddies, began earlier, we see its systematic development during the late Edo period, when Edo became the urban center. Nowhere is the construction of the countryside more vividly depicted than in the woodblock prints (*ukiyo-e*) of the time. Common motifs in the prints by Hokusai and Hiroshige relate to rice and rice agriculture, rice farmers at work, sheaves of harvested rice, and flooded rice paddies. Rice fields against the background of Mt. Fuji became a common way to represent agrarian Japan, that is, the essential Japan. Travelers, often depicted in these woodblocks, symbolize the transient and changing Japan epitomized by Edo, where the travelers are headed, while rice paddies represent "our" land and history, that is, a primordial Japanese identity, uncontaminated by foreign influences and modernity [10] represented by the city. Intellectuals reinforced this sense of agriculture symbolized by a primordial Japanese self through the Meiji period. [11]

Having culturally digested rice, the Japanese later used it to define themselves against the Chinese, after they were replaced by Westerners as the significant Other. The Japanese adopted not only Western science and technology but also many aspects of the ordinary Western life style, as epitomized by the Meiji emperor with his Western-style hair, clothing, and famous Kaiser mustache. The Japanese—who attempted to distinguish themselves from other Asians or Orientals, especially Chinese and Koreans, as well as from Westerners—were almost spellbound by Western civilization, imitating many of its features almost indiscriminately. In public discourse, the distinction between Japanese and Westerners was made and expressed in terms of rice versus meat (or bread). When Commodore Perry made his second visit in 1854, the government staged events in which sumo wrestlers lifted heavy sacks of rice in order to show the strength of the Japanese (Bolitho 1977). Having for centuries adopted rice as an important symbol of their identity, the Japanese found the distinction between themselves and other Asians more difficult; for all are rice consumers. Toward the end of the Early Modern period, domestic rice (*naichimai*) surfaced as a metaphor for the Japanese, contrasted with foreign rice (*gaimai*) as a metaphor for other Asians, although foreign rice had been used in Japan for centuries. Championed by the nativist scholars of the time, the Japanese chose to emphasize their identity by degrading the Chinese and their rice as inferior. This pattern continued throughout the Meiji period. For example, in his novel *Kōfu* (The Miners), Natsume Soseki summarizes life at the coal mine—the lowest type of existence—as "eating Chinese rice and being eaten by Chinese bugs (bed bugs)." Chinese rice is depicted as tasting like mud and being too slippery to hold with chopsticks, unlike Japanese rice, which is called "the silver rice" (*ginmai*) (Natsume Soseki 1984). Thus, the symbolic oppositions of domestic rice/Chinese rice and silver/mud represents the basic opposition of the Japanese self/the marginalized Other, which the Chinese had become by this time in the Japanese view.

Throughout the modernizing period, the military government's construction of Japanese national identity involved the use of foodstuffs, especially rice, as various forms of the motif of the rising sun flag, such as *hinomaru bentoō* (the rising-sun lunch). Importantly, the purity of white rice (*hakumai*) or pure rice (*junmai*) became a powerful metaphor for the purity of the Japanese self. During World War II, white rice had to be saved for the soldiers, while for the rest of the population, Japan's victory promised a return to good times with plenty of domestic white rice, instead of the foreign rice they were forced to eat.

Today, we witness a profusion of foreign foods throughout Japan, in which not only fast foods like hamburgers, chicken, pizza and bagels but also haute cuisine from every culture of the world are available and eagerly sought. In addition to, or, more precisely because of, the profusion of Western foods, Japanese cuisine (*washoku*), has made a phenomenal comeback. Streetcars and newspapers are full of advertisements by restaurants and inns featuring the modern reconstruction of *washoku* with numerous courses of Japanese dishes. From pictures of these colorful and aesthetically arranged dishes, contemporary Japanese often learn what Japanese cuisine is about, even though these dishes are far from the traditional cuisine of the tea ceremony in Kyoto or from any other possible prototypes. Japan now imports most of the ingredients for these Japanese dishes. Amid a flood of Western foods, the Japanese continue to reaffirm their sense of self by reconstructing their own traditional food.

Rice, referred to as the main dish (*shushoku*), is considered the defining feature of traditional Japanese cuisine, although the more elaborate a meal is, the more numerous side dishes are, and less rice is served. For example, Japanese-style steak (*washokushiki suteiki*), a popular menu item today, is served with cooked white rice instead of bread. Memories of Japan's resistance to imported rice in 1993 are still vivid, thanks to the mass media. What American media did not capture was that on Japan's side, the government had engaged in the double-talk all along.[12] Under successive prime ministers, Liberal Democratic Party governments had continued to import rice—a practice observed since the medieval period, even as they told the

Japanese people and the world that they would struggle "until death" to prevent the importation of foreign rice (for details, Ohnuki-Tierney 1995). In a political cartoon, the then-prime minister, Hosokawa, was portrayed as a feudal lord with a long Japanese sword as he met with U.S. President William Clinton, who was shown as Commodore Perry.

The issue of imported rice reinforced the symbolic value of rice for Japanese self-identity even today. Unlike Chinese long-grain rice, Californian rice is virtually identical with Japanese domestic rice, both in appearance and taste. Nonetheless, for some Japanese it is symbolically just as distinct as any other food representing the Other. Not just the government and farmers but also some consumers defended domestic rice and Japanese agriculture, equating Japanese rice and agriculture as symbols of Japanese identity. They argue that rice paddies are essential for Japanese land because they act as dams for flood control, enhance soil conservation, preserve underground water, purify air and water, and beautify the land. We see here the recurrence of the theme of rice paddies as "our" land, a spatial metaphor of the self. Californian rice, in contrast, grown in American paddies thus serves the American land and water, not Japanese. Similarly, the equation of self-sufficiency (*jikyū jisoku*) and the exclusive reliance on domestic rice is a frequently used discursive trope. Other metaphors present rice as a lifeblood crop, the lifeline (*seimeisen*), the last sacred realm (*saigo no seiiki*), the last citadel (that is, of Japanese identity and culture), national life, and the prototype of Japanese culture.

Furthermore, the opponents of rice importation argued that foreign rice contained chemicals from insecticides and processing. Consumer groups became intensely involved in checking foreign rice for chemicals, and individual consumers, especially women, began to voice their fears in newspapers, which introduced the English terms, post-harvest chemicals, into daily parlance. Suddenly worms in rice bags were welcome because they indicated the absence of strong chemicals. Through individual and organized efforts, consumers demanded that the government investigate the processing method used for all foreign rice imported in Japan and opposed the government's plan to mix imported rice with domestic rice.

After agreeing to import rice, as it had intended all along, the government resumed its plan to promote foreign rices by staging, for example, a televised rice-tasting session so that people could taste unlabeled rice. During the session, they reacted more positively than they had anticipated to the taste of various samples of foreign rice, except for that from Thailand, which was "too dry." Even though the government recommended that, in describing the taste of Thai rice, the term *mazui* (distasteful) be replaced by the term *najimi ga usui* (unfamiliar), the Japanese mass media reaffirmed the impurity of imported rices by reporting incidents in which people found a dead mouse in Thai rice or molds and bad odor in Chinese rice.

While an increasing number of Japanese are willing to accept foreign rice for consumption, the twin metaphors of rice as self and rice paddies for

Japanese land were used by those opposing importation. In terms of the reflexive structure, the emphasis on the functions of domestic rice for land beautification and air purification, coupled with the accusation about chemicals in foreign rice, reinforced the symbolic equations of self and other, of purity and impurity.[13] Chemicals and dead mice come to symbolize the impurity of foreign rice, which is portrayed as a threat to the purity of the Japanese self.

As we saw in the myth histories, the Japanese self was in fact born in discourse with the Chinese which required the Japanese to establish their own distinctive identity. They did so by domesticating, literally and figuratively, imported rice. The Japanese self, a hybrid from the very beginning, was fortified just as Japan was introducing Western civilization en masse. With the torrents of global forces breaking on Japanese shores like typhoons, "rice as self" surfaced again at this critical time, even though the economic importance of rice is so insignificant and cheaper California rice can easily replace domestic rice. All through history, then, rice has served as a powerful vehicle for the Japanese to think about themselves in relation to other peoples. That is, the global and the local have been two sides of the same coin: the global (rice) nourishes, literally and figuratively, the local and transforms rice into local (Japanese) rice, enriching its cultural content. The story of rice is indeed a story of hybrid vigor.

Meat as the Other

While Rice as Self has defined and redefined the Japanese self, the story of meat has been unfolding in Japanese culture with its many twists and turns. Although the diet of the people on the Japanese archipelago had no doubt originally consisted of animal meat, fish and plants, meat gradually became taboo. Harada (1993) believes that the basic reason for the prohibition of meat was the development of the polity called *ritsuryōsei*, based on an imperial system that had rice agriculture as its economic base. Both Buddhism and Shintoism also contributed. Buddhism, introduced to Japan from India via China during the sixth century, advocated mercy for all living beings, a principle that nevertheless did not extend to fish. Shintoism complemented Buddhism, extending its own taboo on impurity, which included the deaths of human beings and animals. During the medieval period, the meat of various wild and domestic animals was available in cities (Harada 1993: 258). As Yoshihiko Amino (1980) has pointed out, impurity led to a radically negative stance toward the end of the medieval period (for details, see Ohnuki-Tierney 1987). By the Edo period (1603–1867), meat and butchers had even become "abominable." The severity of the taboo on meat is apparent when we consider that butchering was assigned to the so-called outcaste (Harada 1993; Ohnuki-Tierney 1987) and that both meat and the people who handled it became defiling. The butcher shops were called beast shops (*kemonoya*; *kemono* literally means creatures with hair) or *momonjiya* (*momonji*, a derogative term for creatures with tails and hair or hide) and were located in a spatially marginal area on the other side of a river from a major, more desirable part of the city. Even today one sees a *momonjya* across the Ryōgoku Bridge in Tokyo—the area beyond this bridge was a specially marked area where marginalized people engaged in their stigmatized occupations. Toward the end of the sixteenth century, with the arrival of Portuguese, some Japanese started to eat meat (Endo 1968: 264; Harada 1993: 258). However, meat remained officially taboo, even though there were recipes for beef in a cookbook (Harada 1993: 259).

Just before the Meiji period, in 1857, only two shops in Osaka served beef dishes. Their customers were poor students or shady characters with tattoos (Harada 1993: 21). Some rolled up their kimono sleeves to show their tattoos and flaunted the fact they ate beef as a threat, for no one wanted to tangle with people who ate beef (Gushima 1983: 194). Some who discreetly enjoyed meat did so by giving the names of flowers to animal meat, such as cherry blossoms for horse and peony for wild boar, a custom retained even today. Since meat was defiling, people ran with their eyes closed and pinched their noses when they passed in front of a meat shop. If the procession of a *daimyo* had to pass in front of a meat shop, the carriers lifted his carriage up in the air high enough to keep him from being defiled (Gushima 1983: 188–89).

With the opening up of their country, the Japanese were jolted by the encounter with Western civilization and embarked on seemingly contradictory simultaneous efforts to modernize and industrialize the nation while redefining themselves. Emperor Meiji took the lead in the pro-Western movement by featuring his Kaiser mustache and cutting his hair in a Western style on March 20, 1873. The rush to pursue "the enlightenment" (*bunmei kaika*) of the West entailed the denial and destruction of whatever was thought to be "old and useless," including famous paintings from the past and temples. Even the most famous five-story pagoda was nearly burned down.

The pressing need to negotiate Japanese identity again took the form of us versus them and rice versus meat. Some opposed imitation of the West and claimed that a diet and an agriculture based on rice were evidence of Japanese superiority. Others advocated abandoning rice agriculture and adopting animal domestication, arguing that as long as the Japanese continued to eat only rice, fish, and vegetables, their bodies would never become strong enough to compete with the bodies of meat-eating Westerners (Tsukuba 1986:109–12).[14] Again the emperor took the lead in this matter, eliminating, in December 1871, the prohibition on eating meat at the Imperial Household (Harada 1993: 17). He issued an order that the imperial kitchen should serve mutton and beef regularly, with pork, venison, and rabbit only in small amounts and on occasion (Harada 1993: 17). The emperor was reported to have consumed meat on January 24, Meiji 5 (Gushima 1983:194). French cuisine became the official standard for public entertainment at the imperial court (Harada 1993: 19).[15] Privately, however, the emperor preferred Japanese cuisine, which remained his regular diet in his private quarters.

The drastic change inaugurated by the emperor angered some. In an extremely dramatic incident on February 18, 1872, some members of the *yamabushi*, a shamanistic mountain cult for whom the notion of purity is of paramount importance, attempted to enter the Imperial Palace (Miyake 1978). Clad in white clothing they believed would repel bullets, they came to the palace to appeal to the emperor to prohibit meat eating. Their protest ended in a scuffle with the palace guard (Harada 1993: 18).[16]

Acceptance of meat eating was also facilitated by the strong endorsement of Fukuzawa Yukichi (1835–1901), perhaps the most influential educator of the time and founder of Keiō University. In 1882 he wrote an article explaining on nutritional grounds why meat should not be prohibited, and in 1890 he argued that Japan was not suited for rice cultivation; its people should eat meat and rely on foreign rice (Harada 1993: 20–22). These endorsements from above of a meat diet were effective enough that people began to try meat, which they thought of as a symbol of "enlightenment." In a collection of humorous essays, Kanagaki Robun (1829–94) describes the eager adoption of eating meat at the time in a book entitled, *Aguranabe* (a dish one eats while sitting with legs crossed, rather than sitting properly on one's legs).[17] The book humorously portrays the mood of the day, when cows were seen as providing the miracle of smallpox vaccine and their meat as giving the best nourishment for the body (Kanagaki Robun 1871–72: 77). "Everyone—warriors, farmers, craftsmen, merchants, old and young, men and women, wise and foolish, poor and wealthy—all felt 'uncivilized' unless one ate beef" (Kanagaki Robun 1871–72: 27). Cookbooks on meat dishes started to appear (Harada 1993: 17) and because meat stood for enlightenment, a new dish of sliced beef and vegetables cooked in soy sauce and placed on top of a large bowl of rice was named *kaika donburi* (enlightened bowl) (Nihon Kokugo Daijiten Kankōkai, ed., 1973b: 381).[18]

Still, the concept of defilement from meat continued. Even during the early Meiji, when the Japanese started to eat meat, the inns which served meat to foreigners destroyed and threw away all the cooking utensils and dishes used to cook and serve meat, since they were permanently defiled. This practice made hotel bills quite expensive, resulting in complaints from foreigners (Gushima 1983: 188–89). When Nakagawa Kibei,[19] an entrepreneur, eager to make money on the increasingly popular beef, wanted to set up a slaughterhouse in Tokyo, no one was willing to lend their land for the purpose. He finally set it up in part of a relative's house until he, too, grew afraid of becoming defiled from slaughtering animals. He put up four bamboo poles at the four corners of the slaughter house, hung ritual papers (*shimenawa*) from them for purification, and used a wooden hammer to kill the cows as a way to avoid spilling blood that would defile the area. He took only the upper part of the body to sell and buried the rest in the ground while reciting sutras (Gushima 1983: 190). When Nakagawa wanted to open a shop to sell beef dishes, he still found that few people were willing to lend a place for such a purpose (Gushima 1983: 192–93).

Only in the Taisho period (1912–26) was meat served in individual homes in eastern Japan (*kanto*) (Endo 1968: 264). Meat has been part of the Japanese diet ever since, although the quantity consumed was at first extremely small, not because of psychological resistance, until post-war affluence led to increased meat consumption, especially by the young.

There is an intriguing and important historical development in the propagation of Western foods during Japan's modernizing process. In order to pursue *fukoku kyōhei* (enrich the country and strengthen the military)—the slogan of Meiji Japan—the military was the first to adopt the Western cuisine and did so from the very beginning of this period. A major reason for the military's switch to Western cuisine, especially to dried bread (*kanpan*) and meat, was to combat beriberi, a vitamin B deficiency resulting from a diet of polished white rice. When it first adopted Western cuisine, the navy was successful in reducing the incidence of beriberi but faced complaints from the sailors who were not used to those foods. Mori Ōgai, a medical doctor and a well-known novelist, in 1885 advocated a return to rice, declaring that in terms of nutrition the use of rice was all right as long as it was consumed together with fish, meat and vegetables. His proposal was defeated, but the army chose to combat beriberi by adopting a diet of rice mixed with wheat, meat, fish and vegetables (Harada 1993: 22–23). Thus, before people turned more toward a Western diet at home, soldiers and sailors acquired a taste for Western food (Cwiertka 1996a, 1996b).

The story of meat is more amazing than that of rice. Having rejected meat for centuries, even though the Chinese had been eating it, the Japanese adopted it with such gusto because it stood for Western civilization, when the Westerners became the Other. This occurred despite the real threat it posed to an agrarian ideology more than 2,000 years old and to their social structure and values. Indeed, the blind submission of many Japanese to the cultural imperialism of the West poses a stark contrast to Gandhi's vegetarianism, which stood for his political and ideological opposition in principle and practice to the colonialism of the English whose meat diet gave them the might to rule over the smaller Indian people (Gandhi 1948: 31–37, 60–71; Nandy 1995: 183–85).

It is enormously important to place this development in the larger context of the rise of militarism and extreme patriotism. Since the opening of the country, Meiji Japan fervently engaged in modernization. One goal was to build a strong modern nation, an endeavor that led to a heightened sense of militarism and patriotism that culminated in World War II. Successive governments during Japan's military period adopted the military uniforms, techniques, and strategies of the West while reconstructing Japan's own distinct identity around rice and cherry blossoms. In other words, from near the end of the nineteenth century until the end of World War II, Japan willingly and ardently absorbed Western science, technology, and culture while asserting its own identity.[20] An extreme fortification of the local thus went hand in hand with an eager adoption of the global.

Fast Food Restaurants and McDonald's

If McDonald's golden arches are ubiquitous symbols of "late capitalism"[21] and of fragmented life on the fast track in the United States, they are equally plentiful in the cities of Japan—another society where capitalism languishes after its golden age and where life has been undergoing rapid changes. At first glance, the world-wide expansion of the McDonald's chain seems to offer an ideal case for considering whether this is an example of global culture, a culture that transcends the nation-state and was created as a result of global economic flows.

The McDonald's chain was first introduced to Japan during the economic boom in 1971 by Den Fujita, then a University of Tokyo student, who began with an initial venture of five stores comprising a $1.3 million operation. In 1985, on the New Year's Day, his store in Kamakura, near Tokyo, had the total sales of $47,871—a world record for a single store in one day (Frons 1986:53). By 1986, the sales for his empire of 556 stores increased to an empire of $766.5 million per month, and customers in his restaurants, who included a sizable number of foreigners, consumed 12,000 tons of American beef and 15,000 tons of Idaho potatoes (Frons 1986). By 1994, the number of McDonald's restaurants in Japan had grown to 1,048 stores (Tanaka 1994:46).[22]

Since their introduction to Japan in 1971, McDonald's has targeted the locations highest in real estate value, such as the Ginza in Tokyo, where the first McDonald's was opened,[23] and right next to major train stations. The menu at a Japanese McDonald's has undergone enormous changes in order to increase its popularity. From time to time, various new items appear, including Chinese fried rice (*McChao*), chicken or beef curried rice, fried egg burger,[24] rib burger, hotdog burger, shrimp burgers, chicken *tatsuta* (a soy-sauce flavored chicken sandwich), and bacon-lettuce burgers. The all-time favorite and the standard item is the teriyaki burger, the epitome of McDonald's food to many Japanese.[25] Other items not included in American menus include: iced coffee, hot and cold oolong tea, corn soup, café au lait, and bacon and potato pie.[26]

An important ripple effect of McDonald's on the local cuisine is the birth of the rice burger invented by Mos Burger chains as the result of, and in competition with, McDonald's. Rice burgers are sandwiches made of bun-shaped rice patties which contain meat and salmon patties, vegetables cooked Japanese style, and various other Japanese foods that are staples for lunch (*obento*). Rice burgers thus differ from the old-time Japanese carry-out lunches only in the sense that the rice is prepared in the shape of buns rather than balls. Instead of busy business districts, the Mos Burger chains, since they are quite popular among young people, are often located near universities.[27] Also available in "convenient stores," rice burgers are frozen until sold, then warmed up in microwave ovens.[28]

The ease with which McDonald's was able to make inroads in the enormously competitive food market was in part because of its niche as a fast-food snack and not a bona-fide lunch. Even

Fujita, the founder, concedes that "McDonald's has gained ample recognition among Japanese consumers. However, our image is that of a light restaurant for young people. We are not regarded as a place for adults to have dinner" (Kishi 1992: 40). Thus, his operation did not compete with restaurants offering substantial lunch,[29] let alone dinner,[30] menus.

Even though he refuses to introduce his product as being "from America" (Safranek 1986:7), Fujita capitalized on McDonald's appeal as being "American." He chose not to follow the "suburban approach" in the United States and located his first store on the Ginza, the most fashionable street in Japan. Likewise, he located another restaurant in the Mitsukoshi, the oldest and most prestigious department store (Kishi 1992:39).[31] Both sites, the fashionable Ginza or the prestigious department store, help create the image of McDonald's as an up-scale version of Americana in Japan. The effectiveness of this marketing strategy's success is evidenced by the fact that it convinced some young Japanese that eating while standing—normally a taboo according to Japanese etiquette—could be chic. An extra effort to dramatize the chain's American identity was taken in the summer of 1986, when Den Fujita invited a full troupe of the Broadway musical, "42nd Street," to Japan for a one-month run in Tokyo, even though they sold only 70 percent of the tickets (Frons 1986: 53).

How did consumers perceive McDonald's? Clearly some identify it with what they think of America—that is, the version of Americana constructed by the Japanese. For example, the cover of McDonald's advertising magazine, *McJoy*, indicates the company's effort to promote an image based on its American or Western association. These cover illustrations, solicited from readers,[32] include the cover on the October, 1994 issue that depicts a woman with blond hair, green eyes, star-shaped sun glasses and earrings, and flesh-colored stars on her cheeks. The male artist, Morito Masahiko (a thirty-nine-year-old small-store owner), attempted to "create an image of [an] American type woman with stars and pop [culture]." It is worth noting here that for many Japanese, the mental image of *gaijin* (foreigners) continues to be a person with blond hair and blue eyes.[33] A children's song describes "my blue-eyed doll [who] was born in America and came to a port in Japan." This image, created in the early twentieth century, persists, despite the fact that millions of Japanese have been in personal contact with Westerners of various physical types through their travel abroad and within Japan, where a large number of Westerners have lived over a century. Thus, the picture of an American woman on this magazine cover epitomized the Japanese construction of Americana.

This phenomenon is not confined to Japan, nor was it a construction solely by Den Fujita. In Beijing, McDonald's was introduced for the first time after a long history of China's shunning outside influence, including capitalism. Yunxiang Yan (1997) quotes a Chinese in Beijing:

> The Big Mac doesn't taste great; but the experience of eating at this place makes me feel good. Sometimes I even imagined that I was sitting at a restaurant in New York City or Paris.

This statement reinforces the idea that American commodities are accepted by other countries not simply as neutral or objective goods but as representative of something larger, such as the constructions of Americana in other countries, including China and Japan. Just as Gandhi's nonviolent protest may have had to be Orientalized in the United States in order to be naturalized, as Fox (1997) argues, so McDonald's may have had to be Occidentalized in Japan in order to achieve its success.

The "stranger deity" always has its other side. While a positive image of America is associated with McDonald's, both by managers and consumers, its threatening side is revealed in what the Japanese call *nyan-bāgā densetsu* (the lore of the cat-burger; *nyan* is an onomatopoeia of a cat's cry) or *toshi densetsu* (urban folklore). A tale that first appeared in 1973 and spread among female high school students in Tokyo claimed that skins of cats were seen being dried in back of a McDonald's restaurant (Saitō 1994). In 1974, a story circulated throughout university campuses in Tokyo and Yokohama that McDonald's hamburger meat comes from cats and that a boy who happened to wander into the kitchen saw numerous heads of cats and was bribed with a ¥10,000 bill not to report what he had discovered.[34] The story discouraged students from buying their food from McDonald's for a while, but the rumor died out rather quickly.

McDonald's is not the only target or focus of such urban folklore. In fact almost all foreign fast foods have been victimized by various types of lore. Night crawlers were said to have appeared in the buns at Mos Burger's, and others—Lotteria, Domdom, Kentucky Fried Chicken—have all been targeted for accusations of having food infested with not only cats and night crawlers but also frogs and South American rats. One recent story even claims that there is a factory in Australia that grows night crawlers for food. Targets have included not only fast food imported from America but also from China, such as dumplings (*gyōza*) and even rāmen. Another story claims that *rāmen*, which has been thoroughly "domesticated" in Japan, tastes so good because its broth is made from crows (Saitō 1994). A negative aspect of McDonald's association with the United States is not entirely absent even today. A woman in her late twenties, with whom I engaged in a conversation on a train from Tokyo to Yokohama on August 23, 1994, explained that she seldom goes to McDonald's. Her primary reason was that McDonald's is not only not nutritious but that the "chemical taste" of the burgers proves one cannot trust what they put into these burgers. She added that if you really want to be full, it is expensive to eat there (see note 26 for their prices).

Part of the appeal of McDonald's in the beginning was to young people who wanted to look chic by eating hamburgers while standing, so they would seem to be more American. The young prefer to be chic rather than proper.[35] To eat while standing had long been a taboo for the Japanese, who felt that only animals eat while standing and only human beings know they should sit down when eating. Called *tachigui* (literally, eating while standing), this practice has been a negatively marked behavior in Japanese culture for a very long time. This is part of a larger taboo against doing various things while standing. Kumakura (1990: 108) cites a passage from *Nihonshoki* in 720 A.D., in which putting things down, talking to a superior, pouring wine, and so forth, while standing was considered an extreme breach of taboo, requiring suicide by the offender. In the tea ceremony, in which we see the most developed form of manners, one must kneel down even to open a door (*fusuma*). The term tachigui itself appeared in 1898 in *Genmu Shujaku* by Izumi Kyōka (1873–1939), a well-known novelist. Nagai Kafû (1879–1959), another famous novelist, characterized Chicago as "the place where people grab food and eat while standing" in his *Amerika Monogatari* (Stories about America), published in 1908 (Nihon Kokugo Daijiten Kankōkai 1975: 67). Kafû's observation clearly indicates how tachigui is a custom foreign to the Japanese.

However, the introduction of chairs started the road to an erosion of traditional manners,[36] since it eliminated the most basic of Japanese manners — sitting on one's legs (*seiza*) (Kumakura 1989). At present even small apartments have chairs and tables, rather than *tatami* (straw mats) floors. Even before the introduction of McDonald's, etiquette had for some time become much less formal; hamburgers, pizza, and fried chicken are finger food requiring no plates, tables, or chairs. Indeed, the first McDonald's had neither tables nor chairs (Murakami 1990:133). In short, these fast-food places, especially McDonald's, have allowed eating in ways that are the exact opposite of traditional etiquette.[37]

From the perspective of the "civilizing process," McDonald's and other foreign fast-foods have created an entirely new concept of manners. First, fashion has either merged with, or overridden, manners. Second, as a fashion-based etiquette, it operates only in the public domain and not at home, where traditional manners are learned and remain important. Third, fashion-based manners have a short life. Many far more fashionable foreign goods and activities help Japanese youth to feel "chic," including Bally shoes, Gucci handbags, Polo shirts, a vacation at Waikiki.

McDonald's has become so ingrained in Japanese culture that Den Fujita relishes telling the tale of Japanese Boy Scouts visiting the United States who were relieved to find McDonald's in Chicago (Safranek 1986: 7). In addition to young people who go to McDonald's with their friends, there are two other types of clientele: mothers with young children, for whom celebrating a birthday at the restaurant is as popular as it is in the United States; and working people, who use the store strictly as a quick source of food and literally eat as fast as possible at the crowded counters.[38] Unlike the clean look of the original suburban McDonald's restaurants in the United States, the red-and-yellow signs of many McDonald's in Japan are covered with exhaust gas from millions of cars. Their street frontage is usually very small, often allowing only a counter where orders are placed, with seating on the second and third floors.

If we are to take the world-wide spread of McDonald's as a prime example of a global force, then the Japanese case clearly precludes any possibility that the chain indicates the presence of a universal culture. McDonald's food and mode of operation were thoroughly transformed while in turn changing in Japanese culture. This happened also in other Asian countries (Watson, in press). In order to understand the introduction of McDonald's into other countries as an example of a global force, we must view its introduction and the local reaction to it as part of a continuous process of historical change and a search for the historical antecedents that made the introduction not only possible but behave in a particular way and trigger the ripple effects that occurred.

There are a number of historical antecedents that paved the way for the introduction of McDonald's. As an item of food, McDonald's hamburgers consist primarily of two items: meat and bun. Meat was introduced in early Meiji Japan but was virtually never consumed in any quantity until the 1970s and 1980s, when young people began consuming it in significant quantities, making it a mark of the "post-war-generation."[39] Introduced at the end of the nineteenth century in Yokohama, bread has been enormously popular in Japan;[40] yet buns as such were never used before and sandwiches are not popular. Most important, meals in Japan continue to be characterized by the presence of rice, though its quantity has become smaller as the meal becomes more elaborate and fashionable. The lack of rice in McDonald's food is the reason it remains a snack, despite the company's effort to incorporate rice dishes, such as McChao (Chinese fried rice) and curried rice (Kishi 1992: 40).

Another series of historical antecedents are changes in Japanese society, including the development of a children's and youth culture and as well as changes in eating etiquette. Japanese children, from those who were very small to those in high school at least, used to eat exclusively at home. Now, many often eat out and together, either on a date or with friends.[41] Young students have a great deal of pocket money, coming from their parents, part-time jobs, or both.[42]

The impact of McDonald's on food consumption in Japan is relatively insignificant. Its "invasion" was confined to the realm of snacks that in no way replaced dinners or even lunches. Yet, because it represents Americana, McDonald's, together with other foreign fast-foods, has had a major impact on the continuing changes in the etiquette of eating and other significant aspects of Japanese life. It would not be an exaggeration to claim that McDonald's and other fast foods have had lasting effects on Japanese manners and lifestyle in general.

Summary: Mutual Reconstitution of the Global and the Local: Summary

Not only was the Japanese sense of self born in discourse with the Other, but an imported foreign food, rice, was made a symbol of the self. The story of meat is an equally dramatic case illustrating the impact of the global upon the local. Global forces, represented by the Western practice of eating meat, did not bring about an extensive use of meat in Japan. However, it split open the core of the Japanese belief system and cut through the social fabric, including the caste system, by the introduction of a "defiling" meat diet led by none other than the emperor, whose imperial family symbolized rice and rice agriculture. The introduction of McDonald's was and remains situated in the discourse between the Japanese and Americans but has been gradually domesticated. All three stories of rice and meat in this essay demonstrate beyond a doubt that the global and the local are not antagonistic forces but in fact mutually constituent. The local, that is, the Japanese, has absorbed the external force and attempted to reconstruct Japan's own identity in the face of global tidal waves. They have done so time and again. These forces nourish each other.

Notes

1. This is a common practice among many peoples, including the so-called "primitives."

2. Braudel's own use of the terms the "global" and "total" had altogether different meanings. He meant "globality of all the human sciences." See also Mazlish (1993: 2–4), for differences between the universal history, world history, and global history.

3. Watermelon and catfish were negative markers of the blacks in the culture of the white. Even garlic used to characterize the Jews and Italians when they were distinct minorities. The gender and age also play a part here. In the past, he-men did not eat yogurt and quiche. Other than professional cooks, men baked only bread, not cookies, and barbecued meat in order to preserve the tradition of Man the Hunter. Women the gatherer were the first to prefer salads. In Japan, I once asked my nephew, a bit of a chauvinist, in a coffee shop if he wanted a piece of cake. He looked at me in indignation and replied that it is food for girls (*onnanoko*). Sweets in general are still for

women. In 1993, Professors Noboru Miyata and Tambiah and I were strolling the famous street in Asakusa in Tokyo. Professor Miyata took us to a famous shop for sweets (*oshirukoya*), explaining that they could sneak into the store, catered exclusively to women, because I was with them. Blow fish *sashimi* and live *ayu* used to be eaten only by men; the *ayu* is a fresh water fish that "bravely" travel from the sea in the spring against the current to spawn upstream and live in areas of strong currents.

4. Or, within a contiguous region, the wheat-eating northern Indians versus the rice-eating south Indians; French versus German versus Italian bread; the sorghum of the Pende contrasted with maize of the Mbuun in nineteenth-century central Africa (Vansina 1978:177); or the conflict over oil versus butter that extends east and west across France, with Belgians belonging to the butter side (Joseph Miller personal communication). Similarly, while the Japanese are quite attached to "raw" food, the Ainu take pride in their long, thorough cooking methods and distinguish their "civilized" way from the "barbaric" ways of the Japanese and Gilyaks, their neighbors who eat food "raw." Many Japanese, in turn, distinguish or used to distinguish themselves from the neighboring Koreans and Chinese by pointing out their use of garlic, which is not part of the *washoku* (Japanese cuisine). People have a strong attachment to their own cuisine and, conversely, an aversion to the foodways of others, including their table manners (Ohnuki-Tierney 1990).

5. In the United Kingdom, the daily cuisine now includes foods introduced by peoples from the former colonies—Africa, East and West Indies, Pakistan, Chinese (Hong Kong)—as well as Italian pizza and American hamburgers and "American steak." "Fish and chips" is now sometimes advertised as "traditional," as I observed with amusement in south London.

6. This phrase has been used too frequently and too superficially to hold its original explanatory power. "Invention" is not meant to refer to something that pops out in the air but that which is grounded in particular historical context, especially historical conjuncture.

7. For this process of the dialectic differentiation and representations of Self and Other, not any food will do but only important foods and cuisine are selected as metaphors. The so-called staple foods often play a powerful role—the wheat-eating people in northern India versus rice-eating south Indians; the dark bread of the peasants versus the white bread of the upper-class people in past centuries in Europe; and rice-eating Asians and bread-eating Europeans.

8. The agility with which food travels across political and cultural borders is demonstrated by the "peaceful" co-existence that takes place even under adverse conditions, such as when the two peoples are at war or in hostile relations. There is no other people in the world who, as a group, are as antagonistic to the Japanese as Koreans are. The legacy of Japanese colonialism remains strong today through the teaching of the colonial history in schools. In addition, Korean cuisine is characterized by cooking for a long time and with the use of meat. Yet, sushi and *udon* noodles have become so common and popular among Koreans that they are no longer prominently marked as Japanese foods. Yet, during this process of adopting *sushi*—the food diametrically opposed to the prototypical Korean barbecued beef—Koreans developed their own way of eating raw fish. Thus, unlike the Japanese, who are quite particular about which fishes may be eaten raw, Koreans eat almost all fish raw (Ito 1996: 309–14).

9. It is noteworthy that agrarian cosmology-turned-ideology put a blinder on scholarly eyes so much so that it was not until after World War II that some influential scholars started to unravel evidence that rice was primarily the food for the upper class throughout most of Japanese history and was not a staple food, in quantitative sense, for most Japanese until recently. Nevertheless, it is undeniable that it has always been the most important *symbolic* food for most Japanese.

10. Note, however, that the intimate involvement of space for the Japanese conception of the self does *not* derive from a need to delimit Japan's space, since it is surrounded by the sea. This is in contrast to many situations in which ethnicity and nationalism of social groups in adjacent areas are in physical need of territorial boundaries, as shown by the "Berlin Wall."

11. While many have decried the decay of urban life and exalted the beauty of rural France, Toulouse-Lautrec, for example, celebrated the decadence of Paris and those who lived there, like the can-can dancers with their exquisitely seductive legs. Likewise, the masters of the woodblock prints celebrated the urbane but decadent world of the *geisha*, while others sought refuge in "uncontaminated" rice paddies. Here we see a striking cross-cultural parallel in which urbanization created a need for "the rural." For details of the double nature of both the countryside and the city, see Ohnuki-Tierney (1993).

12. On the *very* day that Hosokawa announced his agreement to open the rice market "in view of the future benefit to Japan," the *Asahi* newspaper broke the "true" story, and a disclosure by Kurokawa of the whole process, dubbed as a "novel," but using all the real names. This appeared in *Chūōkoron*. The newspaper revealed that, unlike Bush, Clinton realized that opening the Japanese rice market would not benefit America, since American rice would lose in the competition against cheaper rice from elsewhere. The United States would benefit far more from exporting other agricultural products, especially wheat, since more than half of Japan's import comes from the United States. Clinton therefore was willing to let the Japanese attach conditions to the opening of the Japanese rice market but expected, incorrectly, that Japan would also open markets for other U.S. products.

13. *Purity* of self is at the symbolic core of ethnicity and nationalism, whether it is the linguistic purity of recent Quebec nationalism (Handler 1988), the "racial purity" of Hitler's Germany, Mao's slogan of "today pure but poor; tomorrow pure and powerful," or the ethnic "cleansing" in Bosnia today. B. Williams (1989) points to "the invention of purity" entailed in all nation-building, as does Yalman (1992) who contrasts the emphasis on purity in ethnicity and nationalism to an imperial system more tolerant of diversity.

14. Some scholars view Tsukuba's work as being too deeply embedded in the *nihonjinron* (theories about the Japanese), a semi-scholarly and semi-journalistic genre of writings that try to identify who the Japanese are, often in a chauvinistic sense. I use his work as an ethnographic source.

15. In March 1996, Prince Mikasa told me that a woman cook sent to France to learn French cuisine at that time set the protocol for the official dinners, which, according to the French tradition at the time, did not include bread plates and did not serve butter. The practice continued until her recent death.

16. The scuffle ended in four dead, one seriously injured, and the remaining six arrested.

17. To eat while sitting with legs crossed signifies a major departure in eating manners from the norm. To sit on one's legs (*seiza*) was and still is regarded as the proper way to eat in Japan. Thus, eating meat brought forth a drastic change in the eating manners.

18. Endo (1968: 264) explains that the dish was called *gyūnabe* (beef pot) in eastern Japan and *sukiyaki* in western Japan, but the latter took over as the generic name for this dish.

However, *sukiyaki* and *gyūdon* are two different dishes today, with the latter more closely resembling *gyūnabe*. *Gyūdon* continues to be a favorite dish, especially for men.

19. Endo (1968: 264) records his name as Nakagawaya.

20. In order to understand how a global force is not neutral, we must take note of the fact that although meat was in the Chinese diet, the Japanese adopted rice but not meat from them. This parallels the ear piercing practiced by the Chinese. The Japanese considered any alteration of the body to be an act of impurity and used the pierced-ear as the negative marker of the Chinese. Thus, an object, whether rice or meat, does not carry an "objective" meaning, but it derives from the discursive space of a given culture.

21. I use F. Jameson's (1991) term here without all of its conceptual properties.

22. In 1991, annual sales rose 18 percent from the previous year to ¥207 billion ($1.6 billion), with 860 stores in Japan (Kishi 1992:39). In terms of total sales among Japan's leading food-service companies, McDonald's was third in 1979 with ¥40 billion but became the leader in 1985, with ¥119 billion and in 1992 with ¥212 billion (*Business Asia* 1993).

23. Initially at Ginza 4-chōme, Mitsukoshimae, now moved to near the Ginza 8-chōme, near the subway station.

24. Called *tsukimi-bagā*, or moon-viewing burger.

25. In July 1994, a man in his mid-forties, who works for the Mitsubishi Automobile Company and had just toured his company's branches in the United States for four weeks, insisted to me that the McDonald's in Japan was much tastier. It became clear that to him McDonald's meant teriyaki burgers with their taste of soy sauce.

26. The prices at McDonald's in August 1994 were hamburger, ¥210; cheeseburger, ¥240; bacon-lettuce-burger, ¥290; fillet-of-fish burger, ¥280; Big Mac, ¥380; Chicken tatsuta (a soy-sauce-flavored chicken sandwich), ¥320; McFried potatoes, ¥260, ¥240, ¥150; Chicken McNugget, ¥780, ¥480, ¥280. They periodically go on sale. For example, a hamburger was sold for ¥100 for 17 days between September 2–18, 1994. Following the Japanese tradition of selling inexpensive foods as a set package (such as soba noodles and inarizushi), a hamburger, French fries and a coke were sold together for ¥400 during the summer of 1994. In August and September of 1994, other sets offered for sale at all McDonald's included: a hamburger or a cheeseburger with French fries and a soft drink for ¥400; fillet of fish sandwich, a larger amount of French fries and a drink, ¥500; a teriyaki burger, a larger amount of French fries and a soft drink, ¥500; Big Mac and a larger amount of French fries, ¥600; and a chicken burger, a larger amount of French fries and a soft drink, ¥600.

27. They are located not in the midst of Tokyo, but close enough, such as the one at Ebisu or the one at Itabashi.

28. The transformation of McDonald's food or hamburgers in general in Japan rests on two key ingredients: soy sauce, used in teriyaki burgers and other "Japanese" items added to the menu, rice, used in rice burgers. Pizza, another recently imported foreign food, was transformed in Japan, with such added items as octopus, squid, and corn. It became a party food for young people since it can be shared—a feature conspicuously lacking in McDonald's.

29. Except soup, Japanese dishes are all at room temperature. Although rice at the dinner table must be piping hot, sushi, rice balls (*onigiri*) and rice in the lunch box are all eaten at room temperature. Lunch boxes are enormously popular and are sold in department stores, supermarkets, and grocery stores as well as by vendors who sell them from minivans and cars parked at busy office areas. Prices range from ¥250 to ¥2,500, with decent-tasting ones averaging around ¥500 (*Asahi* October 26, 1993). Because of the popularity of these lunches, some foreign fast-food companies have moved into the market share in lunches. For example, in the fall of 1992, Kentucky Fried Chicken started an expensive line of lunches, emphasizing the best rice (*akitakomachi*) and fish (*Asahi* Oct. 26, 1993). Even railway stations sell their own *ekiben* (station lunches), which range in price from ¥350 to ¥2,000 (Noguchi 1944:319).

30. A young man from Mino, near Osaka, who just graduated from a university, was flying from Osaka to San Francisco in March 1994. He explained that any food with bread does not really fill the stomach, and thus even for lunch he and his friends at his university would look for *donburi teishoku* — a large bowl of rice on which various ingredients are placed. He prefers the rice burgers to hamburgers; in his opinion, hamburgers are a snack to eat between meals. *Jiyo Jikan* (Free Time), the official magazine of McDonald's aimed at consumers, published in 1994 an article entitled "Hamburgers as Habit and *Gyūdon* (a large bowl of rice with beef and sauce on top) for Full Stomach (*Shūkan to shite no hanbāgā to manpukukan no gyūdon*)," points to how young working men prefer a large bowl of rice with beef or pork on top because it fills their stomach and how hamburgers pose no competition as a lunch item (see also Yamaguchi 1986). On Sundays, when one does not work and thus does not need as much energy at lunchtime, families with small children now often go to McDonald's for lunch.

31. Many of my colleagues and friends told me that companies and individuals would choose this department store to have their gifts sent for them at the annual gift exchange times. Lately, it has become almost the custom to have a store, especially department store, send gifts out to the designated individuals, rather than personally deliver them.

32. Both McDonald's and Mos Burger's in Japan circulate these magazines, which contain essays contributed by customers.

33. My mother was born into a family that first imported foods from France in Yokohama and was in contact with them, as the old photographs indicate. She married my father who was in export business, which brought her into constant contact with foreigners of various types. Even so, after I came to the United States, she kept sending me letters, warning me not to fall in love with a man with blue eyes.

34. Kumakura Isao, professor at the National Museum of Ethnology in Japan and Kindaichi Hideho, professor at Kyôrin University; both personal communications, May 1994.

35. Japan's transnational vertical diffusion was set in motion with its encounter with the Han and Tang civilization of China but was intensified with its encounter with the West. Thus, ever since Japan re-opened its doors to other countries at the end of the nineteenth century, the Japanese people have been compelled to emulate Western civilization. Even after their economic success in the recent past, underscored by its mastery of high technology, the Japanese continued to be under the "cultural imperialism" of the West.

The depth and intensity of this compulsion is instantly recognizable today throughout Japan, where even mannequins for the *kimono* in almost every department store in Tokyo, Kyoto, and Osaka, and other major cities are not only blond but have the body posture of Western men and women. I have been carefully monitoring department stores the past few years. The use of mannequins with the Western look began with the less-prestigious department stores. The Mitsukoshi department store, the aforementioned oldest and most prestigious of all the stores in Japan, held out until 1993 but then changed to mannequins with Western looks in 1994. Today, women, including some middle-aged women, and even men dye their hair red, sometimes even blond. Some women are eager to go through plastic surgery in order to acquire the rounder appearance of Western eyes, instead of their own eyes with its epicanthic fold. Almost all the advertisements for clothes, cameras, you name it, feature western movie stars and models.

It was in this context that Den Fujita was able to "make history," at the time their first store opened in Ginza, Tokyo, by capitalizing on how "chic" it is to eat while standing and to eat using one's hands (*Jiyū Jikan*, p. 32). Young Japanese could identify this new manner with Americans, who are thought and idealized by the Japanese to be "care-free" and casual. The American casualness (*kyajuaru*) caught fire, as it were, introducing casual clothing, barbecues, etc. All of these represented, to the Japanese, the carefree style of Americans, the opposite of the extremely constrained style of Japanese.

To dismiss this phenomenon only as a form of rebellion against their own tradition misses the point, however—the rebellion is embedded in the long tradition of cultural imperialism of the West. Note, for example, that not only are Japan's young people taking to the new chic manner of eating while standing at McDonald's but also some of them, primarily women, now enroll in various "finishing schools" to learn Western manners. The goal of these schools is to produce (by means of reproduction) aristocratic women (*kifujin*)." Some Japanese women spend 9 months to learn manners, at the cost of ¥3,500,000, at a finishing school opened in 1989 in Barcelona. An American finishing school with branches in Tokyo, Osaka, Fukuoka and Hiroshima offers 140 hours of lessons in Western manners for ¥1,000,000. Those enrolled in the school consider this to be cheaper than going abroad to acquire their "international aristocracy" (Murakami 1990: 137).

Indeed, there is a double irony here. The Japanese subscribe willingly to the symbolically more powerful Western culture, whose upper-class life style defined *civilité* for the rest of the population in Western Europe. Not only does this phenomenon represent the "transnational vertical diffusion" of the internal "symbolic violence" within Western society, but it also represents another symbolic violence—a new form of symbolic capital—the internationalization of Japan—successfully transmitted by the government to the people. Note how Den Fujita, the person who introduced

McDonald's to Japan and made it a big success there, has consciously used the Japanese adoration of America: "The secret of my business is to take advantage of the *Japanese inferiority complex* toward Americans" (Frons 1986:53, emphasis added). We recall that the earlier change in the manners to prohibit public urination and breast-feeding was as the result of Japan's interaction with the West, just as the introduction of chairs and tables—the initial force to change the so-called Japanese manners—came from the West.

36. What we call the traditional Japanese manners usually refers to the "Ogasawara-ryū" or Ogasawara School which originated at the beginning of the Muromachi period (1392–1603) (Nihon Kokugo Daijiten Kankokai, ed. 1973a:3, 311).

37. The famous Latin treatise by Erasmus, *Di civilitate morum puerilium* (On civility in children), published in 1530, warns that "it is impolite to greet someone who is urinating or defecating. . . . A well-bred person should always avoid exposing without necessity, the parts to which nature has attached modesty. If necessity compels this, it should be done with decency and reserve" (quoted in Elias 1994 [1939]: 106). Although Erasmus's treatise came at the time of social transformation in Europe, the importance of manners for every human society is well-recognized (see Lévi-Strauss 1978[1968]).

The civilizing process had a quite different contour in Japan, although, as in every society, class differences are significant. Urination in public places has been quite commonly practiced by people from different classes. Around 200 years ago in Kyoto, even (?) women did so quite freely (Inoue, ed. 1990: 97). At the time of the first Olympics in Japan in 1964 the Japanese government issued a plea to Japanese men not to urinate in public and to women not to breast-feed in public because "foreigners are coming, and they might think the Japanese are uncivilized." Unlike in the United States where the body—any part and at all times—is enormously charged with religion and sex, the Japanese used to regard urination or breast-feeding quite apart from the sexual function that these body parts perform at other times. But with the government pressure, breast-feeding in public virtually disappeared, although the men's habit of urinating in the public has not altogether disappeared. The ultimate source for the change, therefore, was the Other.

On the other hand, one of the hallmarks of the Japanese concept of *civilité* is the manner of eating, which have shown far more resilience. Of paramount importance are the practices of not using one's hands for food and not eating while standing. The first derives from the notion that hands are by definition dirty, that is, even after washing, since they touch all sorts of things and thus are always suspect of being contaminated. Symbolically, they stand for a liminal space that demarcates the clean inside—the body, the self—from the dirty outside (Ohnuki-Tierney 1984:28–31). Chopsticks, used since the beginning of the Heian period (794–1185), are by definition clean and thus, except for a few culturally identified foods, one must use chopsticks in eating at all times, that is, even noodles. Thus, traditional fast foods of noodles are eaten also with chopsticks. Many Japanese find it difficult to use hands to eat sandwiches; in Japan sandwiches are often served in tiny pieces, with a toothpick to pick up each piece without using one's hands.

There are certain culturally prescribed foods for which Japanese must use their hands. For example, *nigirizushi* (vinegared rice-balls with raw fish) can be consumed with one's fingers when they are of especially high quality, but they are mostly eaten with chopsticks. *Onigiri* (rice balls), eaten primarily for lunch, almost always require the use of hands. Note, however, when the Japanese use their hands, the hands are cleansed, culturally speaking, by *oshibori*, or wet towels. In fact, whether one uses hands or not, *otefuki* (hand-cleaning towelettes) are often included with fast foods, whether foreign or Japanese.

Concerns with the ritual impurity of hands, especially of the right hand, are almost universal (Hertz 1960 [1907]; Needham, ed. 1973). In the United States, we have lately seen the use of gloves for handling foods. Noting that food containers of fast foods "defy pollution," Kottak (1978: 374) points out how the fast-food chain, Chock Full O'Nuts, assured customers in New York City that "their food was never touched by human hands." The Japanese obsession with clean hands, however, is different from that of the United States and from many other societies not only because the Japanese have a higher level of intensity on this issue but also because they are far more concerned with the impurity of others than the impurity of the self. We recall the insightful remarks by Lévi-Strauss (1978 [1968]:503–04) about "the total opposition between the reasons for good manners believed in by -so-called primitive people and ourselves." "Whereas we think of good manners as a way of protecting the internal purity of the subject against the external impurity of beings and things, in savage societies, they are a means of protecting the purity of beings and things against the impurity of the subject." Although the Japanese in many other respects are closer to the "primitives," that is, societies and cultures not belonging to the High Culture of Western European societies (see Ohnuki-Tierney 1994 for a discussion of the great divide), in this respect, the Japanese are certainly protecting themselves from the contagions of Others that gather, as it were, on their hands.

McDonald's impact on the taboo against eating with hands is restricted. Most Japanese I observed in the summer of 1994 still eat hamburgers in the wrapping, their hands not directly touching the hamburgers, although some explained this practice by pointing to the necessity of using the wrapping so that ketchup and other liquids do not drip down. Furthermore, I do not see a great increase in the Japanese use of hands in eating other foods. Thus, the first rule of the Japanese eating manners seems to have been affected little by the introduction of McDonald's food.

There are other changes in the manner of eating introduced by foreign fast foods. Coke, first, followed by other soft drinks started to culturally sanction *rappa nomi*. Literally, *rappa nomi* means to drink like one is blowing a *rappa* (trumpet), that is, to drink directly from a bottle or lately from a can, rather than using a glass or a cup. Like tachigui, rappa nomi is a negatively marked behavior in a semiotic sense. But now men and women can do so, although this behavior is still confined to young people in certain contexts, such as at a fast-food store.

Another change in the eating manners comes from the whole-scale adoption of ice cream, which is part of the scene of fast foods. The consumption of ice cream used to be restricted due both to the fact that many Japanese were intolerant of lactose and that the Japanese used to avoid cold foods and drinks even during the summer. The Japanese, especially women, used to put only a small amount of food in the mouth, as discreetly as possible. Especially women cover their mouth with a hand, when they eat or laugh. But, ice cream cones require the mouth to be opened to a rather large size. Although many women still use spoons to eat ice cream so that they do not have to open their mouth large, some follow the American way of eating and licking with the tongue.

38. As a fast-food snack, many Japanese use McDonald's restaurants as an equivalent to old-time noodle dishes of *udon*, *soba*, and *rāmen*, originally introduced from China (Ohnuki-Tierney 1990). Of these three types of noodle dishes, *udon* and *soba* can even be considered haute cuisine, if they contain high quality noodles and other ingredients and are served in exclusive restaurants for prices as high as ¥2,500. Shops selling *rāmen* are marked with red awnings, a color symbolizing China, and considered a primary color by Japanese, who make limited use of primary colors.

39. A man in the late forties, an editorial writer for the *Asahi* newspapers, told me during his visit to New York that although he prefers McDonald's, his children prefer Mos Burgers.

40. Only during World War II did the Japanese attempt to purge all foreign-loan words from their daily parlance, including *pan*, a Japanese term for bread which derives from the Portuguese term *pão* for bread. At present, the Japanese have become as discriminating for the taste of bread as they are for rice. Thus, many, who can afford it, buy only from well-known bakeries, often with German or French names. Recently, a newly opened bakery, called *Denen Bēkari* (Pastoral Bakery), which came from out of nowhere near Kyoto, became so famous for the taste of its bread that many people drive to this bakery, often on their way back from golfing. At the only Japanese grocery store in Madison, Wisconsin, they sell what they call Japanese bread (*shokupan*). Likewise, in Cambridge, Massachusetts, stores in the Porter Square shopping center, which is almost exclusively dedicated to Japanese customers, sell Japanese bread so that the local Japanese can enjoy their "traditional Japanese bread" (for details of the use of bread by the Japanese, see Ishige 1982:22–23). The American style bun, used for hamburgers, however, is entirely new to the Japanese, in shape, taste, and use.

The first meal to be "invaded" by foreign foods was breakfast, with bread replacing rice. Dore (1973 [1958]:60) dates the beginning of the adoption of bread for breakfast in 1951. He found that the use of bread was welcomed by housewives, who no longer had to cook rice in the morning and thus could sleep a little longer. Thus, at present many urban Japanese would not think of eating the Japanese breakfast with rice (see for details, Ohnuki-Tierney 1993:41). The popularity of bread is amazing, given the facts that, first, since baking is not a traditional cooking method for the Japanese, most Japanese do not own an oven at home; and that, second, they consume bread only for breakfast and tend not to use it for sandwiches.

41. Dating—a post-war phenomenon—now starts in middle school. As Stanley Tambiah (personal communication), professor at Harvard University, observed in amazement in the summer of 1994, a far greater percentage of young people walk in pairs in Japan's cities than in the United States, or any other place in the world, for that matter.

To give but one example illustrating the power of the youth culture, I noticed beepers, called "Electric Bell," sold at the fax counter of the Takashimaya Department Store in Osaka on September 2, 1994. To my astonishment, they were not for doctors but for young people who do not want to miss a telephone call from their friends. Although youngsters under the age of 18 are supposed to obtain parental permission to purchase one of these beepers, many youths of this age use them. The use of these beepers then eloquently speaks not only for the economic power of Japan's youngsters but also the changes in their culture. Despite the much-publicized "examination hell" which starts at the time of the entrance to a kindergarten, many of these youths are no longer as enslaved to school work as they used be. Instead, a powerful "peer group culture" has created a phenomenon that has in part provided some of McDonald's success (Burros 1994).

42. It used to be that students were supposed to study full time and that they did not usually have part-time jobs for pocket money. During the past decade or so, part-time work for extra money became a common phenomenon, although whether high school students should have a part-time job for pocket money is still being debated. This phenomenon is also related to changes in the system of cultural values that jobs represent. Jobs used to be hierarchically ranked and the lower class jobs, such as waiters and waitresses, were never held, even temporarily, by Japanese of middle- and upper-class background. Such stigma about certain jobs has disappeared, as long as they are held as temporary jobs.

References

Amino, Yoshihiko. 1980. *Nihon Chūsei no Minshūzo—Heimin to Shokunin* (Portrait of the Folk in Medieval Japan—The Common People and the Professionals). Tokyo: Iwanami Shoten.

Appadurai, Arjun. 1991. "Global Ethnoscapes: Notes and Queries for a Transnational Anthropology," in Richard G. Fox, ed. *Recapturing Anthropology: Working in the Present.* Santa Fe: School of American Research Press.

_____. 1996. *Modernity at Large: Cultural Dimensions of Globalization.* Minnesota: University of Minnesota Press.

Augé, Marc. 1992. *Non-lieux: Introduction à une anthropolgie de la sur-modernité.* Paris:Seuil.

_____. 1994. *Pour une anthropologie des mondes contemporains.* Paris: Flammarion.

_____. 1995. *Non-Places: Introduction to an Anthropology of Supermodernity.* New York:Verso. Original French, 1992. English translation, 1992.

_____. 1997a. *L'impossible voyage: Le tourisme et ses images.* Paris: Payot et Rivages.

_____. 1997b. *La guerre des rêves: Exercices d'ethno-fiction.* Paris: Seuil.

Bolitho, Harold. 1977. *Meiji Japan.* Cambridge, UK: Cambridge University Press.

Bourdieu, Pierre. 1984. *Distinction: A Social Critique of the Judgement of Taste.* Cambridge, MA: Harvard University Press. French ed., 1979.

Braudel, Fernand. 1972–73. *The Mediterranean and the Mediterranean World in the Age of Philip II*, vols. I, II. New York: Harper and Row. Original publication in French, 1949.

_____. 1973. *Capitalism and Material Life, 1400–1800.* London: Weidenfeld and Nicolson. Original publication in French, 1967.

Burros, Marian. 1994. "Eating Well." *The New York Times*, April 13, 1994.

Business Asia. 1993. *Business Asia* (October 1993), 25:21,6–7.

Cwiertka, Katarzyna. 1996a. "Western Nutritional Knowledge in Early 20th Century Japan." *Nutrition Bulletin 79*, vol. 21:183–89.

_____. 1996b. "Fighting Foods: Popularizing a Military Diet in Wartime Japan." Presented at the Association of Asian Studies, April 1996. Honolulu.

Dore, Ronald P. 1973 [1958]. *City Life in Japan.* Berkeley: University of California Press.

Endō, Motoo. 1968. "Gyūnabe" (Beef Pot). *Miji Jibutsu Kigen Jiten* (Dictionary of the Origins of Things in Meiji), 264. Tokyo: Shibundō.

Elias, Norbert. 1994 [1939]. *The Civilizing Process.* Oxford: Blackwell.

Featherstone, Michael, ed. 1990. *Global Culture: Nationalism, Globalization and Modernity.* London: Sage Publication.

Fox, Richard G. 1997. "Passage From India," in *In-Between Resistance and Revolution,* Richard G. Fox and Orin Starn, eds. New Brunswick: Rutgers University Press.

Friedman, Jonathan. 1990. "Being in the World: Globalization and Localization." *Theory, Culture and Society,* 7:2–3, 311–28.

Frons, Marc. 1986. "Den Fujita: Bringing Big Macs—and Now Broadway—to Japan." *Business Week* (September 1986), 53.

Gandhi, M. K.(Mahatma). 1948. *Gandhi's Autobiography.* Washington, DC: Public Affairs Press.

Grew, Raymond. 1993. "On the Prospect of Global History," in *Conceptualizing Global History,* B. Mazlish and R. Buultjens, eds., 227–49. Boulder, Colorado: Westview Press.

Gushima, Yanesaburo. 1983. *Bunmei eno Dappi—Meiji Shoki Nihon no Sunbyo* (Exodus Toward Civilization—A Sketch of Early Meiji). Kyūshū: Kyūshū Daigaku Shuppankyoku.

Handler, Richard. 1988. *Nationalism and the Politics of Culture in Quebec.* Madison: University of Wisconsin Press.

Hannerz, Ulf. 1987. "The World in Creolization." *Africa,* 57:4, 546–59.

_____. 1992. *Cultural Complexity: Studies in the Social Organization of Meaning.* New York:

Columbia University Press.

_____. 1996. *Transnational Connections: Culture, People, Places.* New York: Routledge.

Harada, Nobuo. 1993. *Rekishi no Naka no Kome to Niku—Shokumotsu toTennō Sabetsu* (Rice and Meat in History—Food, Emperor and Discrimination). Tokyo: Heibonsha.

Hertz, Robert. 1960. *Death and the Right Hand.* Original publication in French, 1907, 1909. Glencoe, IL: Free Press.

Hobsbawm, Eric J.; Terrence Ranger, eds. 1986 [1983] *The Invention of Tradition.* Cambridge: Cambridge University Press.

Ishige, Naomichi. 1982 [1986]. *Shokuji no Bunmeiron* (Eating and Culture). Tokyo: Chūōkōronsha.

Ito, Abito. 1996. *Korea.* Tokyo: Kawade Shobō.

Jameson, Fredric. 1991 *Postmodernism, or, The Cultural Logic of Late Capitalism.* Durham: Duke University Press.

Jiyū Jikan. 1994. *Shūkan to shite no hanbāgā to manpukukan no gyūdon* (Hamburgers as Habit and *Gyūdon* [a large bowl of rice with beef and sauce on top] for a full stomach). *Jiyū Jikan* (May 5), 32–33.

Kanagaki Robun. 1871–72. *Aguranabe* (The Dish to Eat While Sitting with Legs Crossed), 3 parts in 5 volumes. Tokyo: Iwanami Shoten.

Kishi, Nagami. 1992. "Two Decades of Golden Arches in Japan." *Tokyo Business Today*, 60:4, 38–40.

Kottak, Conrad. 1978. "Rituals at McDonald's." *Journal of American Culture*, 1:2, 370–86.

Kumakura, Isao. 1990. "Zen-Kindai no Shokuji Sahō to Ishiki" (Table Manners and their Concepts Before the Modern Period), in *Shokuji Sahō no Shisō* (Conceptual Structure of the Eating Manners), 107–26, Tadashi Inoue and Naomichi Ishige, eds. Tokyo: Domesu Shuppan.

Lévi-Strauss, Claude. 1978 [1968]. *The Origin of Table Manners*. New York: Harper.

Mazlish, Bruce. 1993. "Global History in a Postmodern Era?," in *Conceptualizing Global History*, 113–27, Mazlish and R. Bunltjens, eds. Boulder, Colorado: Westview Press.

McJoy. 1994. October issue.

Mintz, Sidney W. 1985 [1986]. *Sweetness and Power: The Place of Sugar in Modern History*. New York: Vikings.

Miyake, Hitoshi. 1978. *Shugendō—Yamabushi no Rekishi to Shiso* (*Shugendō*—History and Beliefs of the *Yamabushi*). Tokyo: Kyōikusha.

Murakami, Motoko. 1990. "Gendaijin no Shokuji Manā-kan" (Thoughts on Contemporary Eating Manners), in *Shokuji Sahō no Shisō* (Conceptual Structure of the Eating Manners), 127–43, Tadashi Inoue and Naomichi Ishige, eds. Tokyo: Domesu Shuppan.

Murakami, Shigeyoshi. 1977. *Tennō no Saishi* (Imperial Rituals). Tokyo: Iwanami Shoten.

Nandy, Ashis. 1995. *The Savage Freud and Others Essays on Possible andRetrievable Selves*. Princeton: Princeton University Press.

Natsume Soseki. 1984. "Kōfu" (The Miners), in *Sōseki Zenshū* (Complete Works of Sōseki), vol. 3. [1965] Tokyo: Iwanami Shoten. Originally published as a daily newspaper column beginning January 1, 1907.

Needham, Rodney, ed. 1973. *Right and Left*. Chicago: University of Chicago Press.

Nihon Kokugo Daijiten Kankōkai, ed. 1973a. *Nihon Kokugo Daijiten* (Dictionary of Japanese Language), vol. 3. Tokyo: Nihon Kokugo Daijiten Kankōkai.

_____. 1973b. *Nihon Kokugo Daijiten* (Dictionary of Japanese Language), vol. 5. Tokyo: Nihon Kokugo Daijiten Kankōkai.

_____. 1975. Nihon Kokugo Daijiten (Dictionary of Japanese Language), vol. 13. Tokyo: Nihon Kokugo Daijiten Kankōkai.

Noguchi, Paul. 1994. "Savor Slowly: *Ekiben*—The Fast Food of High Speed Japan." *Ethnology*, XXXIII:4, 317–30.

Ohnuki-Tierney, Emiko. 1984. *Illness and Culture in Contemporary Japan: An Anthropological View*. Cambridge, UK: Cambridge University Press.

_____. 1987. *The Monkey as Mirror: Symbolic Transformations in Japanese History and Ritual*. Princeton: Princeton University Press.

_____. 1990. "The Ambivalent Self of the Contemporary Japanese." *Cultural Anthropology*, 5:196–215.

_____. 1993. *Rice as Self: Japanese Identities Through Time*. Princeton: Princeton University Press.

_____. 1994. "Two Observations of Japanese Religiosity and Rationality," in *The Fourth*. International Congress on Traditional Asian Medicine, *Proceedings*, Part I: 13–74.

_____. 1995. "Structure, Event and Historical *Metaphor*: Rice and Identities in Japanese History." *Journal of the Royal Anthropological Institute*, 30:2 (June 1955), 1–27.

_____. 1997. "McDonald's in Japan: Changing Manners and Etiquette," in *Golden Arches East: McDonald's in East Asia*, James Watson, ed.,161–182. Stanford: Stanford University Press.

Parry, Jonathan. 1985. "Death and Digestion: The Symbolism of Food and Eating in North Indian Mortuary Rites." *Man*, 20:612–30.

Safranek, RoseMary. 1986. "The McDonald's Recipe for Japan." *Intersect* (October 1986), 2:10, 7–10.

Sahlins, Marshall. 1988. "Cosmologies of Capitalism: The Trans-Pacific Sector of 'The World System.'" *Proceedings of the British Academy*, LXXIV:1–51.

_____. 1985. *Islands of History*. Chicago: University of Chicago Press.

Saitō, Hikaru. 1994. "*Nyan-bāgā Densetsu no Nazo*" (The Puzzle of the Cat-burger Lore). *Hanako West*, no. 46 (July), 47.

Schäfer, Wolf. 1993. "Global History: Historiographical Feasibility and Environmental Reality," in *Conceptualizing Global History*, 47–69, B. Mazlish and R. Bunltjens, eds. Boulder, Colorado: Westview Press.

Tanaka, Atsuo. 1994. "Teiku Auto to Ieba Hazusenai Fūsutohūdo Chein Rupo (The "Must" List for Takeouts: Report on Fast Food Chains)." *Hanako West*, no. 46 (July), 45–47.

Tsukuba Tsuneharu. 1986 [1969]. *Beishoku, Nikushoku no Bunmei* (Civilizations of Rice Consumption and Meat Consumption). Tokyo: Nihoon Hōsō Kyōkai.

Vansina, Jan. 1978. *The Children of Woot: A History of the Kuba Peoples*. Madison: University of Wisconsin Press.

Watson, James, ed. 1997. *Goldern Arches East: McDonald's in East Asia*. Stanford: Stanford University Press.

Williams, Brackett F. 1989. "A Class Act: Anthropology and the Race to Nation Across Ethnic Terrain." *Annual Review of Anthropology*, 18:401–44.

Wolf, Eric R. 1982. *Europe and the People Without History*. Berkeley: University of California Press.

Yalman, Nur. 1992. "Ningen Seishin no Kansei:Isuramu ni Okeru Chō-Nashonarizumu no Mondai" (The Perfection of Man: The Question of Supra-Nationalism in Islam). *Shisō*, 823 (January), 34–49.

Yamaguchi, Kikuo. 1986. *Sengo ni Miru Shoku no Bunkashi* (Cultural History of the Post-War Diet). Tokyo: Sanrei Shobō.

Yan, Yunxiang. 1997. "McDonald's in Beijing: The Localization of America," in *Golden Arches East: McDonald's in East Asia*, James Watson, ed., 39–76. Stanford: Stanford University Press.

Chapter Fourteen

Food and the Counterculture: A Story of Bread and Politics

Warren Belasco

Throughout North America and Western Europe, the neo-bohemian youth movement known as the counterculture turned to natural and organic foods in the late 1960s. While this "countercuisine" is still associated with mass-mediated stereotypes of forlorn hippies scratching away in weedy communal gardens ("Easy Rider," 1969) and of dubious New Age repasts of mashed yeast with alfalfa sprouts ("Annie Hall," 1977), it is my argument that the countercuisine represented a serious and largely unprecedented attempt to reverse the direction of dietary modernization and thereby align personal consumption with perceived global needs. If there was a paradigm animating countercultural foodways, it was nicely expressed in the triad of no-non-sense "laws" propounded in *The Whole Earth Catalog* in 1968:

> Everything's connected to everything.
> Everything's got to go somewhere.
> There's no such thing as a free lunch.[1]

For the more conscientious advocates of the countercuisine, food was a way of integrating the world, seeing the social consequences of private actions, and reminding us of our moral responsibilities. Or, as one Berkeley community gardener put it in 1969, food was an "edible dynamic"—a visceral, lived daily link between the personal and the political.[2]

Thirty years after my first brown-rice-with-tofu experience, I still maintain this holistic world view in my food research and teaching. Thus in my courses, "American Food," and "The American Food Chain," I tell students that eating is more than a private, physiological act. It connects us to people and places all over the world—past, present, and future. As an example, I invite them to think about the simple act of toasting and eating a slice of

273

packaged white bread. Growing that wheat helped some Midwestern farmers pay their bills while also polluting their water supply with fertilizers and pesticides, eroding their soil, and, if they used irrigation, lowering their region's water table. The land used to grow the wheat had been acquired—or seized—long ago from other living creatures, human and otherwise, and converted to growing a grass that had originated as a weed in the Middle East and had been gradually domesticated and improved by countless generations of gatherers, peasants, farmers, and, only just recently, scientists. Turning the wheat into bread required the coordinated efforts of numerous companies specializing in food transportation, storage, processing, and marketing, as well as others involved in manufacturing and selling farm equipment.

By extending the bread's shelf life, the plastic wrapping lowered costs and increased profits for corporate processors, distributors, and supermarkets. That packaging also helped to put thousands of neighborhood bakers out of business. Making the plastic from petrochemicals may have helped to foul Cancer Alley in Louisiana and, if the oil came from the Middle East, may have helped to pay for the reconstruction of Kuwait, which was destroyed several years ago by an Iraqi army also financed by petrochemical bread wrappers. The copper in the toaster and electrical wiring may have been mined during the Pinochet dictatorship in Chile or Mobutu's Zaire or Bruce Babbitt's Arizona. The electricity itself probably came from a power plant burning coal, a source of black lung, acid rain, and global warming. And so on. . . . All of this—and more—was involved in making toast. And we have not even mentioned the butter and jam![3]

Since my students already tend to patronize me as a quaint 1960s relic, I do not tell them that my interdisciplinary, global interest in food did in fact originate in the late 1960s and early 1970s, when I was a student at the University of Michigan. This perspective came not so much from my coursework—historians rarely looked at food back then—but from what I was doing off campus. It was in that period that I, like several million other young people, was discovering the political implications of playing with our food. At the coop house where I cooked in 1968, I learned how upset my straighter housemates could be if I left the meat out of the lasagna, injected the roast beef with red dye, or served octopus instead of tuna salad. In 1970 my wife and I met our first macrobiotic, who seemed irritatingly self-righteous and mystical; but soon we too turned vegetarian and came to appreciate the provocative power of refusing steak at the family dinner table. Reading Frances Moore Lappe's *Diet for a Small Planet*, we learned about protein complementarity and the ecological inefficiency of feeding precious grains to cattle. Hoping to secede from the System (or at least from the supermarket), we found *The Tassajara Bread Book* and started baking.[4] *Mother Earth News* and *Organic Gardening* showed us how to make raspberry jam, pickle cucumbers, and grow all the corn and tomatoes we could ever eat on our 20-by-20-foot, chemical-free plot at the nearby community garden. We also brewed dark ale, picked purple clover for wine, and grew our own cannabis. At the anarchistic natural foods coop on South State Street, we bagged our grains, sliced our own cheddar, toted up our bill, and paid whatever we wanted. The new Sikh restaurant in downtown Ann Arbor taught us about vegetable tempura, curried squash soup, and tantric meditation. Cookbook writers Ellen Ewald and Anna Thomas showed us how to make tasty ethnic dishes while saving the Earth.[5] At noisy demonstrations and concerts we scarfed free brown rice and beans served by radical communes dedicated to nourishing "the Revolution." And when, in 1974, someone accidentally mixed fire retardant in dairy cattle feed, we, like every milk drinker in Michigan, learned that in a complex food system, everything really is connected and that there can be no complete escape to nature or self-sufficiency.

My radicalized food awareness translated into sustained scholarship a decade later, when I started a study of the hegemonic process—the way mainstream institutions handle subcultural dissent and deviancy.[6] How does an urban-industrial-capitalist society profit from discontent with urban-industrial-capitalist society? For case studies in what I called "retailing revolt," I chose to examine the fate of blue jeans, "rock 'n' roll," and natural foods. (It does seem that many food studies begin not out of intrinsic interest in food but because of interest in what specific foods can tell us about something else—gender, labor relations, class, ethnicity, imperialism, capitalism, or, in my case, the cooptation of cultural rebellion.) More or less by chance, I started with the food chapter, which soon became a whole book about the counterculture's confrontation with the food industry.[7]

In my research, I tried to set my own nostalgia and amnesia aside and went back to the food-related documents of the late 1960s, especially the Library of Congress's vast collection of countercultural cookbooks, periodicals, catalogs, guides, broadsides, and memoirs. Even today, as I scan this often feverish material with the somewhat sedated perspective of a middle-aged teacher with his own rebellious children, I am still impressed by the core insights of the underground food writers, organic farmers, chefs, entrepreneurs, and consumer activists who articulated the "digestible ideology"[8] of dietary radicalism. Unlike some journalists and historians, I do not dismiss the countercuisine as the latest silly manifestation of the "nuts among the berries" health food faddism that, according to critics, has deceived and diverted gullible Americans since Sylvester Graham, John Harvey Kellogg, Horace Fletcher, and Gaylord Hauser.[9] While postwar crusaders like Adele Davis and J.I.Rodale established some continuity between the earlier health food movement and the countercuisine, it is my argument that the latter was motivated less by concerns about personal vitality or longevity (the traditional health food focus) than by radical politics and environmentalism. Or, just as much food scholarship is really about something other than food, the hip food rebellion was an expression of concerns that extended far beyond the kitchen and dinner table. Alienated by modern culture and anxious about future planetary survival, practitioners of the countercuisine looked to the past for ways to reverse the unsustainable tendencies of the global food supply system.

Using bread as an example, I will first sketch some of the countercultural food-related beliefs, practices, and institutions as they emerged in the late 1960s (content). Then I will speculate about why the countercuisine emerged at that particular time (context). Again focusing on bread, I will briefly overview what happened to the countercuisine over the next few decades (change), and then I will suggest why this all should matter to us today (the moral).

Content

Drawing largely on anthropological sources, I define a cuisine as a set of socially situated food behaviors with these components: a limited number of "edible" foods (*selectivity*); a preference for particular ways of preparing food (*technique*); a distinctive set of flavor, textural, and visual characteristics (*aesthetics*); a set of rules for consuming food (*ritual*); and an organized system of producing and distributing the food (*infrastructure*). Embedded in these components are a set of ideas, images, and values (*ideology*) that can be "read" just like any other cultural "text."[10]

While the countercultural food arrangements I am "reading" were never as well-established and formalized as those of China or France, I do consider them to be intelligible enough to merit the use of the word cuisine.[11] Thus, as every parent who confronted a newly vegetarian teenager discovered, the countercuisine was highly selective, elevating vegetable protein over animal, "natural" foods over those deemed to be "poisoned" by chemicals and processing. Food preparation techniques tended to be labor- and time-intensive, requiring some willingness to make dishes "from scratch" using low-tech manual implements—in opposition to the dominant corporate cuisine's reliance on "quick and easy" automated convenience. The aesthetic principles of taste, texture, and presentation were adapted largely from ethnic styles, particularly Mediterranean, Latin American, and Asian dishes. I use the word "adapted" advisedly because in true post-modern style, the countercuisine was more interested in improvisational creativity than in antiquarian authenticity. (For attracting new recruits, the aesthetic eclecticism of Mexican-Italian Blintzes and sweet-and-sour spaghetti sauce was probably a clear marketing improvement over the earlier health food movement, whose cookbooks favored the ascetic banality of cottage cheese patties and walnut-squash loaf.) Similarly, rituals of consumption tended to be informal, irreverent, and spontaneous—the use of fingers or simple implements (especially chopsticks), much sharing, and a deliberate inattentiveness to matters of time, order, dress, microbial contamination, or conventional decorum. Finally, from the very start many participants in the countercuisine were intensely interested in setting up an alternative infrastructure of organic farms (some operated communally, some individually), farmers' markets, cooperative stores, natural foods processors, group houses, vegetarian restaurants and groceries—as well as an increasingly sophisticated informational distribution system of periodicals, newsletters, cookbooks, guides to simple living, and think tanks devoted to agricultural, nutritional, and entrepreneurial research. This elaborate but decentralized infrastructure of alternative institutions most differentiated the countercuisine from the earlier health food underground, whose primary institutions consisted mainly of a few supplement manufacturers, retail outlets, private clinics, and quasi-religious publishers.[12]

As for an underlying ideology, I have detected three major themes that intertwined to give shape and coherence to countercultural food writings and practices. A consumerist theme targeted foods to be avoided, especially chemicalized "plastic" foods. A therapeutic theme had to do with positive concerns for pleasure and identity, particularly a hunger for craftsmanship, leisure, and tradition. Concerned with the integration of self, nature, and community, an organic motif addressed serious issues of production and distribution, that is, how to reconcile private consumption with wider planetary needs.

To illustrate how these three themes intersected, I will focus on one of the distinctively countercultural food practices that emerged in the late 1960s: the baking of whole wheat bread. When hip cooks began to experiment with soybean stroganoff, curried brown rice, or sesame-garbanzo latkes, they also started to bake the dark, heavy, whole-grained loaves described in books like *The Tassajara Bread Book*, *The Moosewood Cookbook*, and *Laurel's Kitchen*.[13] While the breads were not always very successful, they were a central part of the rebellion. By baking and eating these breads, you were signifying what you were against (consumerist self-protection) and what you were for (therapeutic self-enhancement). In short, bread was part of an oppositional grammar—a set of dichotomies between the devitalized, soft, suburbanized world of Wonder Bread and the vital, sturdy, nutrient-dense peasant world of whole grained breads. In addition to straddling these consumerist and therapeutic elements, this set of dichotomies also pointed towards a holistic or organic sense of how the food system operated.

Plastic versus Natural

Wonder Bread was commonly derided as "plastic bread:" tasteless, completely standardized and homogenized, rendered indestructible—indeed virtually embalmed—by chemical additives and plastic wrapping. Homemade whole wheat breads were, on the other hand, "natural." Natural had two components. First, it meant a lack of additives, preservatives, chemicals, "poisons"; because it lacked these adulterants, it seemed more alive and life-sustaining.

Sourdough was particularly intriguing because it was made from breathing cultures passed down from one generation to another—an expression of the transcendent vital force (much like yogurt cultures, unprocessed beer, and ripened cheese). The second aspect of natural referred to time: It was old-fashioned, traditional, nostalgic—the opposite of the highly rationalized, multinational food industry. The nostalgia tended to look back to ethnic, regional, peasant societies—all seemingly more honest, simple, and virtuous than the bureaucratic urban-industrial state. Thus, in its most romantic sense natural stood for a free form, eccentric, rough-hewn, unstandardized state of mind—a primitive, folksy resistance to the banal, dehumanizing, massifying tendencies of modern culture.[14]

White versus Brown

Paralleling the natural-plastic dichotomy was the opposition between White and Brown: The counterculture did not have much good to say about whiteness, whether in food, clothes, or politics. As one underground newspaper put it, "Don't eat white, eat right, and fight." Whiteness meant Minute Rice, Cool Whip, instant mashed potatoes, white sugar, peeled apples, white tornadoes, white collar, white bucks, bleached cotton, whitewash, white trash, white coats, and, of course, Wonder Bread. Wonder Bread came in for special attack because it was so symbolically rich. Long advertised as the builder of strong bodies in eight ways, Wonder was the best-selling brand. A first cousin by corporate marriage to that other expression of tasteless modern culture, the Twinkie, Wonder Bread's manufacture could be taken to represent the white flight of the 1950s and 1960s. To make clean bread, ITT's bakers removed all colored ingredients (*segregation*), bleached the remaining flour (*suburban school socialization*), and then, to prevent discoloring decay, added strong preservatives and stabilizers (*law enforcement*). Brown bread, on the other hand, may have had a shorter shelf life, but at its peak it seemed hardier, more resilient, more full of innate character. You found this color contrast everywhere. If you visited an underground food coop, you found a preference for brown in everything, from eggs, rice, and sugar to the brown paper bags, wrappers, and signs. The color contrast thus externalized white radicals' alienation from sanitized suburban life—and expressed a neo-primitivist fascination with cultures and struggles of brown people throughout the world.[15]

Convenience versus Craft

A virtue of brown bread was that it took some time and skill to produce, and this leads to another important contrast, convenience versus craft. Wonder Bread represented the ultimate in labor-saving convenience, which was (and is) the food industry's main product and primary hope for global expansion.

It saved time, effort, attention, and money—it even took virtually no time or effort to chew. Sliced white bread thus may have been one of the world's wonders, but the costs in taste seemed enormous. Thanks to the nutrients added back after processing, it may have been "biochemically adequate" but was spiritually vacuous.

Baking your own bread was a considerably less-efficient way to get nutrients, but that was almost the point. Like most Bohemians, hippies wanted to get off the fast track of modern life, to focus on the here and now. Bread baking was a form of craft therapy and meditation: a way to focus attention, a chance to slow down and spend a few hours in intimate contact with the textures, aromas, and chewy sensuality of creating something from scratch. After tasting her first homebaked loaf, hippy cookbook writer Ita Jones (*The Grub Bag*) wrote that she had to bake her own even if it took a whole afternoon—indeed precisely because it took a whole afternoon. "There's no return to the days when I thought that three cluttered hours were preferable to three, long, calm, warm fragrant ones."[16] Those last adjectives—long, calm, warm, fragrant—captured the nostalgic spirit of the counterculture's fascination with traditional crafts, and I believe that if you scratch the surface of the current vogue for artisan and hearth breads, you will find that same hunger for a mythic world of village butchers, bakers, and candle-stick makers.

Product and Process

Finally, closely related to the contrast between convenience and craft was the one between product and process. Mainstream consumer culture put a premium on the end product; how it got to you did not really matter. For the sake of time-saving efficiency, the consumer was alienated from the act of production. The countercuisine, on the other hand, focused on the process—the opportunity to learn by doing, even from the failures. An underground newspaper's food column—called "Bread Bakin': A Garden of Kneadin'"—put it this way: "Don't be discouraged by a few bricks, or even a lot of bricks—they're all building blocks." It was more important how you got there, what you learned along the way, than what you actually wound up with. Hip food writers liked to quote Khalil Gibran: "If a man bakes bread with indifference, he bakes a bitter loaf that feeds but half his hunger." But if you really paid attention to the process of baking bread, you would nourish both stomach and soul.[17]

For the most serious politically minded, this attention to process also resulted in a radical ecological analysis of global food networks. This was the organic theme, the growing awareness of ecological connections between field and fork, production and consumption. In addition to presenting recipes, hip food writers sometimes asked hard questions about the way the wheat was grown, milled, and marketed. Who grew it, what chemicals did they use, where did the water come from, how were farm workers treated, how did the grain conglomerates treat the wheat growers, what ties did the mass-market bread corporations like Wonder's ITT have to the Vietnam War, and so on? Attention to process revealed that the production and distribution of bread, like all food, was intensely political. Similarly, in light of the corporate food system's need to range widely and freely around the globe for the cheapest sources of raw materials, thinking about where one's food came from could become a rather subversive act.[18]

If there was a theme emerging from much of this countercultural experimentation with bread and other foods, it was the one of responsibility: By eating "organically" raised foods (that is, those produced with concern for environmental impact), consumers showed they understood that their eating behavior had roots and consequences—implications not just for their own health but also for the state of the economy, environment, and, ultimately, the planet. (Again, Stewart Brand's "Three Laws.") Out of the ferment of the late 1960s countercuisine came a host of activist nutritionists, agricultural economists, New Age therapists, and radical academics who pushed the analysis.[19] And then there were all the hip business people who combined their social and environmental consciousness with old-fashioned entrepreneurial hustle to establish the organic farms, coops, farmers' markets, natural foods supermarket chains, New American Cuisine restaurants, and designer bread boutiques that feed some of us today.[20]

Context

What *was* going on in the 1960s? Why this rejection of mainstream white bread cuisine and culture? There were two contexts for this rebellion—a mounting dissatisfaction with the prevailing nutritional paradigm coupled with a repositioning of the oppositional left. Harvey Levenstein has clearly documented how the New Nutrition arose in the early part of this century and achieved conventional wisdom status after World War II.[21] As expressed by most nutritionists, agronomists, and food technologists, this modernist paradigm had several main tenets.

First, when evaluating whether a diet is "adequate," the whole is less than its parts. That is, as long as you get the right biochemical nutrients—amino acids, vitamins, minerals, and so on—it does not matter what final form they take. Thus, enriched white bread is nutritionally equivalent to whole wheat. A good diet is more a matter of statistics than of taste or tradition.

Second, a healthy diet is a "well-balanced" one, composed of hefty doses of animal protein from two of the four "basic" food groups; such a high-fat, resource-intensive diet is the envy and goal of "developing" peoples all over the world. (See Adam Drewnowski's chapter in this volume for the still-prevailing assumption that "there is no going back" to a plant-based, low-fat "diet of poverty.")

Third, America has the cheapest, safest, most varied food supply—and for all of that we should thank our modern food industry, with all its agrichemicals and labor-saving farm machinery, food processing, and mass-marketing. Chemicals are our friends. Moreover, only through such high tech production can we ever hope to feed a rapidly expanding world population.

Fourth, conversely, the supposedly good old days before chemicals and agribusiness were really terrible, characterized by the three" P's": plagues, pestilence, and pellagra. Contrary to nostalgia, Grandma did not know best when it came to providing safe, wholesome food; and neither did Old MacDonald, the family farmer, nor the friendly Mama-Papa corner grocery. Information about what constitutes good food should be left to science, not tradition.[22]

This consensus—fondly referred to as the Golden Age by food technologists—crested in the 1950s and early 1960s as marketers successfully rolled out a host of fabricated, synthesized, plastic-wrapped products, as women's magazines taught suburban cooks how to whip up "gourmet" meals using processed foods (my favorite is the "Eight-Can Casserole") and as the nation's much-loved President Eisenhower unapologetically scarfed hash on a tray in front of the TV set.[23] It was also the heyday of the agrichemicals that helped American farmers achieve yield increases that were unimaginable just a decade earlier. Pushing the modernist envelope, technological utopians of the 1950s predicted a push-button future of fully automated farms, restaurants, and kitchens that would "liberate" humanity once and for all from the drudgery of food production and preparation.[24]

These modernist fantasies were not confined to the science-fiction pulp magazines and Sunday supplements. One notable case of technocratic hubris was the widespread belief held by many highly regarded food policy analysts that, in the near future, a crowded world could readily be fed by foods synthesized from chlorella, a high-protein microalgae that, under laboratory conditions, was able to convert upwards of 20 percent of sunlight to usable nutrients.[25] (Conventional "higher" plants like corn and soy, on the other hand, were able to "capture" less than 1 percent.) By "industrializing" photosynthesis, algae manufacturers would be able to bypass inefficient higher plants and anachronistic family farms alogether. Instead, air-conditioned, fully automated "skyscraper farms" would raise algae on raw sewage in enclosed ponds and then pipeline the protein-rich green "scum" to factories fabricating cheap hamburgers, pasta, and animal feed. As for the slimy taste problem—chlorella had what flavorists termed a high "gag factor"—algae's proponents placed great faith in the culinary skills of food engineers. As Cal Tech biologist James Bonner put it in 1957, "the craft of food technology" would soon be able to create "wholly satisfactory" steaks made entirely from vegetable protein flavored with "tasty synthetics" and "made chewy by addition of a suitable plastic matrix." True, such foods might not be up to elite gourmet standards, but Bonner predicted that in the ultra-utilitarian, modernized future, "human beings will place less emotional importance on the gourmet aspects of food and will eat more to support their body chemistry."[26] Here, then, was the apotheosis of what Harvey Levenstein calls the New Nutrition—the progressive-era belief that in a truly efficient world, one would eat just to live, and what one ate would be dictated by biochemical analysis, not frivolous aesthetics.

Unfortunately for the proponents of algae—and for food technology in general—in the 1960s the biochemical paradigm came under assault from a variety of directions. First, the more affluent, urbane, liberal segments of the general public became less receptive to dietary modernism. Inspired by the three "J's"—Julia Child, John F. Kennedy, and jet travel—the new gourmets of the 1960s awakened to food's social and aesthetic dimensions. A renewed interest in roots encouraged many to try traditional ethnic and regional cuisines. Conversely they became more resistant to modernistic advice to eat just for biochemical efficiency, especially as consumer advocates questioned the safety of additives that preserved, fortified, and flavored highly processed foods.[27] By the end of the decade, many Americans could appreciate social critic Lewis Mumford's blast at "the brave new world of totalitarian technics." According to Mumford, promoters of algae and other processed panaceas ignored food's role in enhancing conversation, pleasure, and the landscape. The "pathological technical syndrome" of the efficiency experts was "based on a desire to displace the organic with the synthetic and the prefabricated with the scientifically controlled." The world needed more small farms, Mumford suggested, and with that a greater sensitivity to localness and diversity.[28]

Mumford's advocacy of small-scale, decentralized farming had strong roots in American populist culture, but for most of this century proponents of modern agribusiness had successfully argued that the only way to keep up with rapid population growth (the Malthusian trap) was through extensive industrialization and consolidation of agriculture. The Malthusian threat loomed large in the 1960s, as world population increased at an unprecedented rate of 2.5 percent a year—leading to warnings of impending food wars not just from the apocalyptic Paddock brothers and Paul Ehrlich but also from the Food and Agriculture Organization of the United Nations (FAO), National Academy of Sciences, and U.S. Department of Agriculture (USDA).[29] While the USDA encouraged further agricultural rationalization as a way to feed a hungry world, doubts mounted about the safety and efficacy of modern farming's primary tools, especially pesticides, synthetic fertilizers, subsidized irrigation projects, and heavy machinery that destroyed soil while bankrupting over-mortgaged farmers.[30]

Concerns about the environmental impact of modern agriculture dovetailed with new worries about another key tenet of the reigning nutritional paradigm: the necessity and superiority of animal protein. Most of America's postwar agricultural productivity gains went not into feeding the world's hungry but into producing the corn and soybeans that fattened cattle, which in turn fattened consumers of steaks and fast-food hamburgers. Mainstream food marketers responded to the cholesterol scare of the 1960s with a proliferation of low-calorie, low-fat products, but disaffected youth looked for more comprehensive, subversive solutions. Thus, in the late 1960s a Berkeley graduate student, Frances Moore Lappe went to the library to look for research on feed-grain ratios, protein complementarity, and the ecological impact of animal production. The result—*Diet for a Small Planet*—was perhaps the best-selling book of the countercuisine. Lappe's basic point was simple: By feeding grains to farm animals, Americans were literally throwing away most of their food. A grain-fed North American steer ate twenty-one pounds of vegetable protein for every pound of protein it delivered to the steak eater. In addition to squandering food and clogging our arteries, the animal industry depleted soil, water, and energy resources—all of which would be in short supply in a world whose population was doubling every few decades.[31]

Lappe's argument was by no means new. For many years Malthusians had been saying that rapid population growth, coupled with degradation of farmlands, threatened to reduce Anglo-American beef eaters to "coolie rations"—an "Asian" peasant cuisine based on grains and legumes, with little or no animal protein. But rather than advocate a reduction in steak consumption, most Malthusians urged a reduction in the number of steak consumers, that is, birth control. (Or, as an alternative way to stave off an involuntarily vegetarian future, Cornucopians pushed high-tech agriculture.)[32] Where Lappe differed was not in her statistics but in her willingness to advocate the once unthinkable route—the diet of grains and beans. Calling the scaremongers' bluff, Lappe suggested that perhaps those "coolie rations" were not so unpalatable after all! To prove it, after presenting her research, she provided tasty peasant recipes—and headed off to become "the Julia Child of the Soybean Circuit."

Lappe's book sold millions of copies because her holistic, ecological perspective on meat struck a responsive chord with a young white, largely middle-class audience who shared her need to "think globally, act locally"—the working motto of the new environmental movement. Environmentalism filled an oppositional void left by dissatisfaction with the civil rights and anti-war movements, far-leftist revolutionary socialism, and the druggy urban counterculture. Whereas liberal white youths had once rallied to the cause of racial integration, by the end of the decade that movement had been taken over by exclusionary Black Power advocates. The anti-war movement was also in a rut, especially after the Democratic Convention debacle of 1968 produced the election of Richard Nixon and the lunatic rantings of the Weathermen. While demonstrations continued, peaceful protest was sporadic and only partially effective; yet the confrontational "street-fighting" tactics of the "revolutionary" left were dangerously counterproductive. The internal disputes of assorted Marxist-Leninist factions seemed irrelevant to more pressing worries about oil spills, urban smog alerts, insecticides like DDT in breast milk, poisoned birds, and burning industrial rivers, not to mention the warnings of overpopulation and famine. This sense of impending catastrophe also induced many young people to think twice about the hip drug culture, which by the end of the decade was producing far too many "bad trips." If civilization was about to collapse, perhaps the best hip survivalist strategy was to toughen up, cleanse the body of "poisons," and eat right. Thus, *The Last Whole Earth Catalog* recommended a natural foods cookbook (*Passport to Survival*): "Emergency procedures and forethoughts stored here will serve you come holocaust, catastrophe, or unemployment."[33]

In this polarized, apocalyptic climate of 1968–70, environmentalism emerged as a peaceful, pastoral, pragmatic alternative. Environmentalism gave dissidents a safe cover; even *Time* and President Nixon praised Earth Day (April 22, 1970). But underneath its placid feel-good surface, ecology could be, in the words of one popular text, "the subversive science"; for to fix the mess that industrial society had created, everything would have to be changed. As eco-poet Gary Snyder put it, "You can't be serious about the environment without being a revolutionary."[34] Like the women's movement that emerged at about the same time, environmentalism improved on the "revolutionary" rhetoric surrounding other leftist activities by requiring that you walked the way you talked. Environmentalism entailed more than attending demonstrations and reading radical tracts; you had to change the way you lived: transportation, housing, energy use, and, most of all, food.

Of all the household reforms dictated by ecological living, dietary change seemed the most radical and least cooptable step (especially for young people who did not yet have large investments in energy-hogging cars, houses, and appliances). Dietary radicalism could be lived 365 days a year, three times a day. If, as all leftists knew, the personal was political, what could be more personal than eating? And what could be more political than challenging America's largest industry, the food business? Given the deep-seated, ultra-conservative nature of socialized food habits, radical dietary change required considerable self-scrutiny and self-sacrifice. It was also quite inconvenient, since finding natural foods and preparing them involved effort and skill—hence the strong push to establish an alternative infrastructure to supply and inform the countercuisine. But those who successfully completed the transition could experience the consumerist security of avoiding "poisons," the therapeutic high of a newfound identity, and the organic tranquility that came from living in tune with planetary needs in the long run.

Change

Of course, it did not quite work out as the countercuisine's rhapsodists hoped. The hegemonic incorporation process soon came into play and much of the natural foods movement was safely contained by a food industry that, if anything, is more consolidated, chemicalized, and globalized now than it was in the 1960s. It is safe to say that corporate food executives were not too thrilled by the more subversive aspects of the countercuisine—particularly the emerging radical analysis of the food system. Organic agriculture, in particular, underwent very strong ridicule in the early 1970s, as journalists echoed the claims of industry-subsidized food scientists that, without agrichemicals, millions would starve. The news media also belittled the organic movement's preference for localized, small-scale production and distribution, which was obviously contrary to the multinational direction of the food industry. But food marketers also appreciated that some of the hip critics struck a deep chord in middle-class urban culture—especially the nostalgia for slower, simpler, more honest and intimate times wrapped up in the interest in natural and ethnic foods and the lost craftsmanship of cooking and baking. Also, as the news media highlighted mounting scientific debate about the old nutritional paradigm, more Americans in the 1970s began to worry about pesticides, additives, meat, and cholesterol. In the 1980s the U.S. government's Dietary Guidelines would reinforce some of these health concerns—particularly the negative consumerist uneasiness about fat, sugar, and sodium. Reports about the protective qualities of fiber seemed to confirm the countercuisine's veneration of brown breads, whole grains, and fresh vegetables.[35]

Consumer "demographics" also impressed food marketers. The fact that these nostalgic, health-conscious consumers tended to come from the more affluent part of the population made it even more imperative that the food industry respond in some way, as modern marketing theory was coming to appreciate the virtues of market segmentation. Gone were the days when a company could try to capture a single mass market with one product—say Kellogg's Corn Flakes or Continental Baking's Wonder Bread. Now it appeared that they would need to cater to different "segments" and especially to the people with the more upscale demographics. If the richer half or third of the population wanted natural, old-fashioned foods, then the modern food industry would just have to give it to them—perhaps not quite the same stuff that the hip gourmets of Berkeley were creating but a close enough facsimile to appease most patrons of suburban supermarkets and casual theme-restaurant chains. And that is how we got some of the products that now take up considerable supermarket shelf space, such as natural cereals, the granolas and granola bars, yogurts, ethnic frozen dinners, veggie burgers, salad bars with alfalfa sprouts and sunflower seeds, Celestial Seasonings herbal teas, Ben and Jerry's ecologically righteous premium ice cream, and "lite" versions of virtually everything.[36]

Rather than recapitulate the full progression from countercuisine to Lean Cuisine, I will focus on the evolution of those early hippy wholewheat "bricks" into what the food industry calls "variety or specialty breads," the consumption of which surpassed that of plain white bread among the more affluent shoppers of the 1980s. The incorporation process was gradual. At first, mass-market bread companies simply tried to coopt countercultural symbols: the loaves in brown wrappers with key words like "natural," "wholesome," and "whole-grained," even though the whole wheat was only a tiny percentage of the flour and the extra fiber sometimes came from wood pulp. Or the old-fashioned, craftsman-like feel of "rustic" or "country" breads from Pepperidge Farm, an acquisition of Campbell's Soup. Or the vaguely ethnic or European aura of Stella D'Oro, Lender's, or Entenmann's, all also acquired by major food conglommerates.[37]

While these packaged baked goods captured some of the look of tradition, they lacked the texture, aroma, and taste. Filling that niche were new "boutique" bakeries, many of them established and staffed by ex-hippies who, once the counterculture disbanded in the early 1970s, professionalized their food interests by traveling to Europe to study with top chefs and bakers who were catering to similar longings felt elsewhere in the West. Returning home, they showed Americans what real peasant bread tasted like, first in the California-Cuisine style of panethnic bistros (also set up by countercuisine veterans) that dotted the chic gourmet ghettoes of coastal cities, university towns, and upper-class resorts, and then (in the later 1980s and 1990s) in their own craft bakeries, which retailed rustic sourdough, sesame semolina, and savory olive breads for four to six dollars a loaf.[38] Ironically, by importing these Old World foods, they furthered the culinary globalization of foodways that had begun with the Columbian Exchange, if not before.

The middle class's flirtation with these "artisan breads" was a bit unsettling for packaged bread manufacturers. Instead of reviving the once-ubiquitous neighborhood "made-from-scratch" bakeries, the new hip bread boutiques probably accelerated their disappearance, for supermarkets responded with their own in-store bakeries, which increased from about 2,000 in 1972 to over 30,000 today (compared with around 350 of the independent boutiques). Retailing limp baguettes for 99 cents or pale imitations of seven-grain bread for $1.98, the in-store bakeries now account for about half of the nation's $18 billion sales of baked goods. Like the supermarket produce sections, which also boomed in response to affluent shoppers' demand for healthier foods, these in-store bakeries are quite profitable, for the fresh-baked variety loaves command a higher price than packaged breads, although they do not cost a lot more to produce.[39]

The supermarket in-store unit is the corner bakery of our day and has some of the same appeal on the surface: the personal, over-the counter service, the inviting racks of warm loaves and sugary confections, the cute awnings, free samples, and most important, the freshly baked aroma that pervades the whole store. Sometimes you can even see what looks like an oven and thus vicariously participate in the baking process, much as diners at chic restaurants with exposed demonstration kitchens think they are watching dinner being cooked. But it is mostly an illusion. There simply are not enough scratch bakers left to staff every supermarket, and no big chain wants to pay the high costs of training and keeping them, so most of the skilled mixing work—and much of the baking, too—is done at centralized wholesale locations, often in highly automated German tunnel ovens that are capable of turning out fairly sophisticated crusty loaves and flat breads. (As is always the case when labor is too expensive or troublesome, Fordist automation rules.) If anything is actually baked in the store, it is usually from frozen dough, or more likely it is a pre-cooked "par-baked" loaf that is heated (or "finished') just enough to provide the warmth and yeasty smell. And the crunchiness of the crust can be adjusted by the type of plastic bag it is sold in.[40]

The main reason for this persistence of the status quo is that convenience—the food industry's strongest suit—still sells. While consumers have shown a nostalgia for craftsmanship, most really do not want to spend much time or energy baking, or even shopping for bread. (Similarly, while many of us envy the impressive health profile of the traditional Mediterranean diet, few want the hard labor that went along with it.) Most consumers would rather buy a finished product that looks as if a skilled craftsman did it; and to save time, they would just as soon buy it in the same supermarket where they pick up their milk, laundry detergent, and drug prescription.

To be sure, the truly discerning (and richest) bread gourmets may still take the time to patronize the boutiques, where the craftsmanship, quality, and freshness are real—and there is no doubt that these are increasing. Some industry observers see a potential for as many as 3,000 more over the next few years. But it is doubtful that they will remain independent for long as they undergo the same pressures for conglomeration that drives the mainstream food industry. A few franchise operations are already underway, and it is likely that we will soon see a shakeout and consolidation similar to what has happened in premium ice cream, bagels, and coffee. Indeed, one gourmet bread franchiser recently stated that he hopes to do for bread what Starbuck's has done for coffee. So beware the illusion of the folksy corner bakery. The retail units may have righteous populist names like Northern Plains, Prairie Grain, and Montana Gold, but they will be centralized corporate affairs ripe for eventual takeover by the really big players—General Mills, Campbell's, Phillip Morris, and so forth. True, McDonald's aborted its recent Hearth Express experiment in which unwrapped, locally baked loaves of "hearth breads" were sold along with take-out roasted chicken and meat loaf, but just because McDonald's backed off does not mean that Boston Market or T.G.I.Friday's will do the same. Like the processors and supermarkets, the restaurant chains are very interested in high-profit variety breads.[41]

But why should I care about these trends? If we, the upper-middle-class writers and readers of this volume, can find and afford this great bread, is not that what counts? I suppose the answer is "yes," if one is content with a purely privatistic, myopic view of food. But, as this chapter shows, I am too much a child of the 1960s. I keep thinking about the global picture. As my hippy mentors wrote, it is not the product, it is the process. If we think only about the end product rather than the process by which it was made, then the food industry will always be able to come up with products that at least superficially cater to our worries about health, skill, tradition, and community. But if we start asking questions about the process by which grain was transformed into the bread that sustains and entertains us, then we are not likely to be so easily appeased. What actually is in this stuff anyway? Is it really so wholesome? Who baked it and under what conditions? Thinking about process means asking why a peasant bread costs $5.00, while real peasants abroad cannot buy plain wheat and poor people here can barely afford store-bought white bread. And it means asking about environment and agriculture: Where did the plastic bag come from and where will it go after I discard it? How will the greenhouse effect affect grain production? Is our global seed stock genetically diverse enough to withstand the inevitable attack of the next pesticide-resistant fungus or fly? Did the farmer get a fair share of the profits? And down the road will that farmer's land be in good enough condition to feed our grandchildren's grandchildren? These are the questions that really matter.[42] And no amount of postmodern marketing wizardry will answer them or make them go away.

Notes

1. *The Last Whole Earth Catalog* (Menlo Park, Calif.: Portolo Institute, 1971), 43.

2. "People's Pods," *Good Times*, July 24, 1969, p. 14.

3. What I am describing here is an analysis of product's "ecological wake." For more on this type of environmental auditing, see Alan Durning, *How Much is Enough? The Consumer Society and the Future of the Earth* (New York: Norton, 1992); Mathis Wackernagel and William Rees, *Our Ecological Footprint: Reducing Human Impact on the Earth* (Barioola Island B.C.: New Society Publishers, 1996); Martin Teitel, *Rain Forest in Your Kitchen: The Hidden Connection between Extinction and Your Supermarket* (Washington, D.C.: Island Press, 1992); Alessandro Bonanno, et al., *From Columbus to Conagra: The Globalization of Agriculture and Food* (Lawrence: University Press of Kansas, 1994); Geoff Tansey and Tony Worsley, *The Food System: A Guide* (London: Earthscan, 1995). Two particularly fine historical audits of individual foodstuffs are Sidney W. Mintz's *Sweetness and Power: The Place of Sugar in Modern History* (New York: Viking, 1985), and the chapters on grain and meat in William Cronon's *Nature's Metropolis: Chicago and the Great West* (New York: Norton, 1991), pp. 97–147, 207–59.

4. Frances Moore Lappe, *Diet for a Small Planet* (New York: Ballantine, 1971); Edward Espe Brown, *The Tassajara Bread Book* (Berkeley: Shambala Publications, 1970).

5. Ellen Buchman Ewald, *Recipes for a Small Planet* (New York: Ballantine, 1973); Anna Thomas, *The Vegetarian Epicure* (New York: Vintage, 1972).

6. On hegemony theory: Dick Hebdige, *Subculture: The Meaning of Style* (London: Methuen, 1979); Stuart Hall, et al., *Resistance through Rituals* (London: Hutchison, 1976); Todd Gitlin, *The Whole World is Watching: Mass Media in the Making and Unmaking of the New Left* (Berkeley: University of Calfornia Press, 1980).

7. Warren Belasco, *Appetite for Change: How the Counterculture Took on the Food Industry* (Ithaca: Cornell University Press, 1993).

8. Berkeley gardener, "People's Pods," 14.

9. For the most biased historical treatment of "food faddism," see Gerald Carson, *Cornflake Crusade* (New York: Rinehart, 1957); Ronald Deutsch, *The Nuts Among the Berries* (New York: Ballantine, 1961). For more recent and balanced appraisals: James C. Whorton, *Crusaders for Fitness: The History of American Health Reformers* (Princeton: Princeton University Press, 1982); Harvey Green, *Fit for America: Health, Fitness, and American Society* (New York: Pantheon, 1986); Ronald G. Walters, *American Reformers, 1815-1860* (New York: Hill and Wang, 1978), 145-72; Harvey Levenstein, *Revolution at the Table: The Transformation aof the American Diet* (New York: Oxford University Press, 1988), 86-97; and Levenstein, *Paradox of Plenty: A Social History of Eating in Modern America* (New York: Oxford, 1993), 178-94. For journalistic treatment of the countercuisine: *Appetite for Change,* 154-82.

10. My understanding of "cuisine" has been shaped particularly by Peter Farb and George Armelagos, *Consuming Passions: The Anthropology of Eating* (Noston: Houghton Mifflin Co., 1980), 190–98; Elizabeth Rozin, "The Structure of Cuisine," in Lewis M. Barker, ed., *The Psychobiology of Human Food Selection* (Westport CT: AVI Publishing, 1982), 189–203; Roland Barthes, "Toward a Psychosociology of Contemporary Food Consumption," in Robert Forster and Orest Ranum, eds., *Food and Drink in History* (Baltimore: Johns Hopkins University Press, 1979), 166–73; Charles Camp, *American Foodways* (Little Rock: August House, 1989).

11. The "reading" of the countercuisine in the rest of this section is drawn from Belasco, *Appetite for Change,* 15–108.

12. On the countercultural infrastructure in general: John Case and Rosemary C. R. Taylor, eds., *Co-ops, Communes, and Collectives: Experiments in Social Change in the 1960s and 1970s* (New York: Pantheon, 1979).

13. Brown, *Tassajara Bread Book*; Mollie Katzen, *The Moosewood Cookbook* (Berkeley: Ten Speed Press, 1977); Laurel Robertson, Carol Flinders, and Bronwen Godfrey, *Laurel's Kitchen* (New York: Bantam Books, 1978).

14. Belasco, *Appetite for Change,* 37–42.

15. *Ibid.,* 48–50. In a sense the neo-primitivistic attraction to brown-ness had deeper roots in the ambivalence of affluent Westerners towards the fruits of their own political and economic mastery of third-world societies. Thus, in the 1920s rich metropolitan intellectuals on both sides of the Atlantic found themselves attracted to black music (jazz), sexuality (Josephine Baker), and pigments themselves (Coco Chanel's tanning craze). Jan Nederveen Pieterse, *White on Black: Images of Africa and Blacks in Western Popular Culture* (New Haven: Yale University Press, 1992).

16. Ita Jones, "Grub Bag," *Liberation News Service* #135, January 30, 1969, p. 4; Belasco, *Appetite for Change,* 50–54.

17. · mother bird, "Bread Bakin': A Garden of Kneadin'," *Northwest Passage*, January 10, 1972, p.4; Belasco, *Appetite for Change*, 46–48.

18. Belasco, *Appetite for Change*, 32–34, 68–76. Claude Fischler makes a related point in his chapter in this volume on "The Mad Cow Crisis": The modern food system's vast distance between process and product leads to considerable consumer distrust and anxiety, but while Fischler tends to dismiss such sentiment as verging on paranoia, I see it as merited and, if channelled constructively, politically useful.

19. Examples of early radical analysis of the food system by countercuisine veterans: Jim Hightower, *Eat Your Heart Out: Food Profiteering in America* (New York: Crown Publishers, 1975); Catherine Lerza and Michael Jacobson, eds., *Food for People, Not for Profit* (New York: Ballantine Books, 1975); Frances Moore Lappe, *Diet for a Small Planet* (New York: Ballantine, 1971); Gene Marine and Judith Van Allen, *Food Pollution: The Violation of Our Inner Ecology* (New York: Holt, Rinehart and Winston, 1972); Joan Dye Gussow, ed., *The Feeding Web: Issues in Nutritional Ecology* (Palo Alto: Bull Publishing, 1978). Post-countercultural think tanks devoted to alternative approaches include: Michael Jacobson's Center for the Study of Science in the Public Interest, Frances Moore Lappe's Institute for Food and Development Policy, Wes Jackson's Land Institute, John Todd's New Alchemy Institute, and Amory and Hunter Lovins' Rocky Mountain Institute.

20. On hip entrepreneurs: Belasco, *Appetite for Change*, 94–108. Two of the most influential hip businesses of the 1980s and 1990s: Alice Water's Chez Panisse, the Berkeley training school for countless environmentally aware chefs and bakers, and Whole Foods, the quasi-organic/gourmet supermarket chain from Austin that is rapidly expanding throughout the United States.

21. Levenstein, *Revolution at the Table*, especially 72–85, 147–60; *Paradox of Plenty*, 3–23, 53–130; Ross Hume Hall, *Food for Nought: The Decline in Nutrition* (New York: Vintage, 1976); Laura Shapiro, *Perfection Salad: Women and Cooking at the Turn of the Century* (New York: Farrar, Straus, and Giroux, 1986); Gussow, ed., *The Feeding Web*, 119–204.

22. For the response of nutritional "orthodoxy" to the countercuisine: Belasco, *Appetite for Change*, 111–31.

23. Jane and Michael Stern, *Square Meals*, 274; Levenstein, *Paradox of Plenty*, 120; Gerry Schremp, *Kitchen Culture: Fifty Years of Food Fads* (New York: Pharos Books, 1991), 1–96.

24. On agricultural yields: Lester Brown, et al., *Vital Signs: The Trends that are Shaping Our Future* (New York: Norton, 1994), 29; Gilbert C. Fite, *American Farmers: The New Minority* (Bloomington: Indiana University Press, 1981), 80–197. For technological utopian visions: Robert Brittain, *Let There Be Bread* (New York: Simon and Schuster, 1952); Jacob Rosin and Max Eastman, *The Road to Abundance* (New York: McGraw-Hill, 1953); Victor Cohn, *1999: Our Hopeful Future* (Indianapolis: Bobbs-Merrill, 1956); Joseph J., Corn, ed., *Imagining Tomorrow: History, Technology, and the American Future* (Cambridge: MIT Press, 1986).

25. For a fuller treatment of the chlorella story: Warren Belasco, "Algae Burgers for a Hungry World? The Rise and Fall of Chlorella Cuisine," *Technology and Culture* (July 1997).

26. *Proceedings of "The Next Hundred Years": A Symposium* (New York: Seagram's, 1957), 31.

27. Levenstein, *Paradox of Plenty*, 131–43; Jane and Michael Stern, *American Gourmet* (New York: Harper Collins, 1991); Warren Belasco, "Ethnic Fast Foods: The Corporate Melting Pot," *Food and Foodways*, 2 (1987), 1–30; Rachel Carson, *Silent Spring* (Boston: Houghton Mifflin, 1962); Beatrice Trum Hunter, *Consumers Beware! Your Food and What's Been Done to It* (New York: Simon and Schuster, 1971).

28. Lewis Mumford, "Closing Statement," in *Future Environments of North America*, F. Fraser Darling and John P. Milton, eds. (Garden City, NY: Natural History Press, 1966), 724–25.

29. Paul Ehrlich, *The Population Bomb* (New York: Bantam, 1968); William and Paul Paddock, *Famine 1975! America's Decision: Who Will Survive?* (Boston: Little Brown, 1967); P. V. Sukhatme, "The World's Hunger and Future Needs in Food Supplies," *Journal of the Royal Statistical Society*, 124:4 (1961), 463–525; National Academy of Sciences, *Resources and Man* (San Francisco: W. H. Freeman, 1969), 43–108; Joseph W. Willett, "A Single Chariot with 2 Horses: The Population and Food Race," *Contours of Change* (Washington: USDA, 1970), 247–50.

30. Carson, *Silent Spring*; Hightower, *Eat Your Heart Out*, 154–217; Hall, *Food for Nought*, 88–205.

31. Lappe tells her story in *Diet for a Small Planet: Tenth Anniversary Edition* (New York: Ballantine, 1982).

32. Earlier Malthusian warnings about the Asian population/culinary menace are discussed in Walter B. Pitkin, *Must We Fight Japan?* (New York: Century, 1921); Edward M. East, *Mankind at the Crossroads* (New York: Charles Scribner's Sons, 1924); William Vogt, *The Road to Survival* (New York: Wlliam Sloane Associates, 1948). Cornucopian versions: J. Russell Smith, *The World's Food Resources* (New York: Henry Holt, 1919); Robert J. McFall, "Is Food the Limiting Factor in Population Growth?," *The Yale Review*, January 1926, pp. 297–316; E. E. DeTurk, ed., *Freedom from Want: A Survey of the Possibilities of Meeting the World's Food Needs* in *Chronica Botanca*, 2:4 (1948), 207–84. For an excellent overview of the food/population debate, see Joel E. Cohen, *How Many People Can the Earth Support?* (New York: Norton, 1995).

33. *The Last Whole Earth Catalog* (Menlo Park, CA: Portola Institute, 1971), 198; Belasco, *Appetite for Change*, 15–42.

34. Peter R. Jannsen, "Where the Action Is," *Ecotactics: The Sierra Club Handbook for Environmental Activists*, John G. Mitchell, ed. (New York: Pocket Books, 1970), 55; Paul Shepherd and David McKinley, eds., *The Subversive Science—Essays Toward an Ecology of Man* (Boston: Houghton Mifflin, 1969).

35. Belasco, *Appetite for Change*, 109–99.

36. *Ibid.*, 185–251.

37. "Analysis of Baked Goods," *Food Engineering*, August 1980, 81–82; Danielle K. Mooney, *Mass-Merchandised Healthy Foods: Markets, Trends* (Stamford CT: Business Communications Co., 1982), 62–69; "Easing of Bread Ad Ban Asked," *Advertising Age*, June 27, 1983, p. 16. Kenneth Wylie, "Bread Returns to Its Humble Beginnings," *Advertising Age*, May 3, 1984, p. M62; "It's Natural, It's Organic, Or Is It?" *Consumer Reports*, July 1980, p. 411; Belasco, *Appetite for Change*, 218–24, 229–36.

38. "New Restaurant-Bakery Combinations Taking Off," *Nation's Restaurant News*, February 3, 1986, p. 1; Florence Fabricant, "Fresh from the Baker: A New

Staff of Life," *The New York Times*, November 11, 1992, p. C1; Danielle Forestier, Joe Ortiz, Steven Sullivan, "The Making of the Ultimate Loaf," panel at the symposium, "Bread: A Language of Life," California Academy of Sciences, San Francisco CA, March 2, 1996.

39. Doug Krumrei, "Great Harvest of Specialty Breads," *Bakery Production and Marketing*, September 1994, p. 44; "Instore Bakeries: the Top 10 Categories," *Supermarket Business*, June 1994, p. 89; "Let the Good Times Roll," *Bakery Production and Marketing*, June 24, 1995, p. 1; Roseanne Harper, "Bred to Rise," *Supermarket News*, January 30, 1995, p. 21.

40. Dan Malovany, "How New Products Drive Automation," *Bakery Production and Marketing*, June 24, 1995, p. 18; Pat Lewis, "Evolution of In-Store Bakeries," *Supermarket News*, December 28, 1992, p. 70; "Savor the Flavor," *Bakery Production and Marketing*, March 24, 1995, p. 42.

41. "Doing for Bread What Starbucks Has Done for Coffee," *Brandweek*, April 10, 1995, p. 30; "Bake Shop Bonanza," *Restaurant Hospitality*, September 1994, p. 78; Louise Kramer, "McDonald's Deep-Sixes Test of Hearth Express Concept," *Brandweek*, July 17, 1995, p.1.

42. For important questions about the global food system: Lester Brown, *Who Will Feed China?* (New York: Norton, 1995); Brown, *Tough Choices: Facing the Challenge of Food Scarcity* (New York: Norton, 1996); Joan Dye Gussow, *Chicken Little, Tomato Sauce and Agriculture: Who Will Produce Tonorrow's Food?* (New York: Bootstrap Press, 1991); Jack Ralph Kloppenburg, *First the Seed: The Political Economy of Plant Biotechnology, 1492–2000* (Cambridge: Cambridge University Press, 1988); Cary Fowler and Pat Mooney, *Shattering: Food, Politics, and the Loss of Genetic Diversity* (Tucson: University of Arizona Press, 1990); Elizabeth Ann R. Bird, et al., eds., *Planting the Future: Developing an Agriculture that Sustains Land and Community* (Ames: Iowa State University Press, 1995); Lawrence Busch, et al., ed., *Plants, Power and Profit* (Oxford: Basil Blackwell, 1991); Robin Mather, *A Garden of Unearthly Delights: Bioengineering and the Future of Food* (New York: Penguin, 1996).

Food in Global History: List of Contributors

JOELLE BAHLOUL is associate professor of anthropology and jewish studies at Indiana University.

WARREN BELASCO is professor of history and american studies at the University of Maryland, Baltimore County.

ADAM DREWNOWSKI is professor of epidemiology and internal medicine at the University of Washington.

CLAUDE FISCHLER is directeur de recherche at the Centre National de Recherche Scientifique and Maitre de Conference at the Ecole des Hautes Etudes en Sciences Sociales.

HARRIET FRIEDMANN is professor of sociology at the University of Toronto.

RAYMOND GREW, former editor of *Comparative Studies in Society and History*, is professor of history at the University of Michigan.

ELISABET HELSING, formerly with the World Health Organization in Europe, is a member of the board of health of Norway.

SUCHETA MAZUMDAR is professor of history at Duke University.

WILLIAM ALEX McINTOSH is professor of sociology at Texas A & M University.

DELLA E. McMILLAN is a research scientist of anthropology and of the Center for African Studies at the University of Florida.

EMIKO OHNUKI-TIERNEY is professor of anthropology at the University of Wisconsin.

THOMAS A. REARDON is professor of international agircultural development and food and agricultural marketing in the agricultural economics department at Michigan State University.

JEFFERY SOBAL is professor of nutritional sociology at Cornell University.

NOEL W. SOLOMONS is senior scientist and scientific coordinator at the Center for Studies of Sensory Impairment, Aging, and Metabolism in Guatemala City.

REBECCA L. SPANG is lecturer in the department of history, University College, London.

Printed in the United States
218994BV00001B/13/A